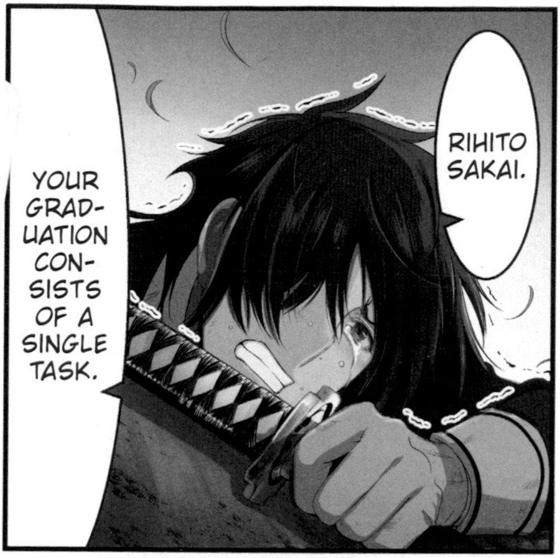
RIHITO SAKAI.
YOUR GRADUATION CONSISTS OF A SINGLE TASK.

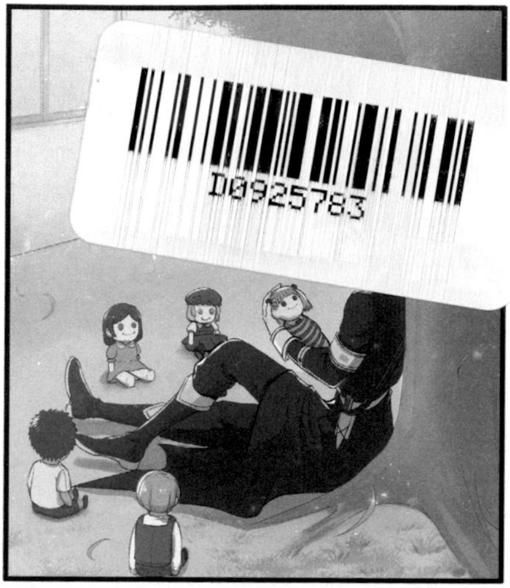
D0925783

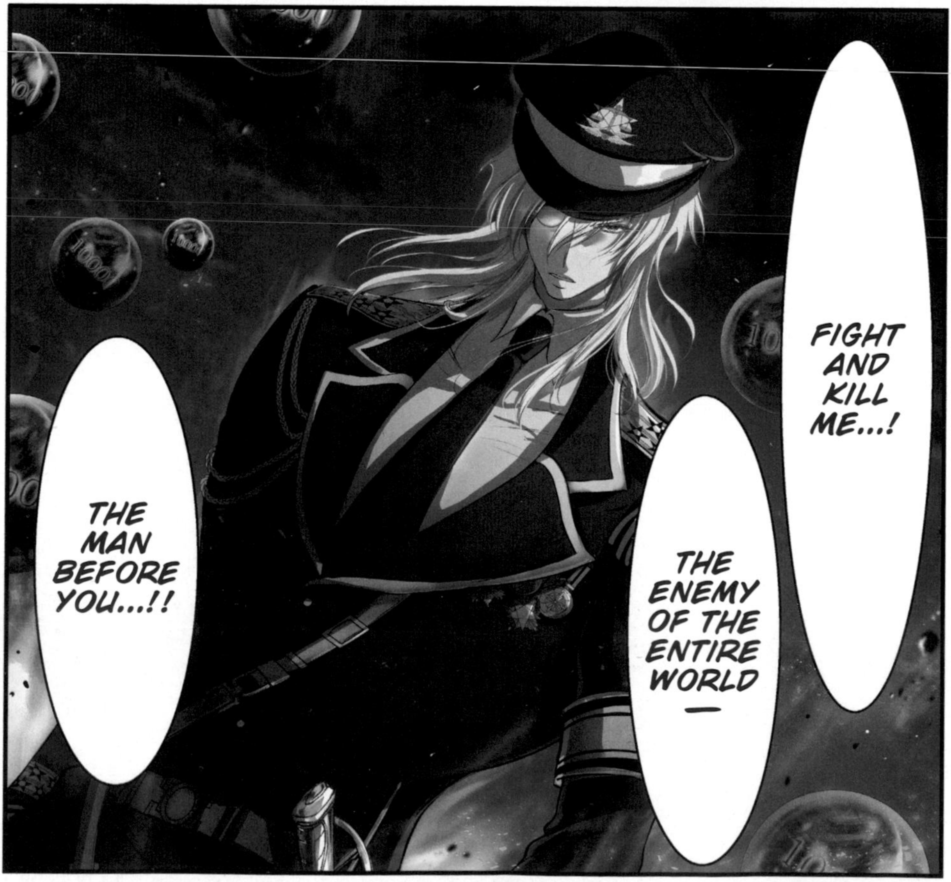
FIGHT AND KILL ME...!
THE ENEMY OF THE ENTIRE WORLD—
THE MAN BEFORE YOU...!!

CHAPTER 80: THE ENEMY OF THE ENTIRE WORLD

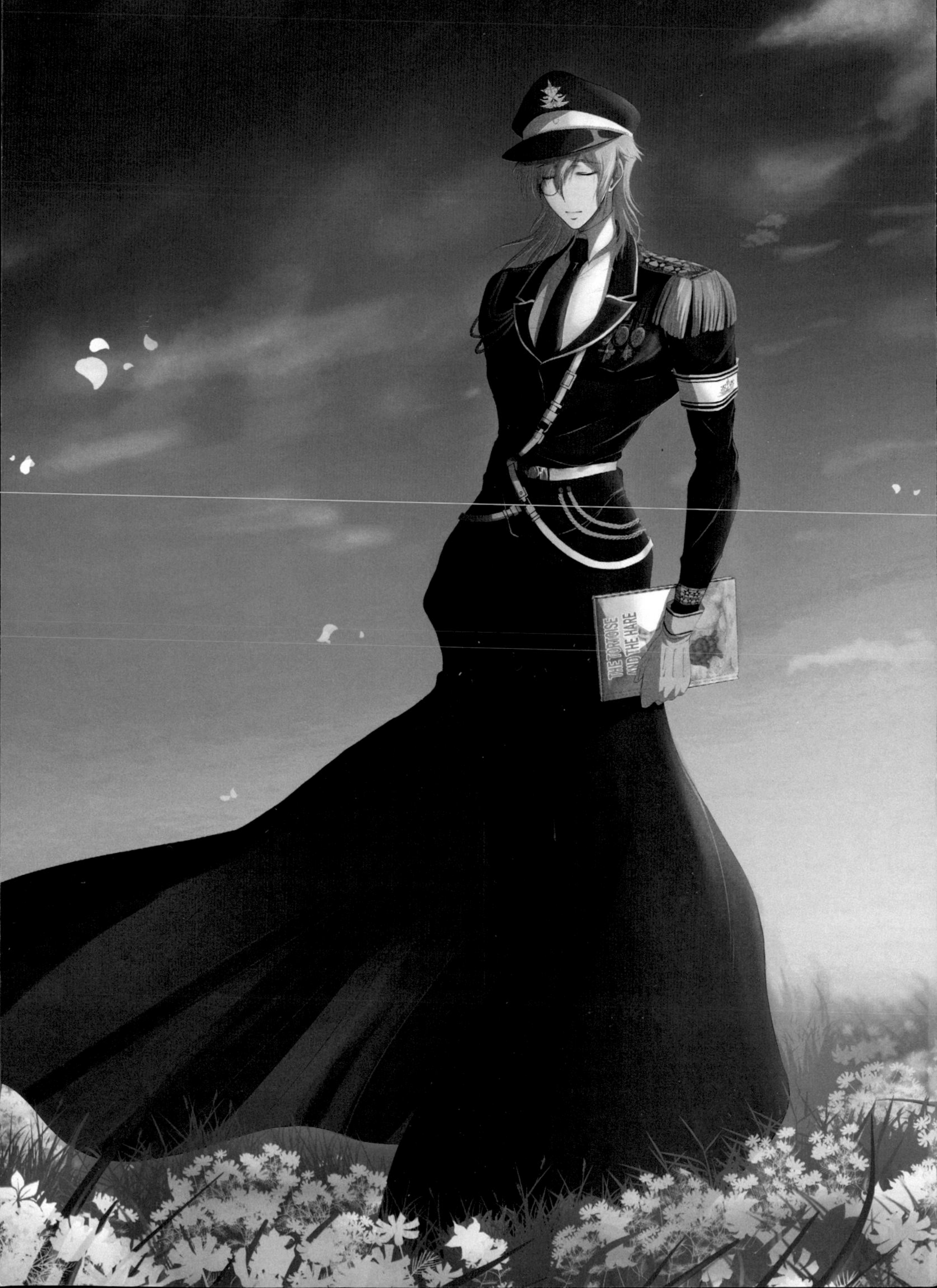
THE TORTOISE AND THE HARE

PLUNDERER
11

CONTENTS

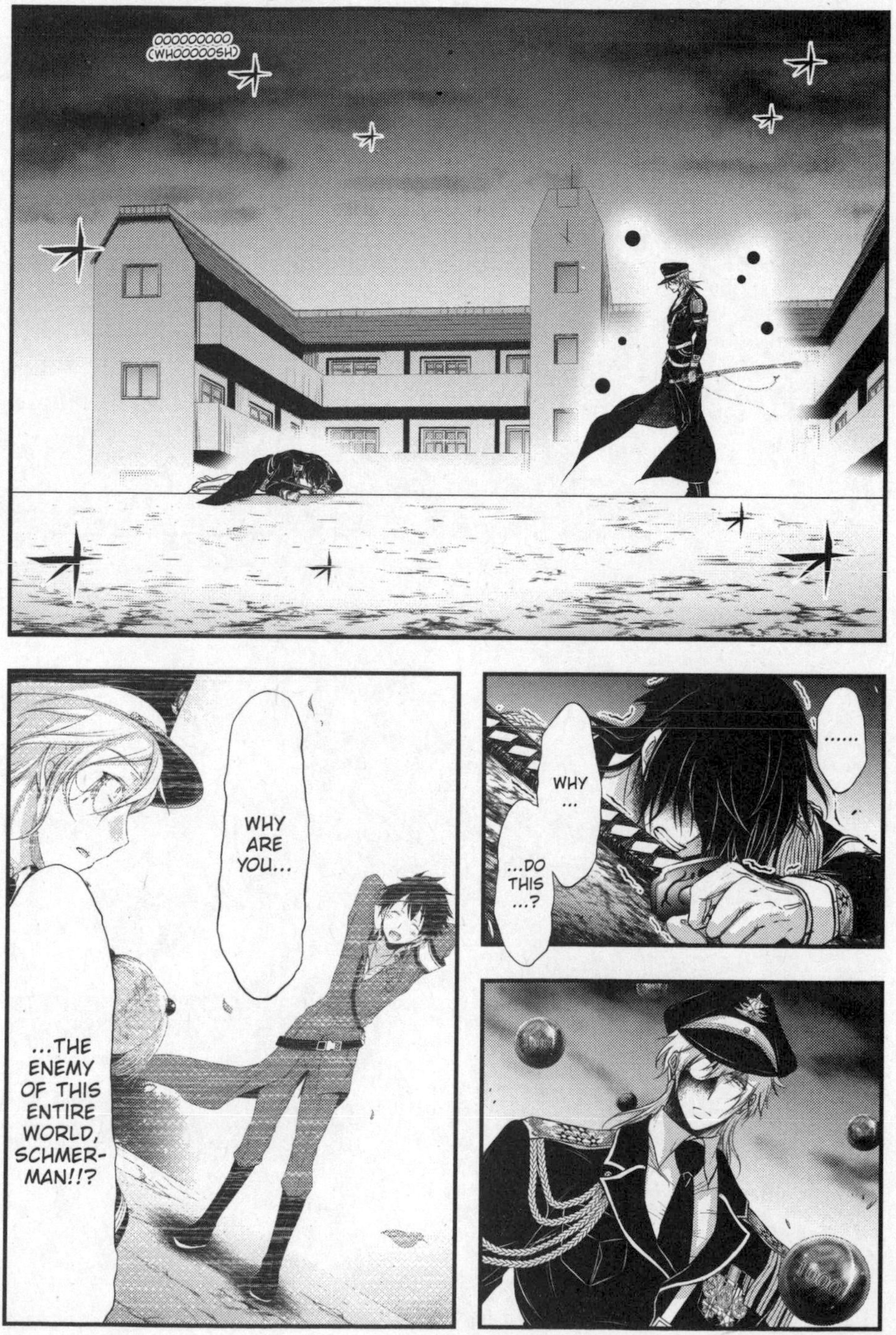
OOOOOOOOO
(WHOOOOOSH)
......
WHY ...
...DO THIS ...?
WHY ARE YOU...
...THE ENEMY OF THIS ENTIRE WORLD, SCHMER-MAN!!?

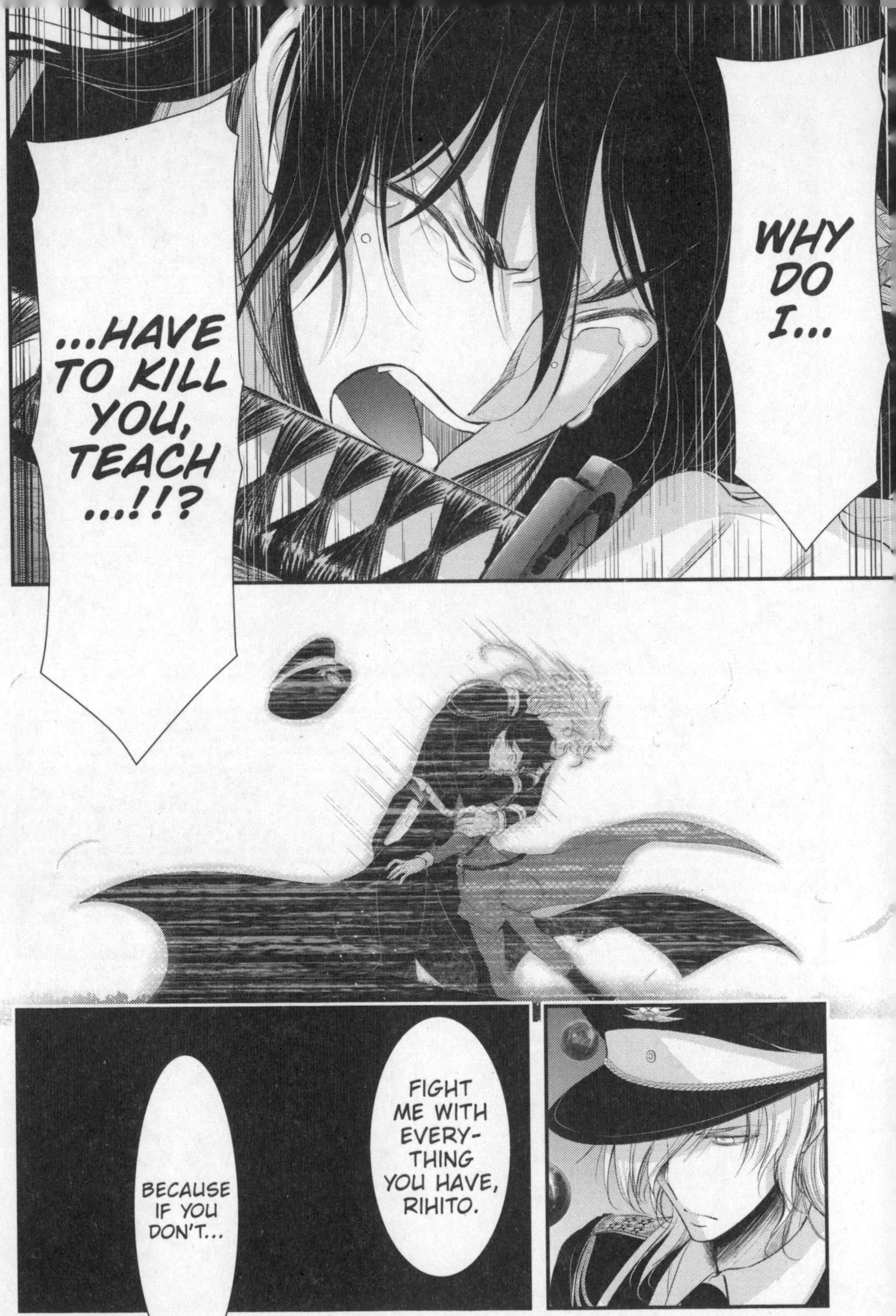
WHY DO I...
...HAVE TO KILL YOU, TEACH ...!!?
FIGHT ME WITH EVERY-THING YOU HAVE, RIHITO.
BECAUSE IF YOU DON'T...

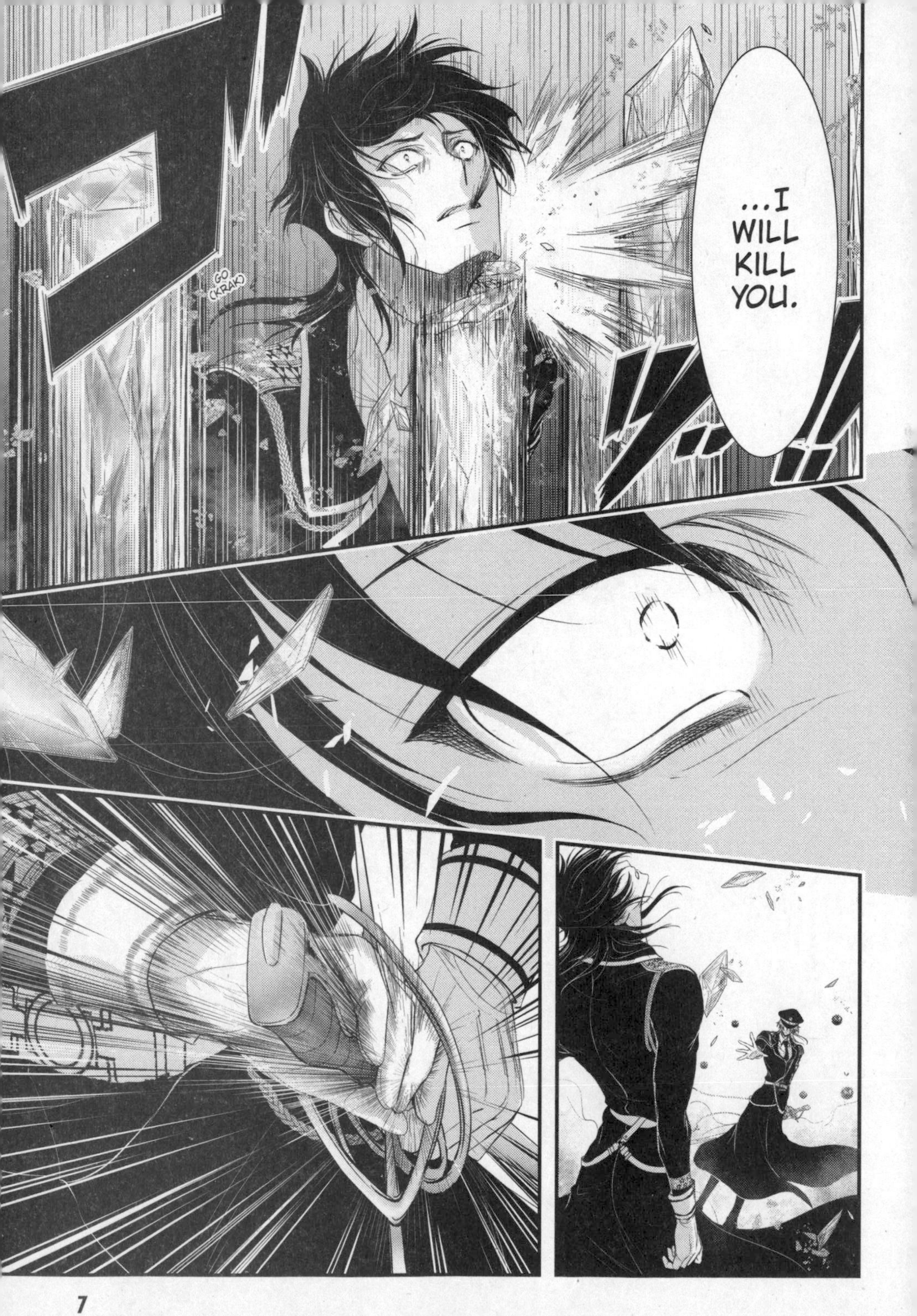
...I WILL KILL YOU.
GO (KRAK)

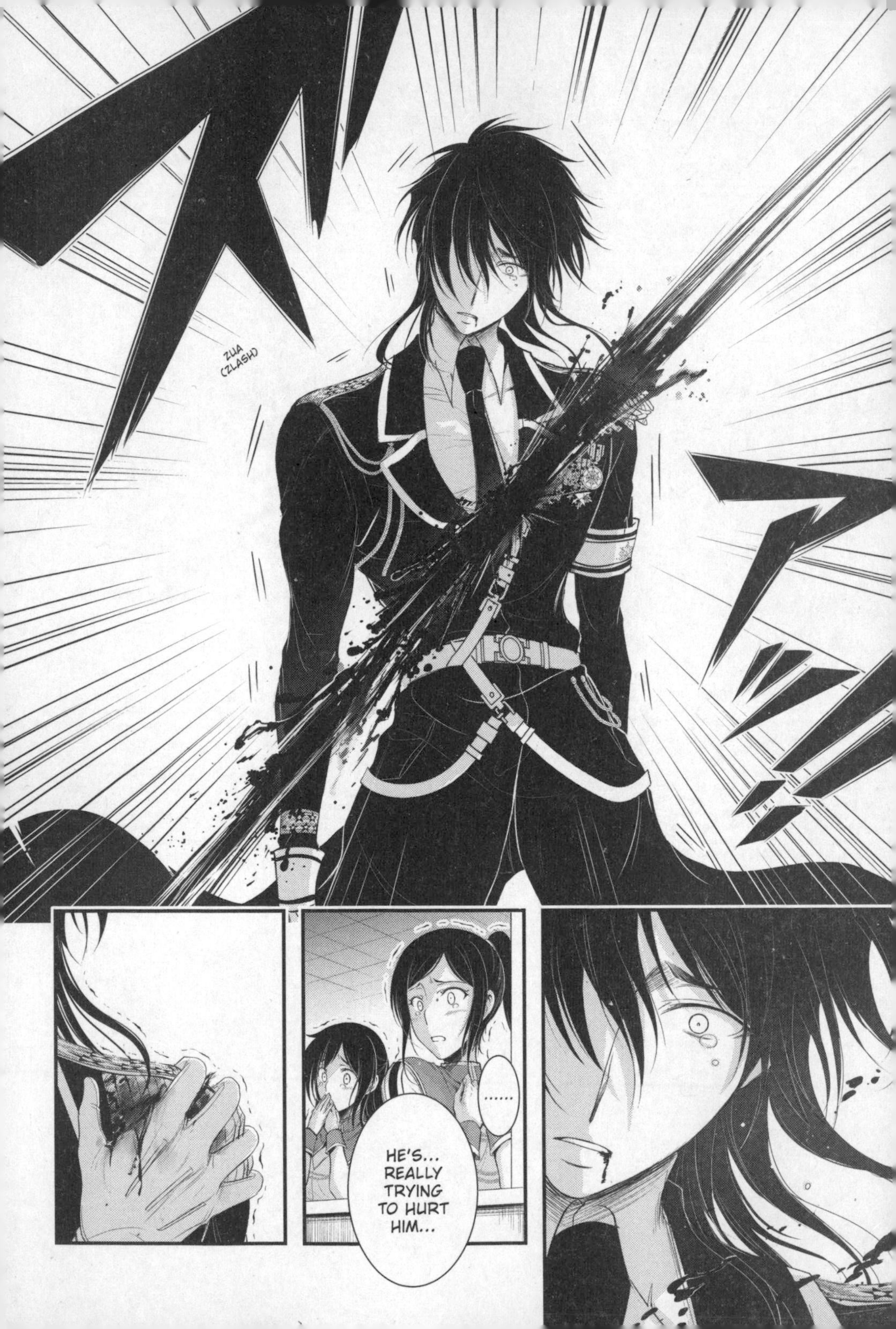
ZUA
(ZLASH)
......
HE'S... REALLY TRYING TO HURT HIM...

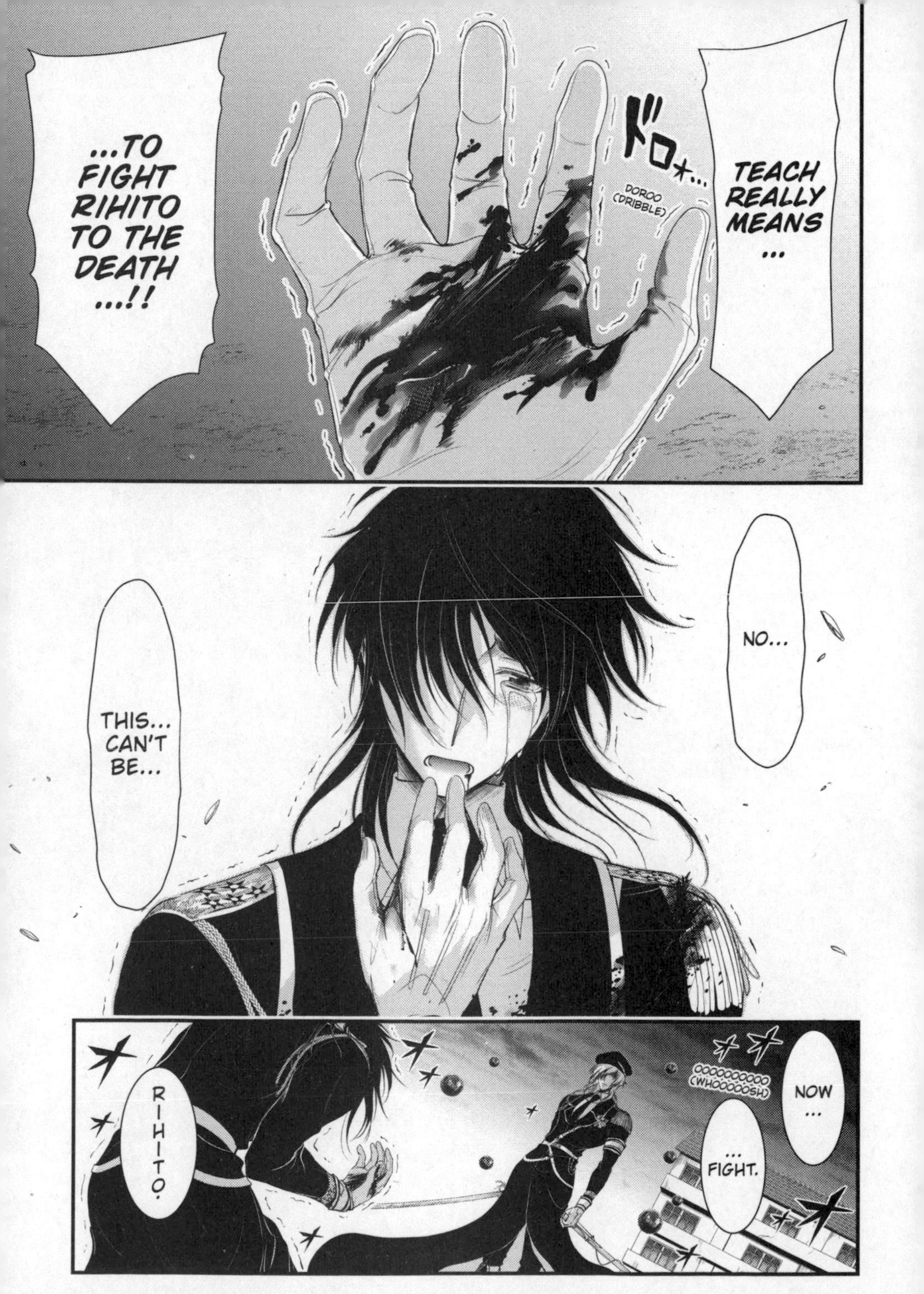
TEACH REALLY MEANS ...
DOROO (DRIBBLE)
...TO FIGHT RIHITO TO THE DEATH ...!!
NO...
THIS... CAN'T BE...
NOW ...
... FIGHT.
OOOOOOOOOO (WHOOOOOSH)
RIHITO.

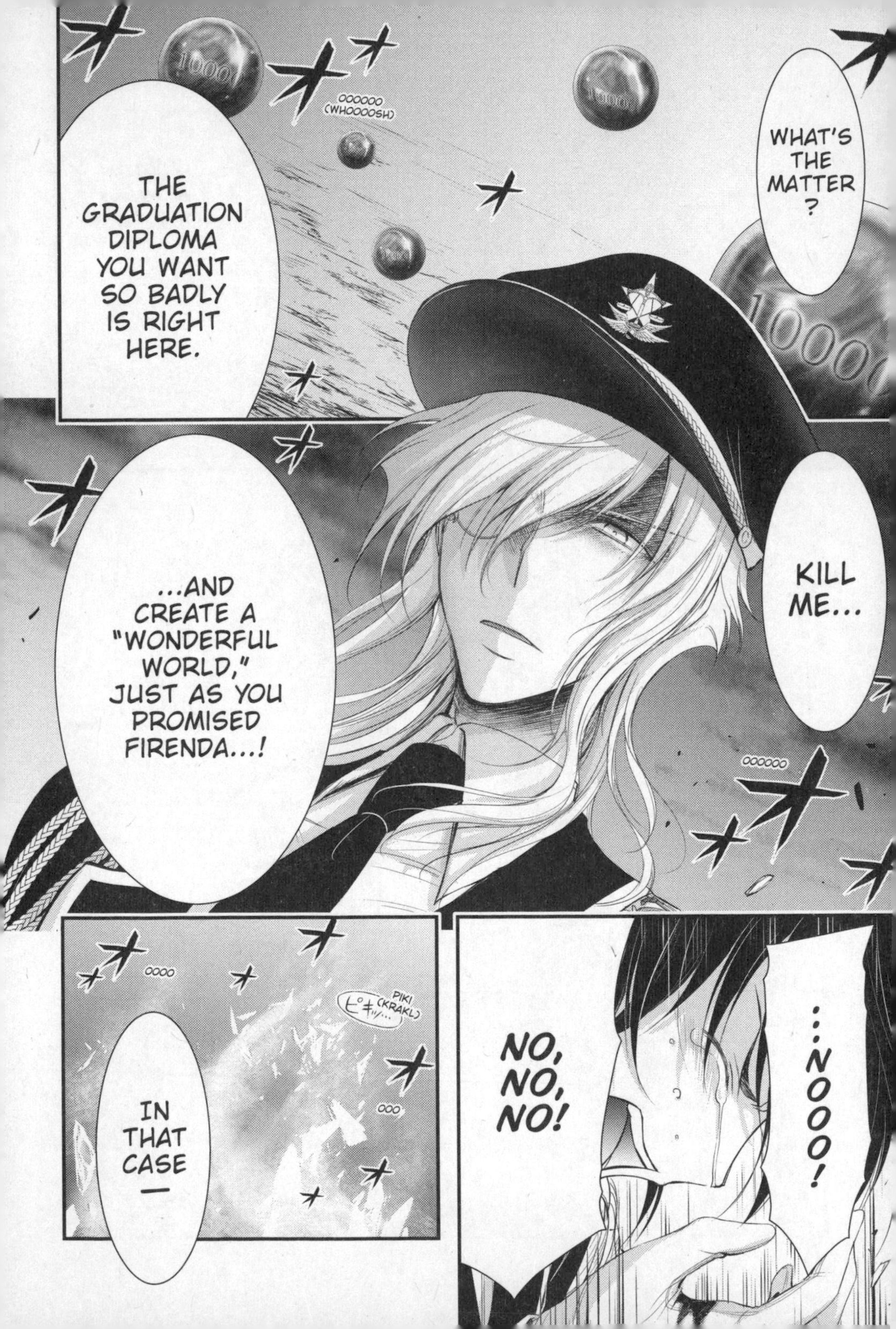
WHAT'S THE MATTER?
OOOOOO (WHOOOOSH)
THE GRADUATION DIPLOMA YOU WANT SO BADLY IS RIGHT HERE.
KILL ME...
OOOOOO
...AND CREATE A "WONDERFUL WORLD," JUST AS YOU PROMISED FIRENDA...!
...NOOOO!
NO, NO, NO!
PIKI (KRAKL)
OOOO
OOO
IN THAT CASE—

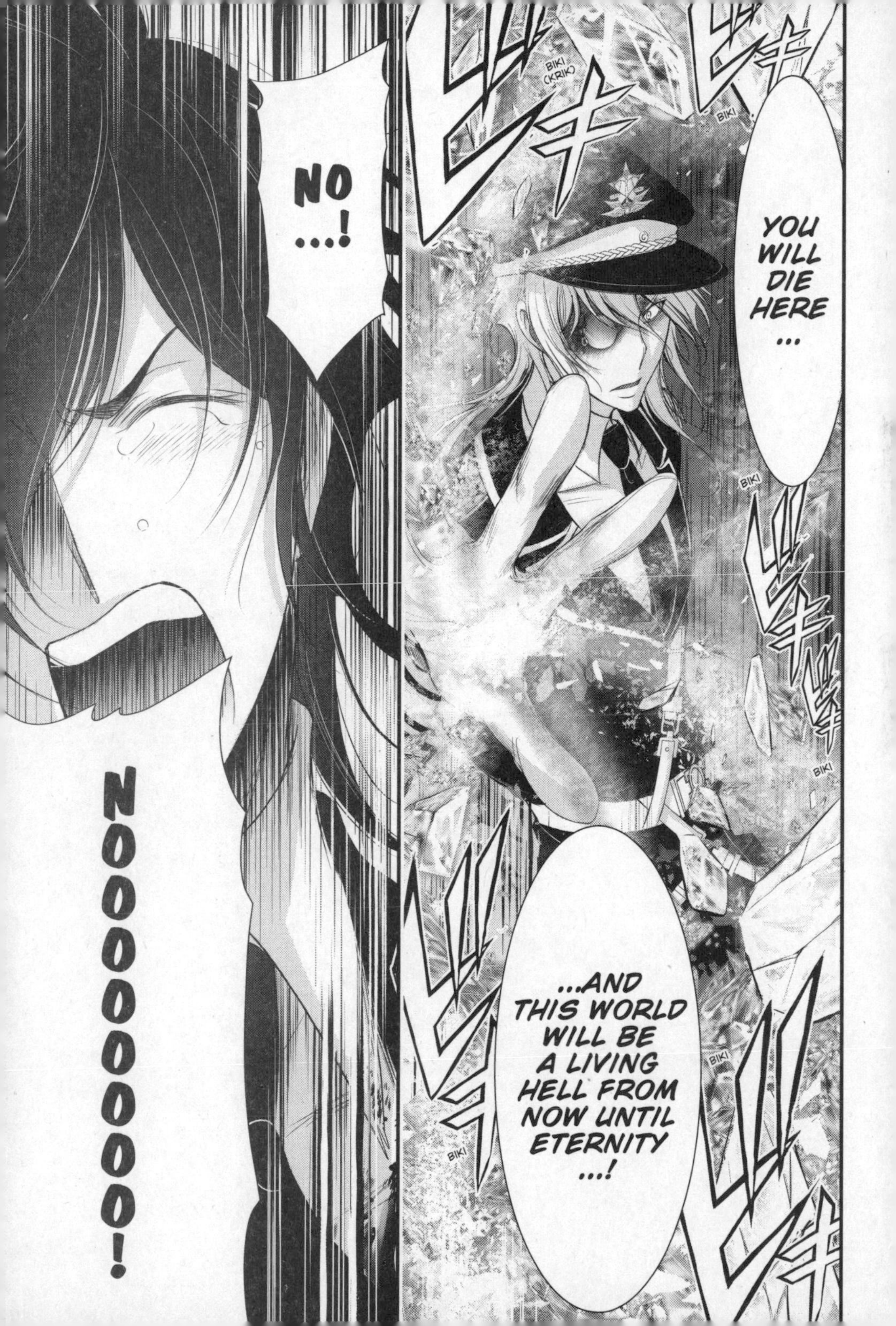
BIKI (KRIK)
BIKI
YOU WILL DIE HERE ...
BIKI
BIKI
...AND THIS WORLD WILL BE A LIVING HELL FROM NOW UNTIL ETERNITY ...!
BIKI
BIKI
NO ...!
NOOOOOOOO!

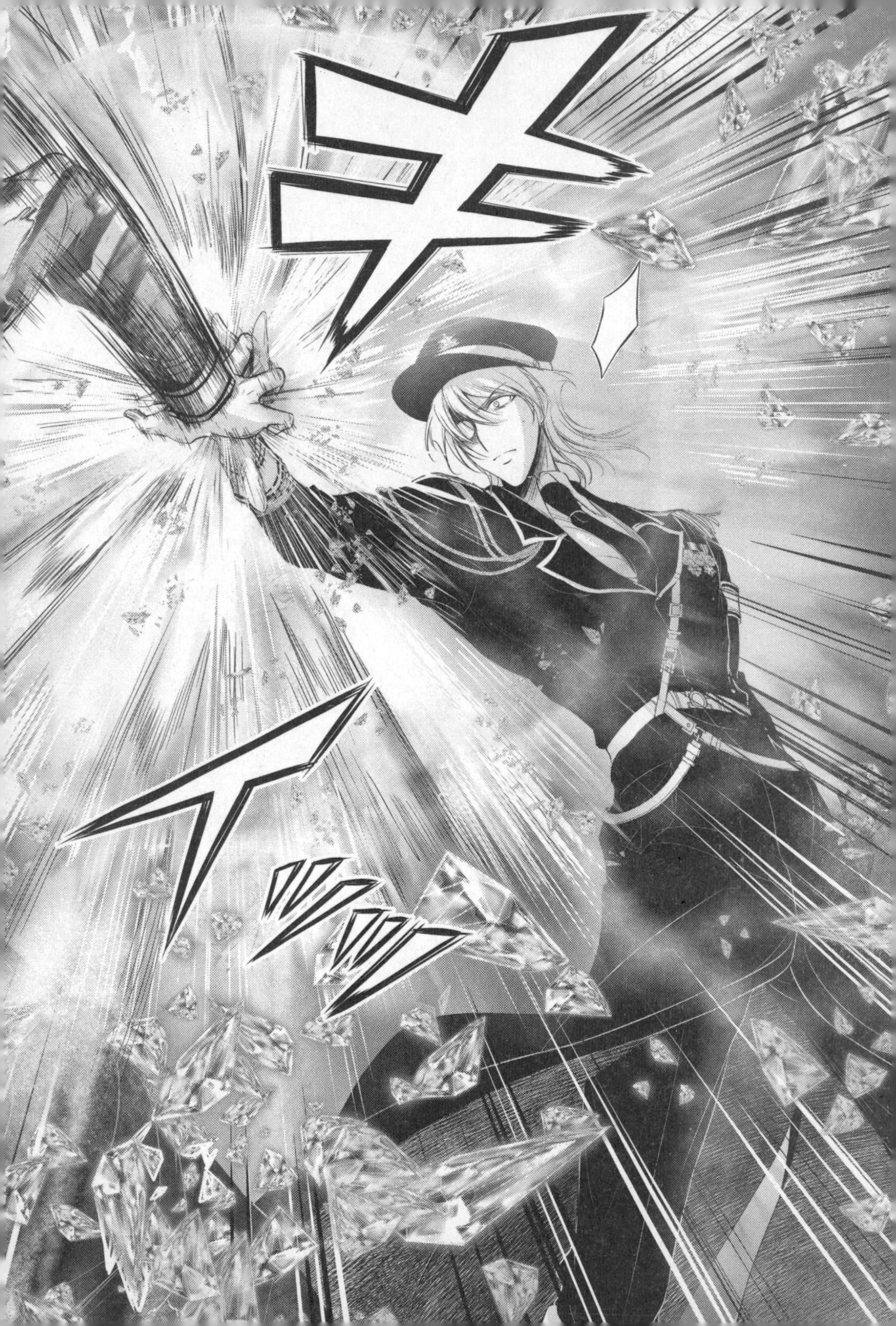

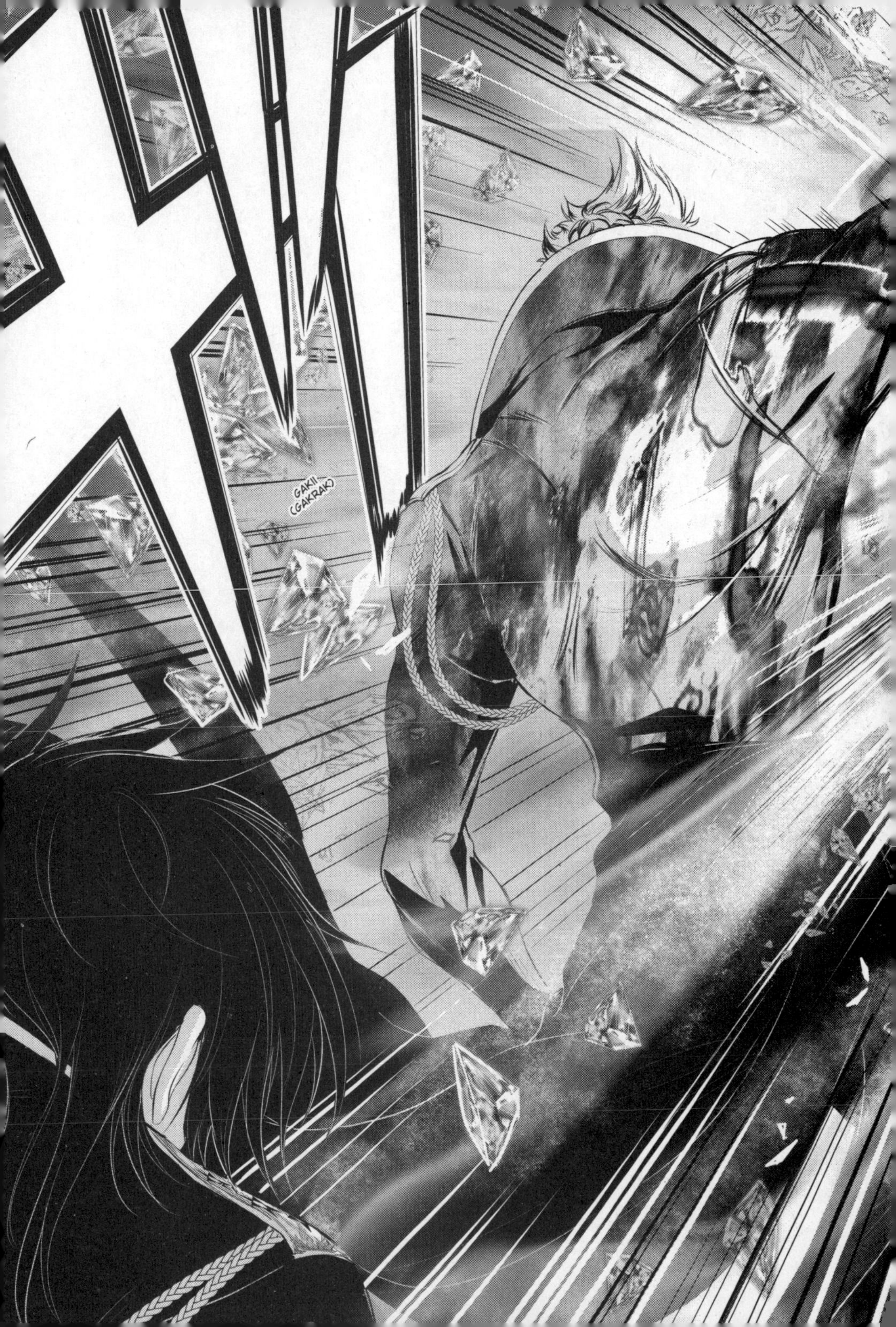
GAKII
(GAKRAK)

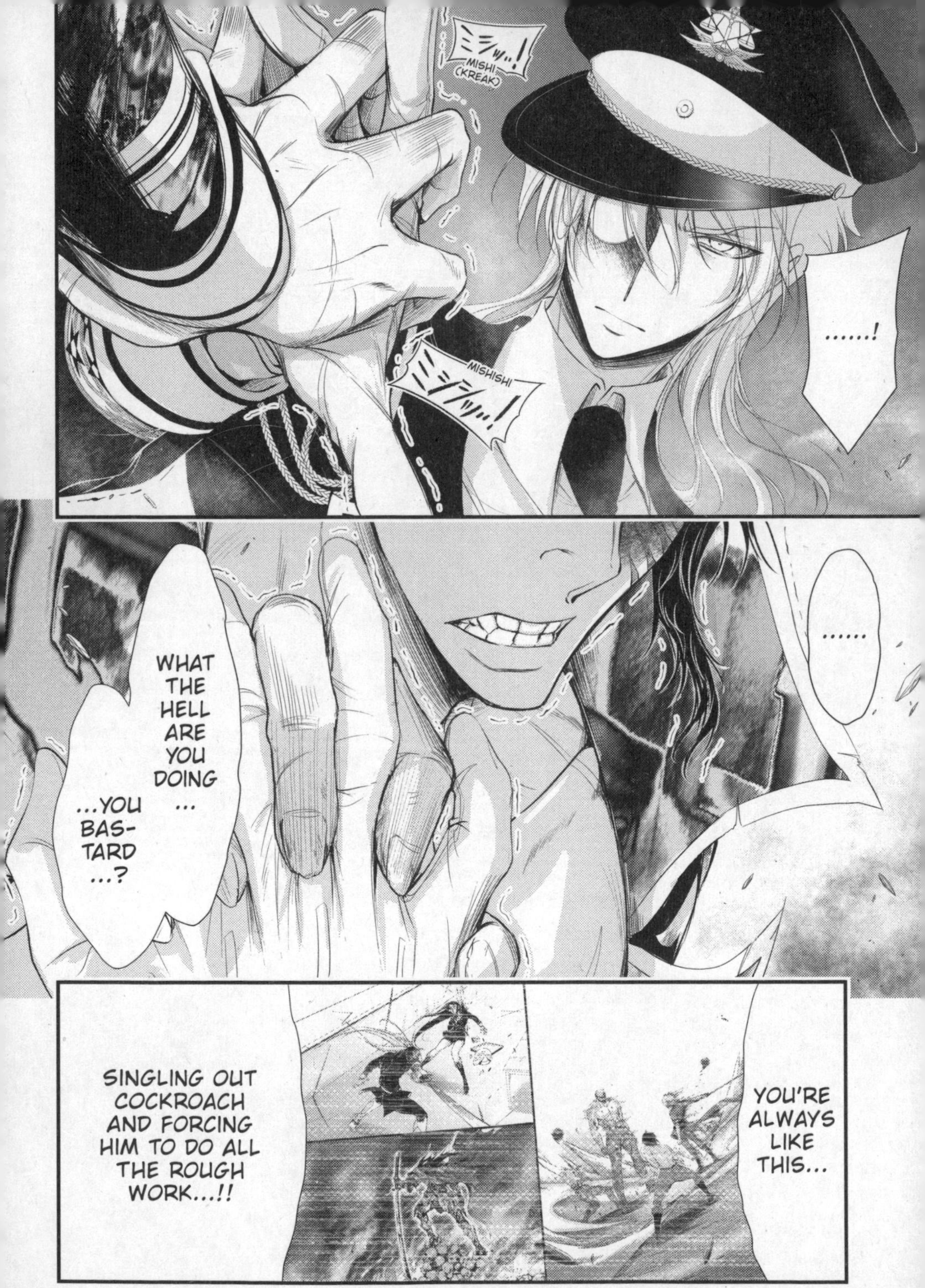
ミシッ..!
MISHI (KREAK)
......!
ミシシッ..!
MISHISHI
......
WHAT THE HELL ARE YOU DOING...
...YOU BASTARD...?
YOU'RE ALWAYS LIKE THIS...
SINGLING OUT COCKROACH AND FORCING HIM TO DO ALL THE ROUGH WORK...!!

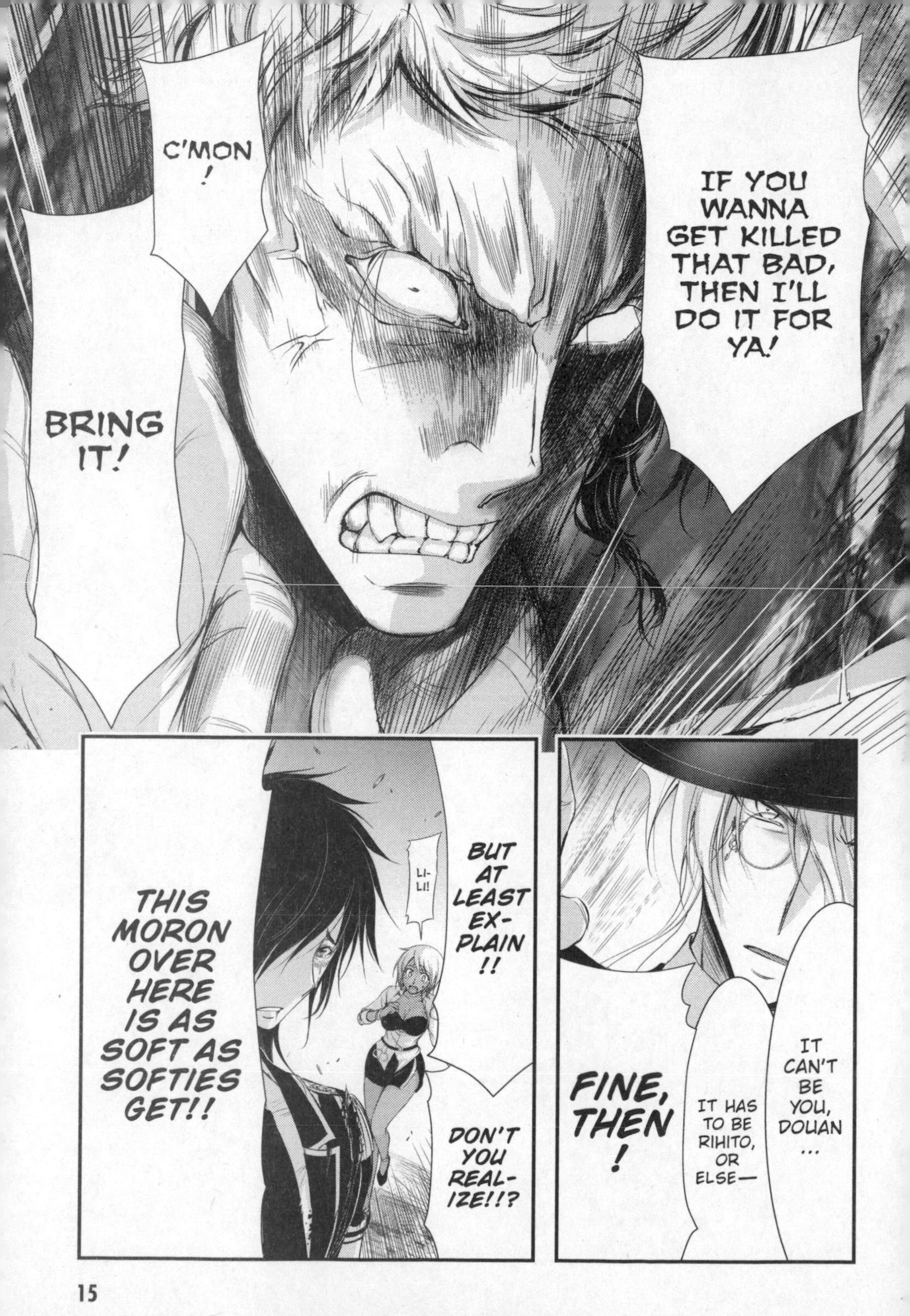
IF YOU WANNA GET KILLED THAT BAD, THEN I'LL DO IT FOR YA!
C'MON!
BRING IT!
IT CAN'T BE YOU, DOUAN...
IT HAS TO BE RIHITO, OR ELSE—
FINE, THEN!
BUT AT LEAST EX-PLAIN!!
LI-LI!
THIS MORON OVER HERE IS AS SOFT AS SOFTIES GET!!
DON'T YOU REAL-IZE!!?

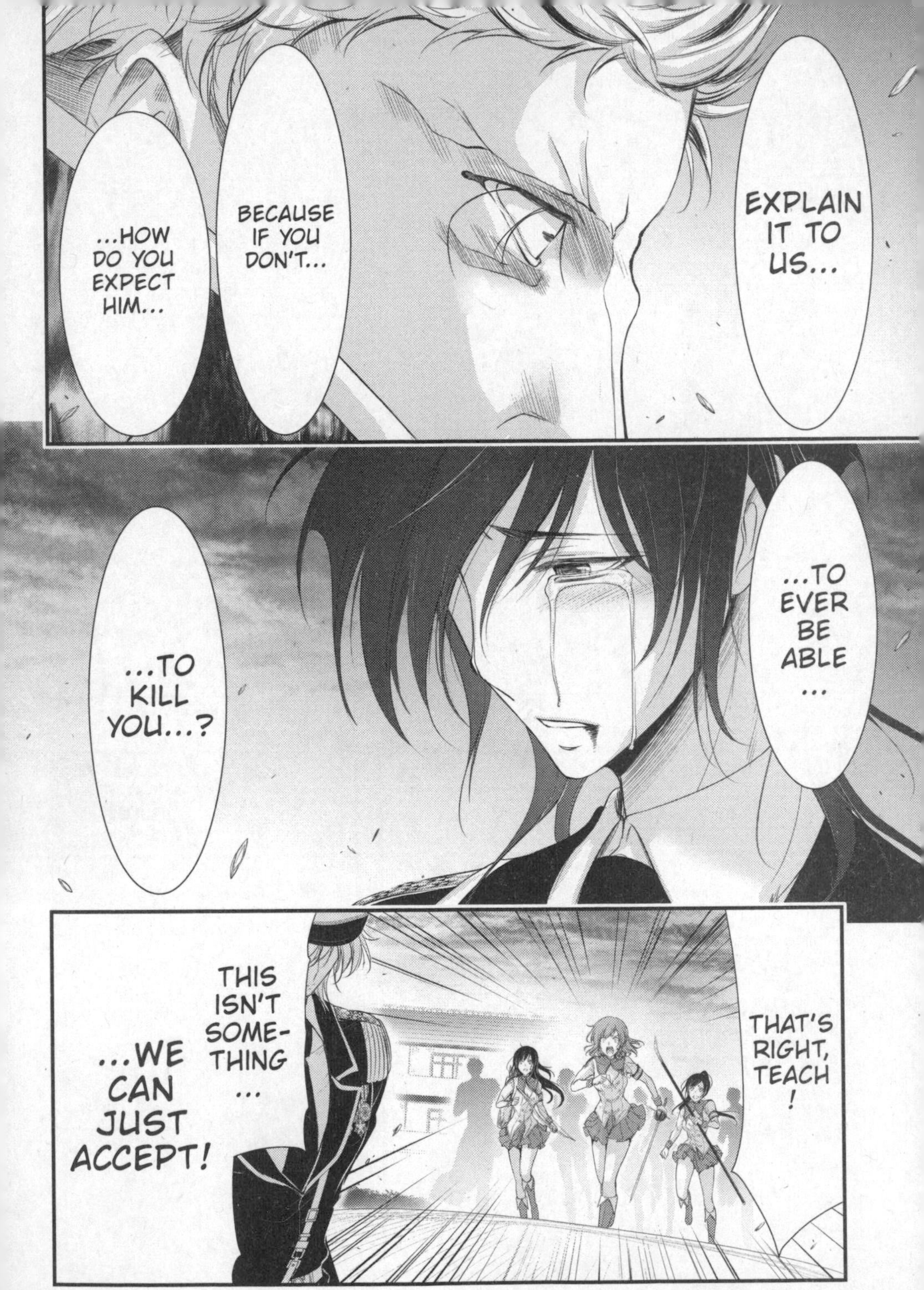
EXPLAIN IT TO US...
BECAUSE IF YOU DON'T...
...HOW DO YOU EXPECT HIM...
...TO EVER BE ABLE...
...TO KILL YOU...?
THAT'S RIGHT, TEACH!
THIS ISN'T SOME-THING...
...WE CAN JUST ACCEPT!

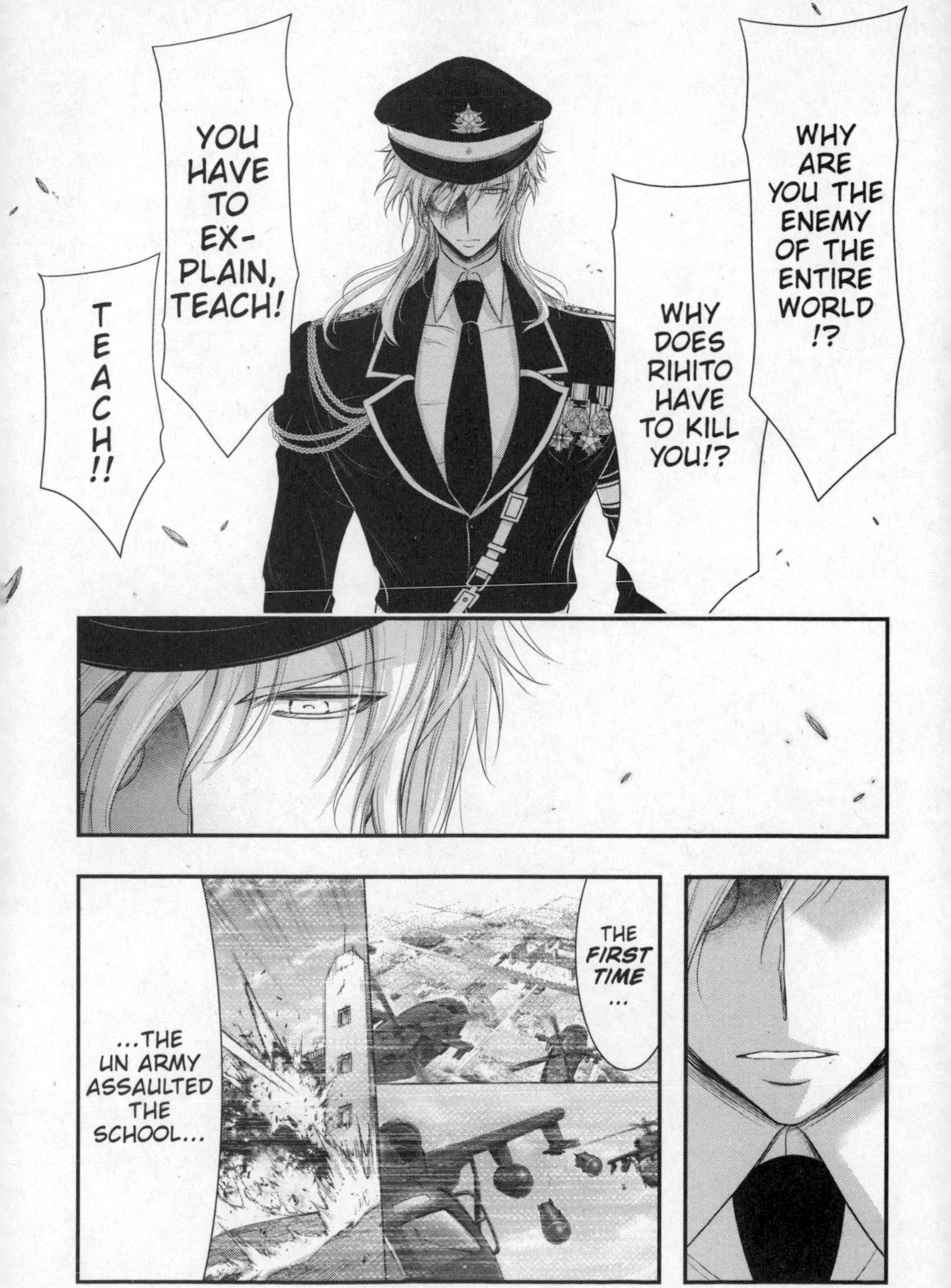
WHY ARE YOU THE ENEMY OF THE ENTIRE WORLD!?
WHY DOES RIHITO HAVE TO KILL YOU!?
YOU HAVE TO EX-PLAIN, TEACH!
TEACH!!
THE *FIRST TIME* ...
...THE UN ARMY ASSAULTED THE SCHOOL...

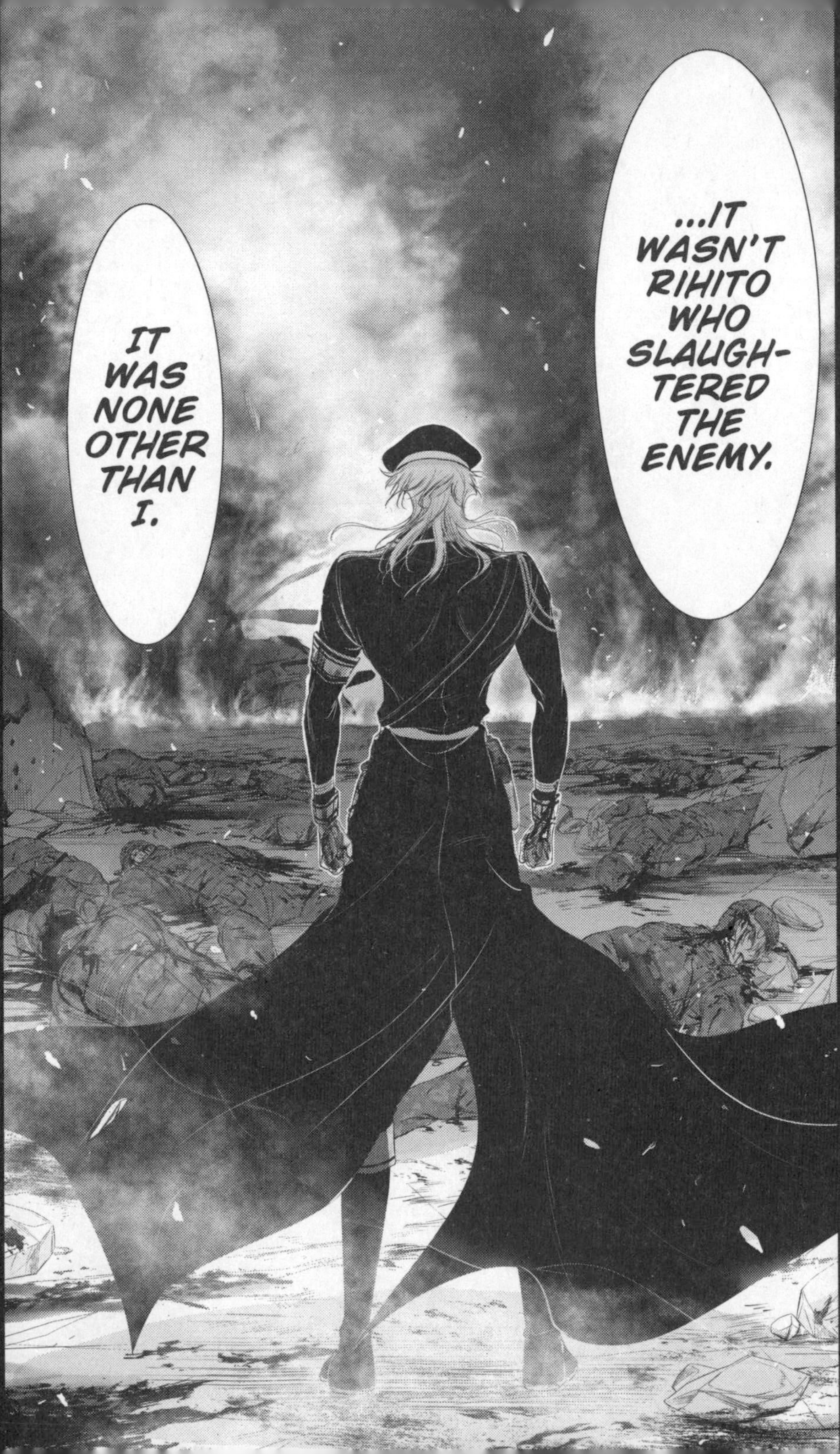
...IT WASN'T RIHITO WHO SLAUGHTERED THE ENEMY.
IT WAS NONE OTHER THAN I.

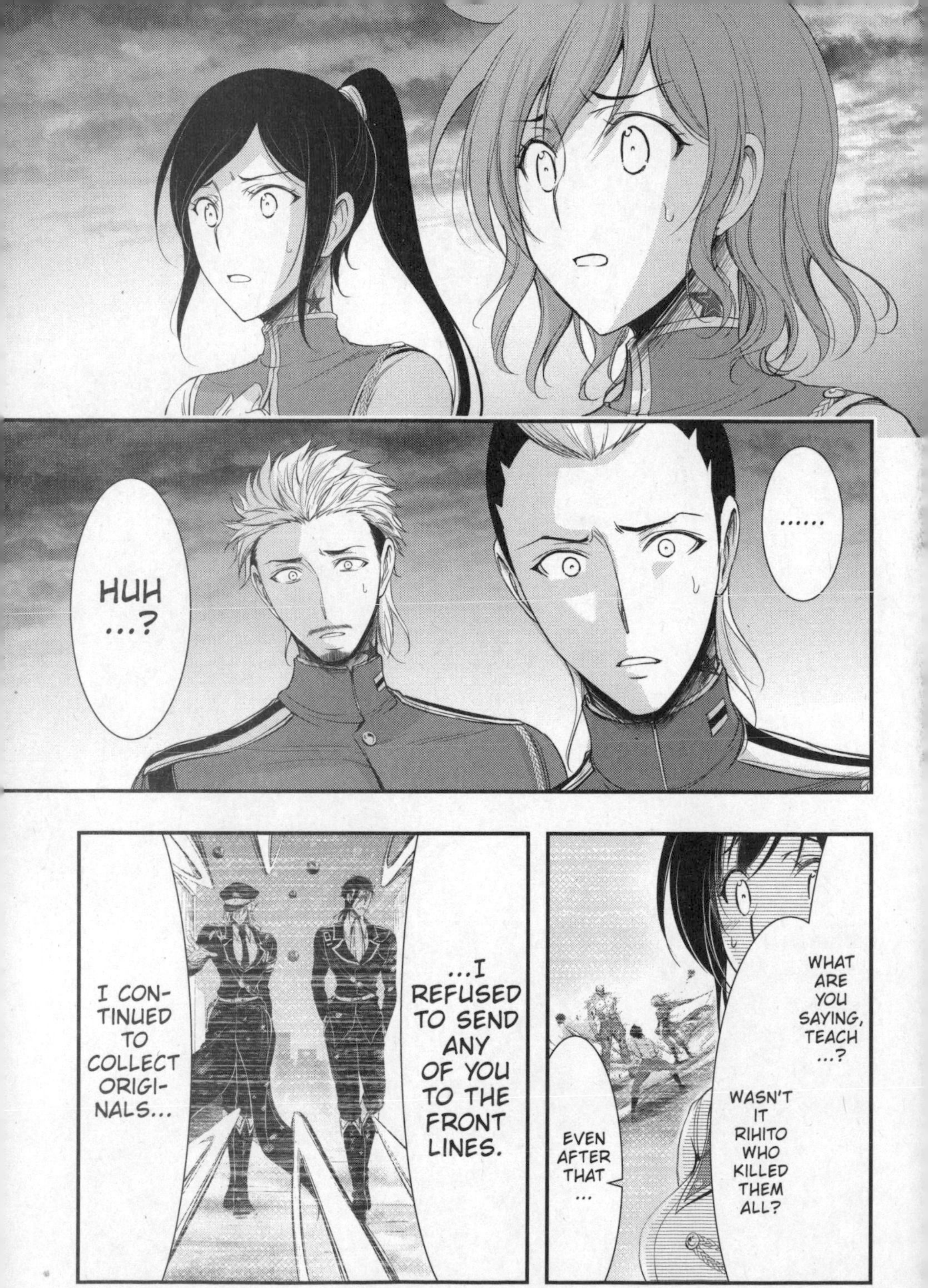
......
HUH ...?
WHAT ARE YOU SAYING, TEACH ...?
WASN'T IT RIHITO WHO KILLED THEM ALL?
EVEN AFTER THAT ...
...I REFUSED TO SEND ANY OF YOU TO THE FRONT LINES.
I CON-TINUED TO COLLECT ORIGI-NALS...

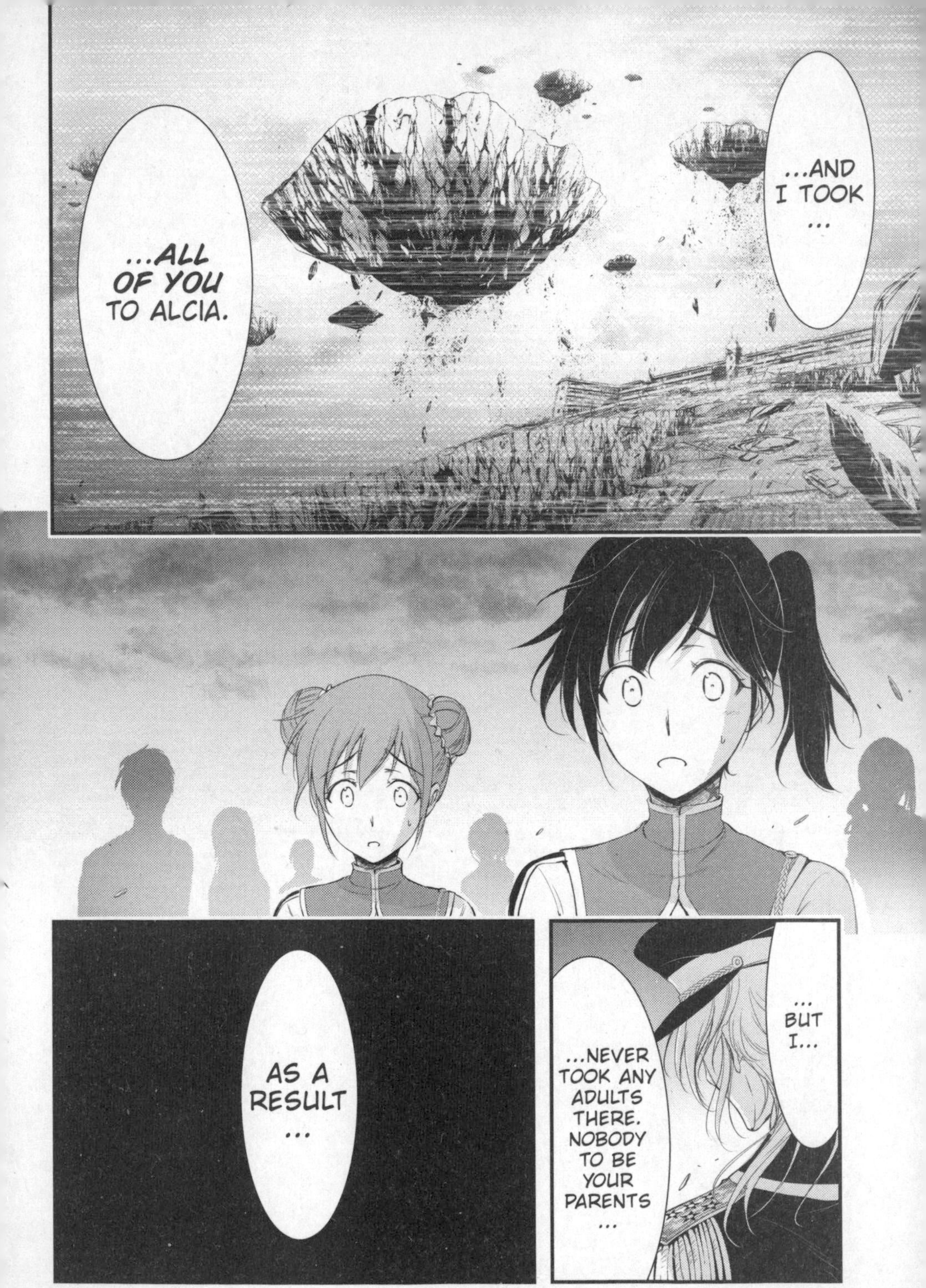
...AND I TOOK ...
...ALL OF YOU TO ALCIA.
... BUT I...
...NEVER TOOK ANY ADULTS THERE. NOBODY TO BE YOUR PARENTS ...
AS A RESULT ...

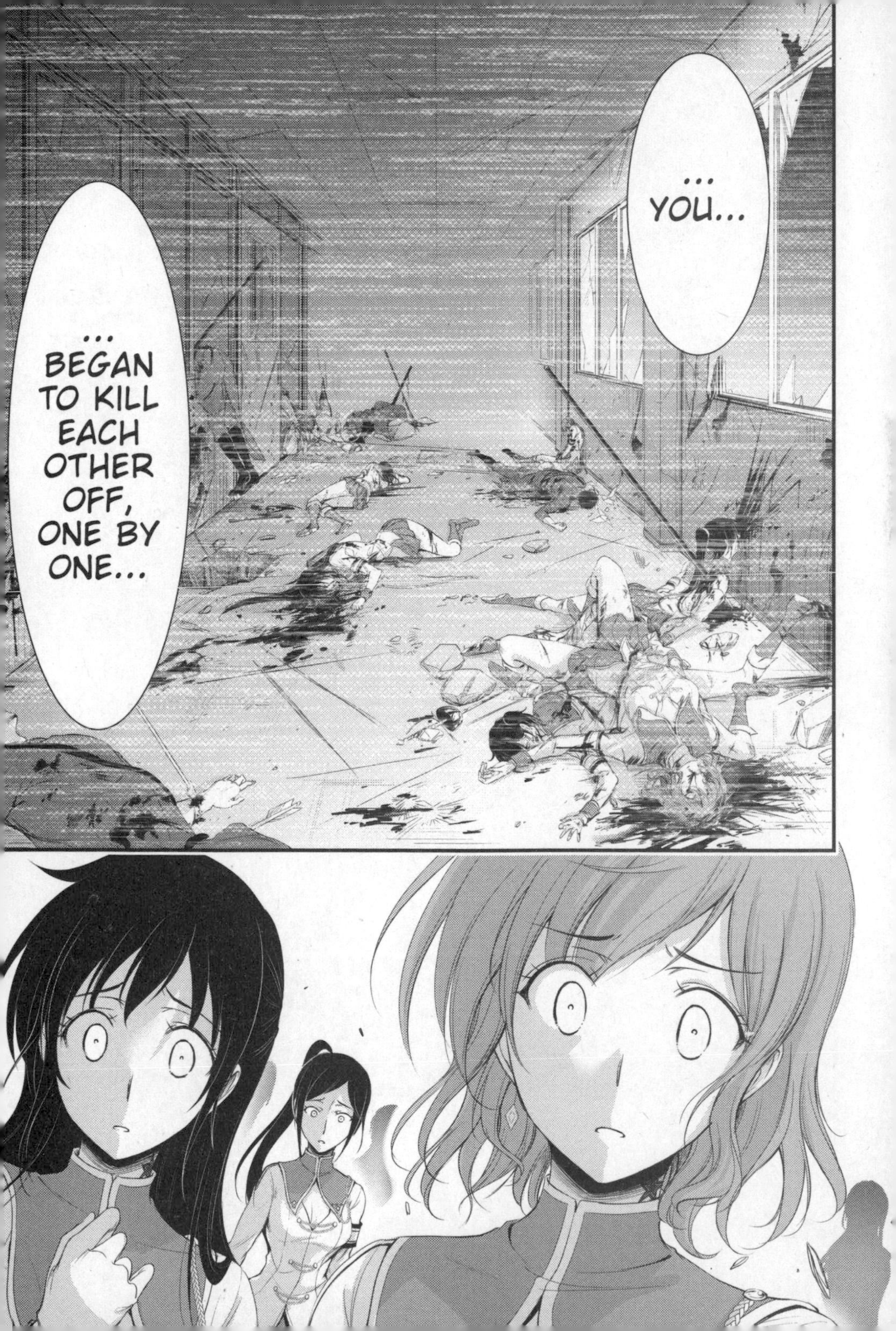
... YOU...
... BEGAN TO KILL EACH OTHER OFF, ONE BY ONE...

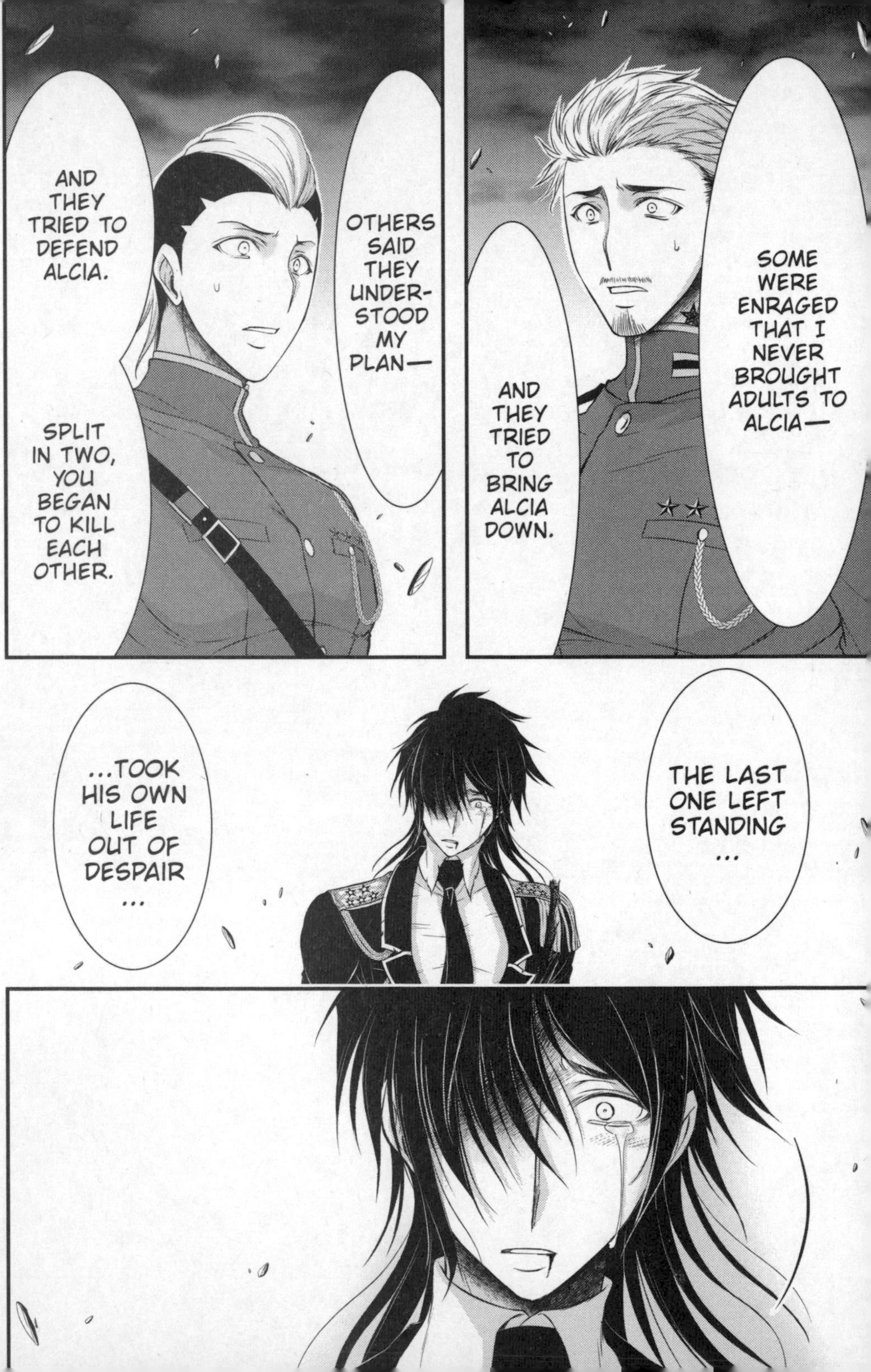
SOME WERE ENRAGED THAT I NEVER BROUGHT ADULTS TO ALCIA—
AND THEY TRIED TO BRING ALCIA DOWN.
OTHERS SAID THEY UNDER-STOOD MY PLAN—
AND THEY TRIED TO DEFEND ALCIA.
SPLIT IN TWO, YOU BEGAN TO KILL EACH OTHER.
THE LAST ONE LEFT STANDING ...
...TOOK HIS OWN LIFE OUT OF DESPAIR ...

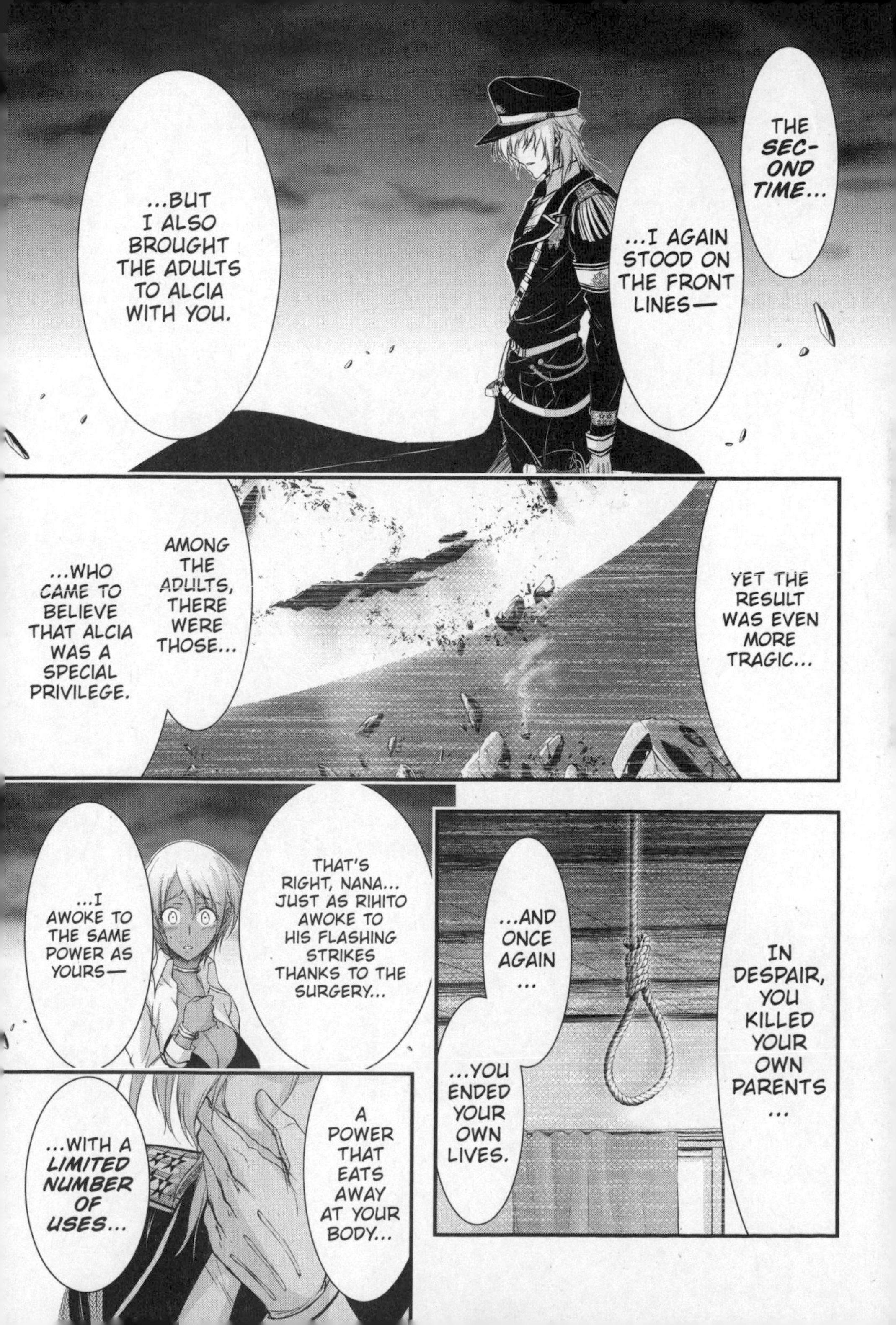
THE *SECOND TIME*...
...I AGAIN STOOD ON THE FRONT LINES—
...BUT I ALSO BROUGHT THE ADULTS TO ALCIA WITH YOU.
YET THE RESULT WAS EVEN MORE TRAGIC...
AMONG THE ADULTS, THERE WERE THOSE...
...WHO CAME TO BELIEVE THAT ALCIA WAS A SPECIAL PRIVILEGE.
IN DESPAIR, YOU KILLED YOUR OWN PARENTS...
...AND ONCE AGAIN...
...YOU ENDED YOUR OWN LIVES.
THAT'S RIGHT, NANA... JUST AS RIHITO AWOKE TO HIS FLASHING STRIKES THANKS TO THE SURGERY...
...I AWOKE TO THE SAME POWER AS YOURS—
A POWER THAT EATS AWAY AT YOUR BODY...
...WITH A *LIMITED NUMBER OF USES*...

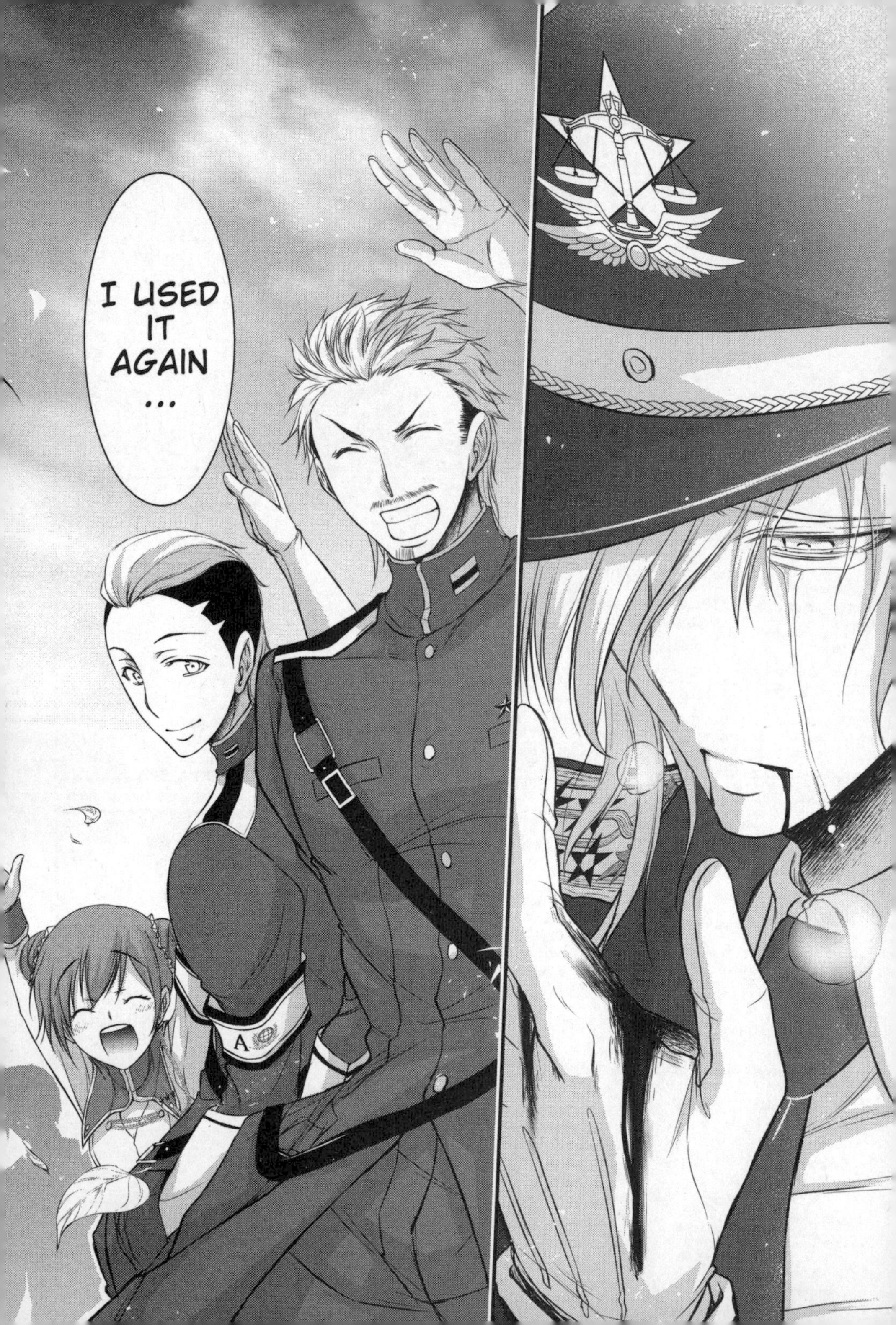
I USED IT AGAIN...

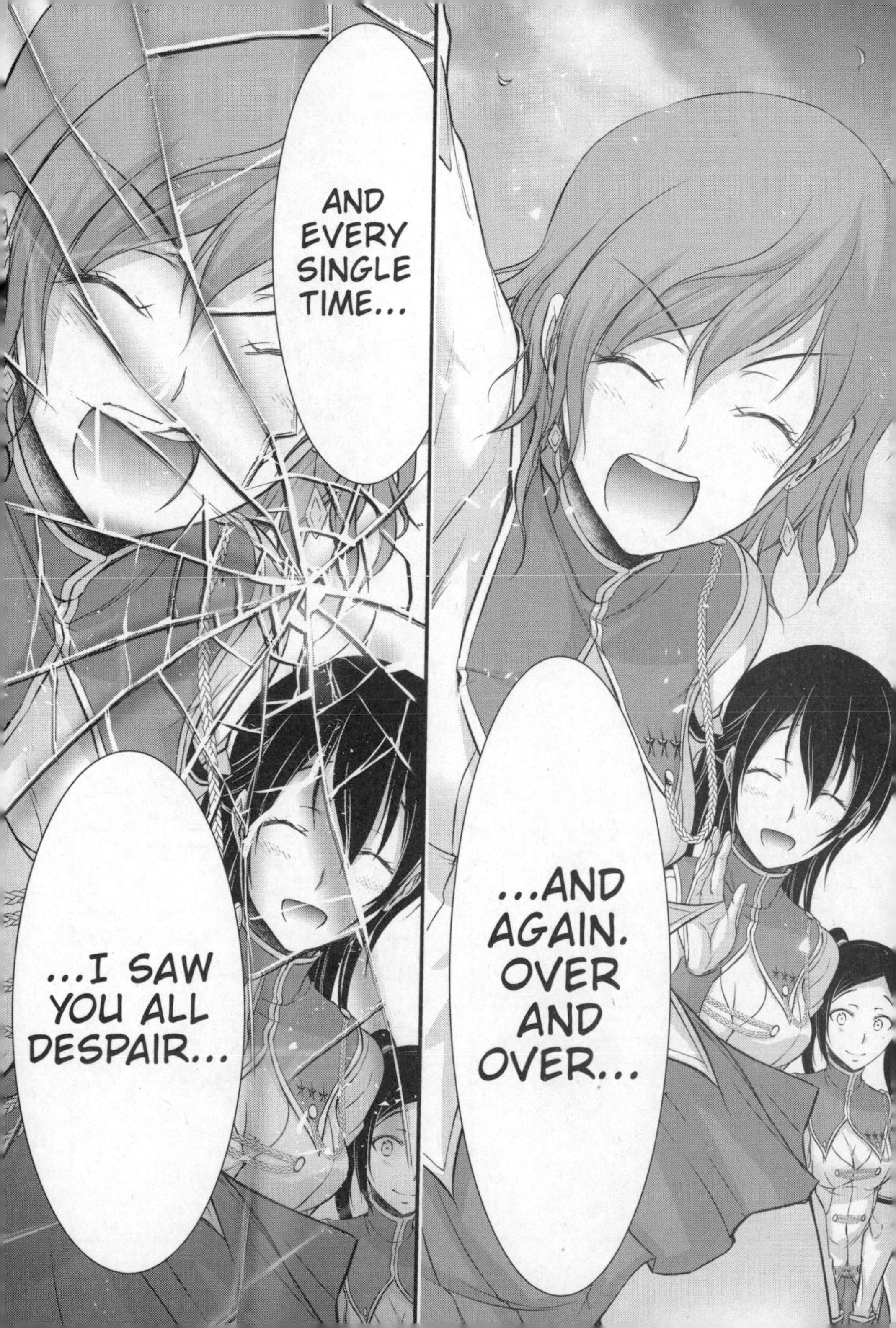
...AND AGAIN. OVER AND OVER...
AND EVERY SINGLE TIME...
...I SAW YOU ALL DESPAIR...

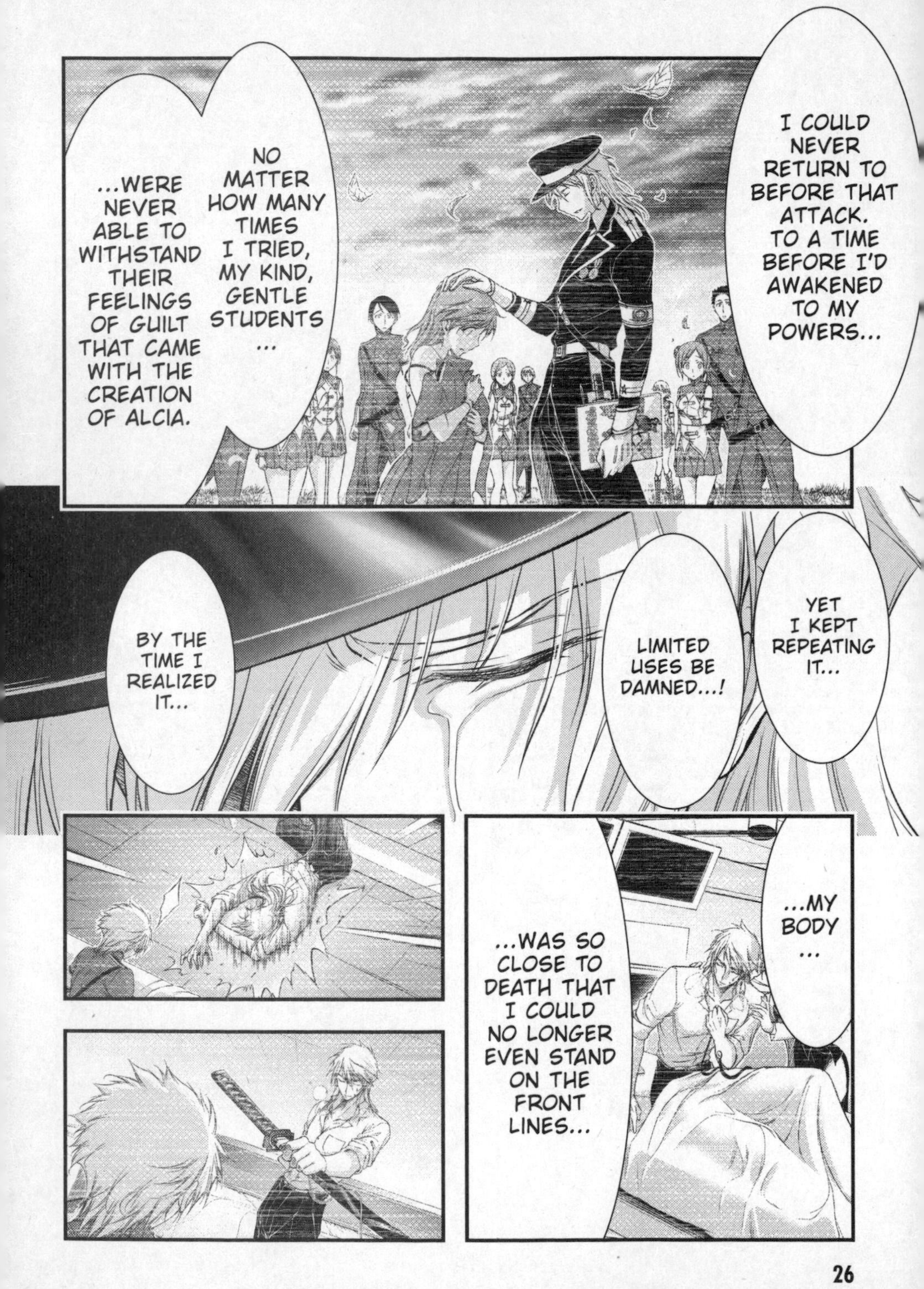
I COULD NEVER RETURN TO BEFORE THAT ATTACK. TO A TIME BEFORE I'D AWAKENED TO MY POWERS...
NO MATTER HOW MANY TIMES I TRIED, MY KIND, GENTLE STUDENTS ...
...WERE NEVER ABLE TO WITHSTAND THEIR FEELINGS OF GUILT THAT CAME WITH THE CREATION OF ALCIA.
YET I KEPT REPEATING IT...
LIMITED USES BE DAMNED...!
BY THE TIME I REALIZED IT...
...MY BODY ...
...WAS SO CLOSE TO DEATH THAT I COULD NO LONGER EVEN STAND ON THE FRONT LINES...

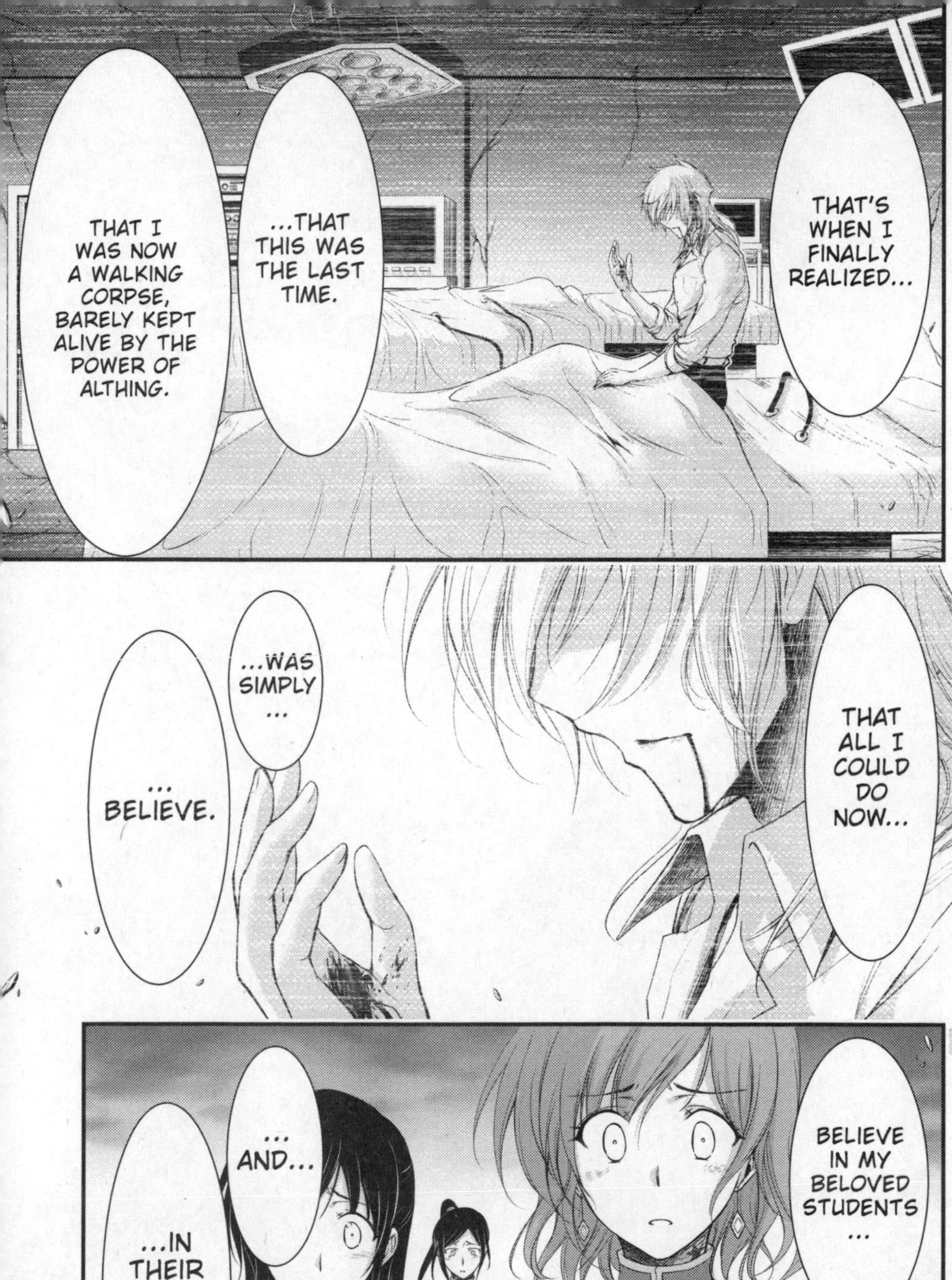
THAT'S WHEN I FINALLY REALIZED...
...THAT THIS WAS THE LAST TIME.
THAT I WAS NOW A WALKING CORPSE, BARELY KEPT ALIVE BY THE POWER OF ALTHING.
THAT ALL I COULD DO NOW...
...WAS SIMPLY...
...BELIEVE.
BELIEVE IN MY BELOVED STUDENTS...
...AND...
...IN THEIR CAPTAIN—

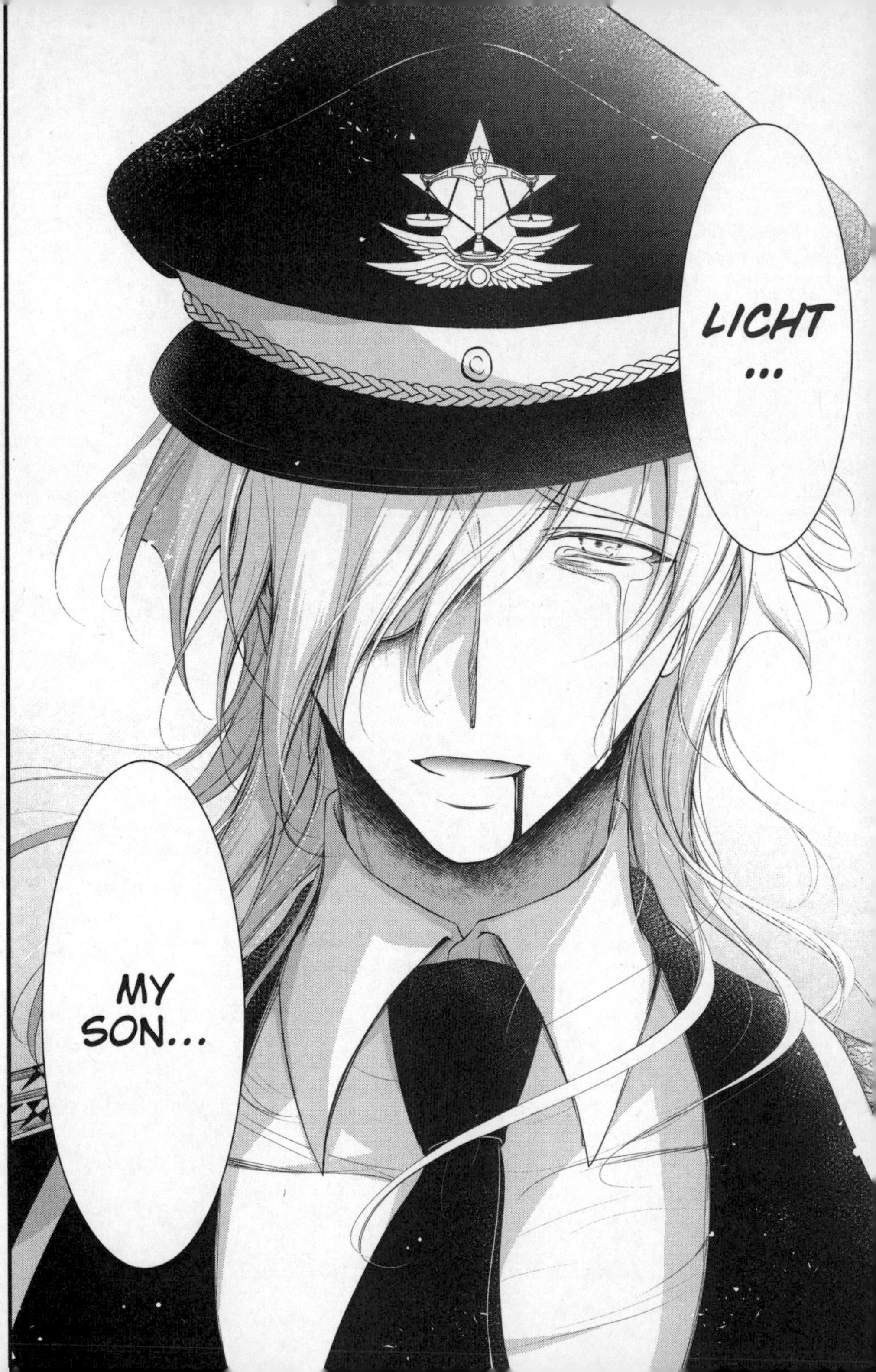
LICHT ...
MY SON...

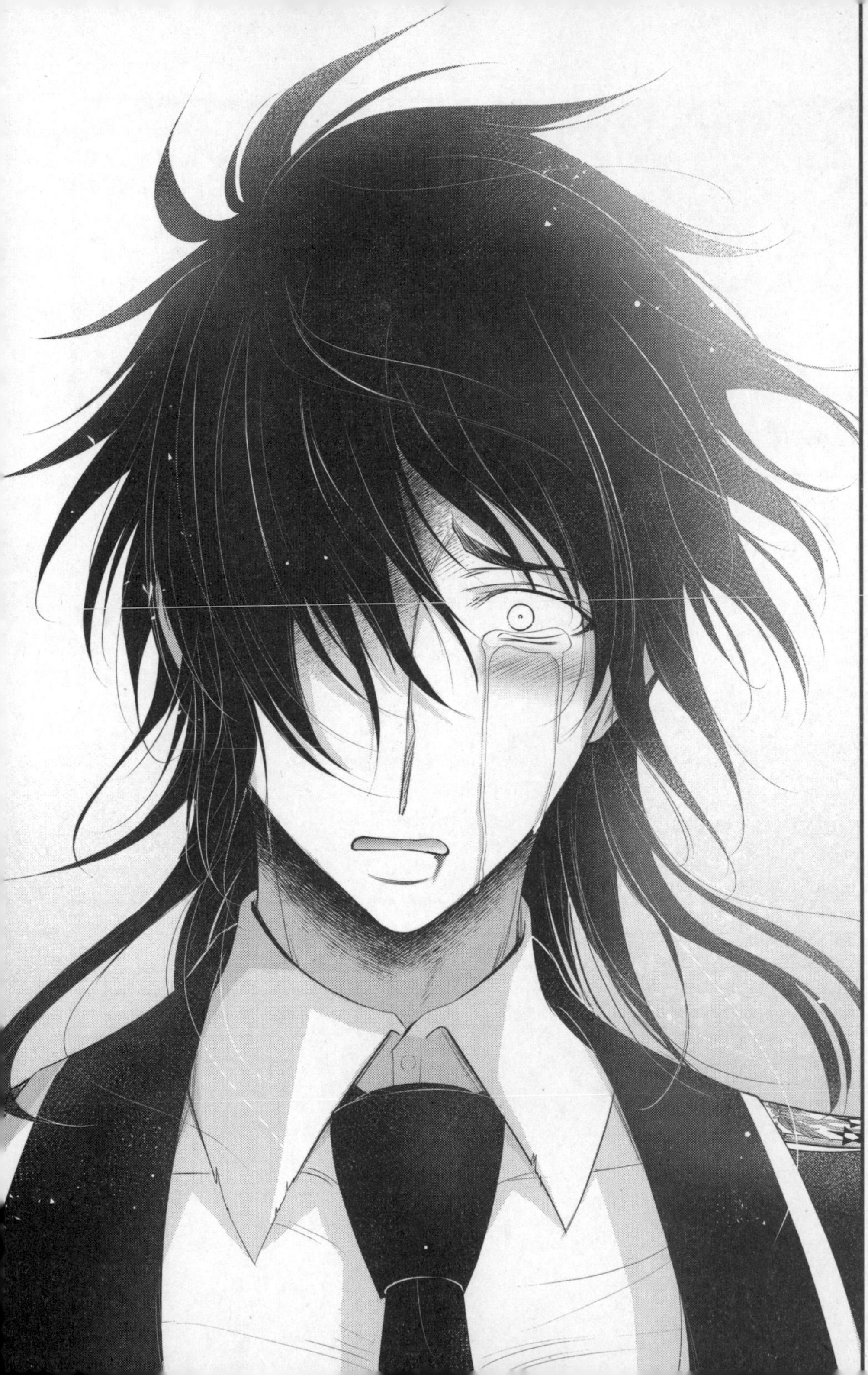

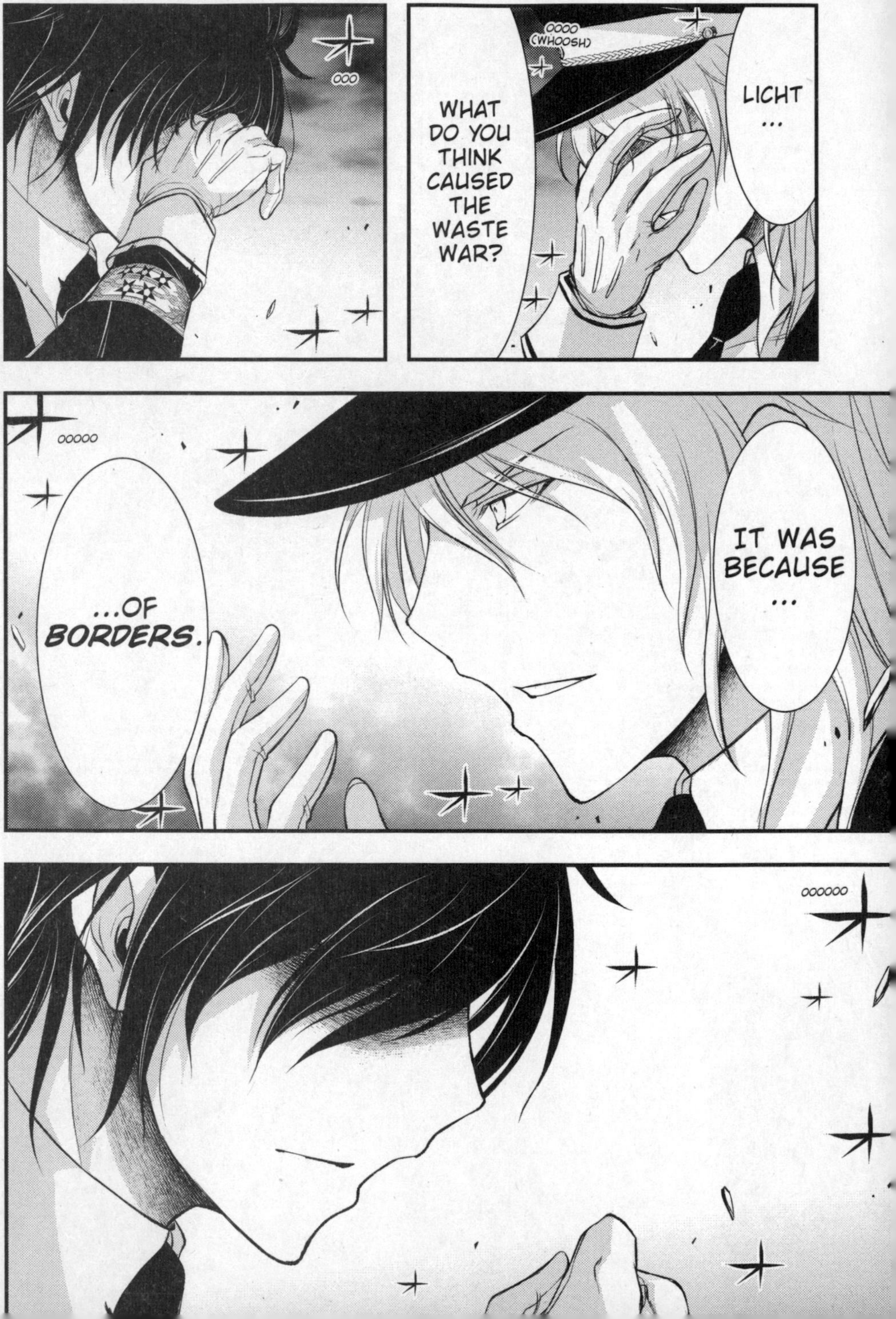
(WHOOSH)
LICHT ...
WHAT DO YOU THINK CAUSED THE WASTE WAR?
IT WAS BECAUSE ...
...OF BORDERS.

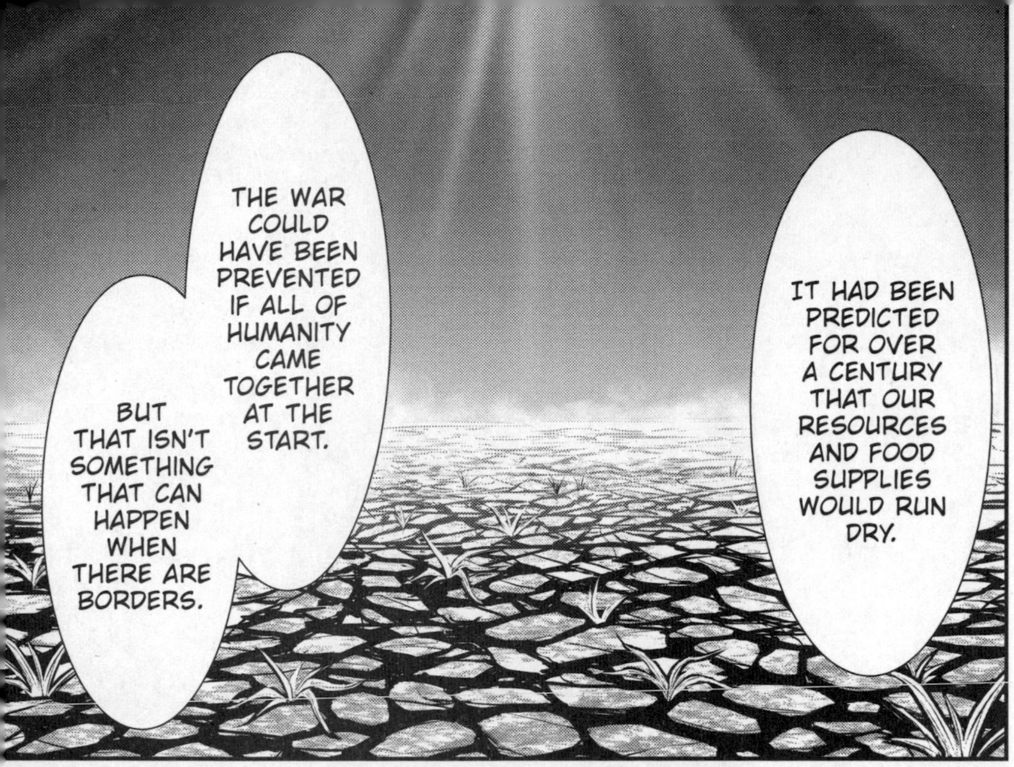
IT HAD BEEN PREDICTED FOR OVER A CENTURY THAT OUR RESOURCES AND FOOD SUPPLIES WOULD RUN DRY.
THE WAR COULD HAVE BEEN PREVENTED IF ALL OF HUMANITY CAME TOGETHER AT THE START.
BUT THAT ISN'T SOMETHING THAT CAN HAPPEN WHEN THERE ARE BORDERS.
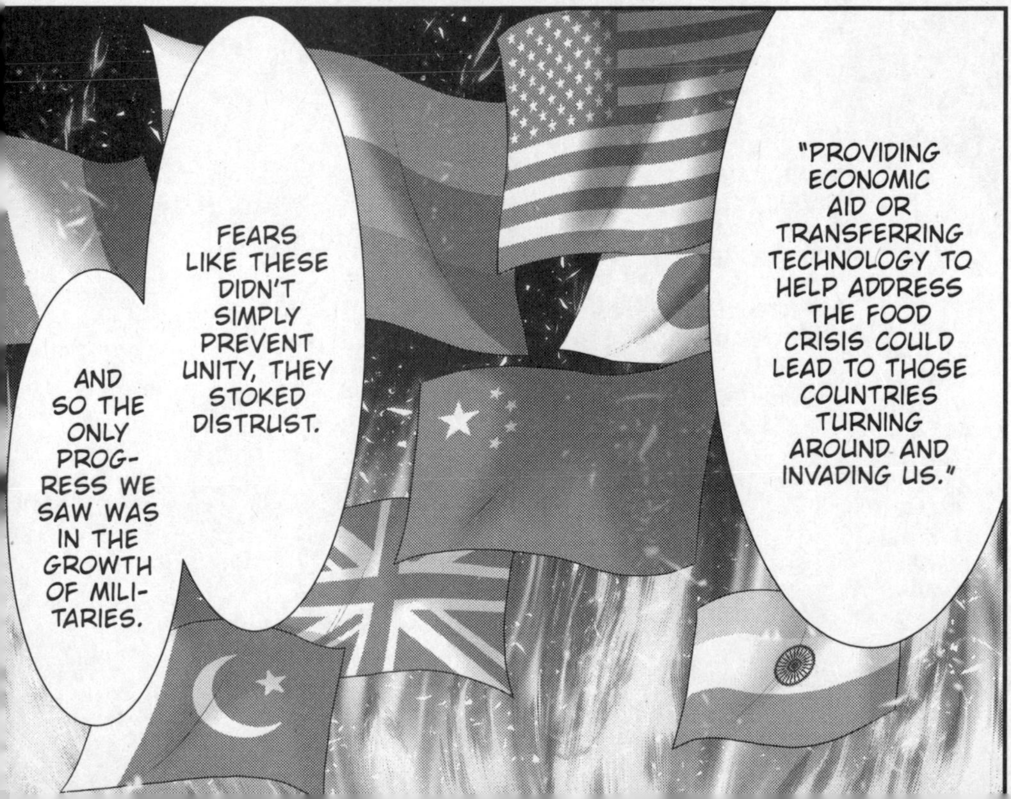
"PROVIDING ECONOMIC AID OR TRANSFERRING TECHNOLOGY TO HELP ADDRESS THE FOOD CRISIS COULD LEAD TO THOSE COUNTRIES TURNING AROUND AND INVADING US."
FEARS LIKE THESE DIDN'T SIMPLY PREVENT UNITY, THEY STOKED DISTRUST.
AND SO THE ONLY PROG-RESS WE SAW WAS IN THE GROWTH OF MILI-TARIES.

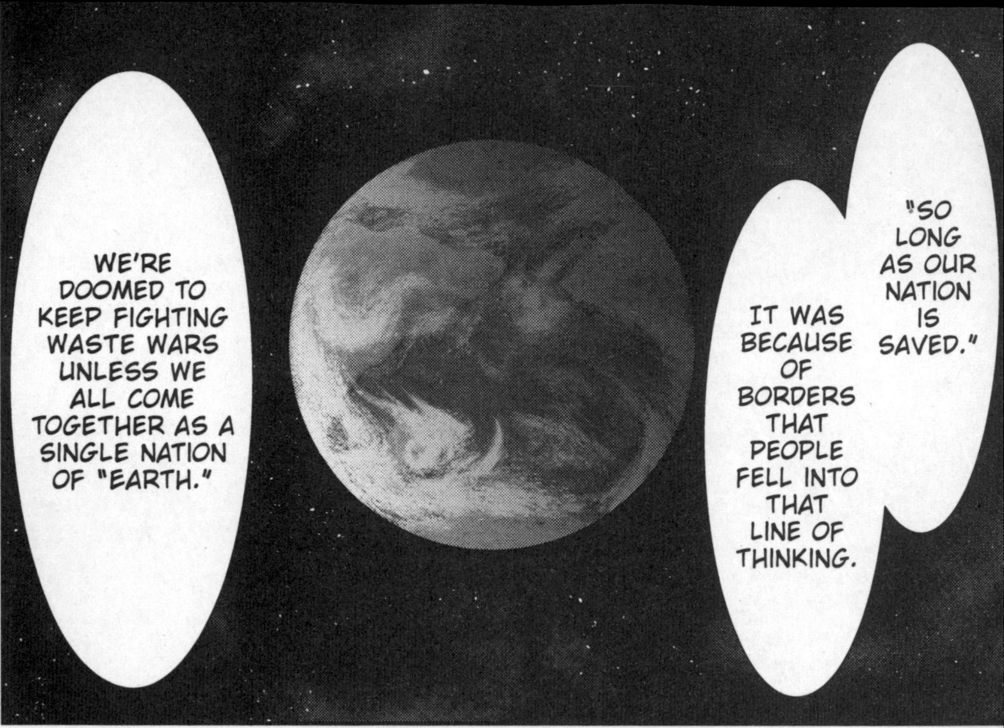
"SO LONG AS OUR NATION IS SAVED."
IT WAS BECAUSE OF BORDERS THAT PEOPLE FELL INTO THAT LINE OF THINKING.
WE'RE DOOMED TO KEEP FIGHTING WASTE WARS UNLESS WE ALL COME TOGETHER AS A SINGLE NATION OF "EARTH."

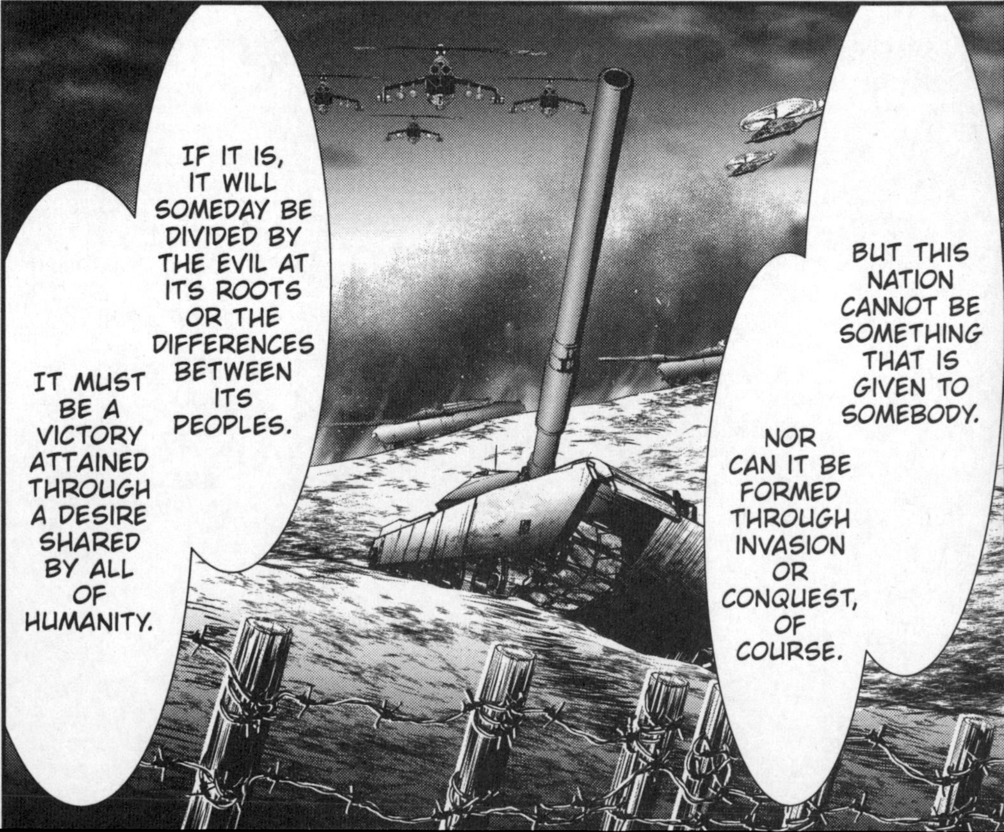
BUT THIS NATION CANNOT BE SOMETHING THAT IS GIVEN TO SOMEBODY.
NOR CAN IT BE FORMED THROUGH INVASION OR CONQUEST, OF COURSE.
IF IT IS, IT WILL SOMEDAY BE DIVIDED BY THE EVIL AT ITS ROOTS OR THE DIFFERENCES BETWEEN ITS PEOPLES.
IT MUST BE A VICTORY ATTAINED THROUGH A DESIRE SHARED BY ALL OF HUMANITY.

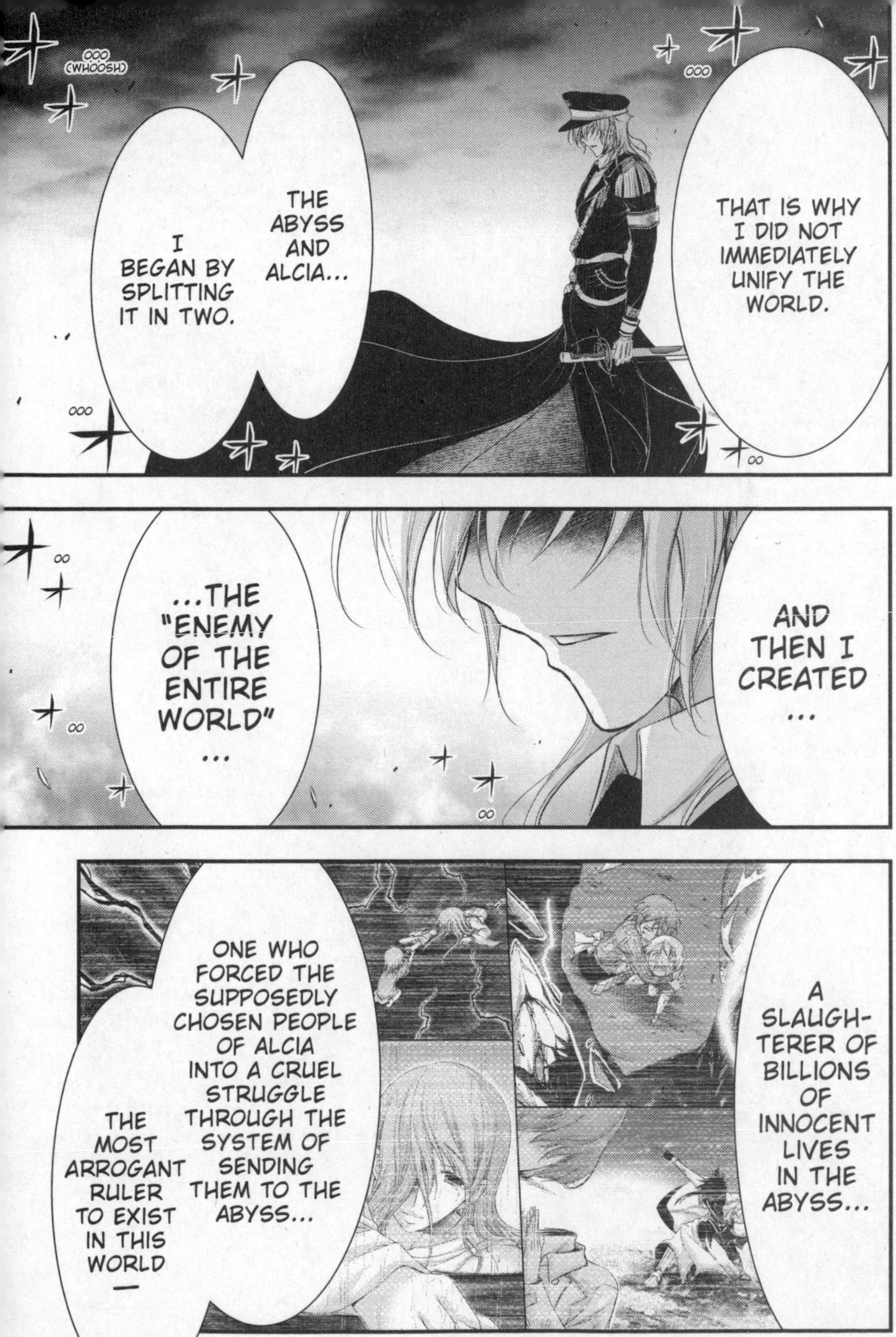

(WHOOSH)
THAT IS WHY I DID NOT IMMEDIATELY UNIFY THE WORLD.
THE ABYSS AND ALCIA... I BEGAN BY SPLITTING IT IN TWO.
AND THEN I CREATED...
..."THE ENEMY OF THE ENTIRE WORLD"...
A SLAUGHTERER OF BILLIONS OF INNOCENT LIVES IN THE ABYSS...
ONE WHO FORCED THE SUPPOSEDLY CHOSEN PEOPLE OF ALCIA INTO A CRUEL STRUGGLE THROUGH THE SYSTEM OF SENDING THEM TO THE ABYSS...
THE MOST ARROGANT RULER TO EXIST IN THIS WORLD—

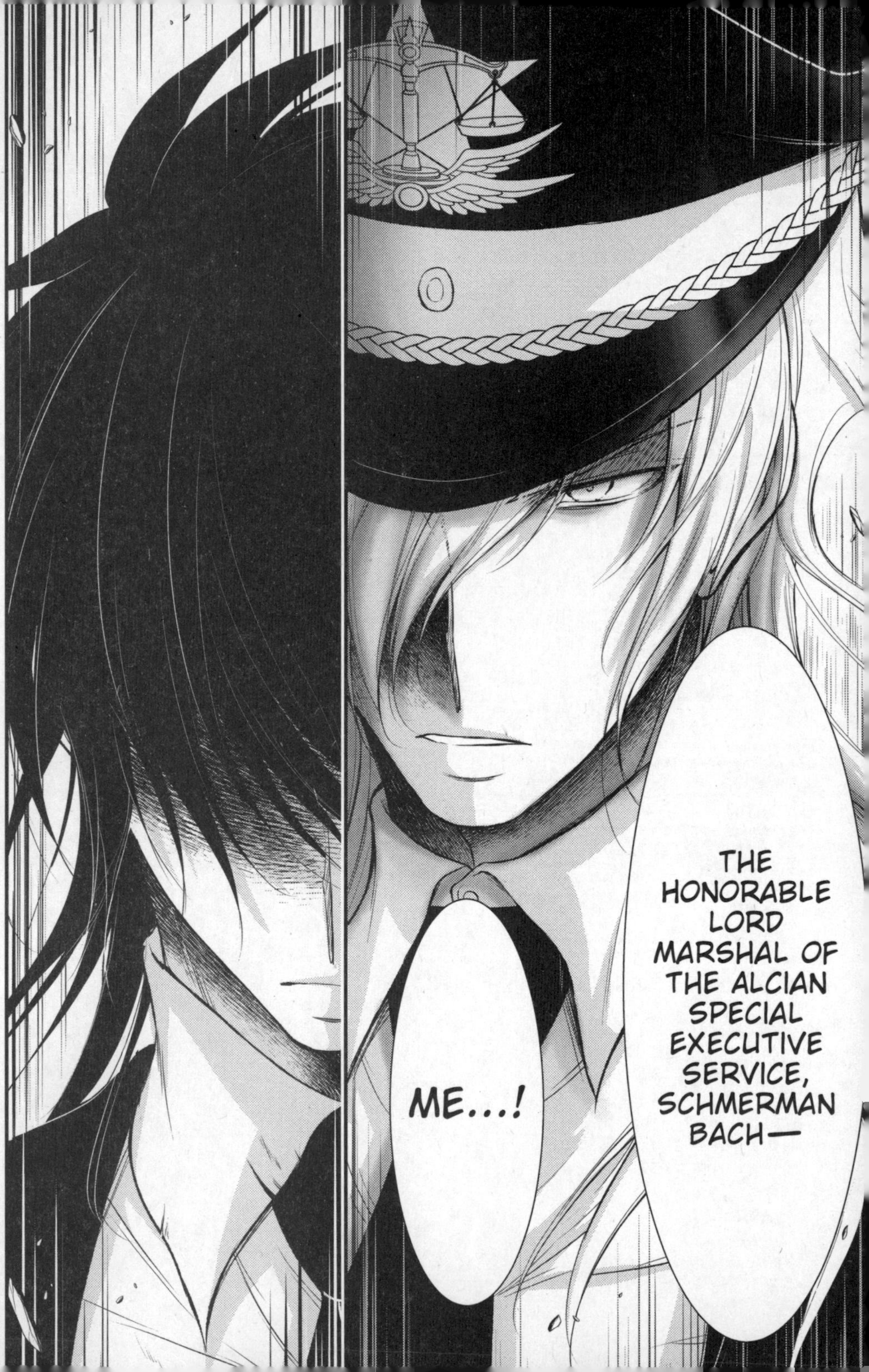
THE HONORABLE LORD MARSHAL OF THE ALCIAN SPECIAL EXECUTIVE SERVICE, SCHMERMAN BACH—
ME...!

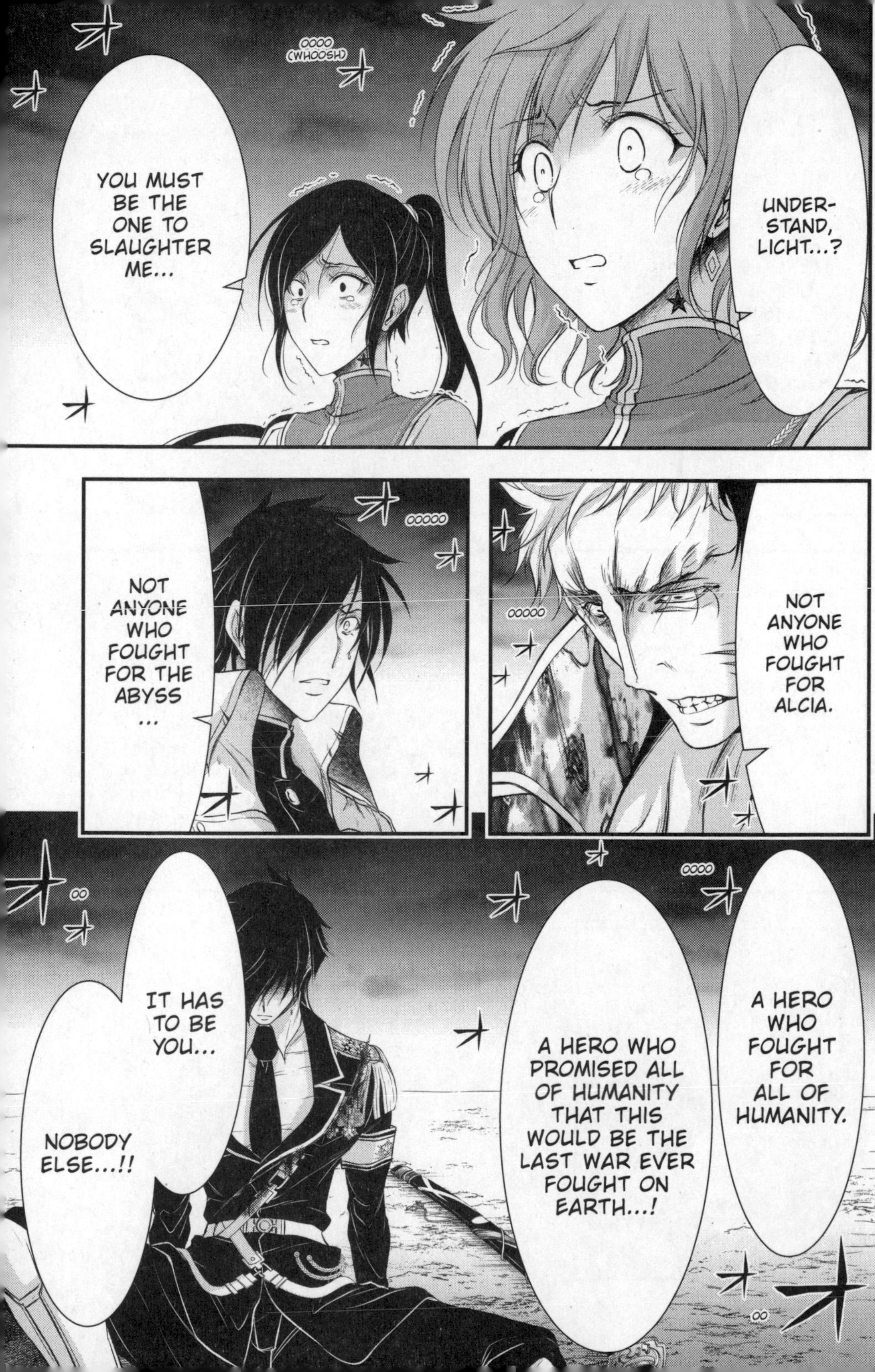
UNDER-STAND, LICHT...?
OOOO (WHOOSH)
YOU MUST BE THE ONE TO SLAUGHTER ME...
NOT ANYONE WHO FOUGHT FOR ALCIA.
OOOOO
OOOOO
NOT ANYONE WHO FOUGHT FOR THE ABYSS ...
A HERO WHO FOUGHT FOR ALL OF HUMANITY.
OOOO
A HERO WHO PROMISED ALL OF HUMANITY THAT THIS WOULD BE THE LAST WAR EVER FOUGHT ON EARTH...!
IT HAS TO BE YOU...
NOBODY ELSE...!!

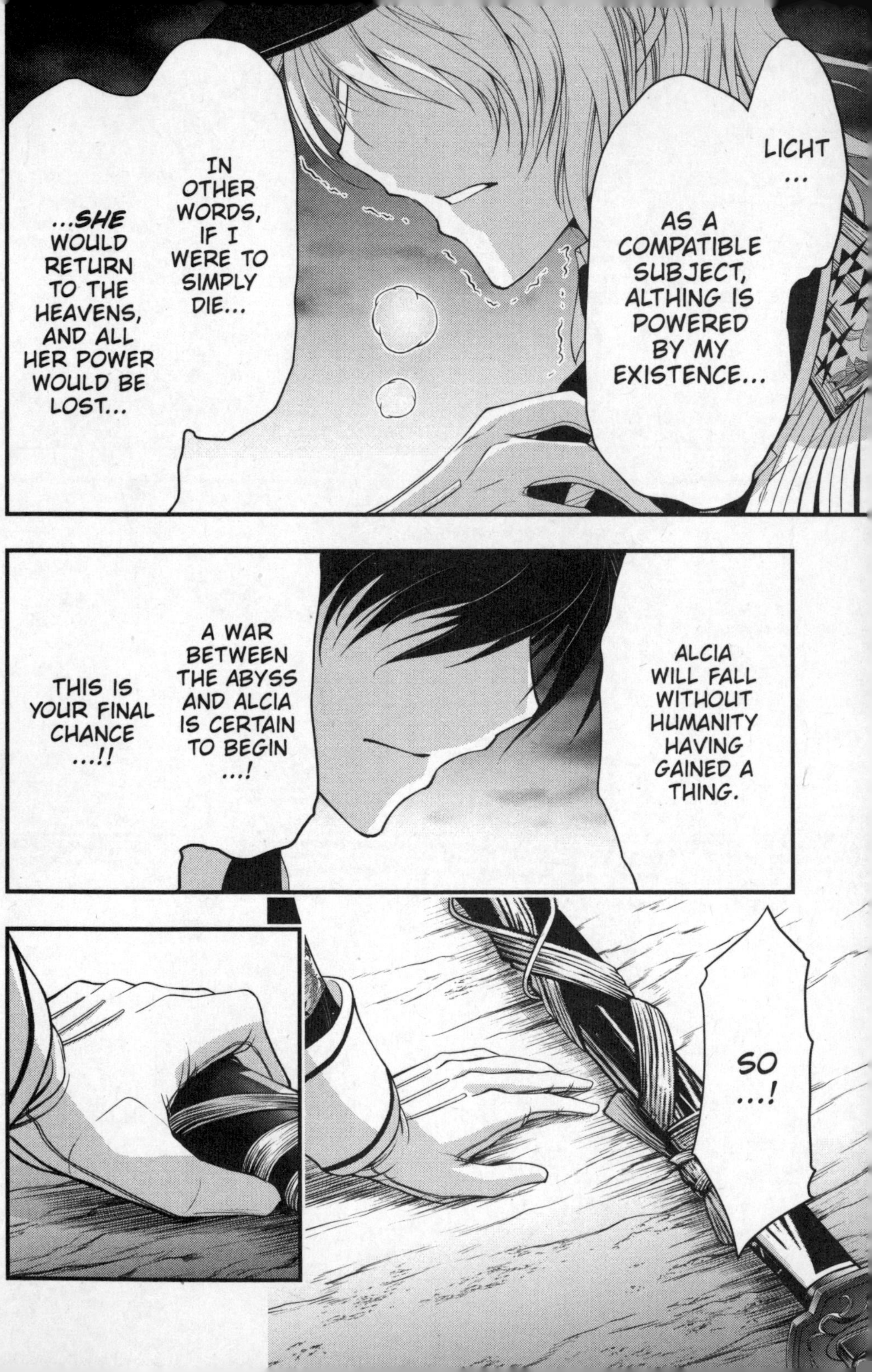
LICHT ...
AS A COMPATIBLE SUBJECT, ALTHING IS POWERED BY MY EXISTENCE...
IN OTHER WORDS, IF I WERE TO SIMPLY DIE...
...*SHE* WOULD RETURN TO THE HEAVENS, AND ALL HER POWER WOULD BE LOST...
ALCIA WILL FALL WITHOUT HUMANITY HAVING GAINED A THING.
A WAR BETWEEN THE ABYSS AND ALCIA IS CERTAIN TO BEGIN ...!
THIS IS YOUR FINAL CHANCE ...!!
SO ...!

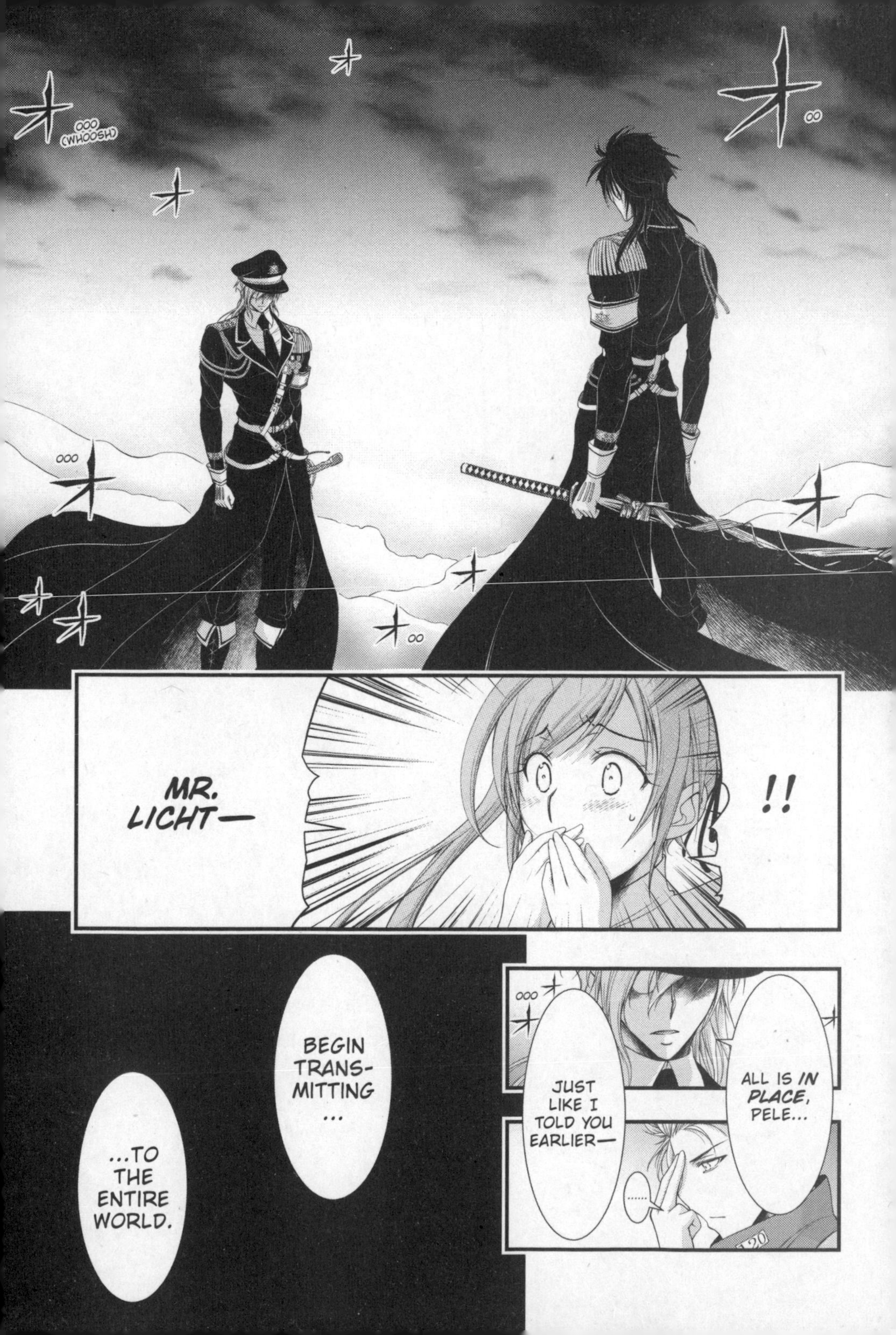
OO
OOO (WHOOSH)
OOO
OO
!!
MR. LICHT—
OOO
ALL IS IN PLACE, PELE...
JUST LIKE I TOLD YOU EARLIER—
......
BEGIN TRANSMITTING...
...TO THE ENTIRE WORLD.

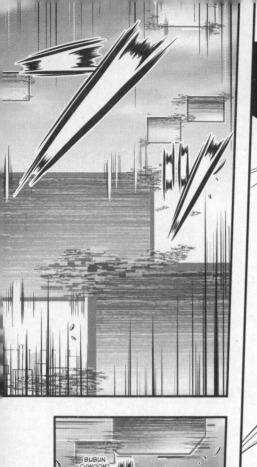

BUBUN
(VWOOM)

SHOW
ALL OF
HUMANITY
...

...THE
SIGHT
OF THEIR
HERO
DEFEATING
THEIR
COMMON
FOE.

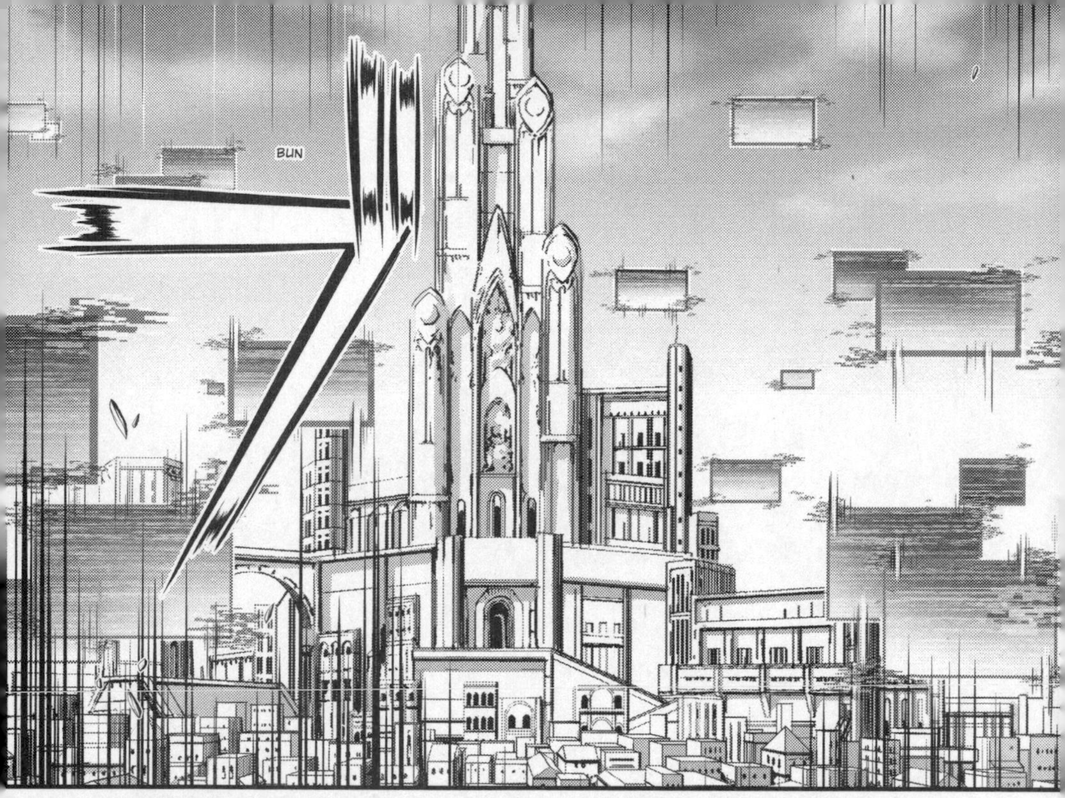
BUN
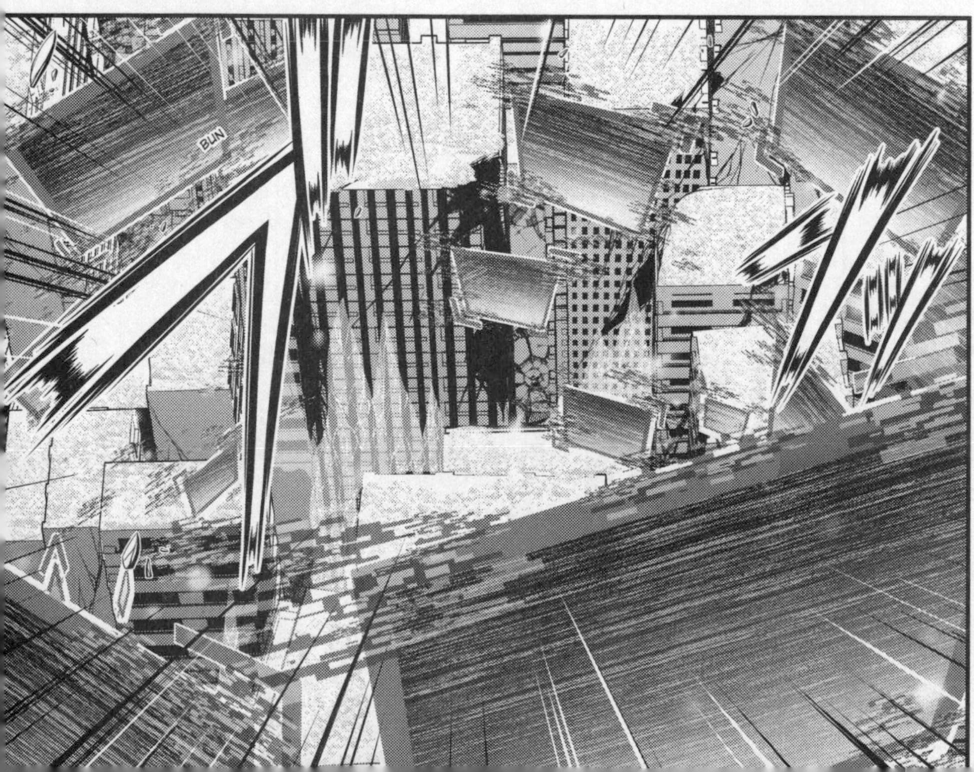
BUN

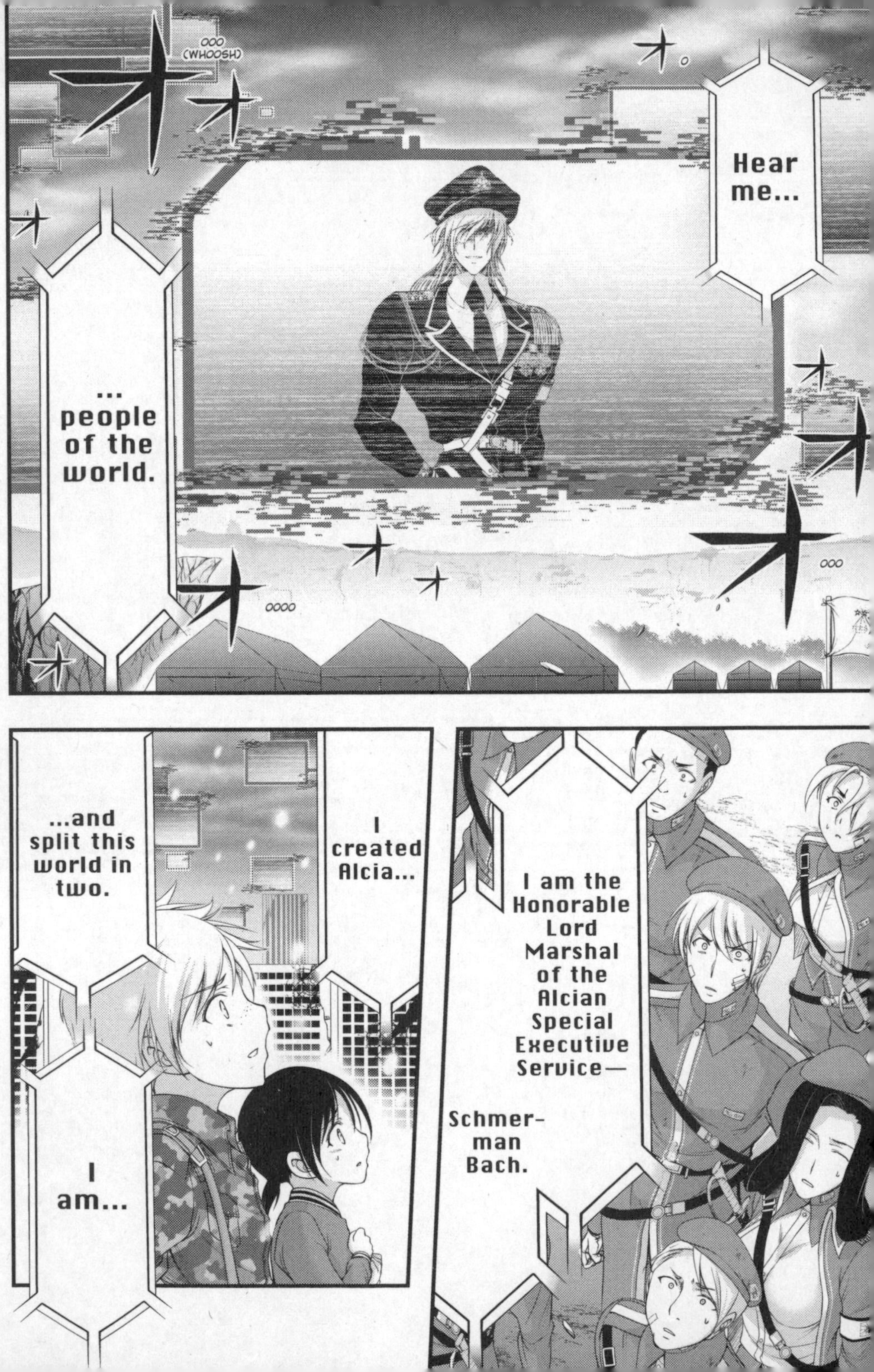
Hear me...
...people of the world.
ooo
OOO (WHOOSH)
oooo
I am the Honorable Lord Marshal of the Alcian Special Executive Service—
Schmer-man Bach.
I created Alcia...
...and split this world in two.
I am...

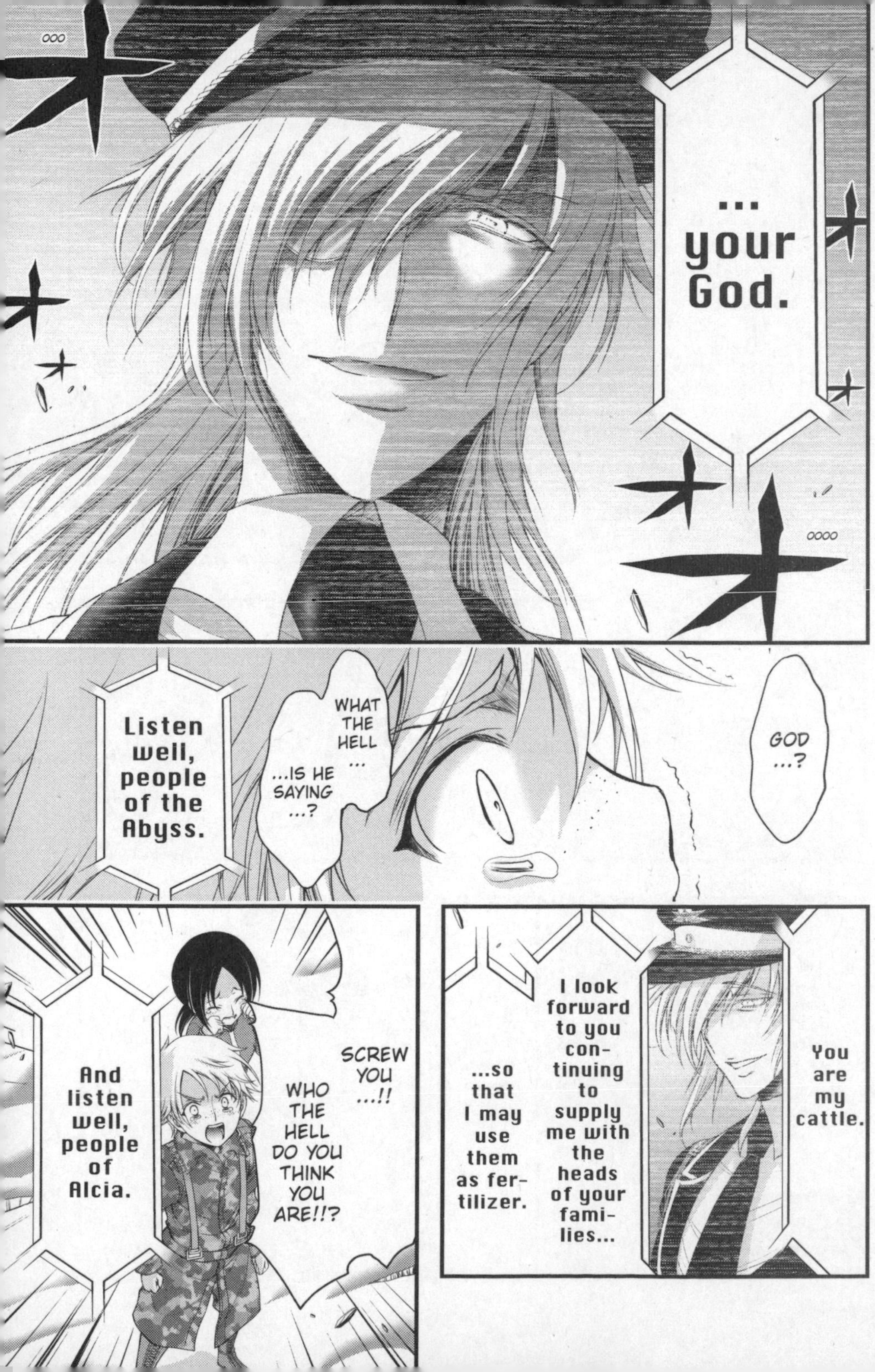

ooo
... your God.
oooo
GOD ...?
WHAT THE HELL ...
...IS HE SAYING ...?
Listen well, people of the Abyss.
You are my cattle.
I look forward to you con-tinuing to supply me with the heads of your fami-lies...
...so that I may use them as fer-tilizer.
SCREW YOU ...!!
WHO THE HELL DO YOU THINK YOU ARE!!?
And listen well, people of Alcia.

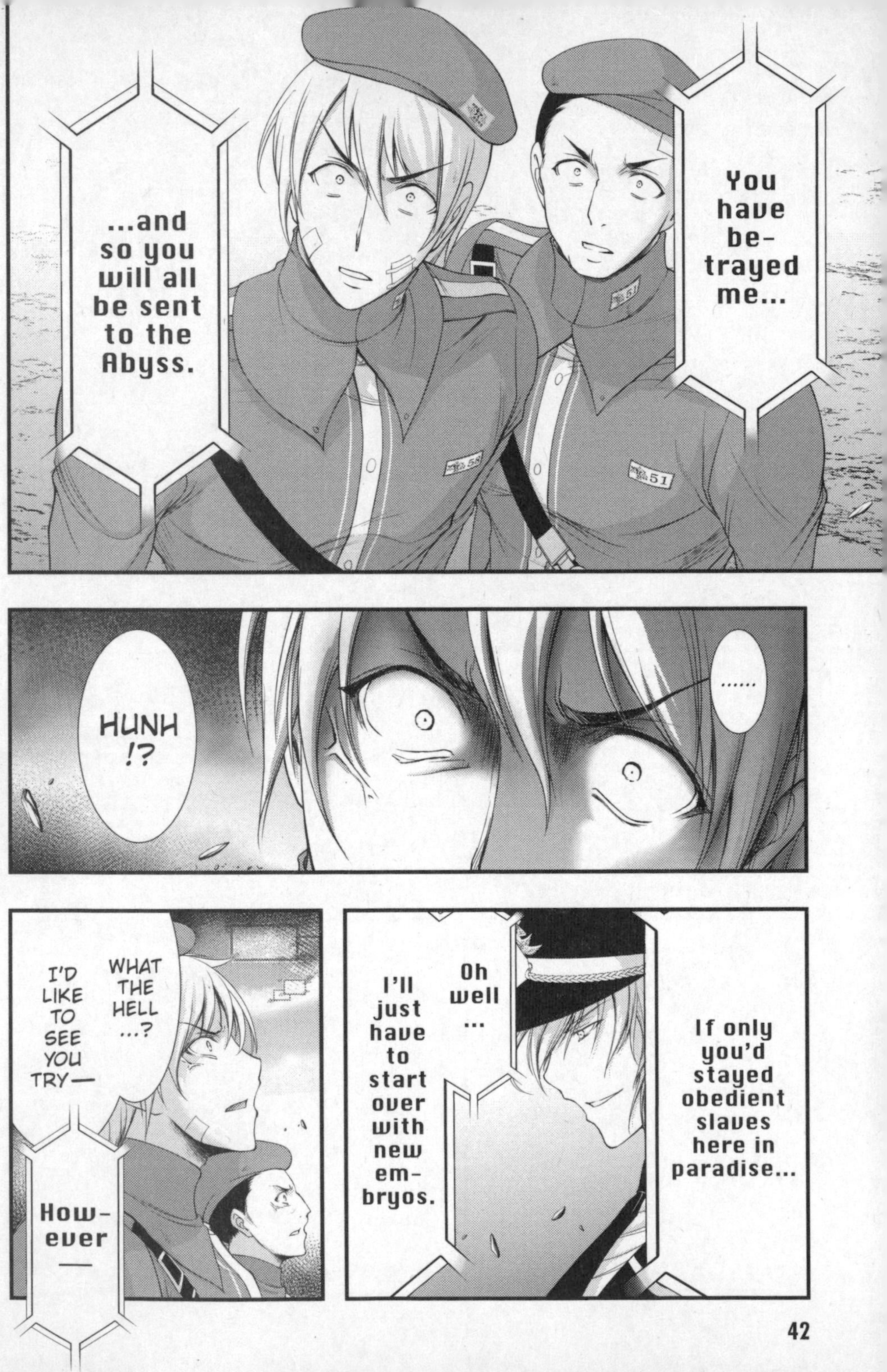
You have be-trayed me...
...and so you will all be sent to the Abyss.
......
HUNH !?
If only you'd stayed obedient slaves here in paradise...
Oh well ...
I'll just have to start over with new em-bryos.
WHAT THE HELL ...?
I'D LIKE TO SEE YOU TRY—
How-ever—

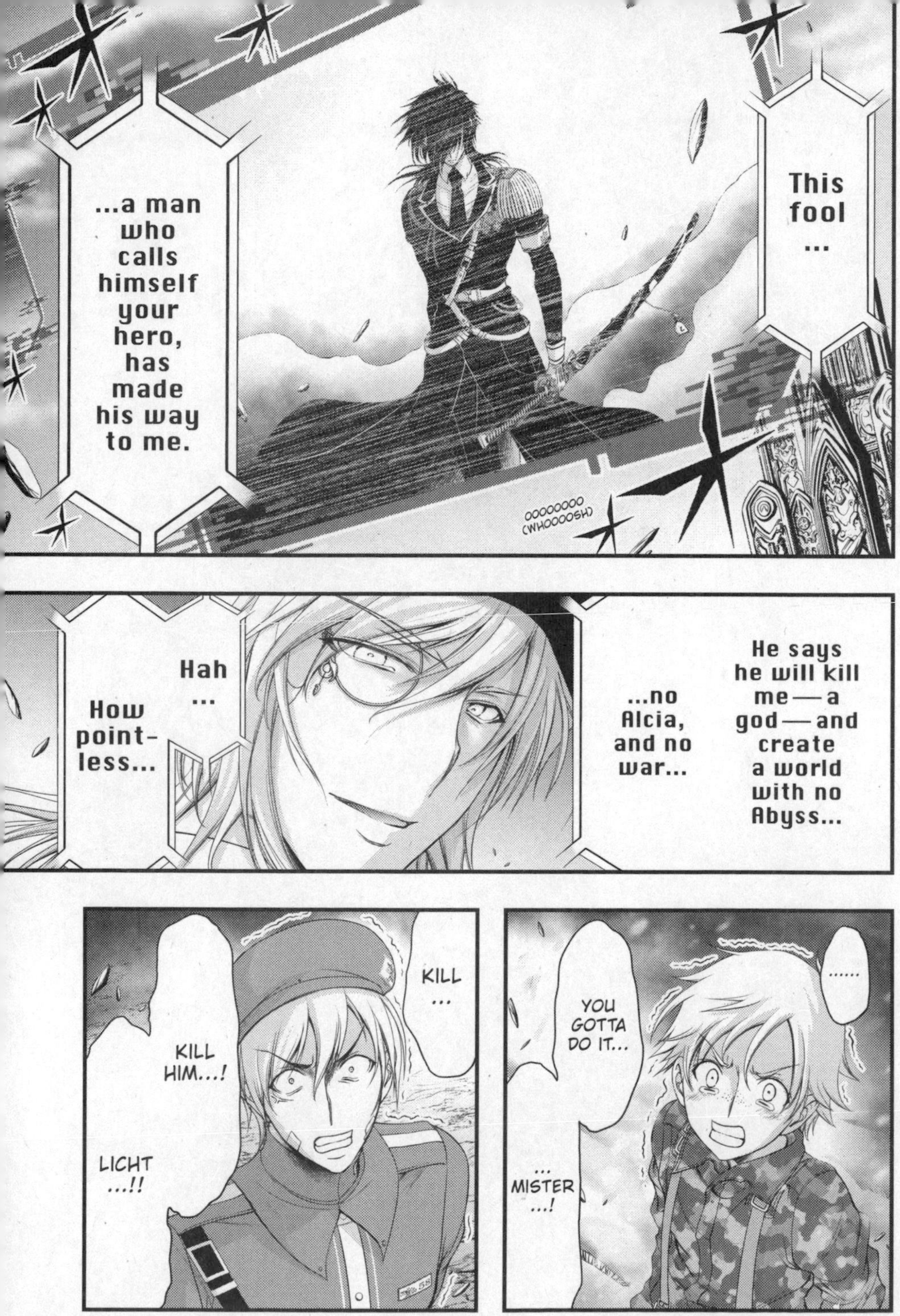
This fool ...
...a man who calls himself your hero, has made his way to me.
OOOOOOOO (WHOOOOSH)
He says he will kill me — a god — and create a world with no Abyss...
...no Alcia, and no war...
Hah ...
How pointless...
......
YOU GOTTA DO IT...
... MISTER ...!
KILL ...
KILL HIM...!
LICHT ...!!

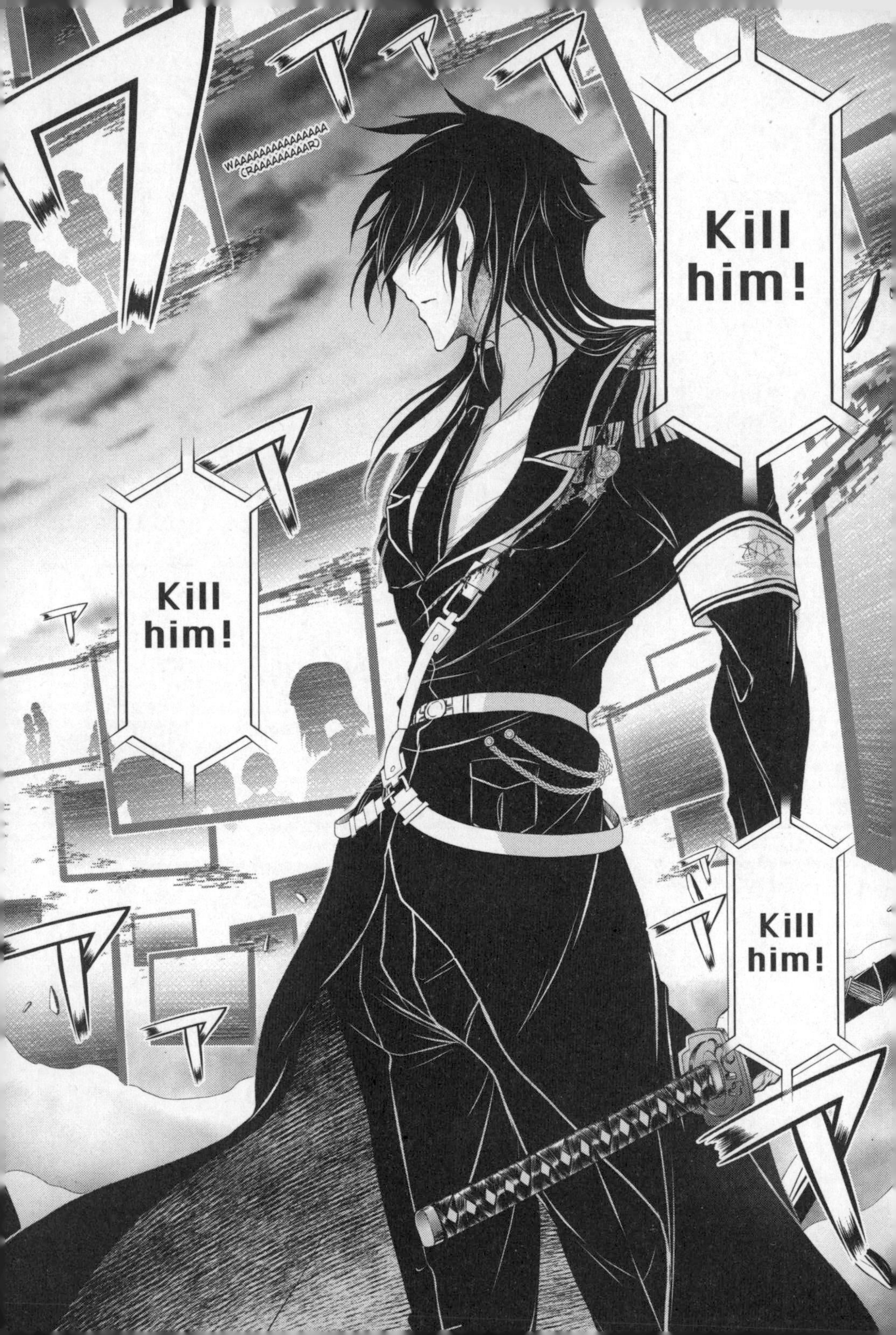
Kill him!
WAAAAAAAAAAAAAAA
(RAAAAAAAAAAR)
Kill him!
Kill him!

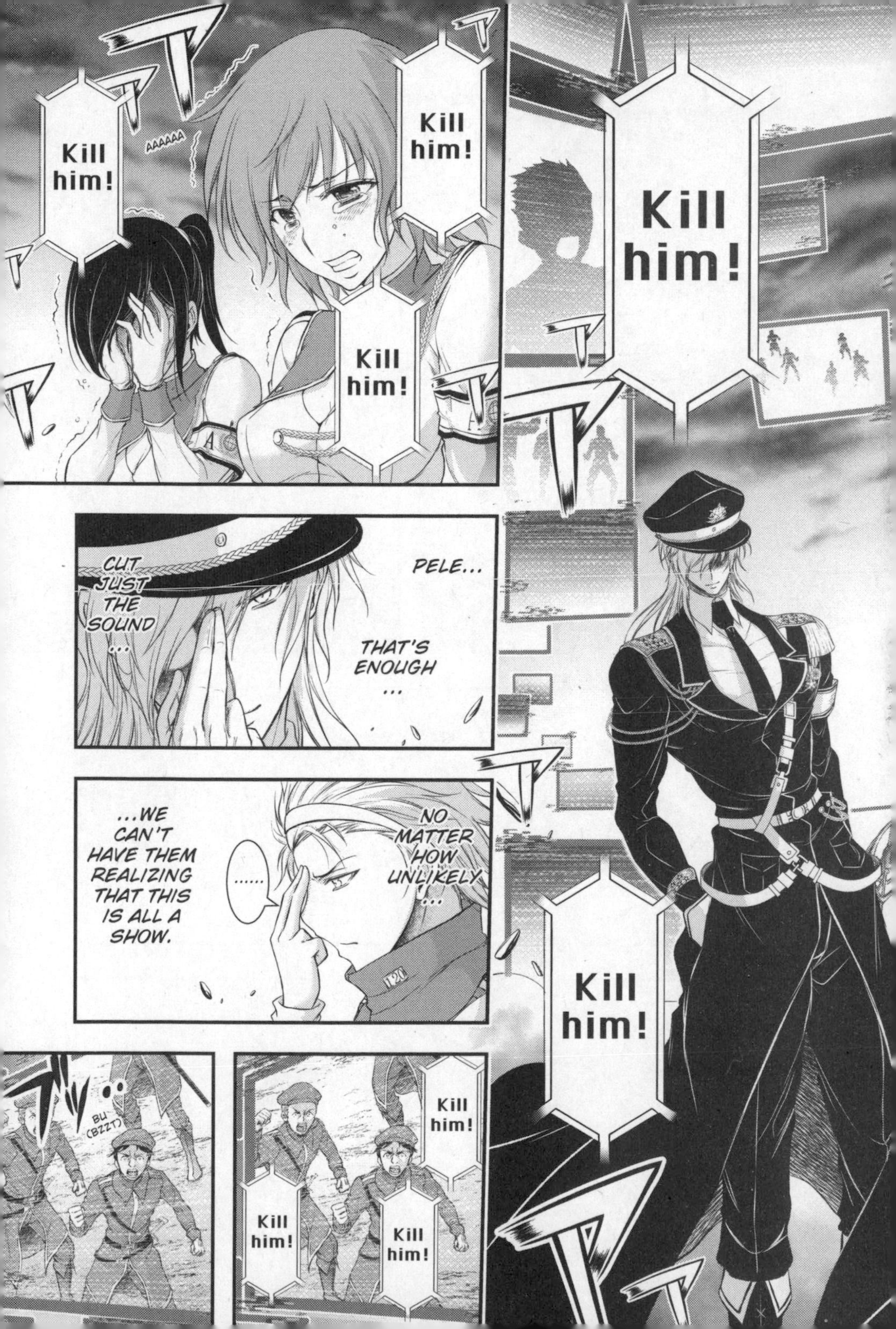
Kill him!
Kill him!
Kill him!
Kill him!
AAAAAA
Kill him!
Kill him!
PELE...
THAT'S ENOUGH...
CUT JUST THE SOUND...
NO MATTER HOW UNLIKELY...
......
...WE CAN'T HAVE THEM REALIZING THAT THIS IS ALL A SHOW.
Kill him!
Kill him!
Kill him!
BU (BZZT)

NOW
...

LET'S
BEGIN,
LICHT...

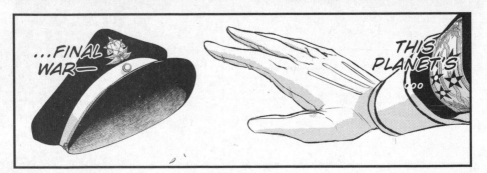

...FINAL
WAR—

THIS
PLANET'S
...

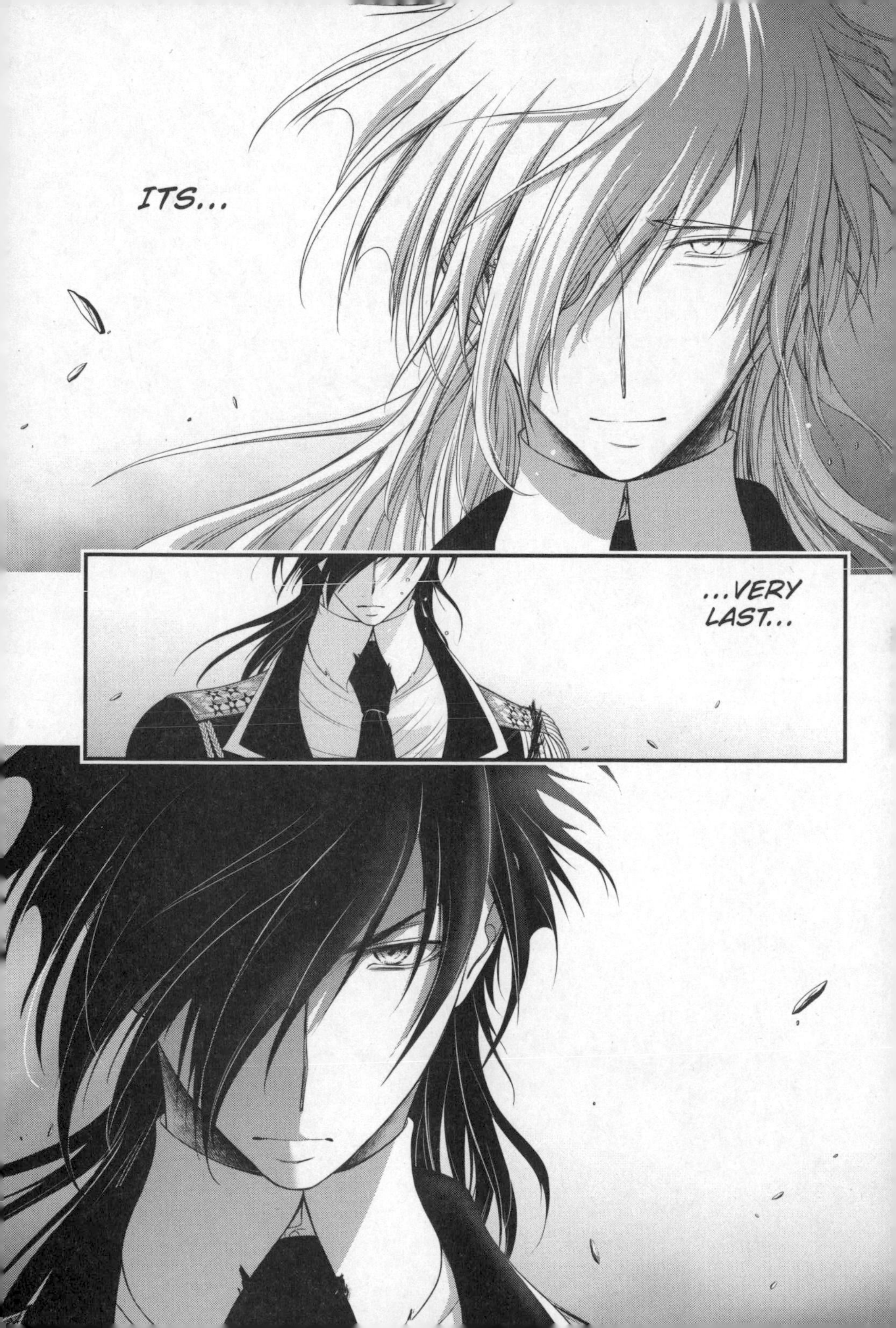
ITS...
...VERY LAST...

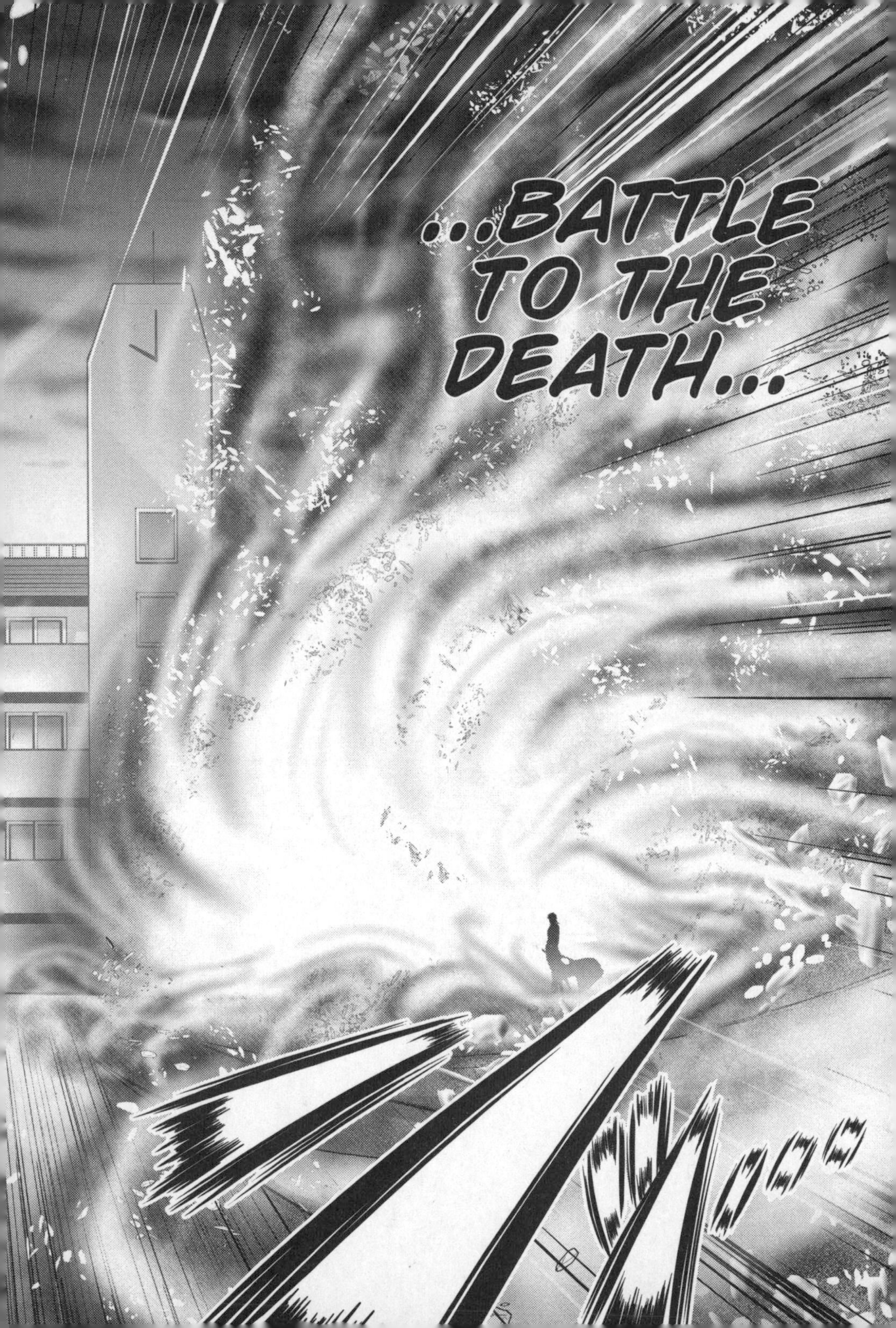
...BATTLE TO THE DEATH...

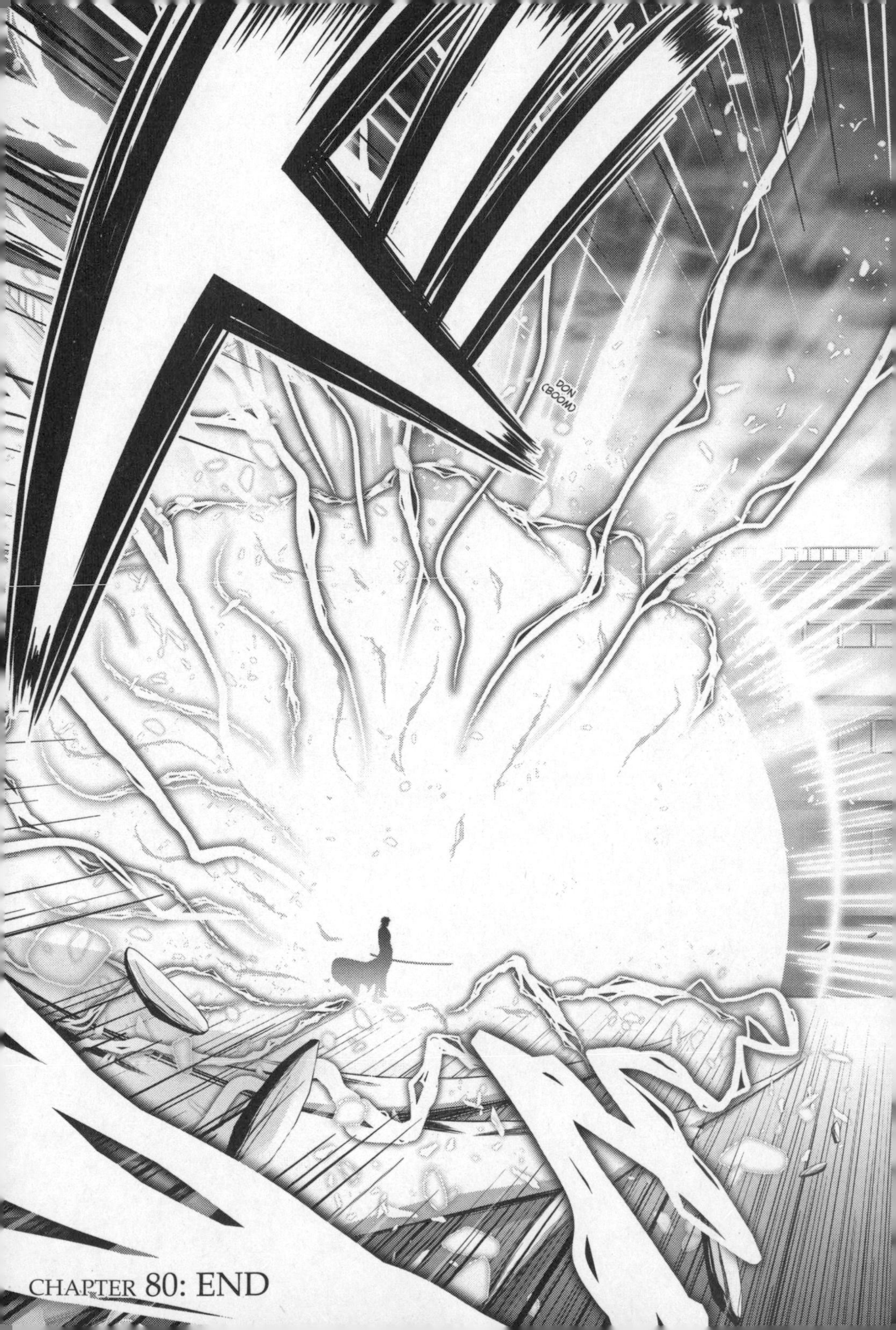
DON (BOOM)

CHAPTER 80: END

PLUNDERER

CHAPTER 81

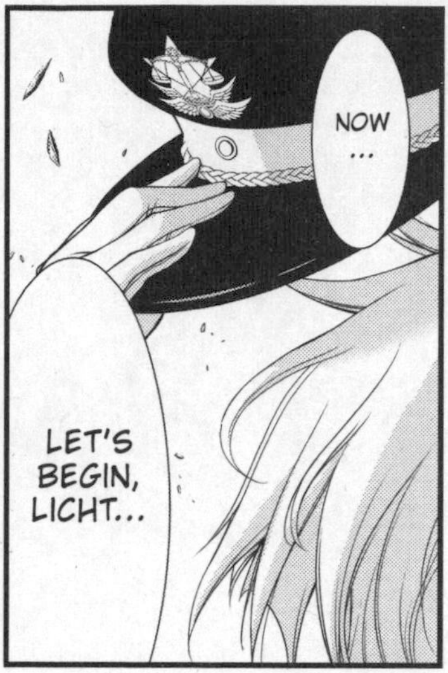
NOW ...
LET'S BEGIN, LICHT...

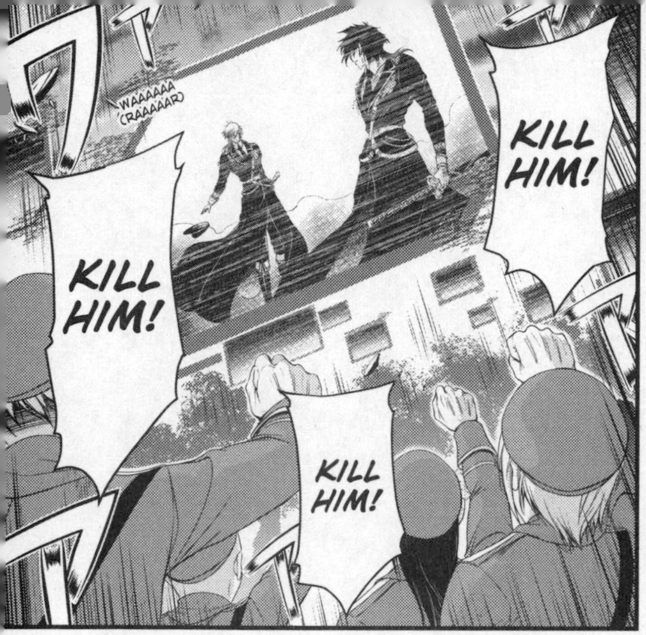
KILL HIM!
WAAAAAA (RAAAAAR)
KILL HIM!
KILL HIM!

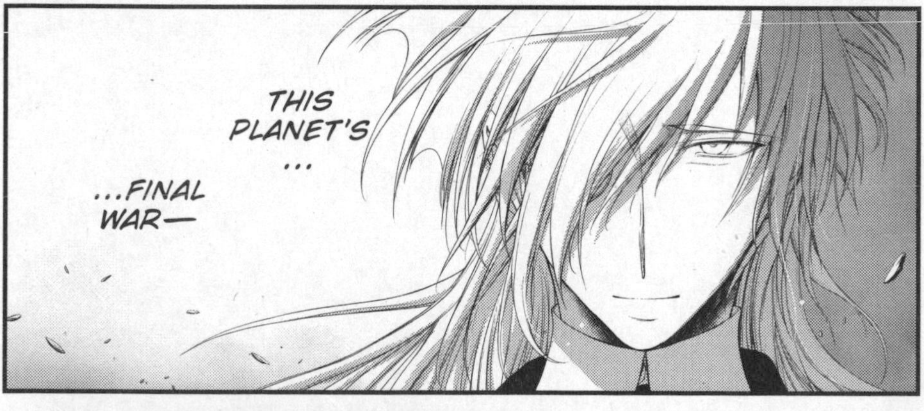
THIS PLANET'S ...
...FINAL WAR—

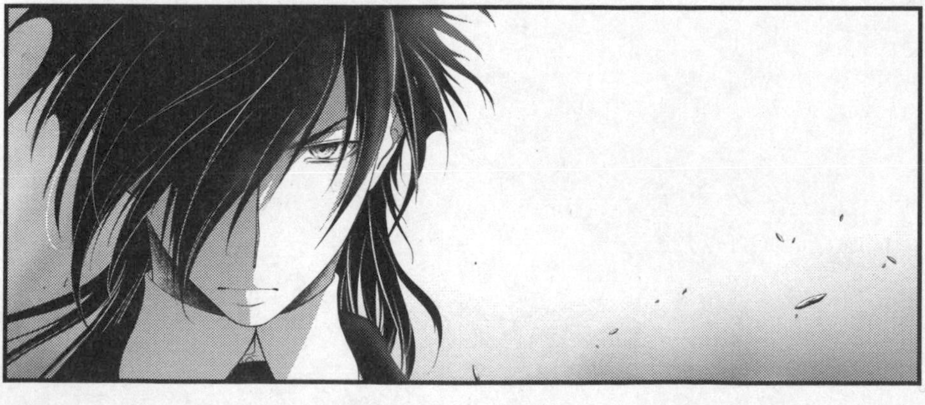

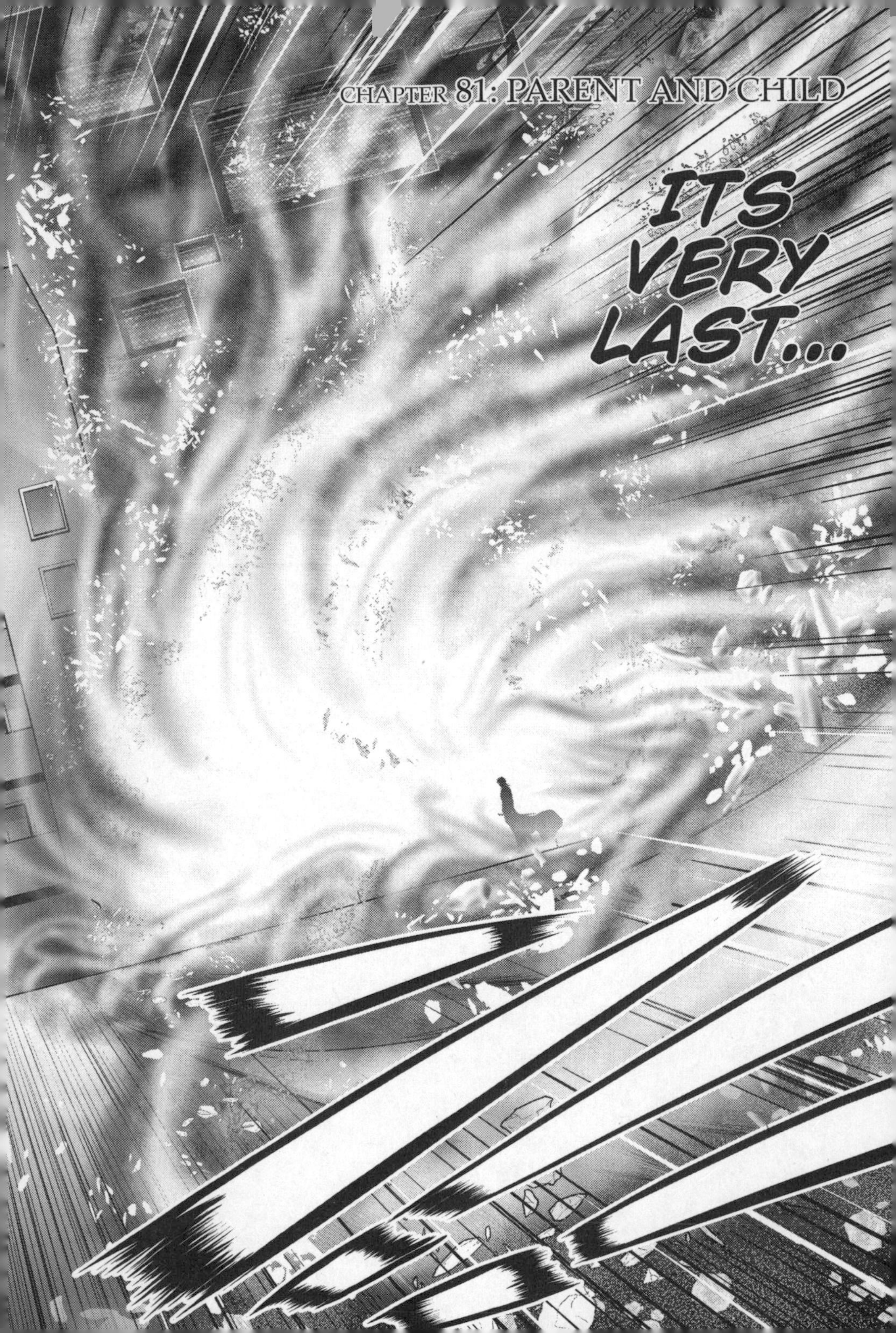
CHAPTER 81: PARENT AND CHILD
ITS VERY LAST...

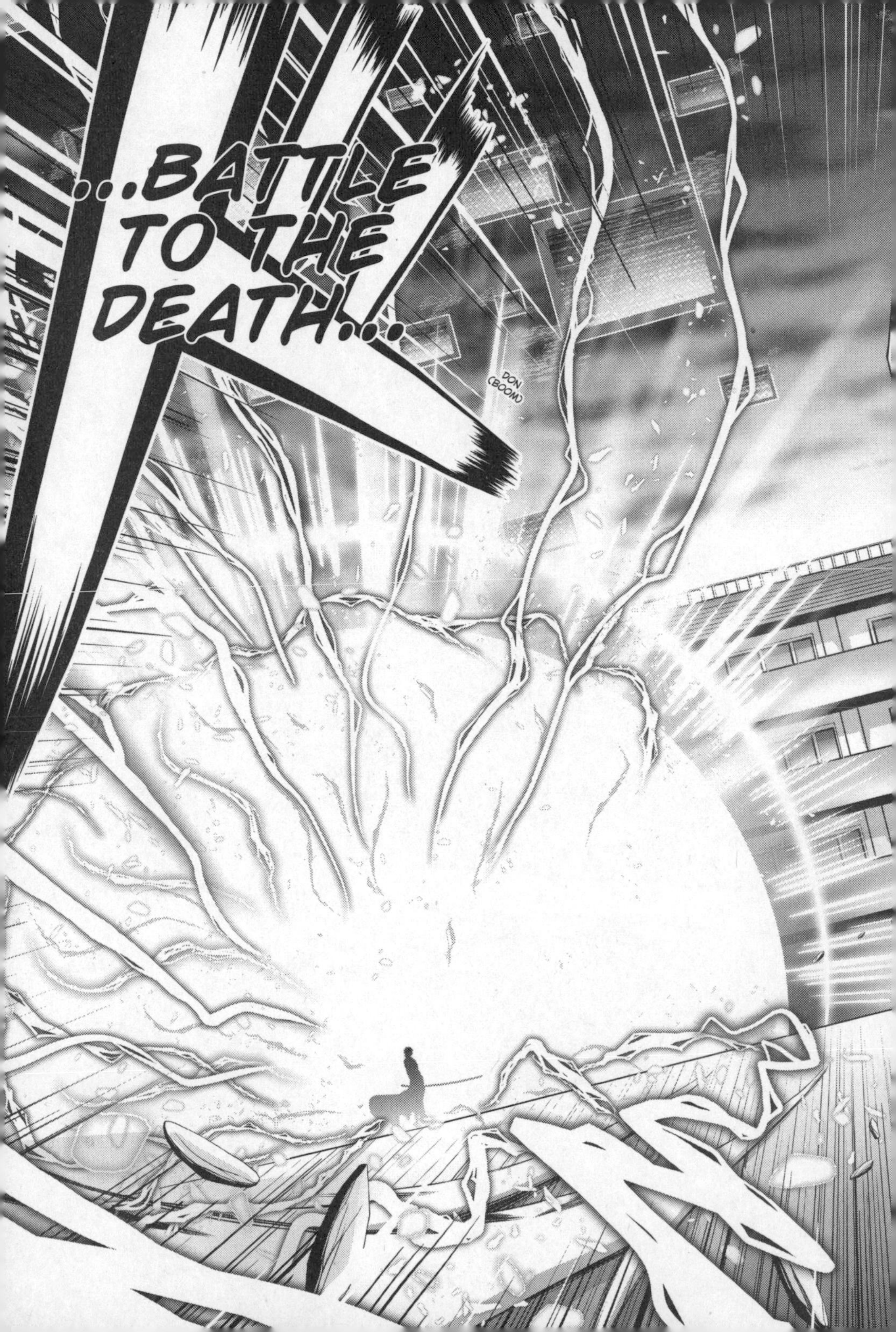
...BATTLE TO THE DEATH...
DON (BOOM)

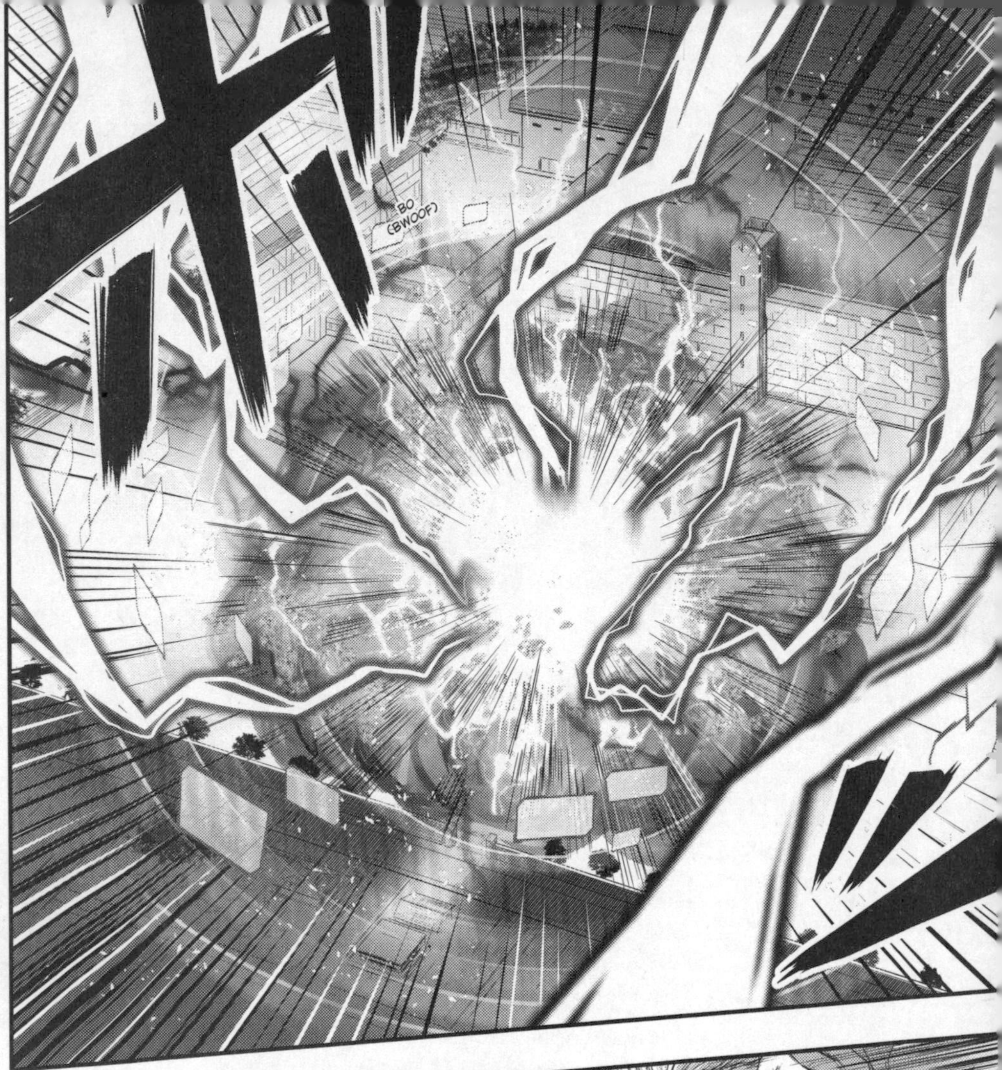
BO
(BWOOP)
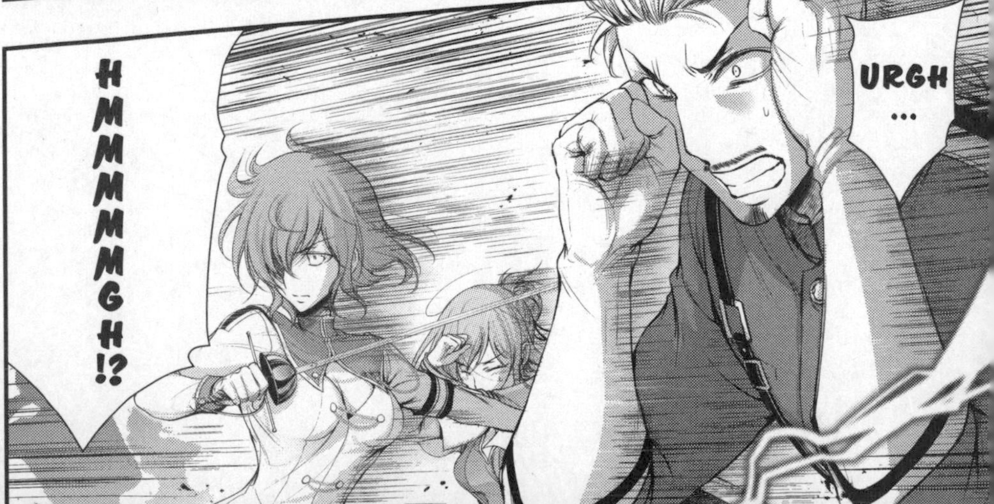
URGH
...
HMMMMMGH!?

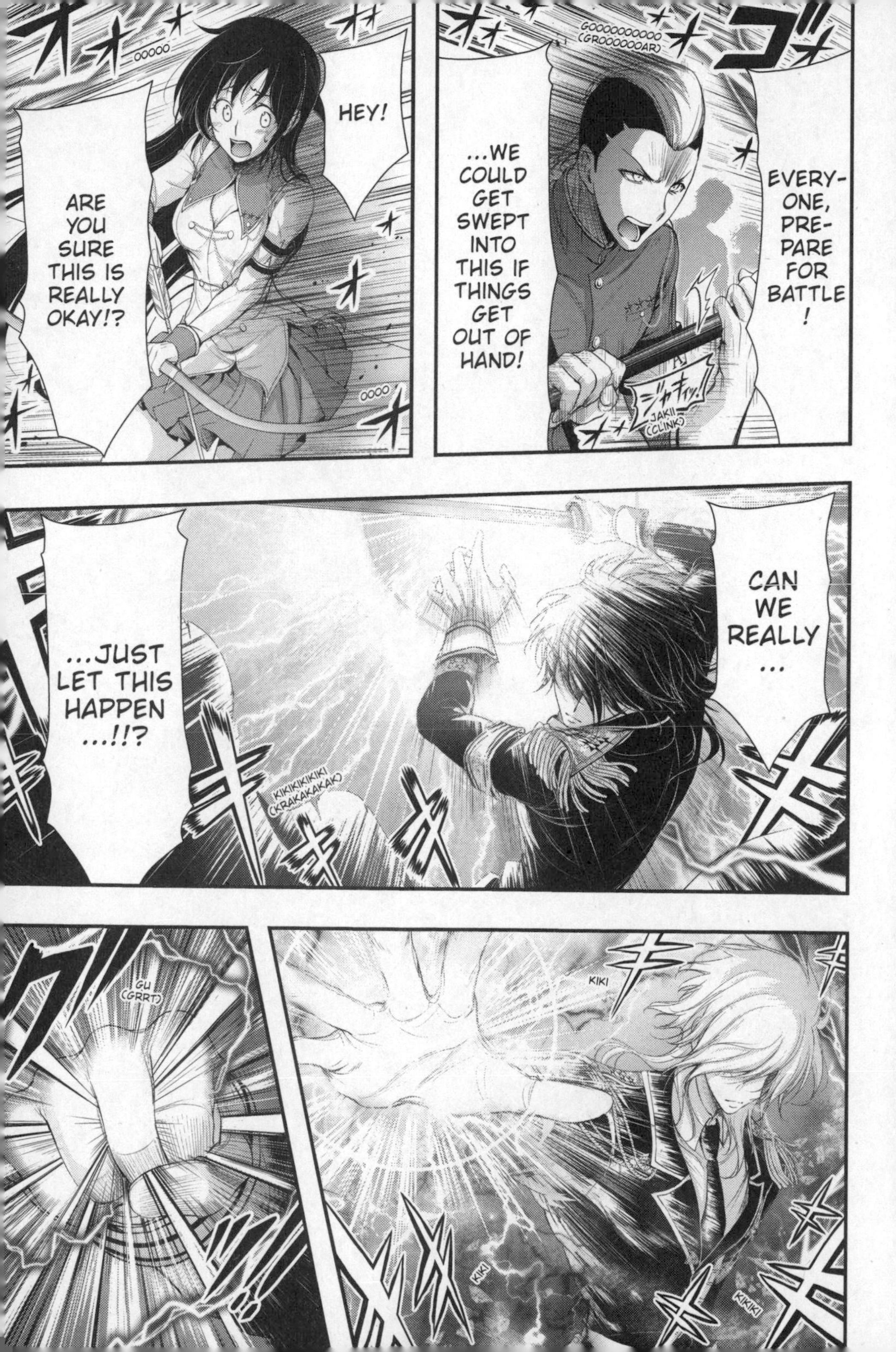
GOOOOOOOOOOO (GROOOOOOAR)
EVERY-ONE, PRE-PARE FOR BATTLE!
...WE COULD GET SWEPT INTO THIS IF THINGS GET OUT OF HAND!
JAKI! (CLINK)
OOOOO
HEY!
ARE YOU SURE THIS IS REALLY OKAY!?
OOOO
CAN WE REALLY ...
...JUST LET THIS HAPPEN ...!!?
KIKIKIKIKIKI (KRAKAKAKAK)
KIKI
KIKI
KIKIKI
GU (GRRT)

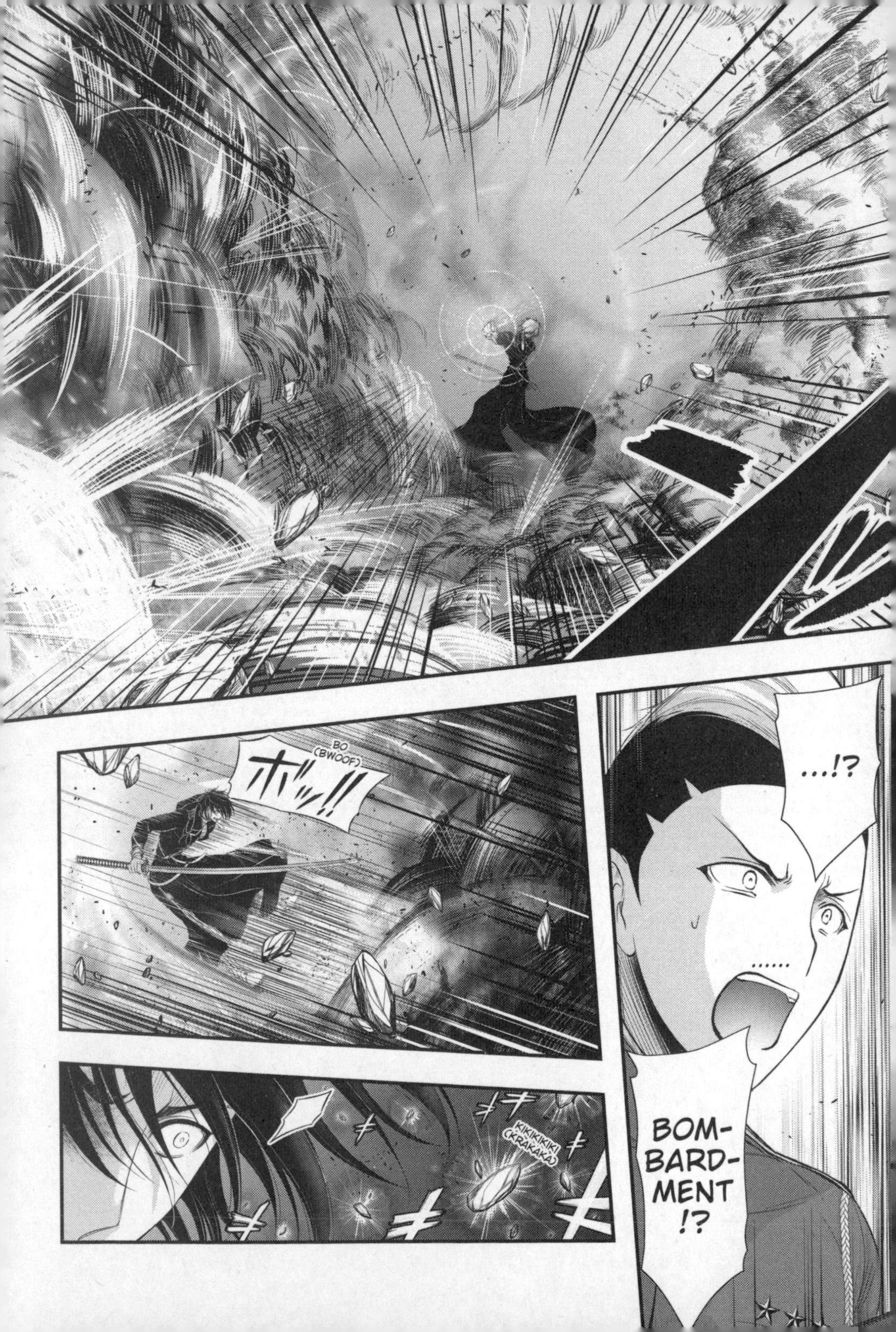
...!?
......
BOM-BARD-MENT !?
BO (BWOOF)
ボッ!!
KIKIKIKIKI (KRAKAKA)

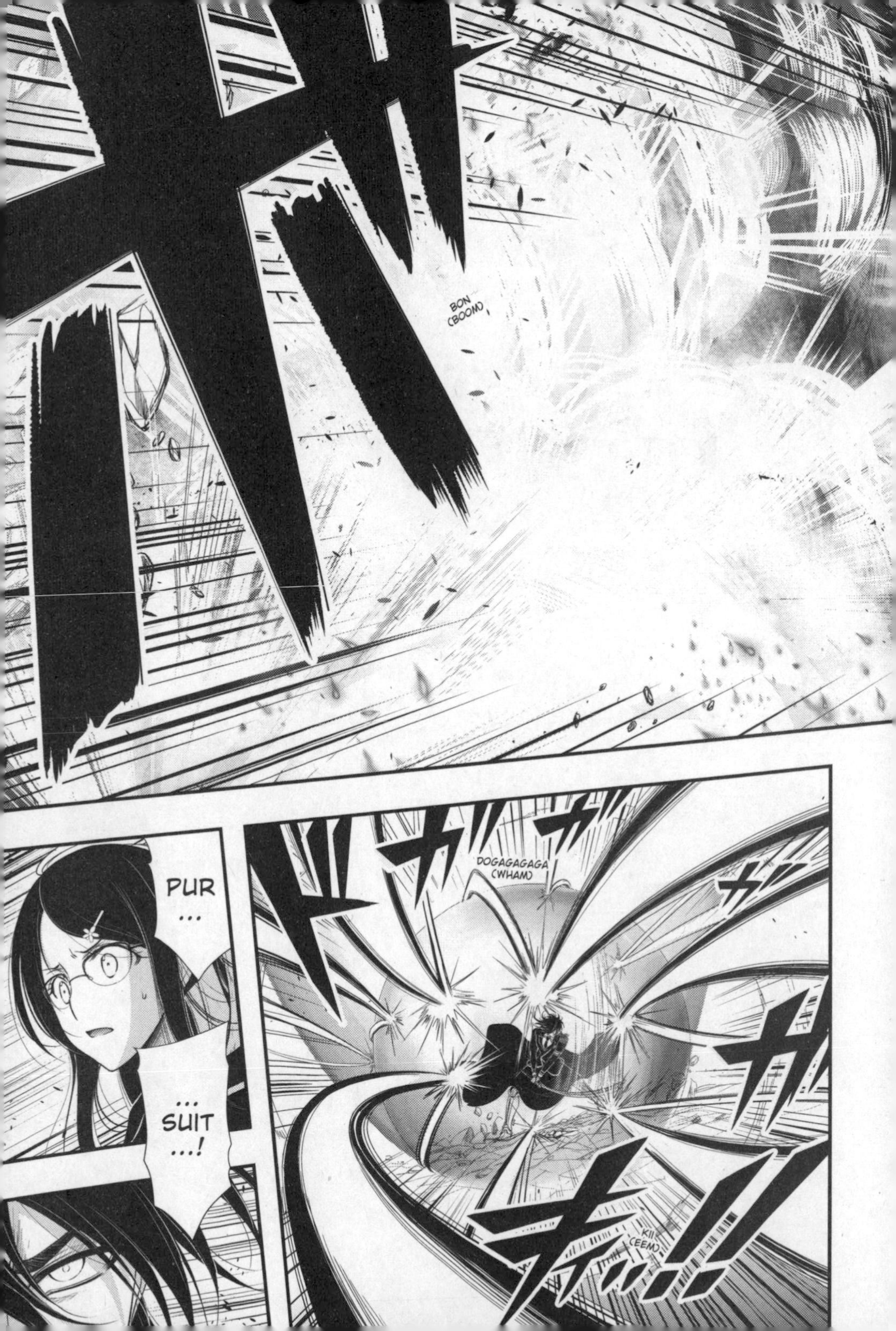
BON (BOOM)
DOGAGAGAGA (WHAM)
KII (EEEM)
PUR...
...SUIT...!

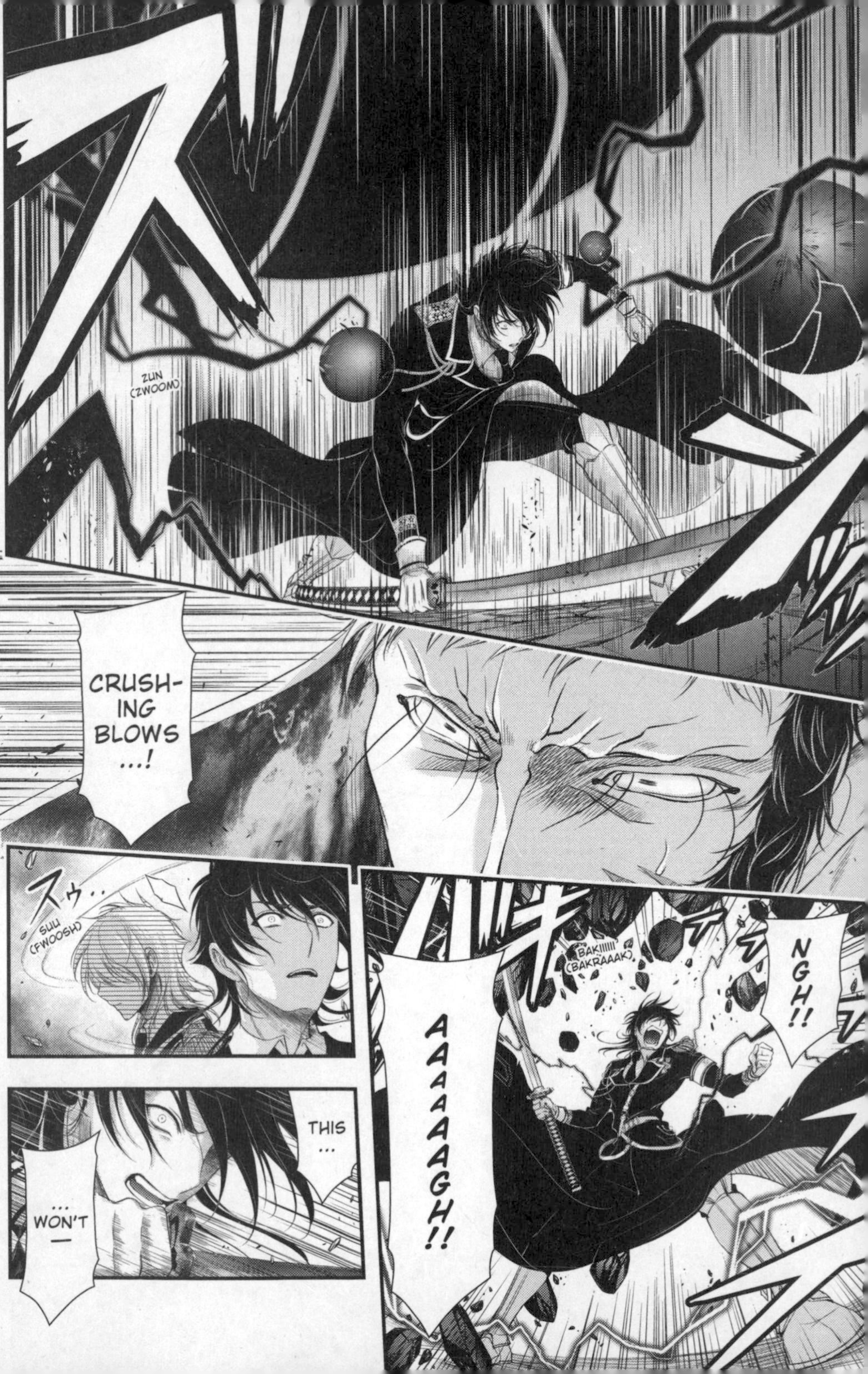
ZUN (ZWOOM)
CRUSHING BLOWS ...!
BAKIIIIIII (BAKRAAAK)
NGH!!
AAAAAAAGH!!
スゥ.. SUU (FWOOSH)
THIS ...
... WON'T —

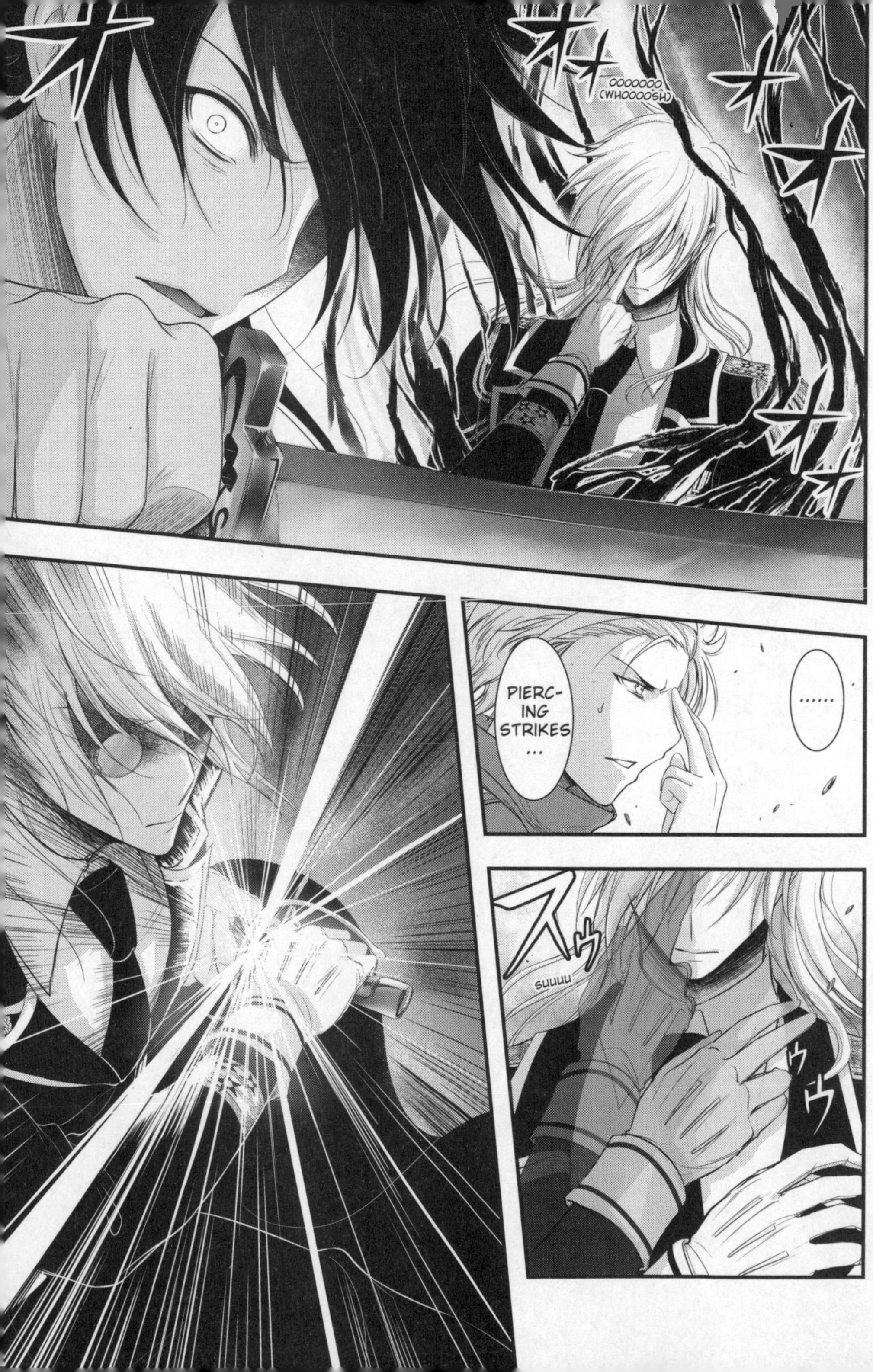
OOOOOOO (WHOOOOSH)
......
PIERC-ING STRIKES ...
SUUUU

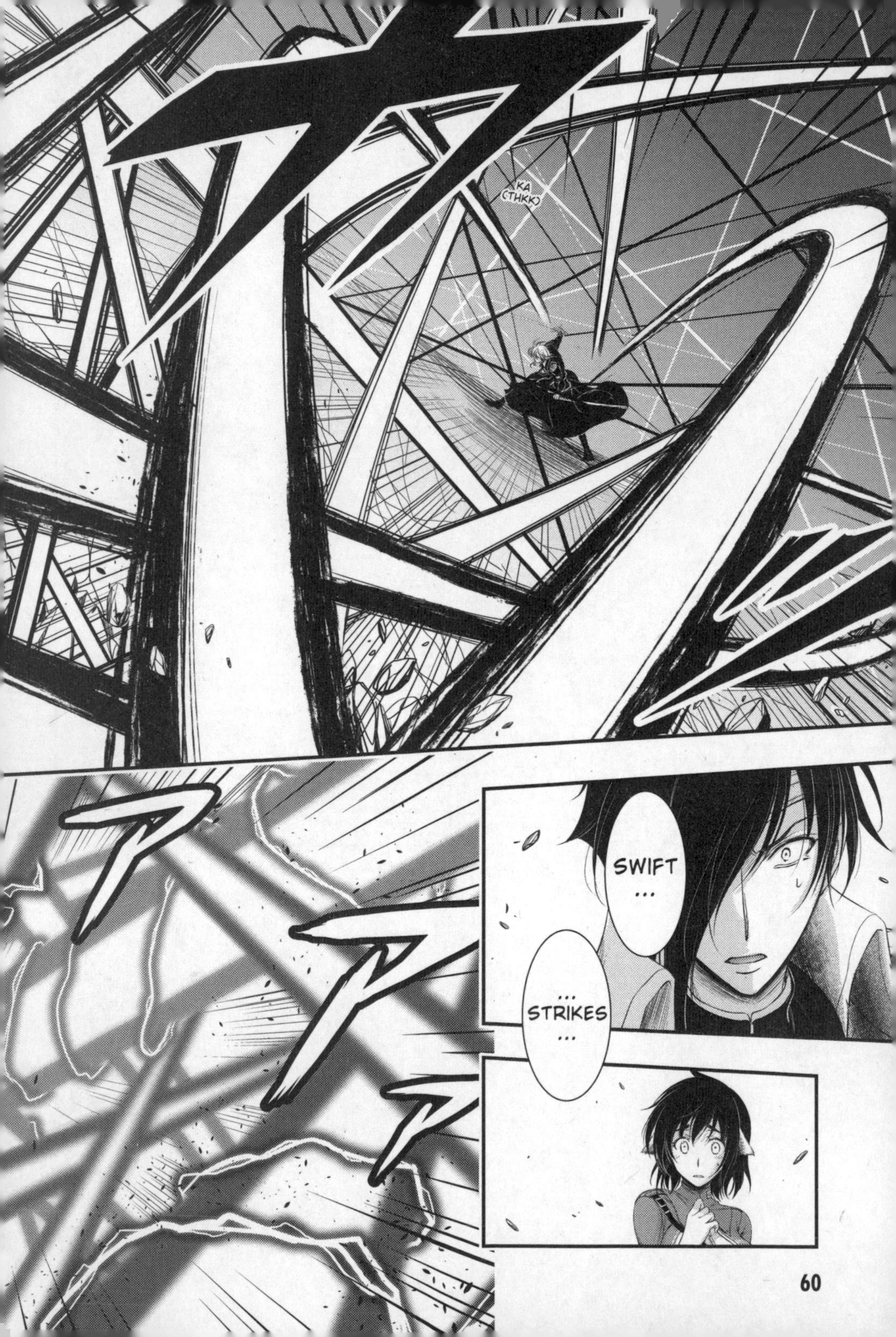
KA
(THKK)
SWIFT
...
...
STRIKES
...

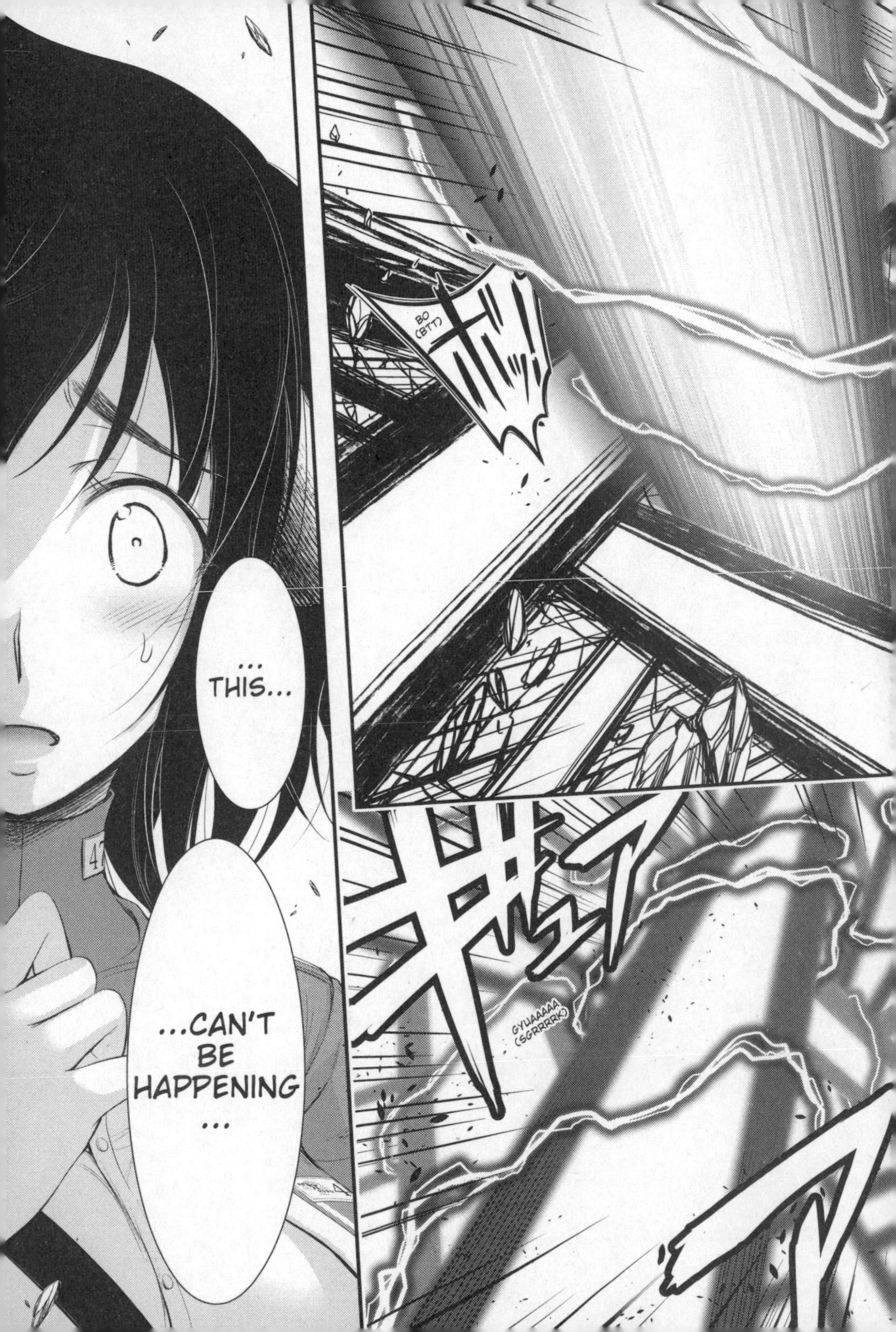
BO (BTT)
GYUAAAAA (SGRRRRK)
... THIS...
...CAN'T BE HAPPENING ...

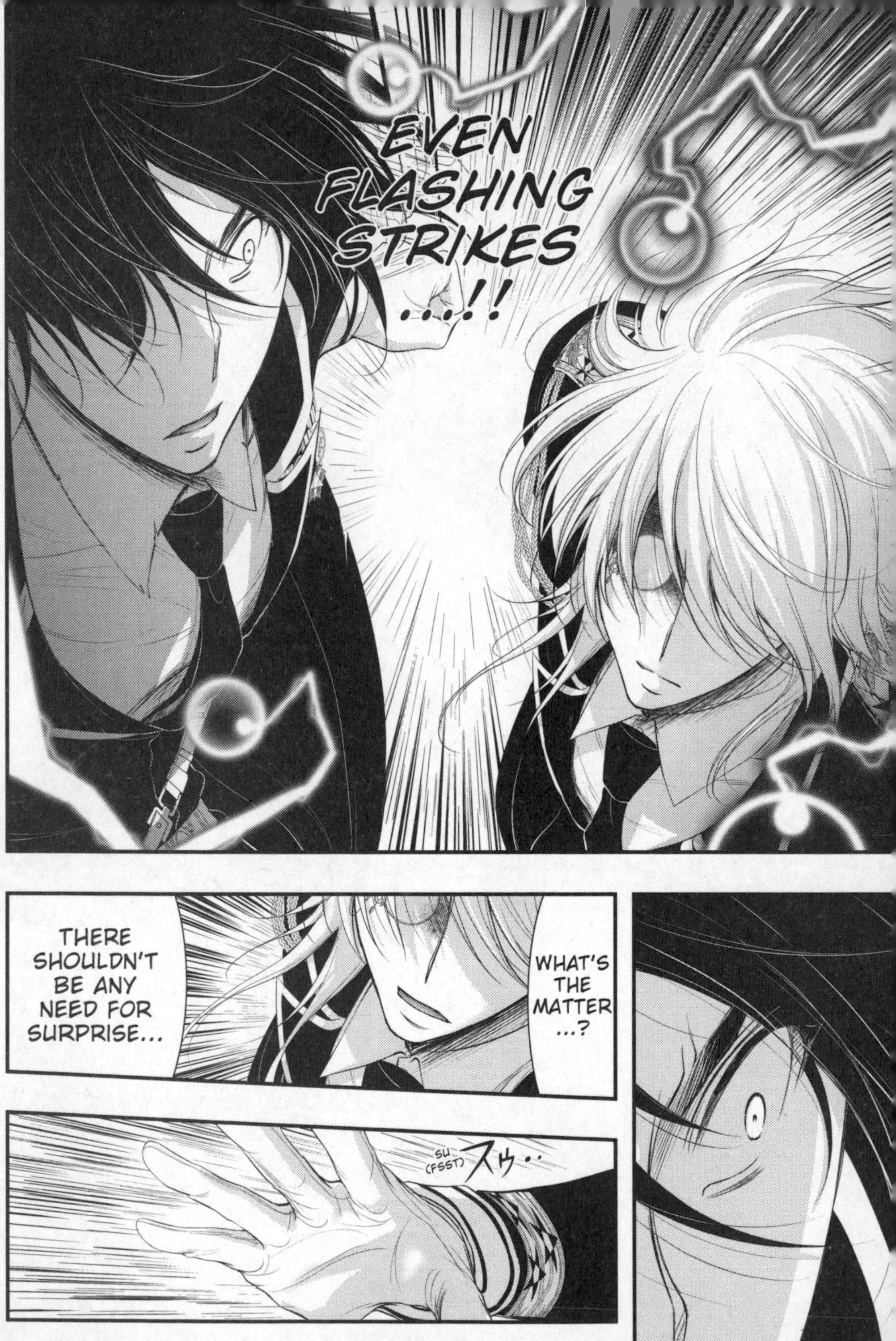
EVEN FLASHING STRIKES ...!!
WHAT'S THE MATTER ...?
THERE SHOULDN'T BE ANY NEED FOR SURPRISE...
SU (FSST) スゥ‥

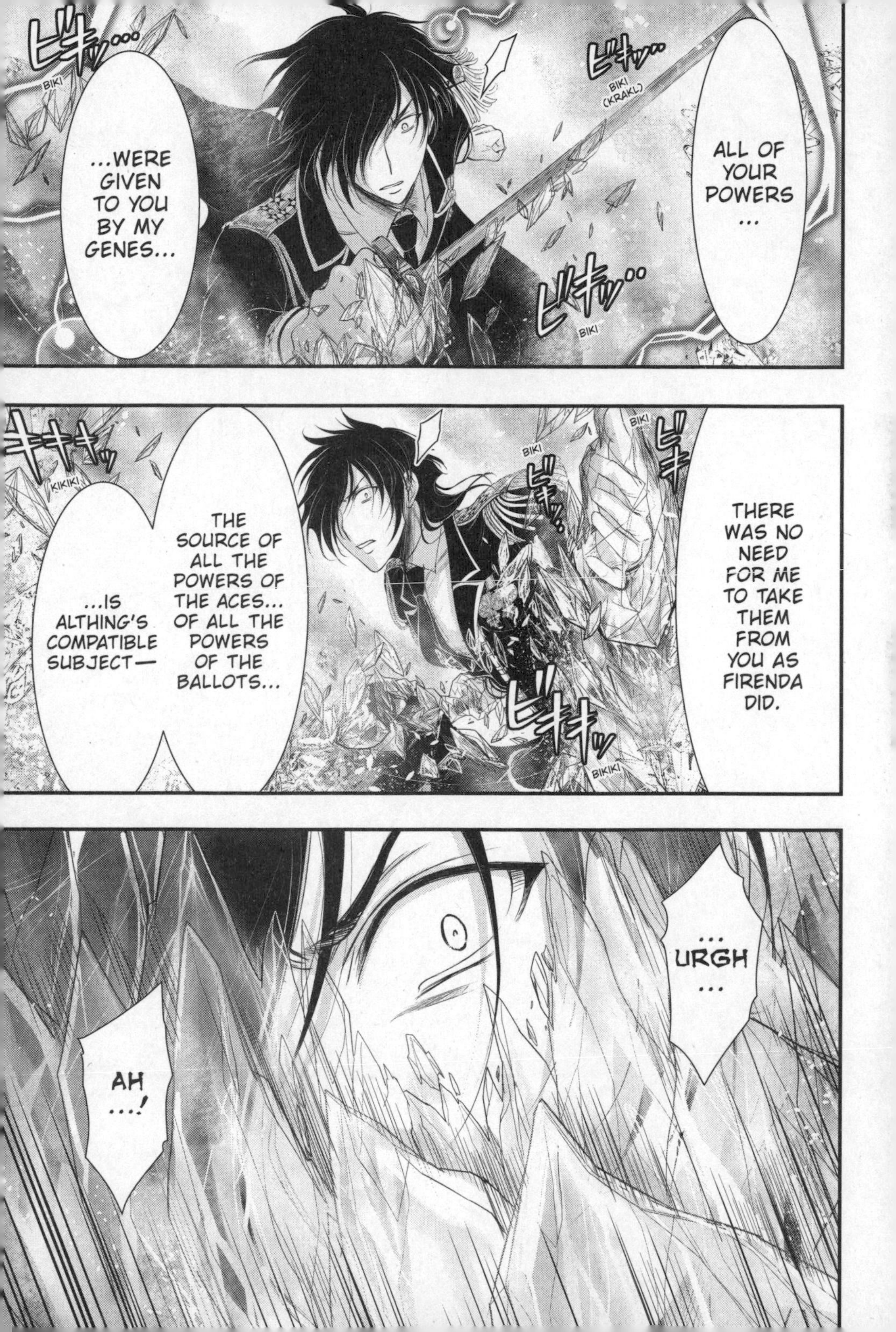
ビキッ…
BIKI
BIKI (KRAKL)
ALL OF YOUR POWERS …
…WERE GIVEN TO YOU BY MY GENES…
ビキッ…
BIKI
ビキッ…
BIKI
ビキ
BIKI
ビキッ
THERE WAS NO NEED FOR ME TO TAKE THEM FROM YOU AS FIRENDA DID.
THE SOURCE OF ALL THE POWERS OF THE ACES… OF ALL THE POWERS OF THE BALLOTS…
…IS ALTHING'S COMPATIBLE SUBJECT—
キキキッ
KIKIKI
ビキキッ
BIKIKI
… URGH …
AH …!

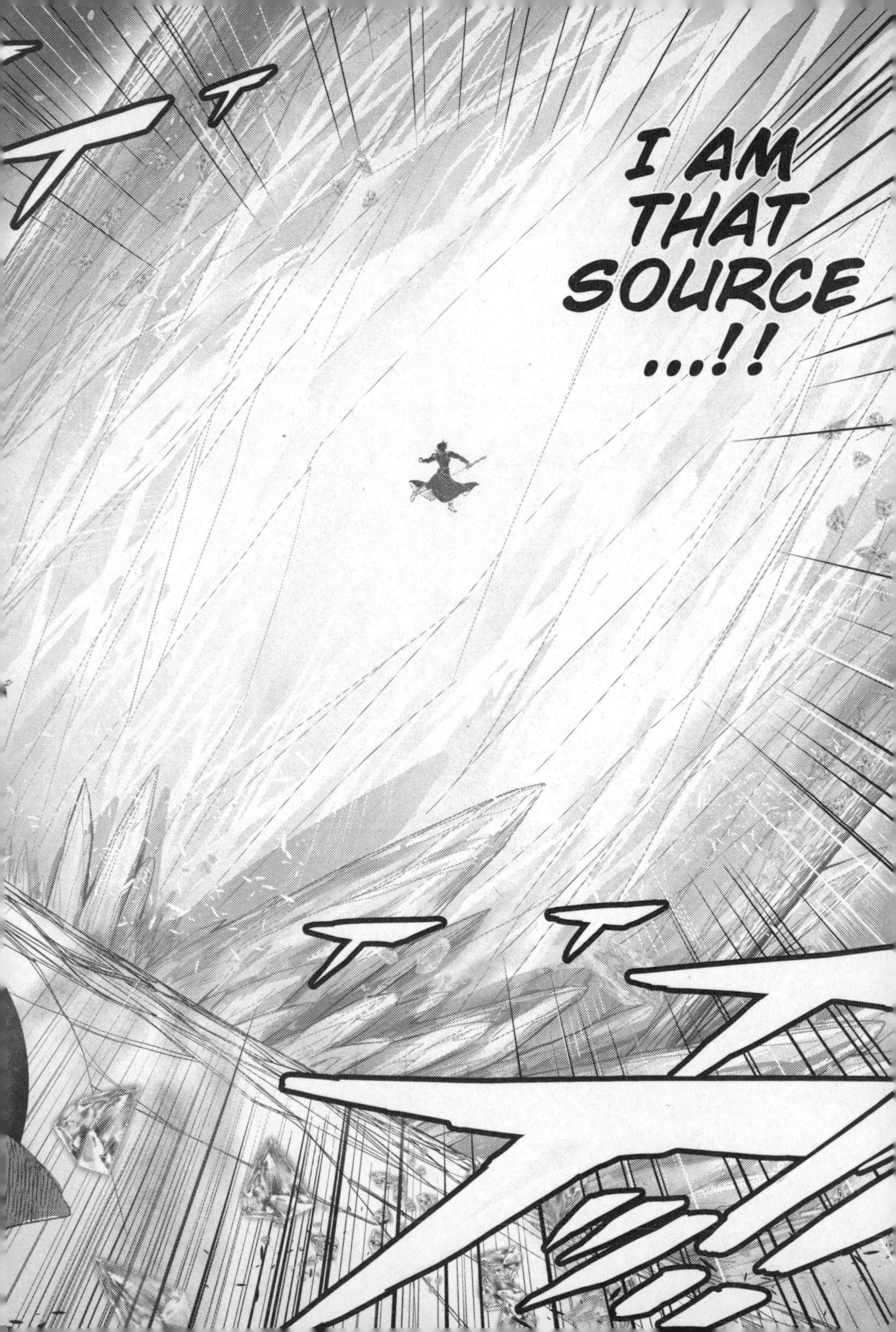
I AM THAT SOURCE ...!!

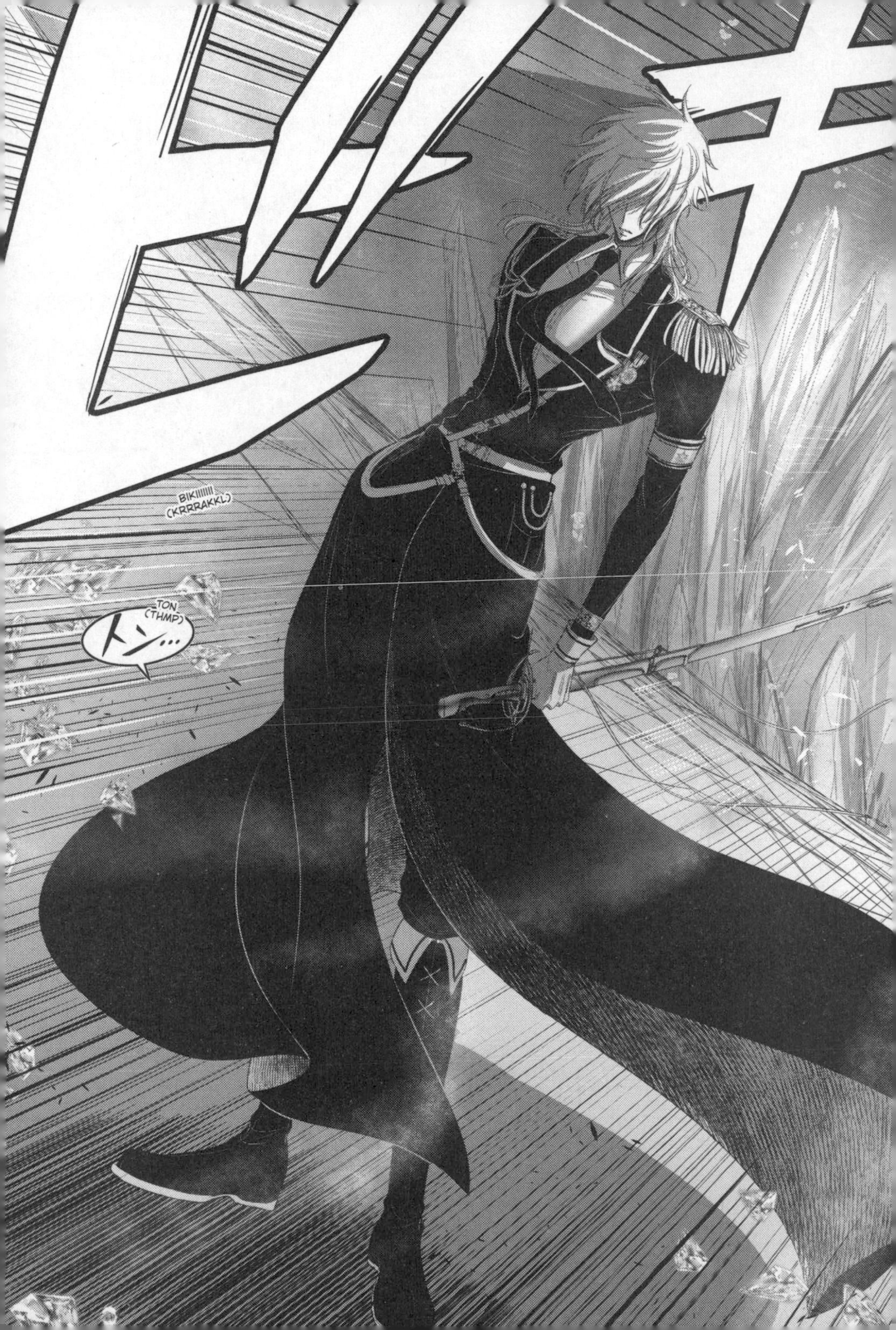
ビキ
BIKIIIIIIIII
(KRRRAKKL)
TON
(THMP)
トン…

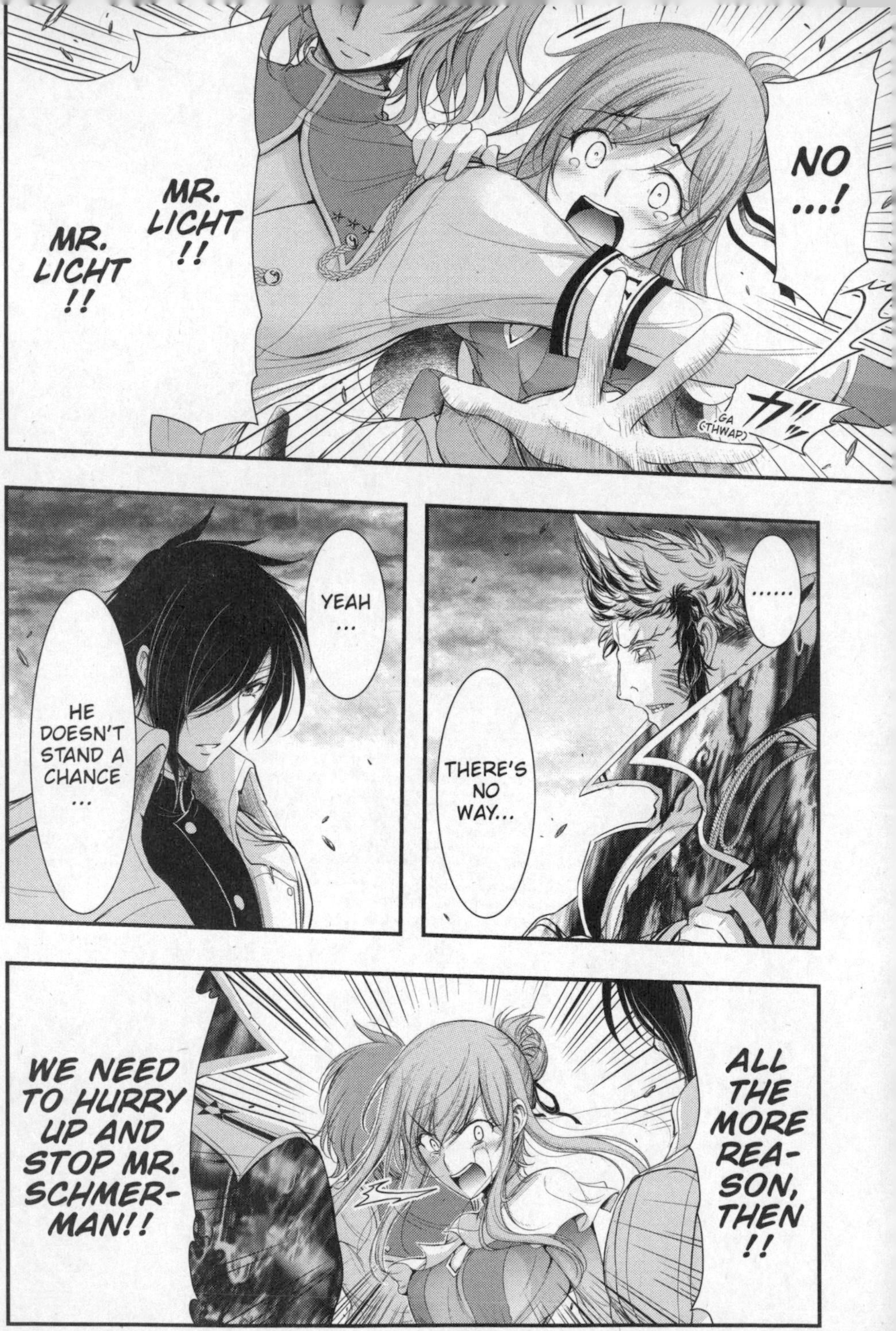
NO ...!
MR. LICHT !!
MR. LICHT !!
GA (THWAP)
......
THERE'S NO WAY...
YEAH ...
HE DOESN'T STAND A CHANCE ...
ALL THE MORE REA-SON, THEN !!
WE NEED TO HURRY UP AND STOP MR. SCHMER-MAN!!

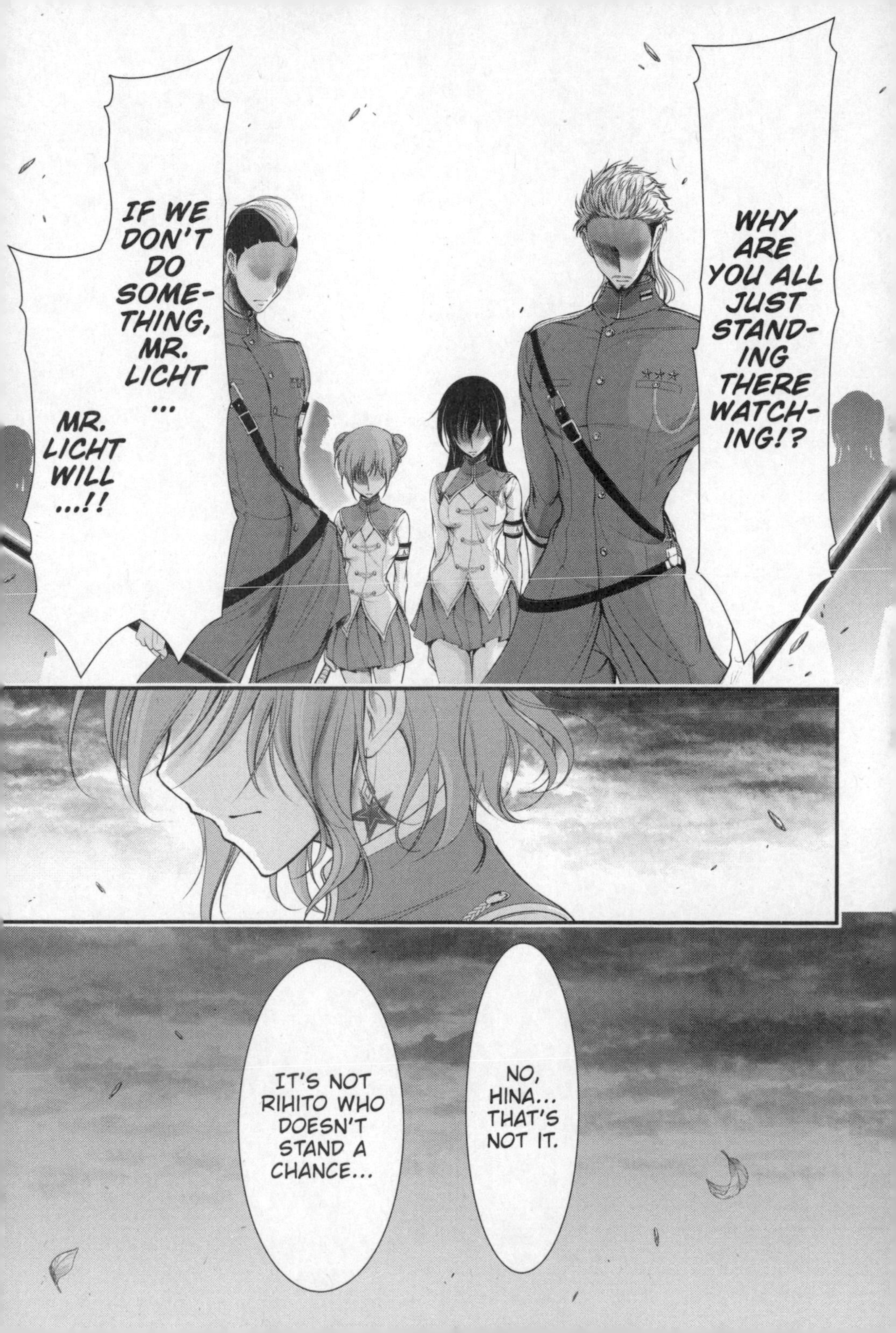
WHY ARE YOU ALL JUST STANDING THERE WATCHING!?
IF WE DON'T DO SOMETHING, MR. LICHT ...
MR. LICHT WILL ...!!
NO, HINA... THAT'S NOT IT.
IT'S NOT RIHITO WHO DOESN'T STAND A CHANCE...

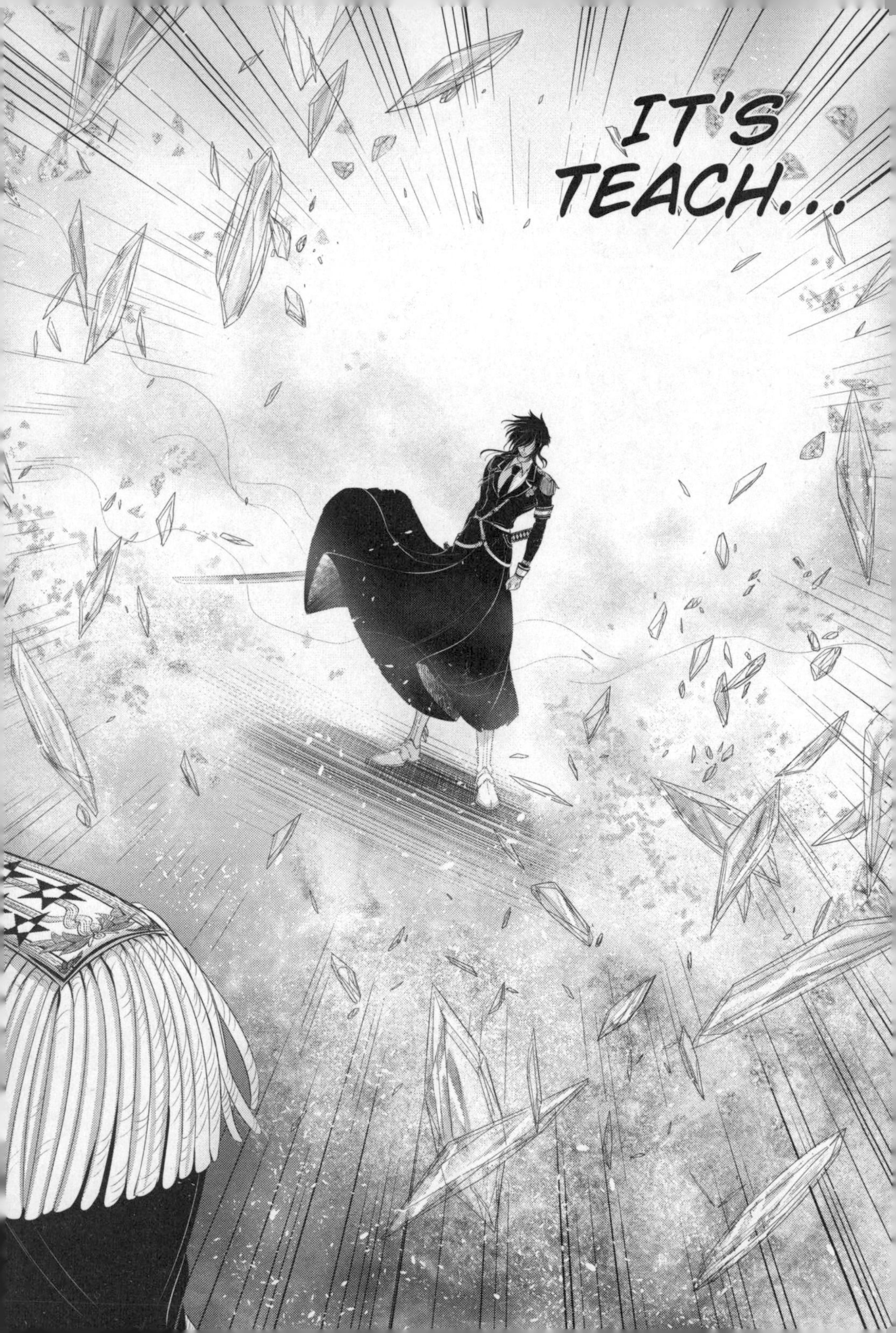
IT'S TEACH...

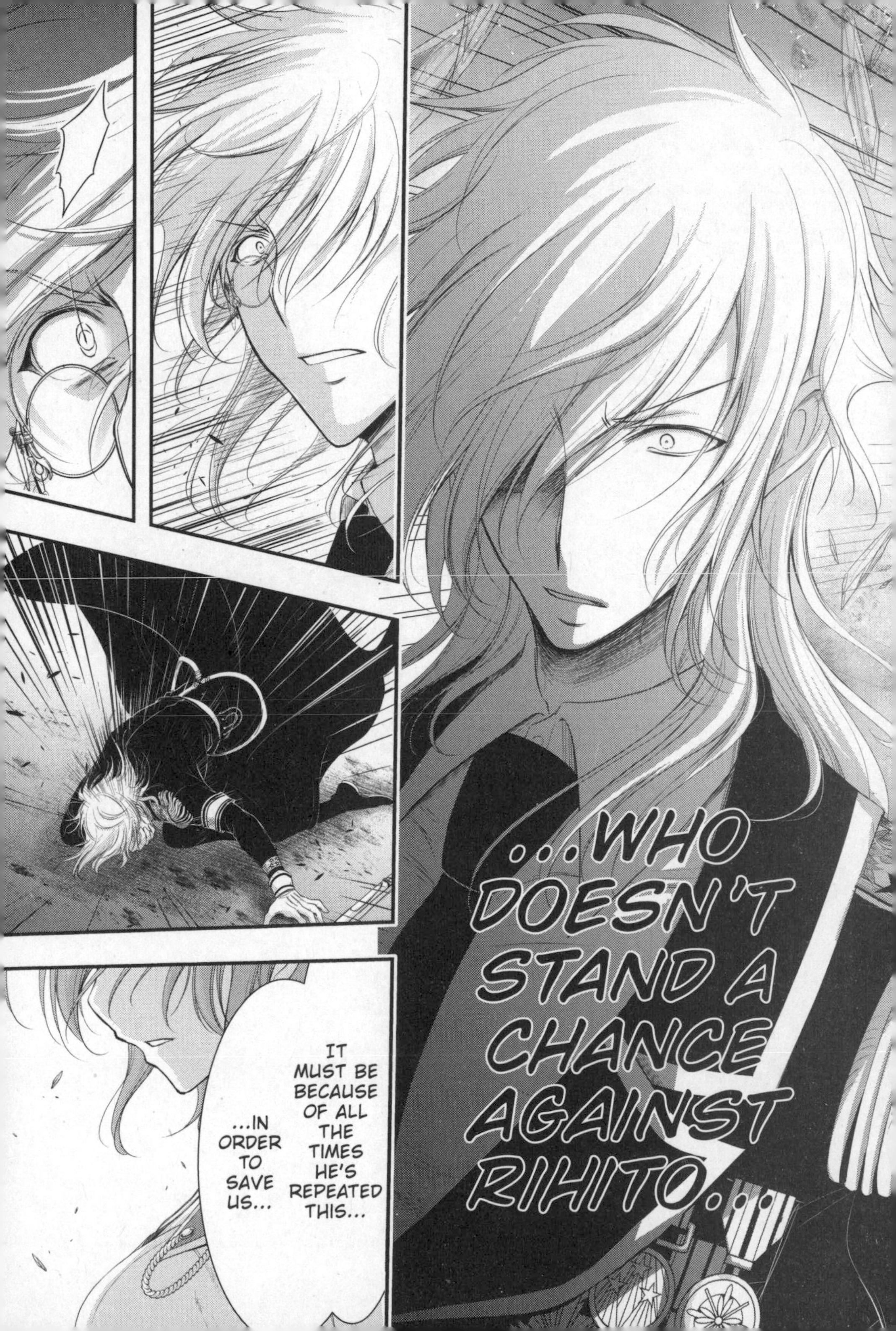
IT MUST BE BECAUSE OF ALL THE TIMES HE'S REPEATED THIS...
...IN ORDER TO SAVE US...
...WHO DOESN'T STAND A CHANCE AGAINST RIHITO...

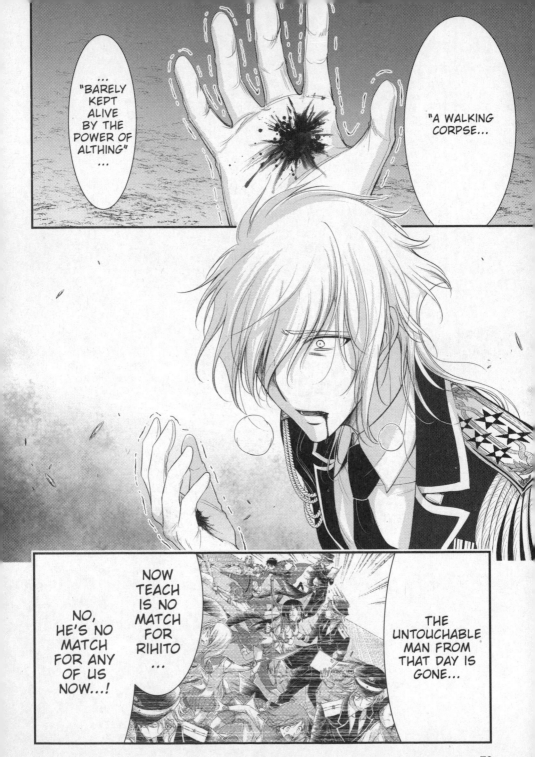

"A WALKING CORPSE...
... "BARELY KEPT ALIVE BY THE POWER OF ALTHING" ...
THE UNTOUCHABLE MAN FROM THAT DAY IS GONE...
NOW TEACH IS NO MATCH FOR RIHITO ...
NO, HE'S NO MATCH FOR ANY OF US NOW...!

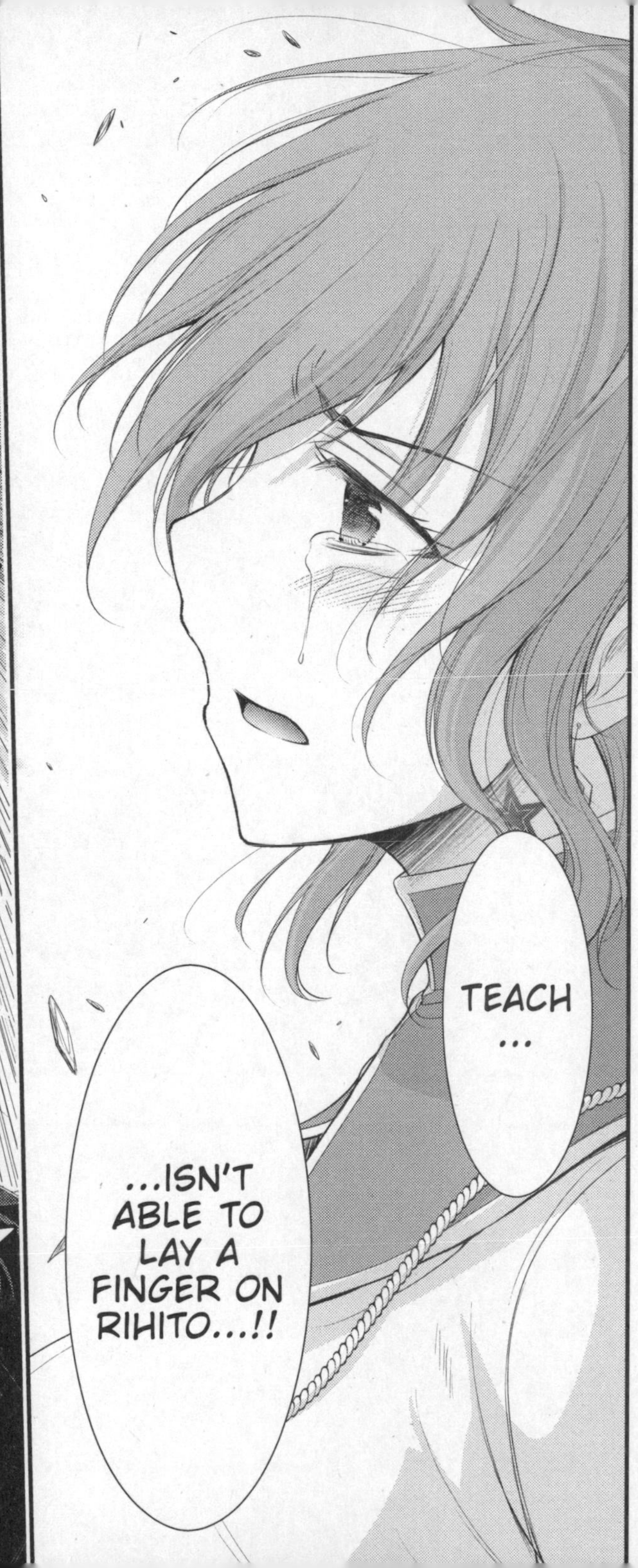
TEACH ...
...ISN'T ABLE TO LAY A FINGER ON RIHITO...!!
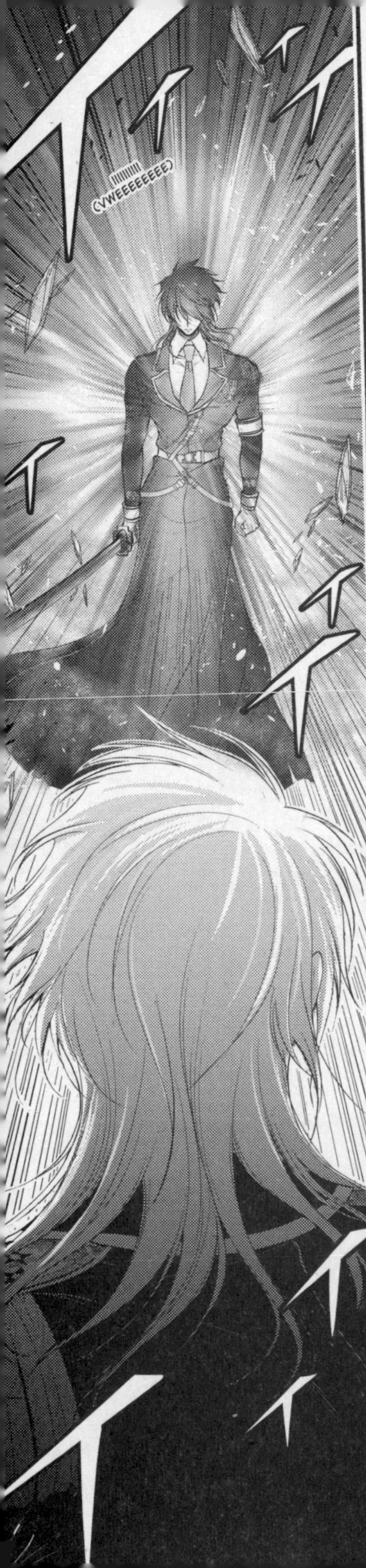
(VWEEEEEEEE)

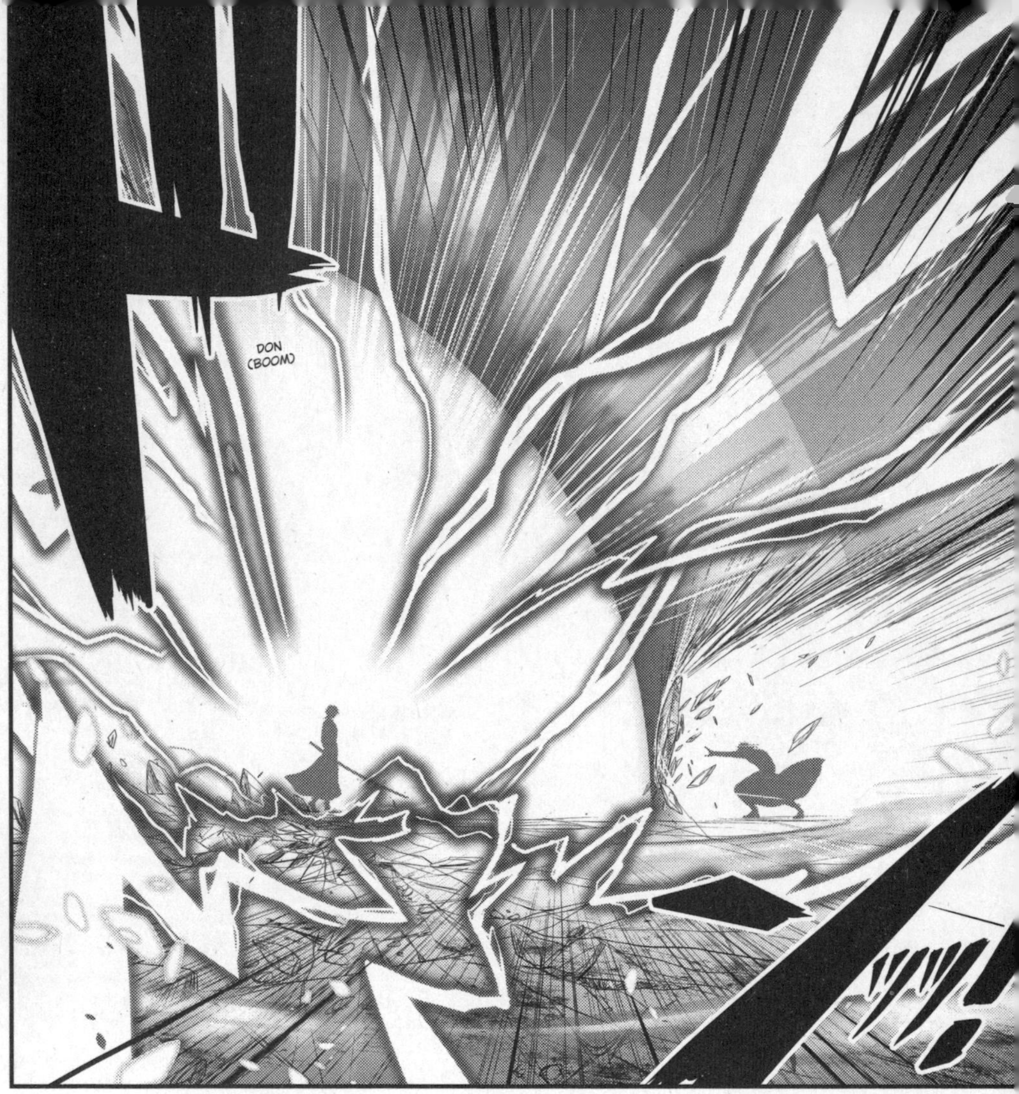
DON (BOOM)
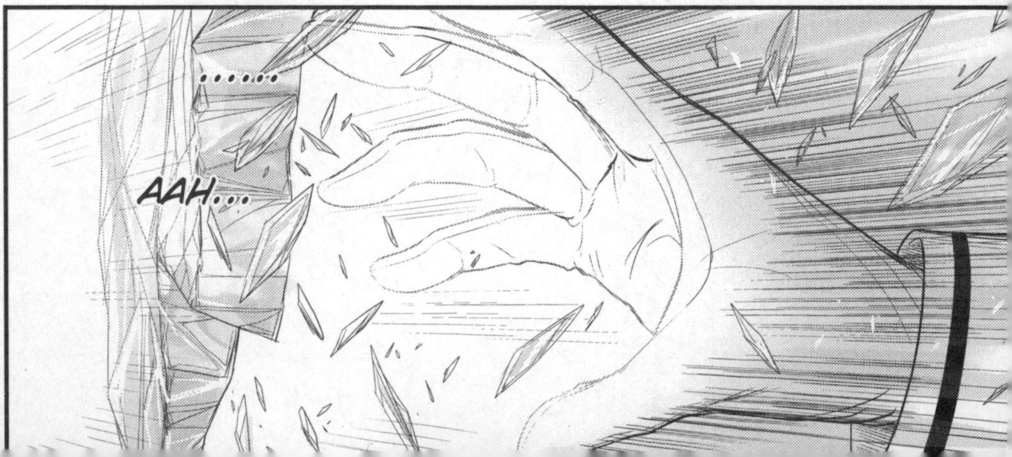
......
AAH...

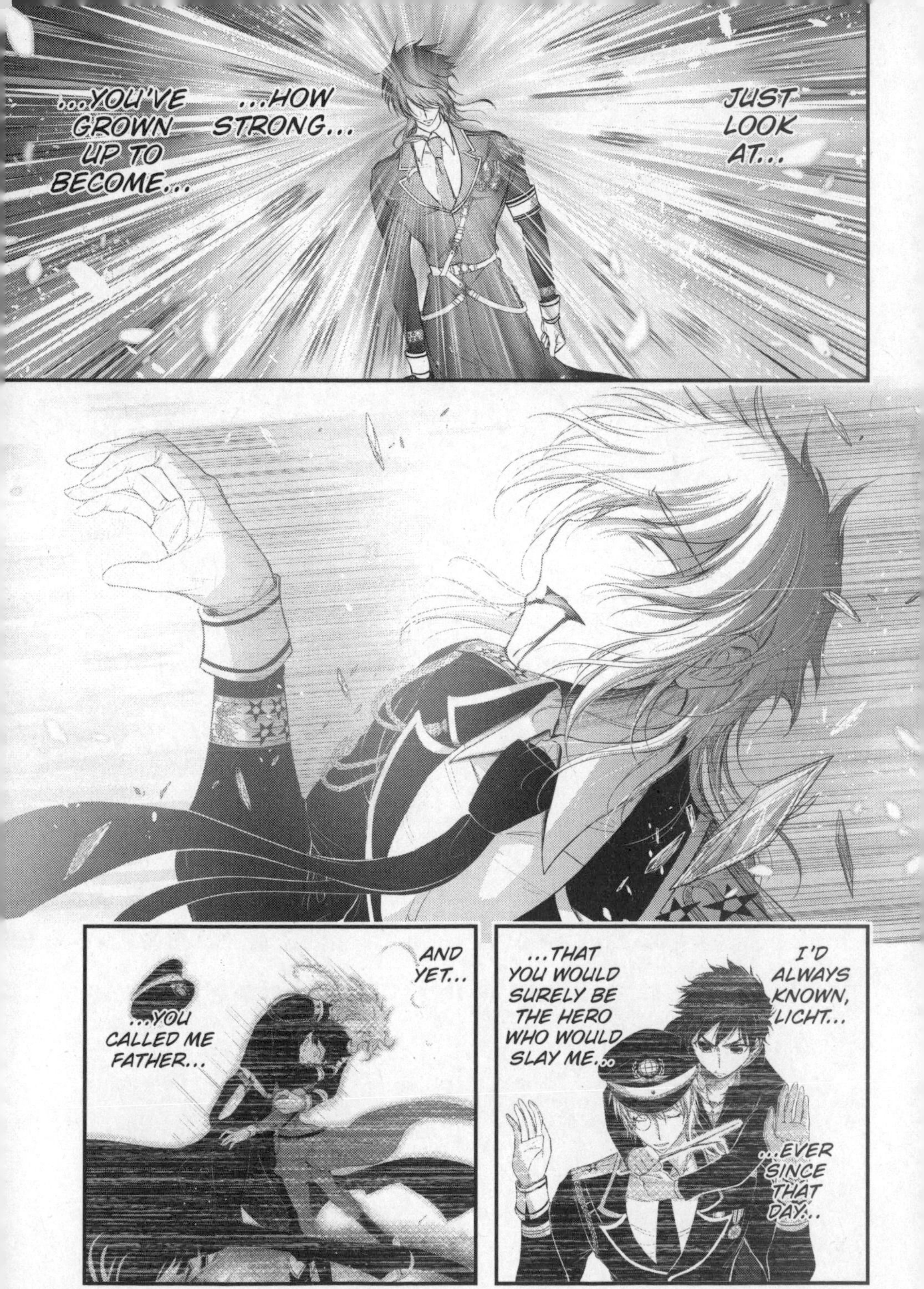
JUST LOOK AT...
...HOW STRONG...
...YOU'VE GROWN UP TO BECOME...
I'D ALWAYS KNOWN, LICHT...
...THAT YOU WOULD SURELY BE THE HERO WHO WOULD SLAY ME...
...EVER SINCE THAT DAY...
AND YET...
...YOU CALLED ME FATHER...

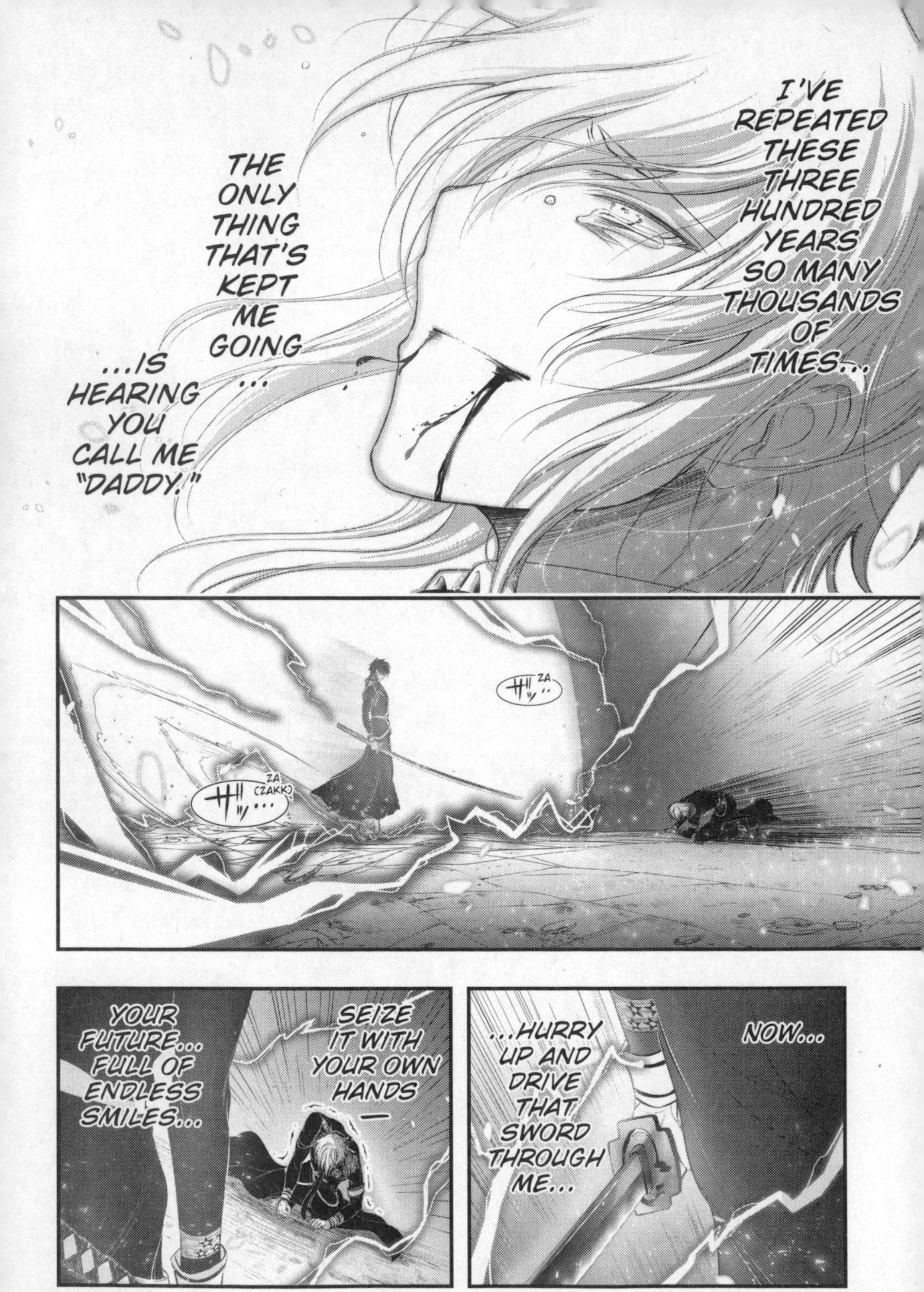
I'VE REPEATED THESE THREE HUNDRED YEARS SO MANY THOUSANDS OF TIMES...
THE ONLY THING THAT'S KEPT ME GOING...
...IS HEARING YOU CALL ME "DADDY."
ZA
ZA (ZAKK)
NOW...
...HURRY UP AND DRIVE THAT SWORD THROUGH ME...
SEIZE IT WITH YOUR OWN HANDS —
YOUR FUTURE... FULL OF ENDLESS SMILES...

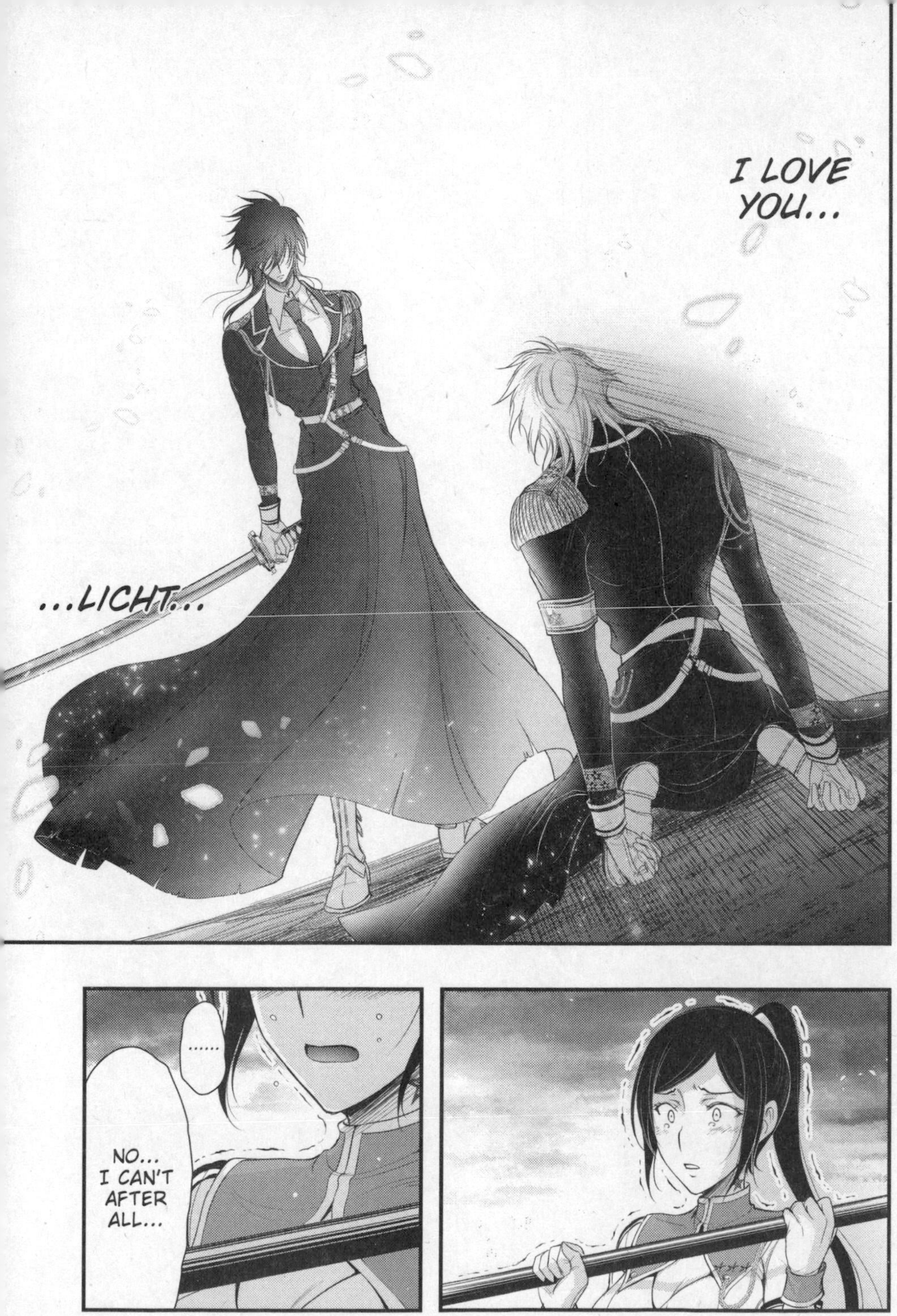
I LOVE YOU...
...LICHT...
......
NO... I CAN'T AFTER ALL...

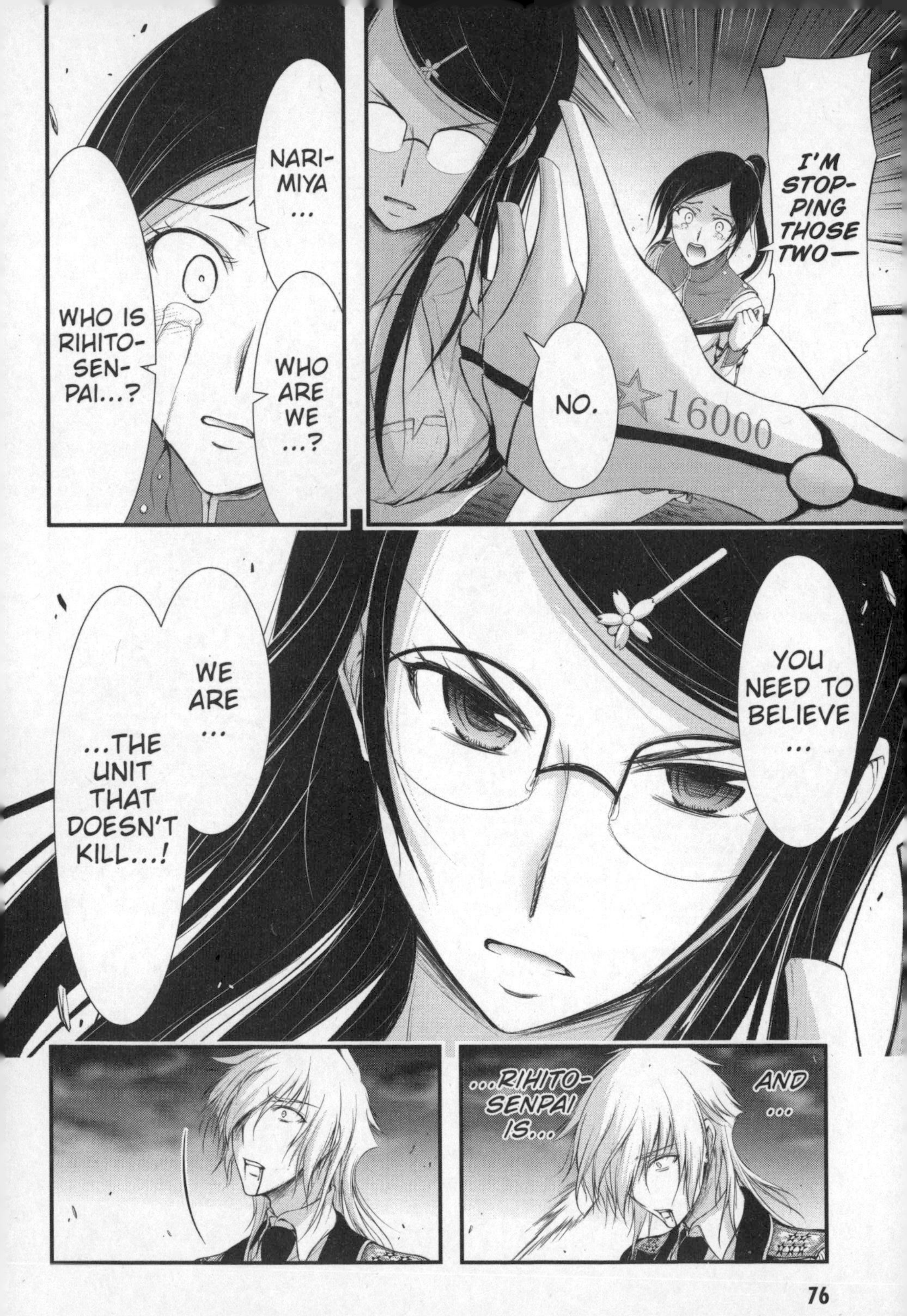
I'M STOPPING THOSE TWO—
NO.
16000
NARIMIYA...
WHO ARE WE...?
WHO IS RIHITO-SENPAI...?
YOU NEED TO BELIEVE...
WE ARE...
...THE UNIT THAT DOESN'T KILL...!
AND...
...RIHITO-SENPAI IS...

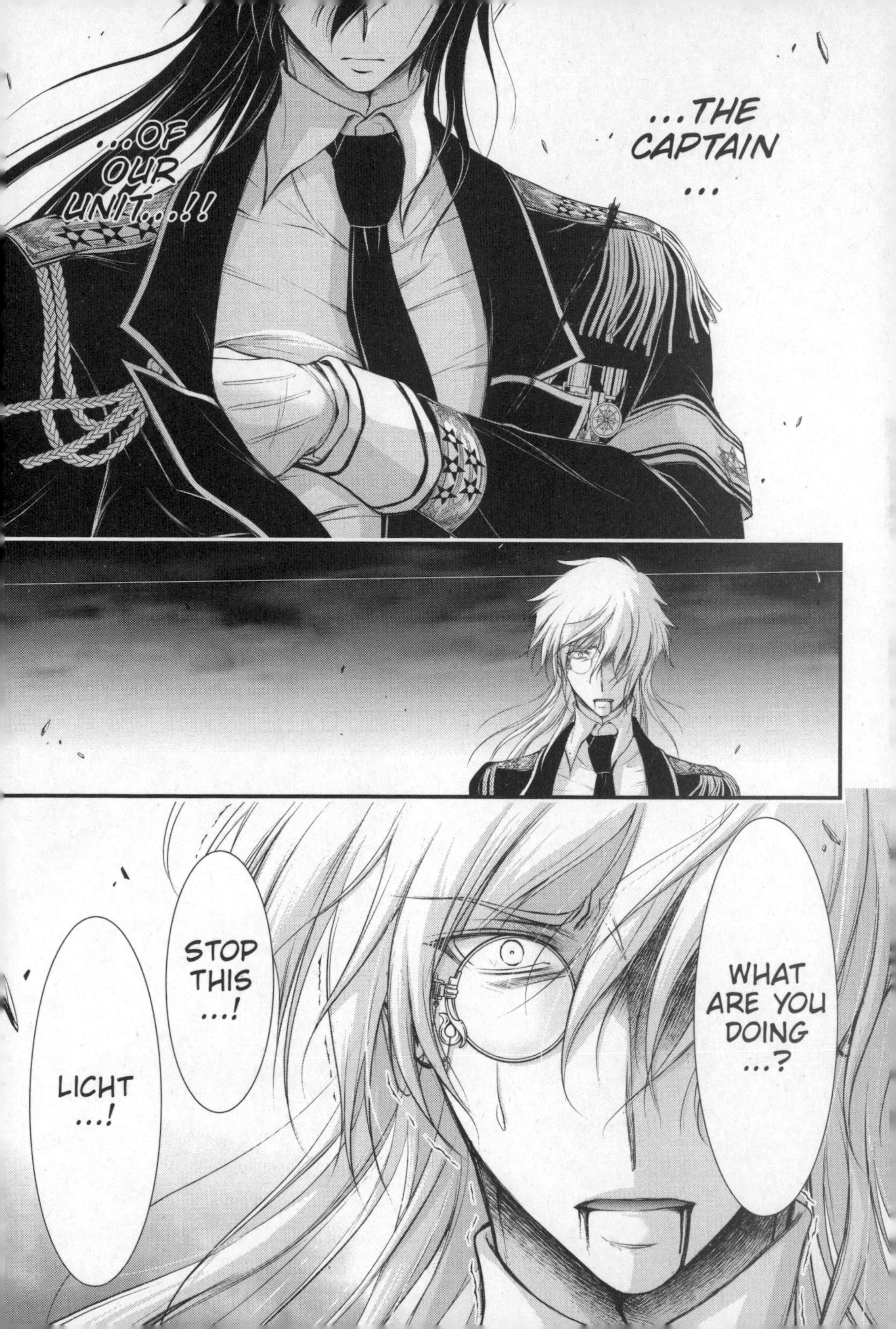
...THE CAPTAIN ...
...OF OUR UNIT...!!
WHAT ARE YOU DOING ...?
STOP THIS ...!
LICHT ...!

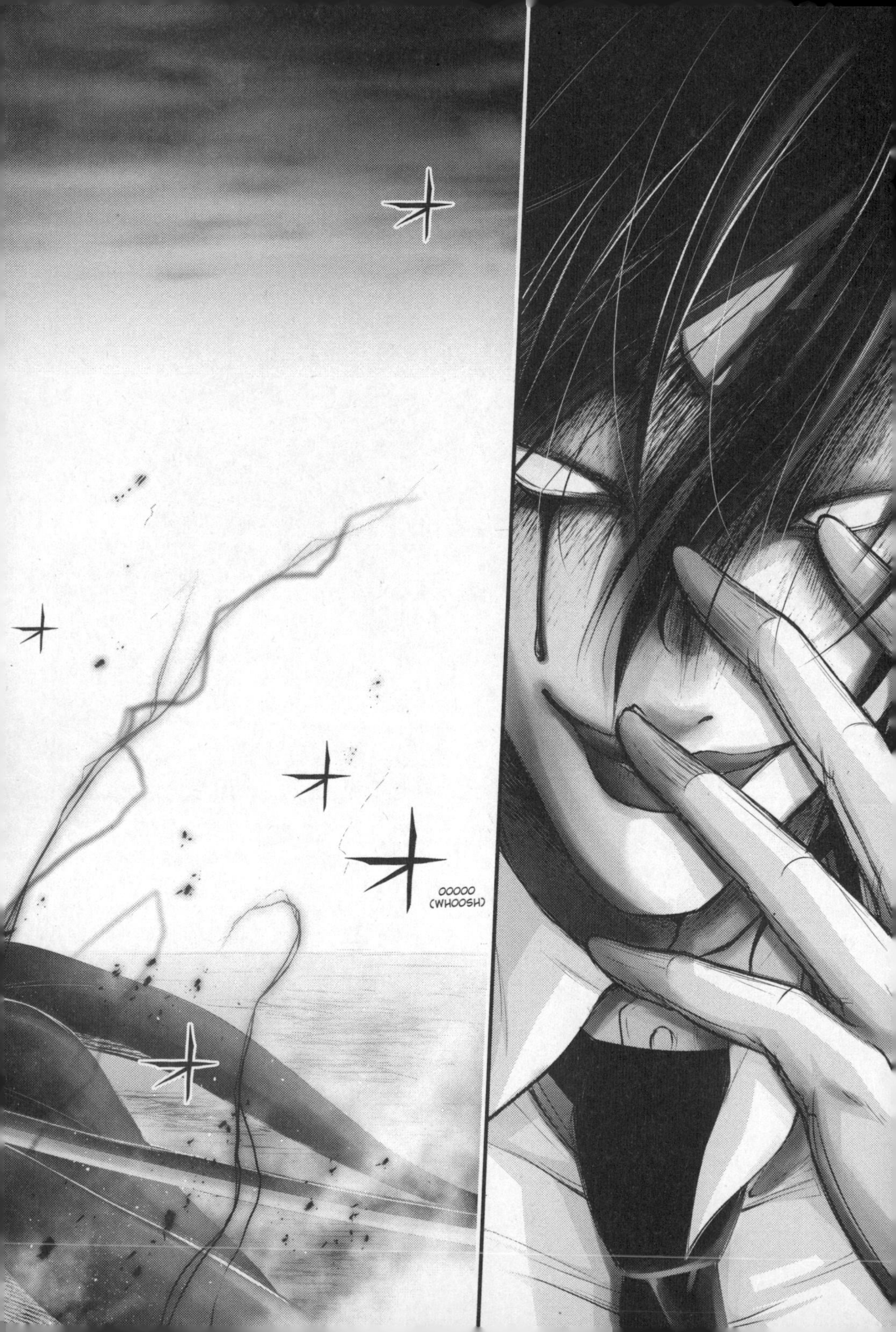
OOOOO
(WHOOSH)

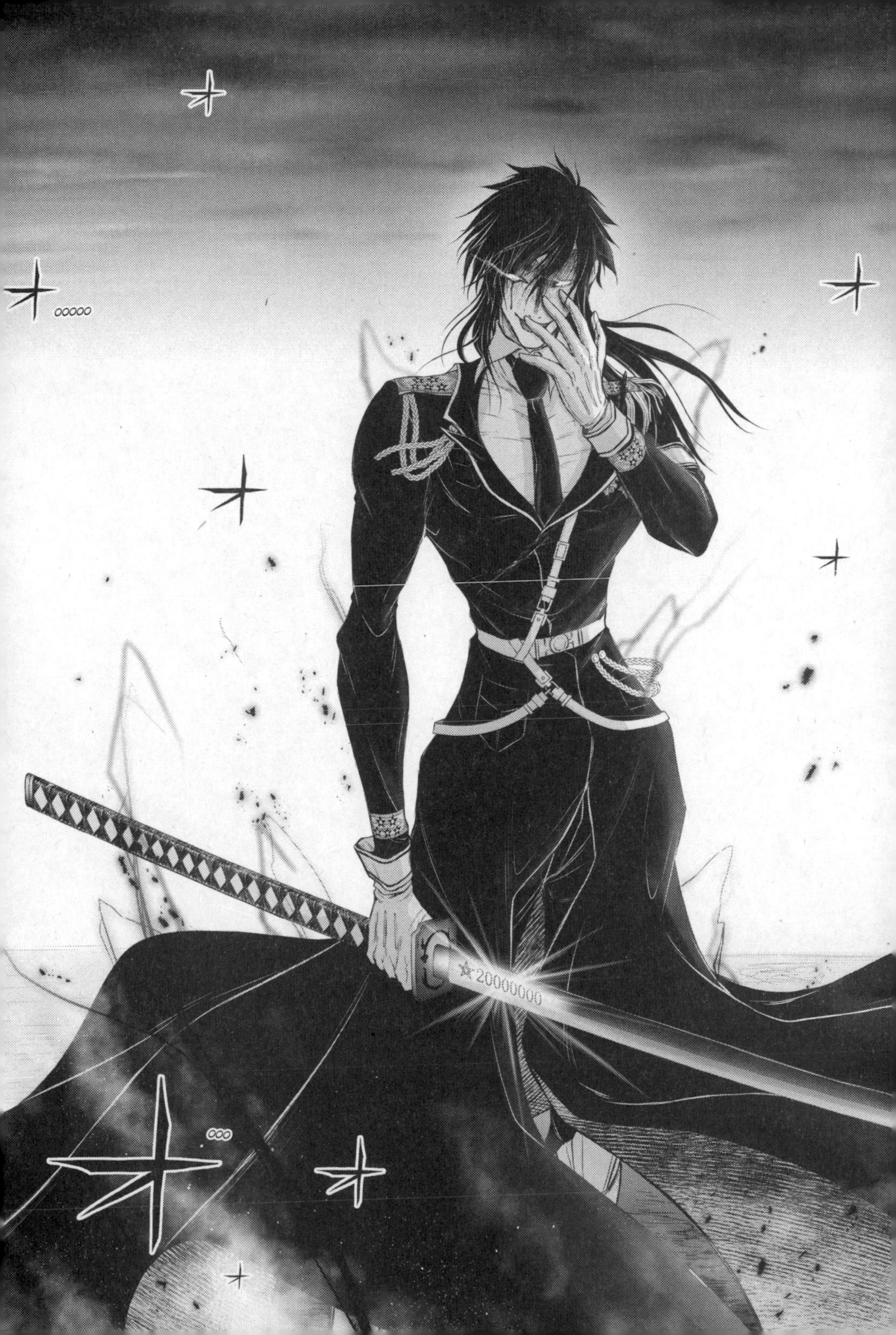
20000000

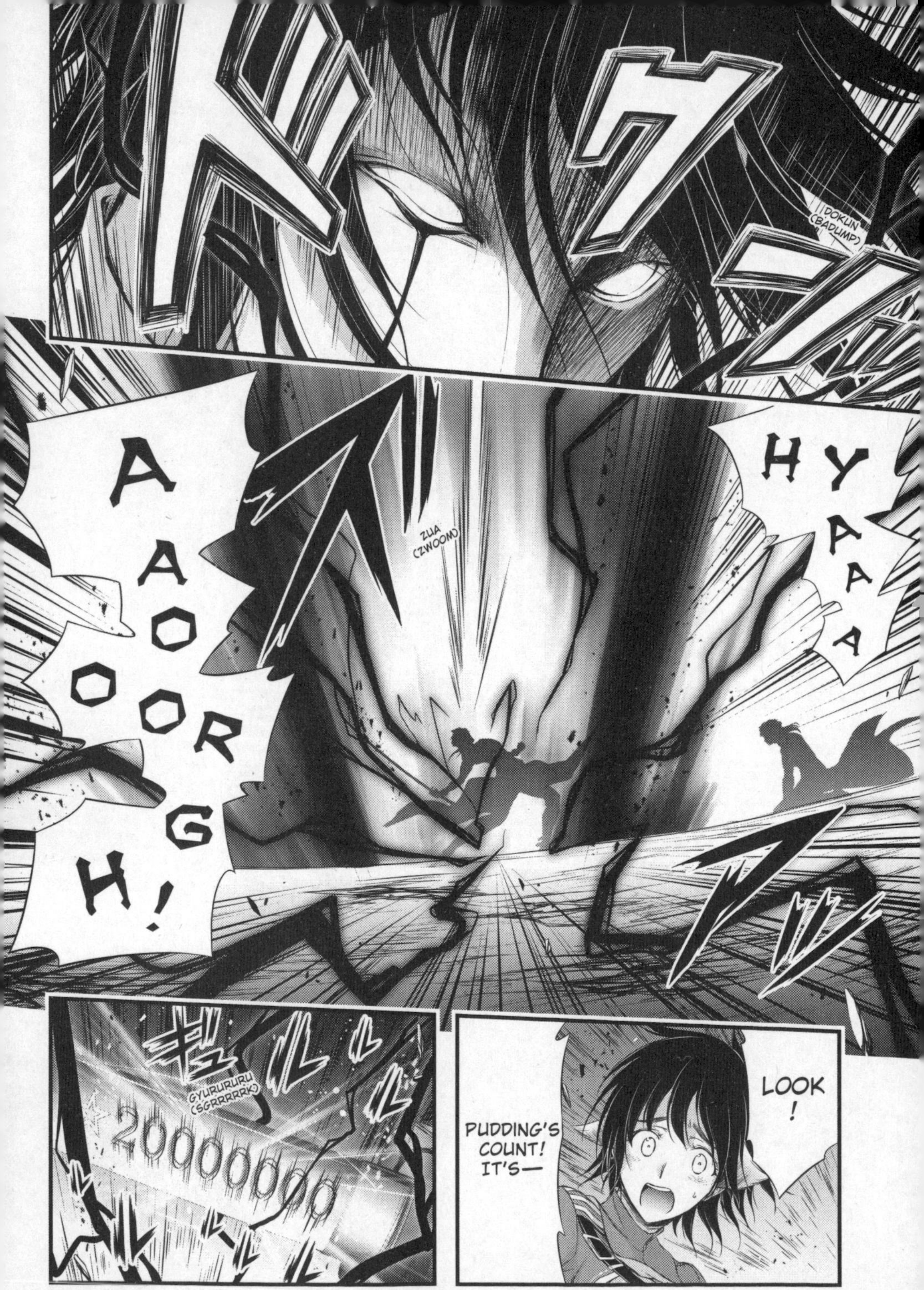
DOKUN (BADUMP)
HYAAA
ZUA (ZWOOM)
AAOOORGH!
LOOK!
PUDDING'S COUNT! IT'S—
GYURURURU (SGRRRRRK)
20000000

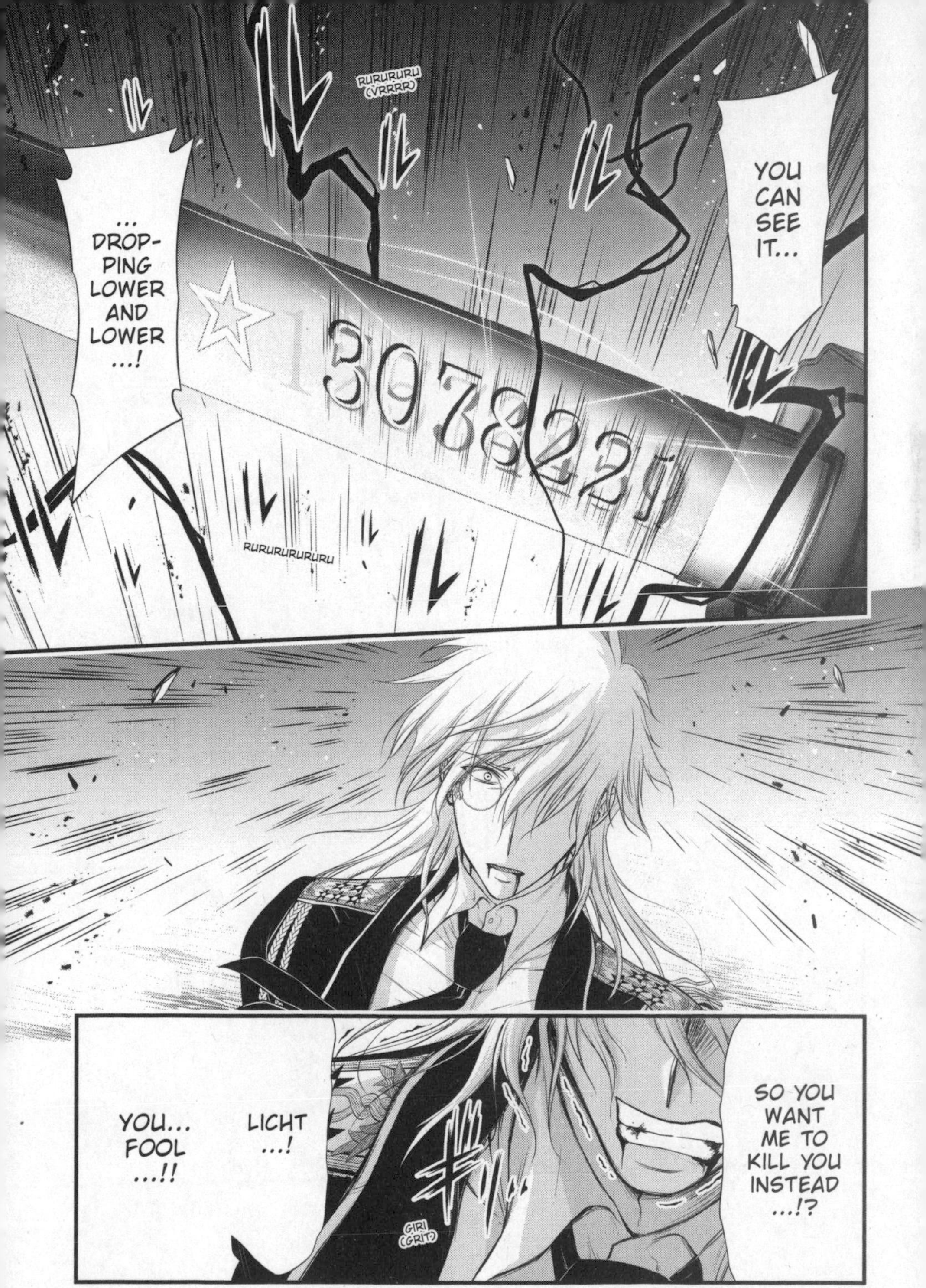
YOU CAN SEE IT...
RURURURU (VRRRR)
...DROP-PING LOWER AND LOWER...!
RURURURURURU
SO YOU WANT ME TO KILL YOU INSTEAD...!?
GIRI (GRIT)
LICHT...!
YOU... FOOL...!!

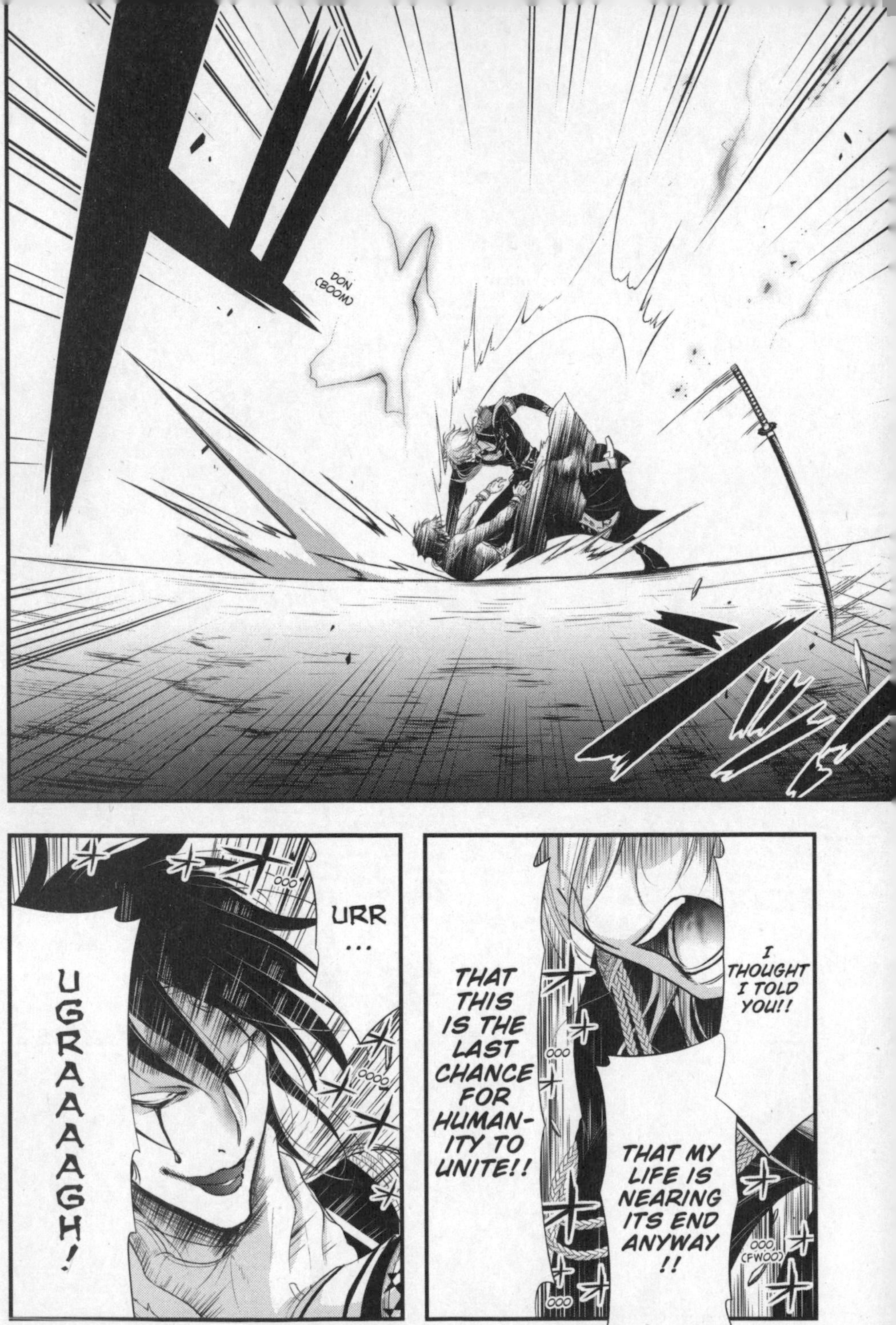
DON (BOOM)
I THOUGHT I TOLD YOU!!
THAT THIS IS THE LAST CHANCE FOR HUMANITY TO UNITE!!
THAT MY LIFE IS NEARING ITS END ANYWAY!!
OOO (FWOO)
URR...
UGRAAAAAGH!

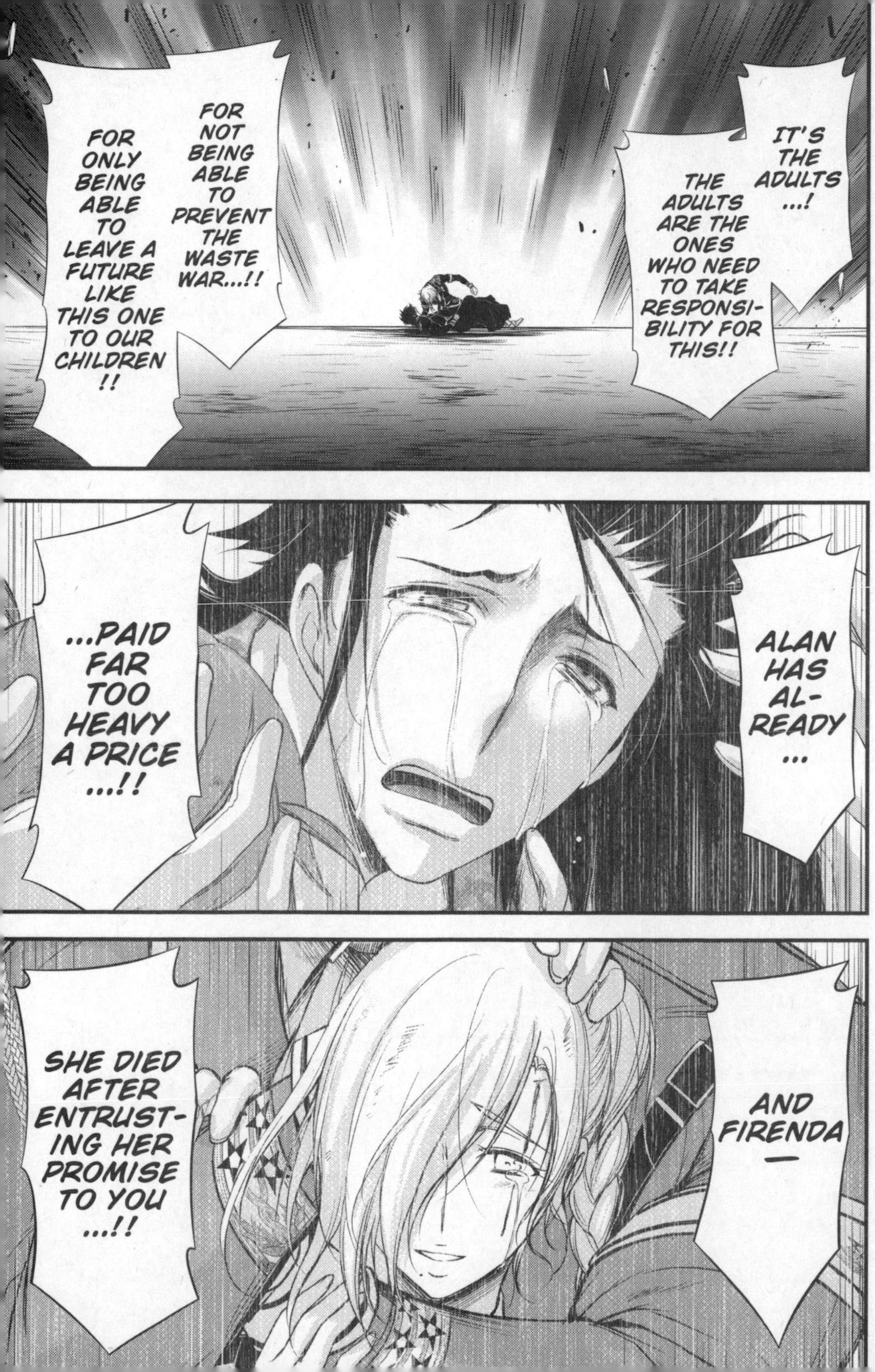
IT'S THE ADULTS...!
THE ADULTS ARE THE ONES WHO NEED TO TAKE RESPONSIBILITY FOR THIS!!
FOR NOT BEING ABLE TO PREVENT THE WASTE WAR...!!
FOR ONLY BEING ABLE TO LEAVE A FUTURE LIKE THIS ONE TO OUR CHILDREN!!
ALAN HAS ALREADY...
...PAID FAR TOO HEAVY A PRICE...!!
AND FIRENDA—
SHE DIED AFTER ENTRUSTING HER PROMISE TO YOU...!!

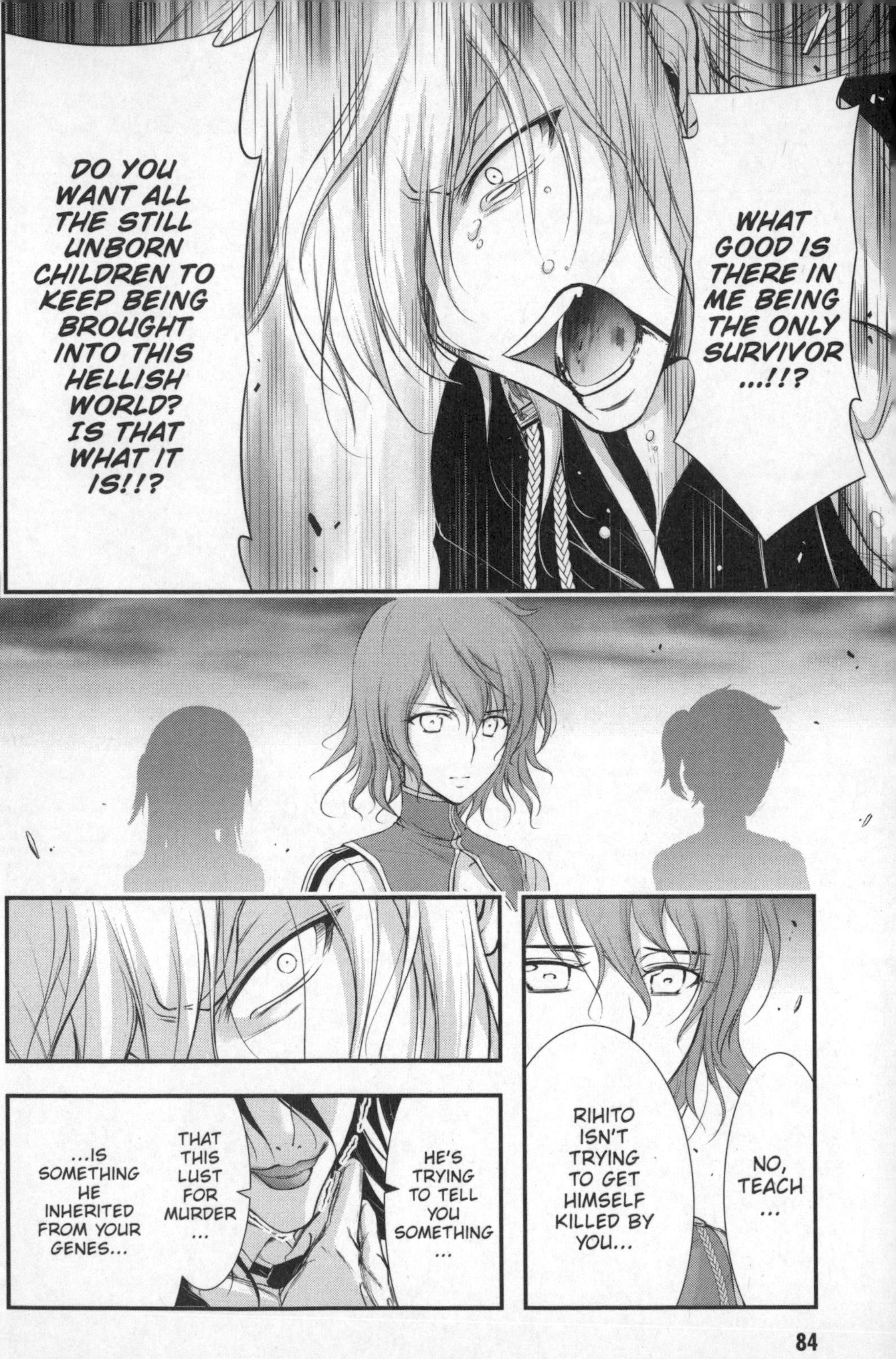
WHAT GOOD IS THERE IN ME BEING THE ONLY SURVIVOR ...!!?
DO YOU WANT ALL THE STILL UNBORN CHILDREN TO KEEP BEING BROUGHT INTO THIS HELLISH WORLD? IS THAT WHAT IT IS!!?
NO, TEACH ...
RIHITO ISN'T TRYING TO GET HIMSELF KILLED BY YOU...
HE'S TRYING TO TELL YOU SOMETHING ...
THAT THIS LUST FOR MURDER ...
...IS SOMETHING HE INHERITED FROM YOUR GENES...

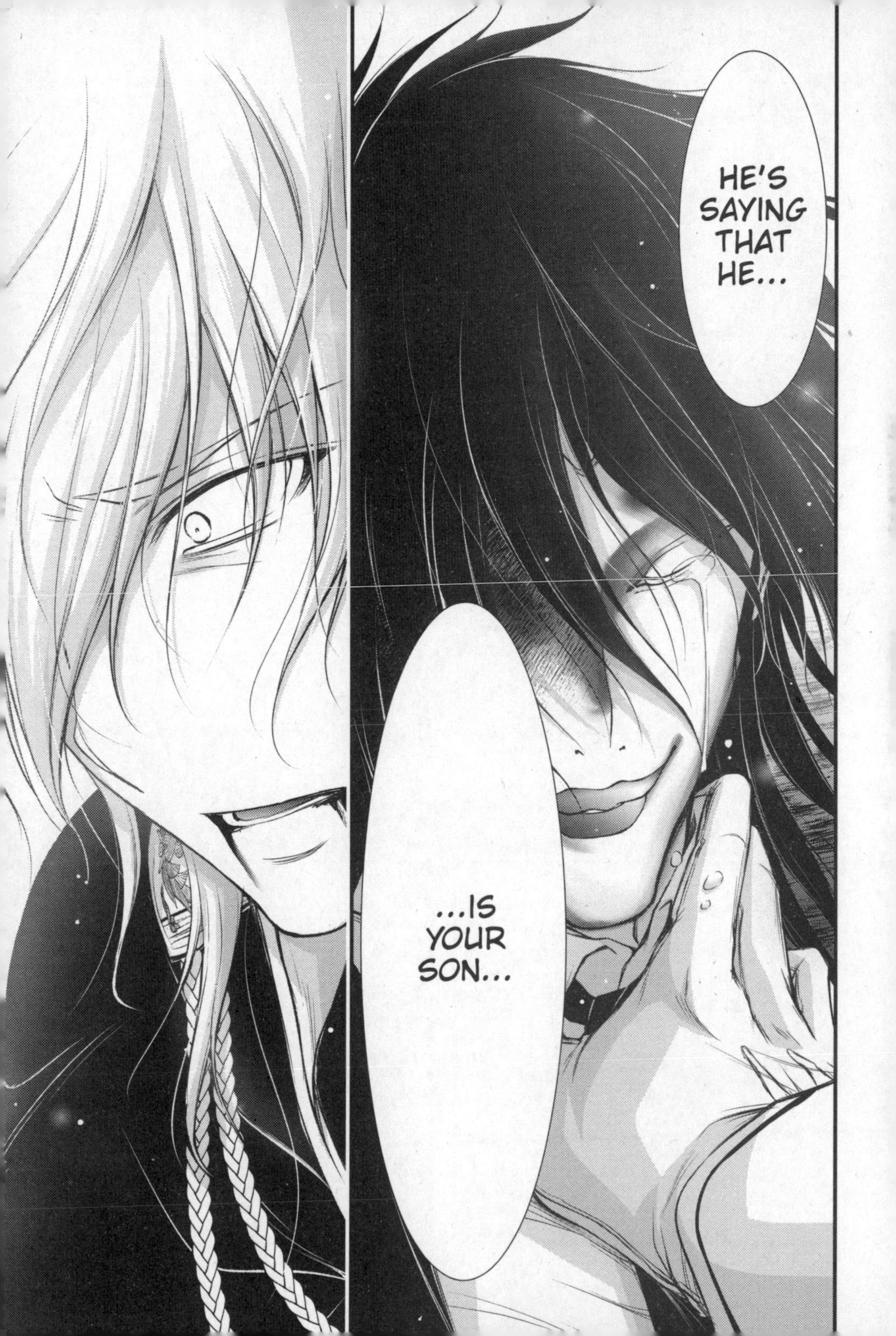
HE'S SAYING THAT HE...
...IS YOUR SON...

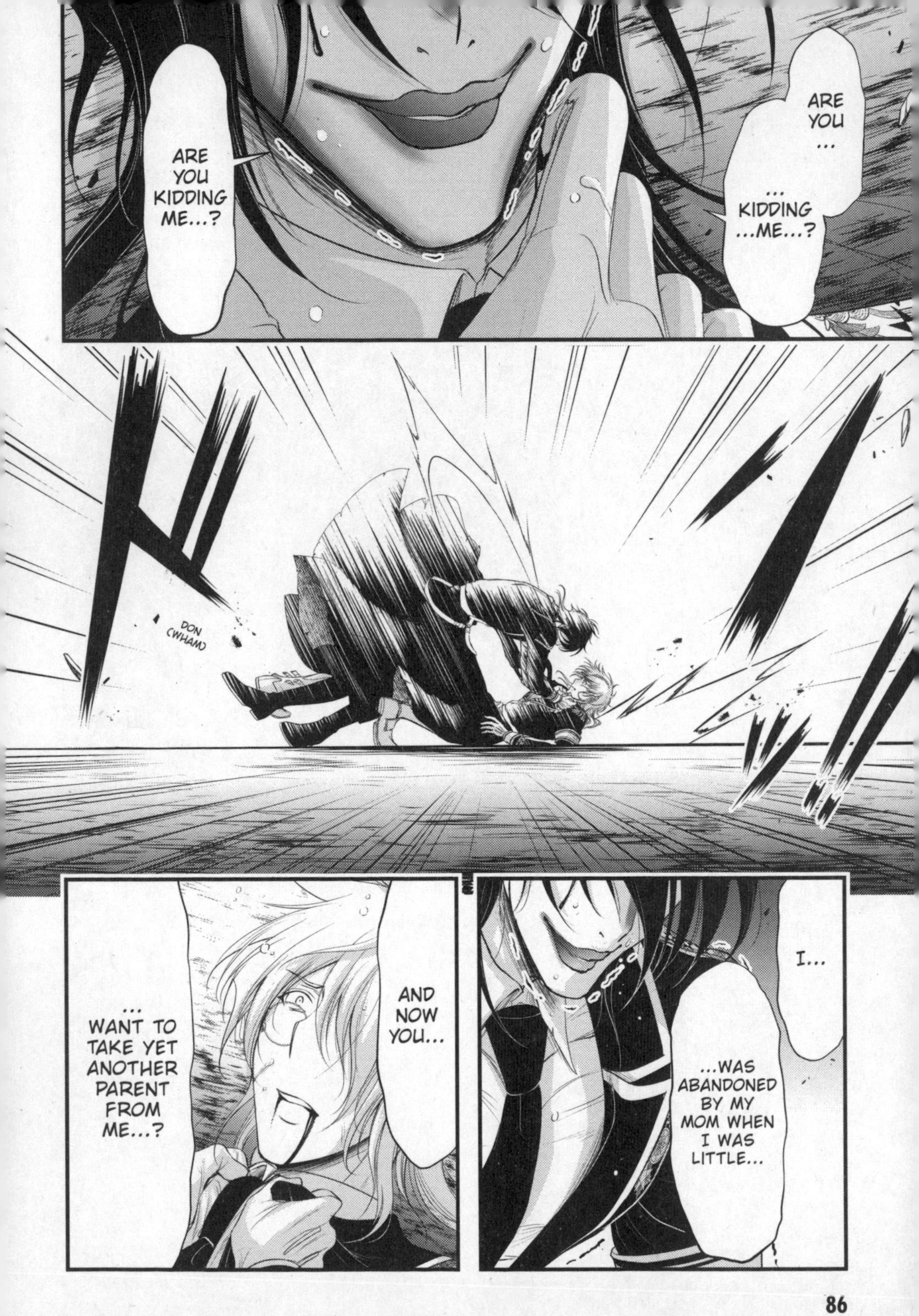

ARE YOU ... ... KIDDING ...ME...?
ARE YOU KIDDING ME...?
DON (WHAM)
I...
...WAS ABANDONED BY MY MOM WHEN I WAS LITTLE...
AND NOW YOU...
... WANT TO TAKE YET ANOTHER PARENT FROM ME...?

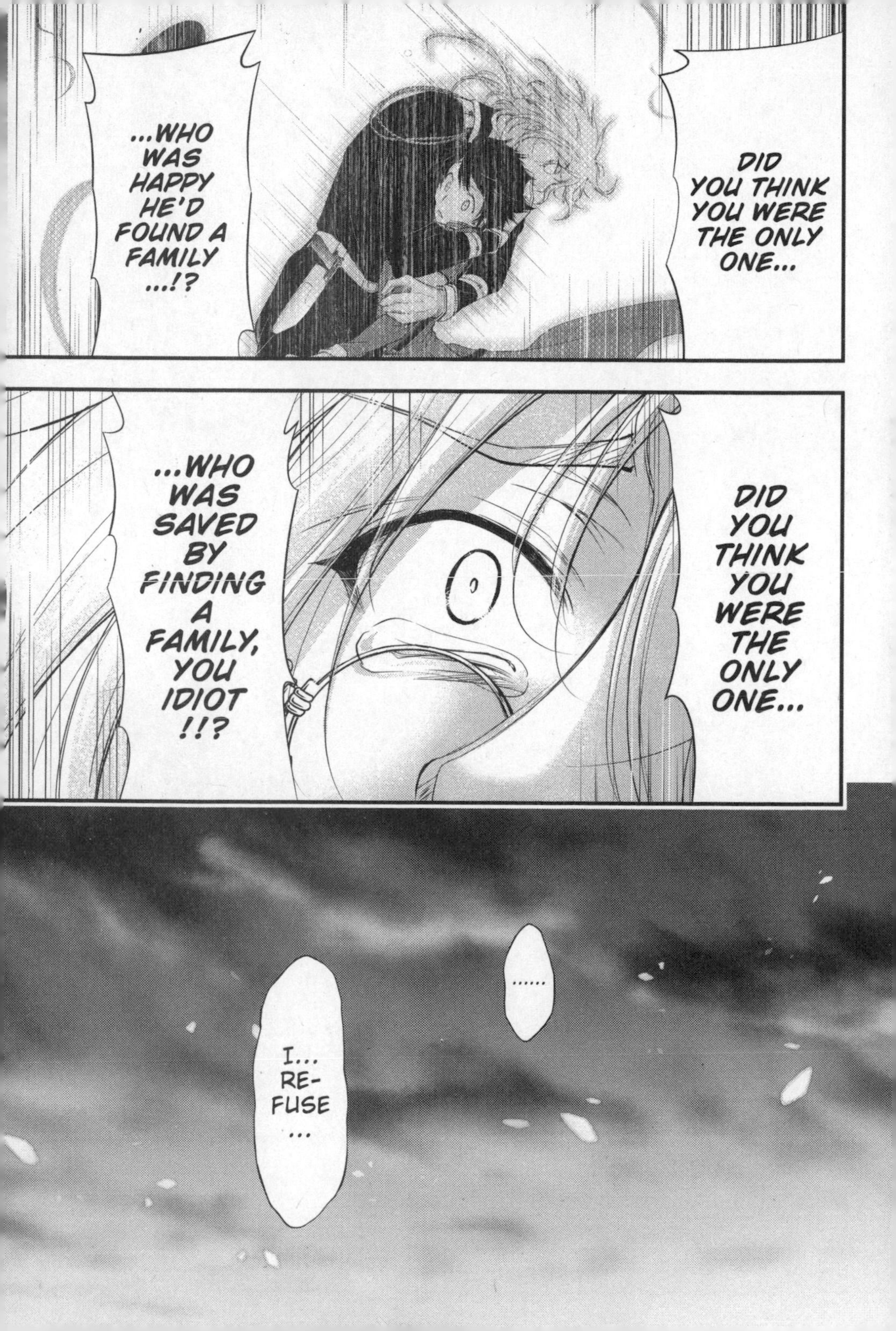
DID YOU THINK YOU WERE THE ONLY ONE...
...WHO WAS HAPPY HE'D FOUND A FAMILY ...!?
DID YOU THINK YOU WERE THE ONLY ONE...
...WHO WAS SAVED BY FINDING A FAMILY, YOU IDIOT !!?
......
I... RE- FUSE ...

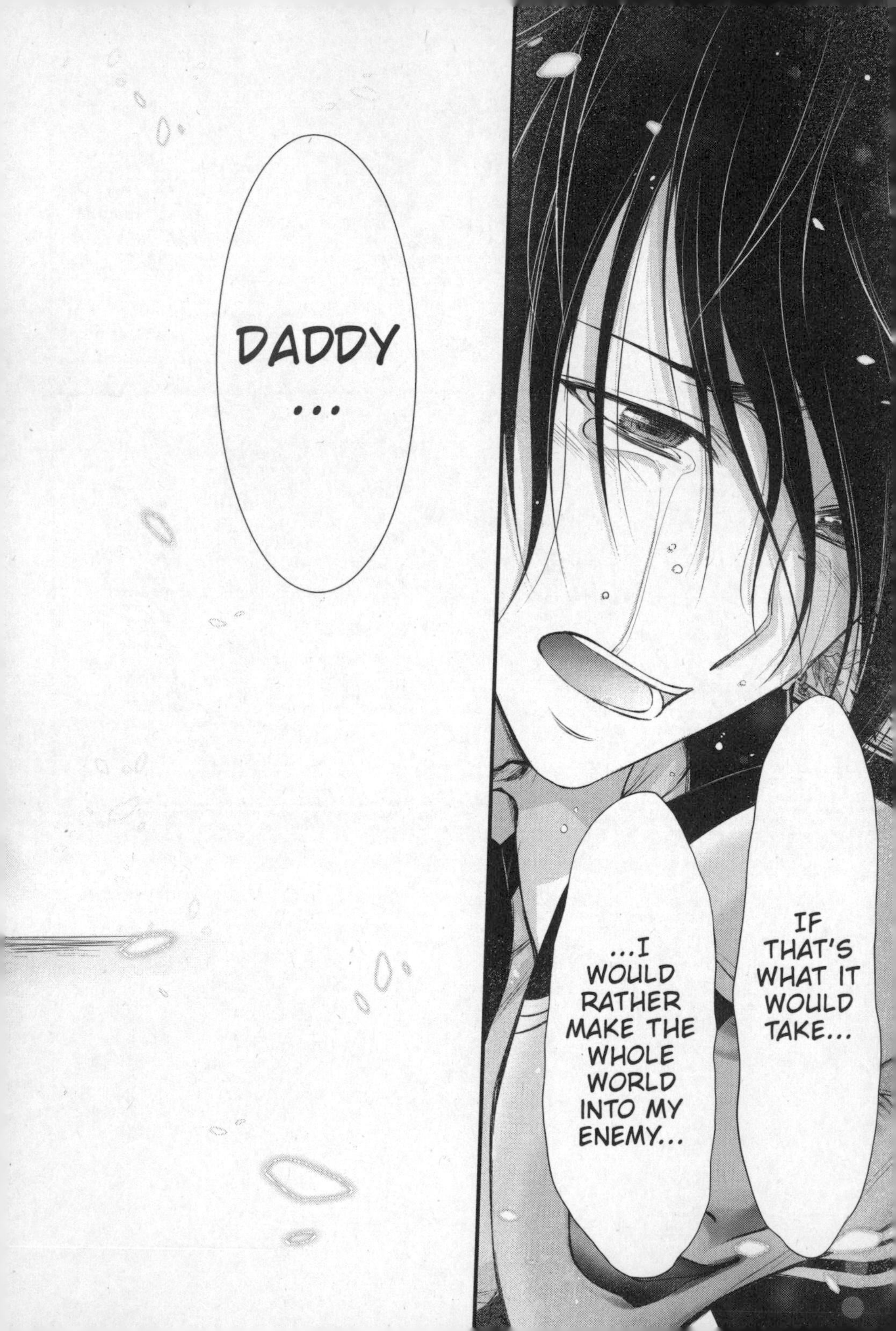
IF THAT'S WHAT IT WOULD TAKE...
...I WOULD RATHER MAKE THE WHOLE WORLD INTO MY ENEMY...
DADDY ...

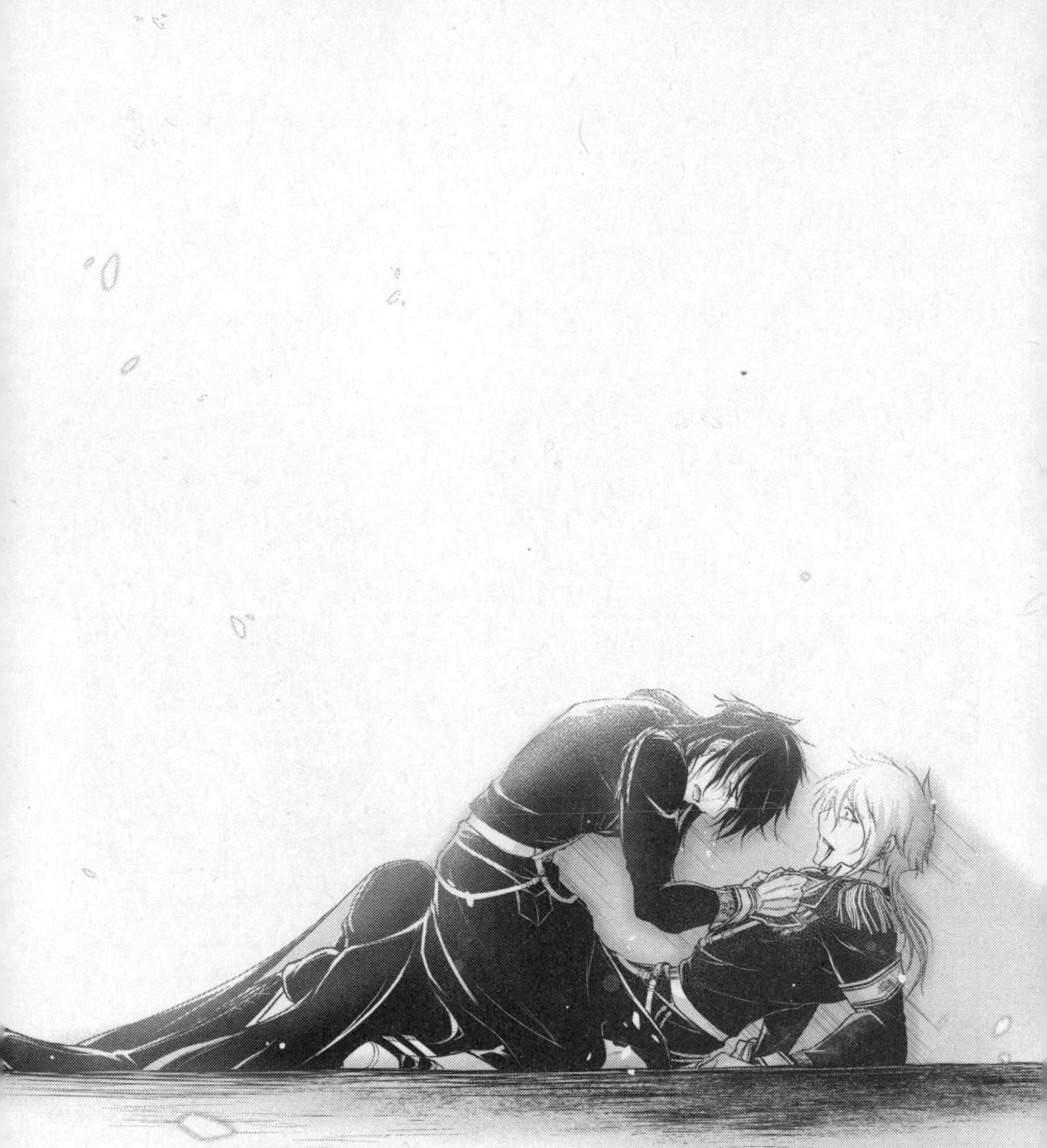

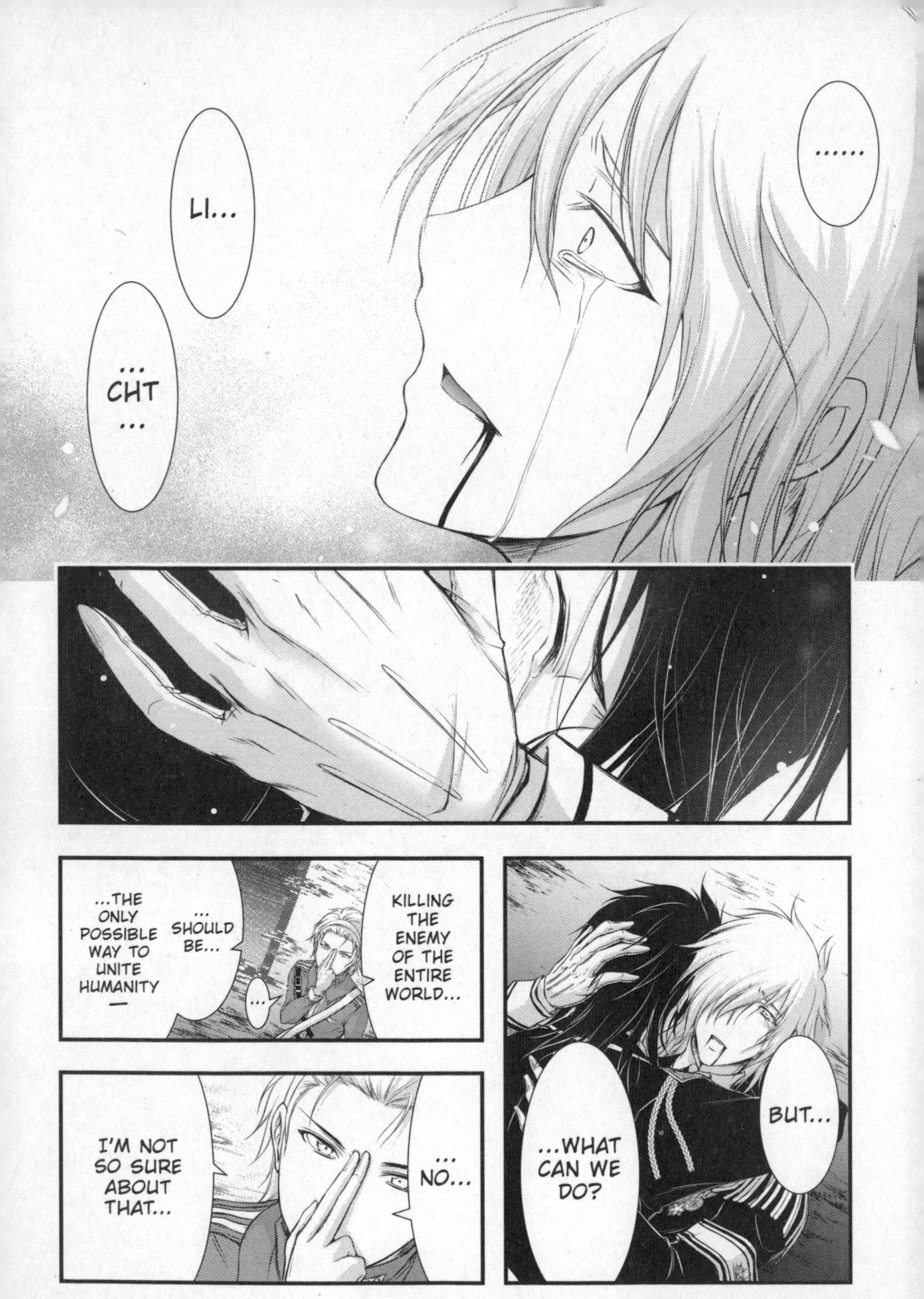
......
LI...
... CHT ...
BUT...
...WHAT CAN WE DO?
KILLING THE ENEMY OF THE ENTIRE WORLD...
...
... SHOULD BE...
...THE ONLY POSSIBLE WAY TO UNITE HUMANITY —
... NO...
I'M NOT SO SURE ABOUT THAT...

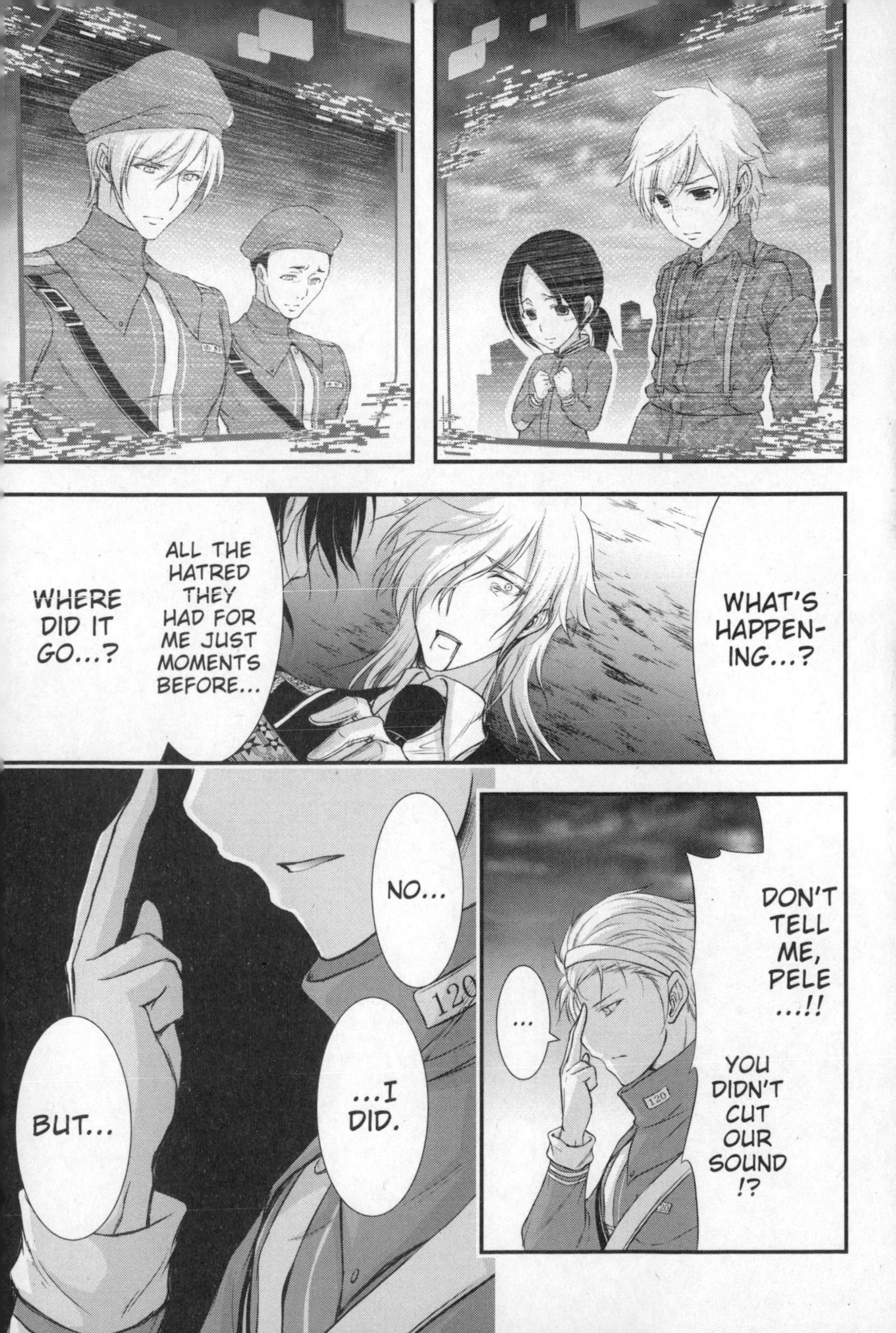
WHAT'S HAPPEN-ING...?
ALL THE HATRED THEY HAD FOR ME JUST MOMENTS BEFORE...
WHERE DID IT GO...?
DON'T TELL ME, PELE...!!
YOU DIDN'T CUT OUR SOUND!?
...
NO...
...I DID.
BUT...
120

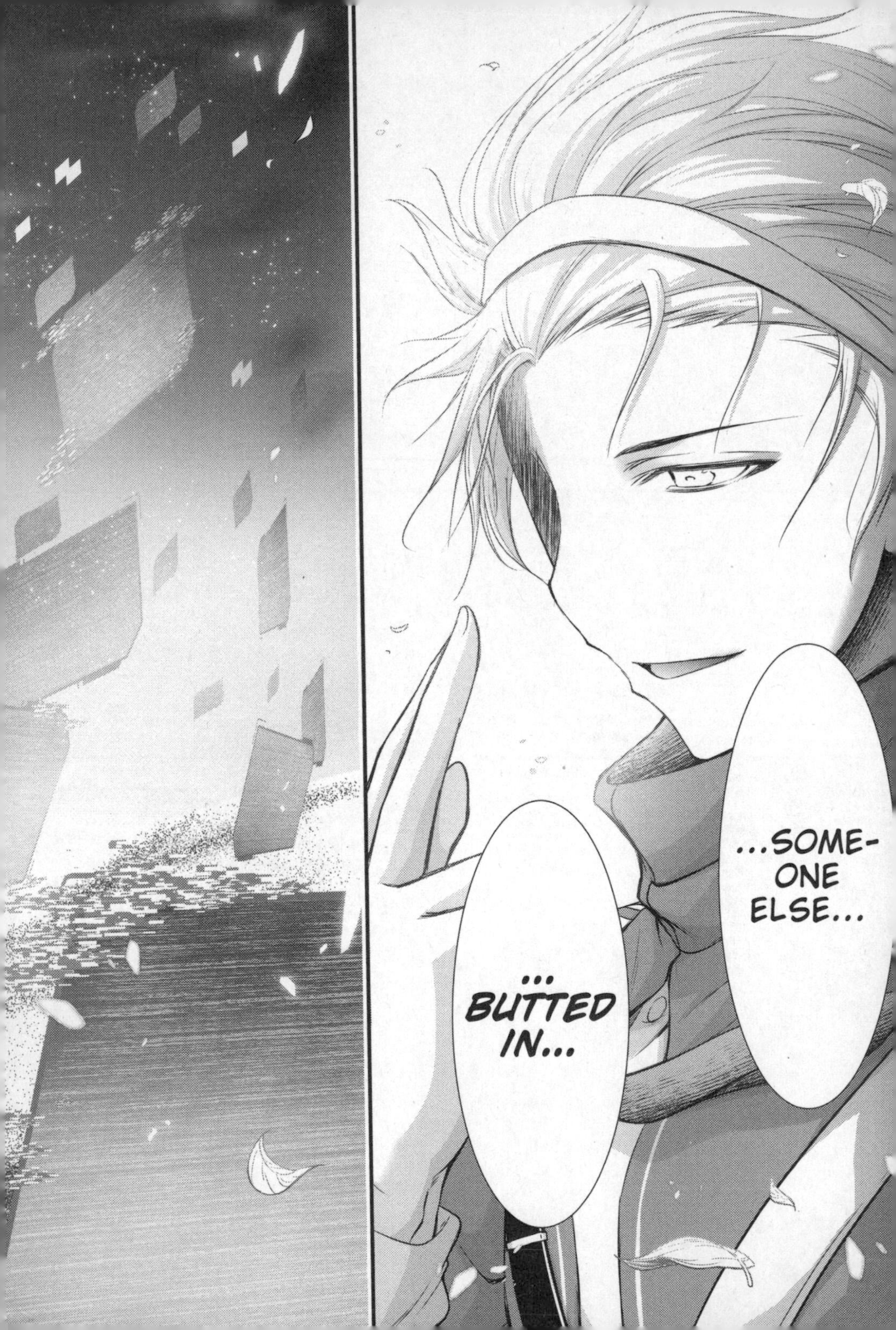
...SOME-ONE ELSE...
...BUTTED IN...

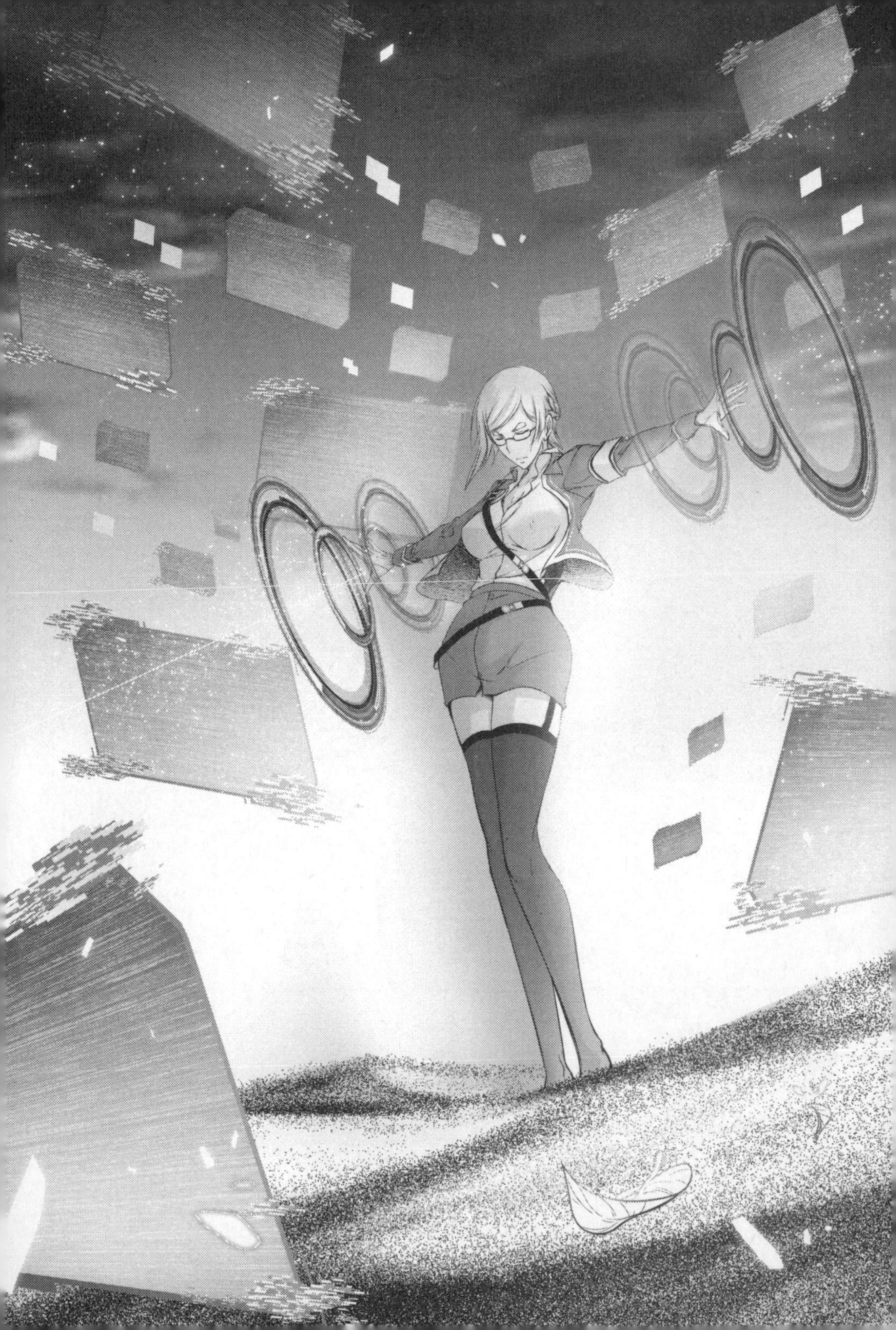

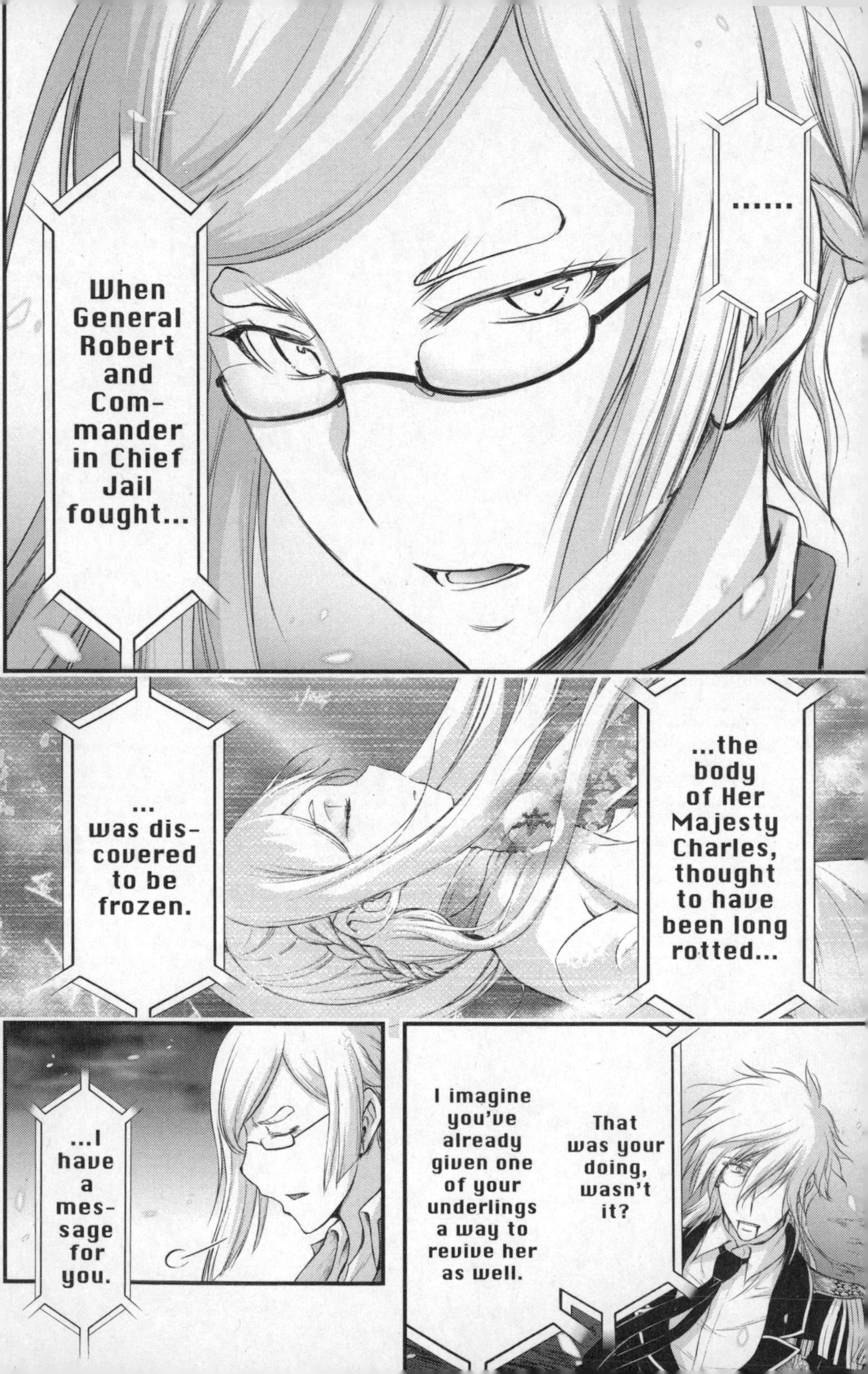
......
When General Robert and Com-mander in Chief Jail fought...
...the body of Her Majesty Charles, thought to have been long rotted...
... was dis-covered to be frozen.
That was your doing, wasn't it?
I imagine you've already given one of your underlings a way to revive her as well.
...I have a mes-sage for you.

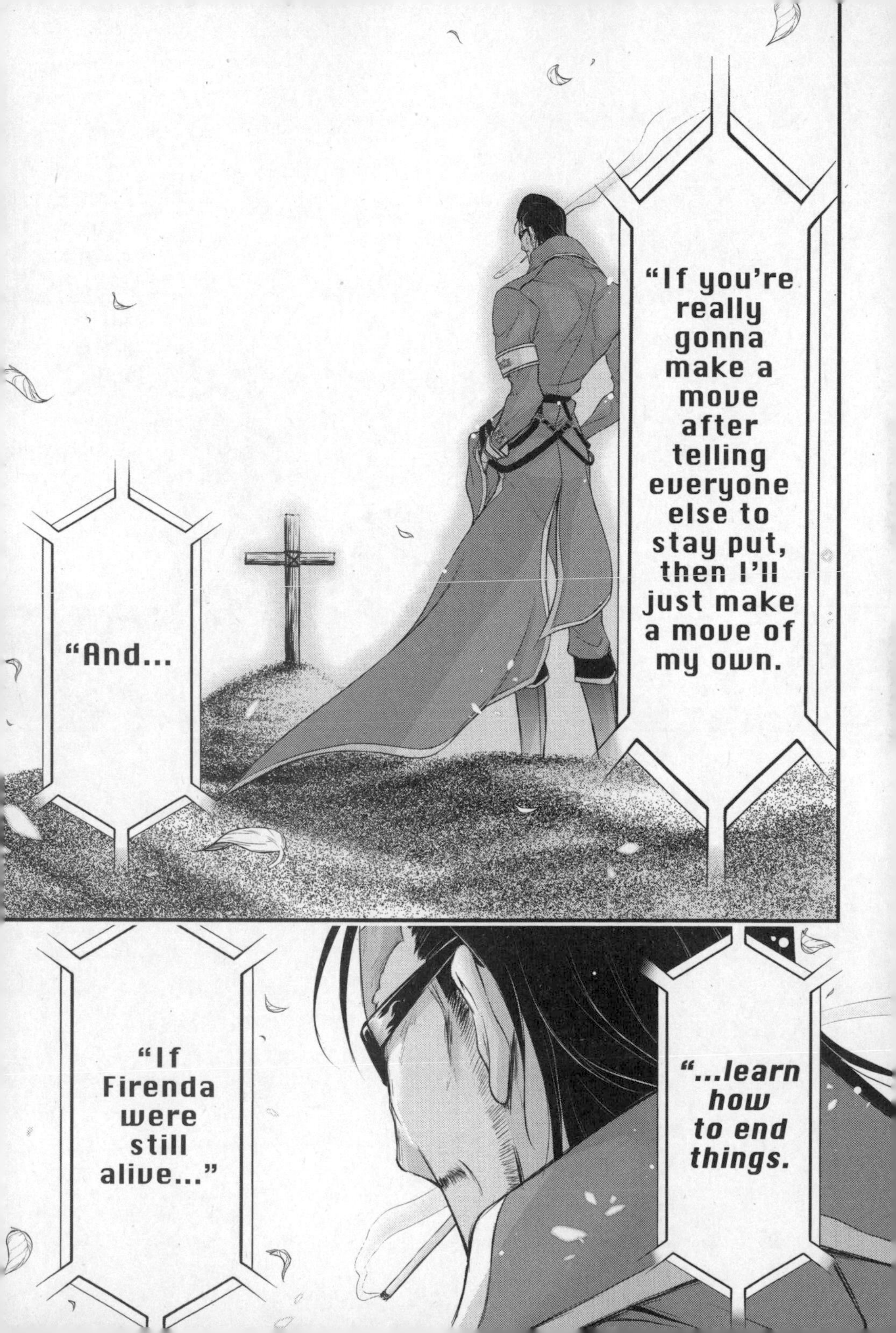
"If you're really gonna make a move after telling everyone else to stay put, then I'll just make a move of my own.
"And...
"...learn how to end things.
"If Firenda were still alive..."

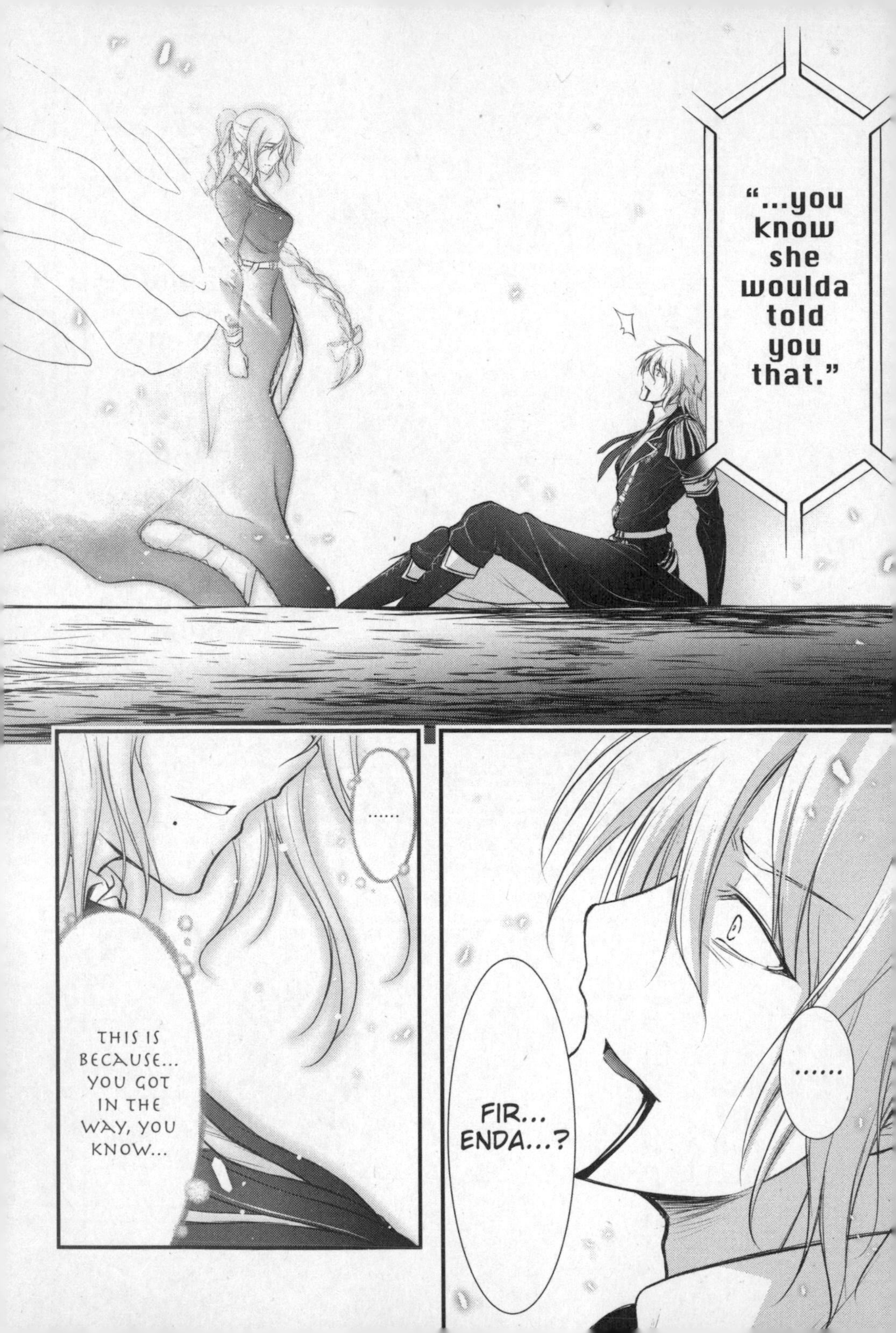
"...you know she woulda told you that."
......
FIR... ENDA...?
......
THIS IS BECAUSE... YOU GOT IN THE WAY, YOU KNOW...

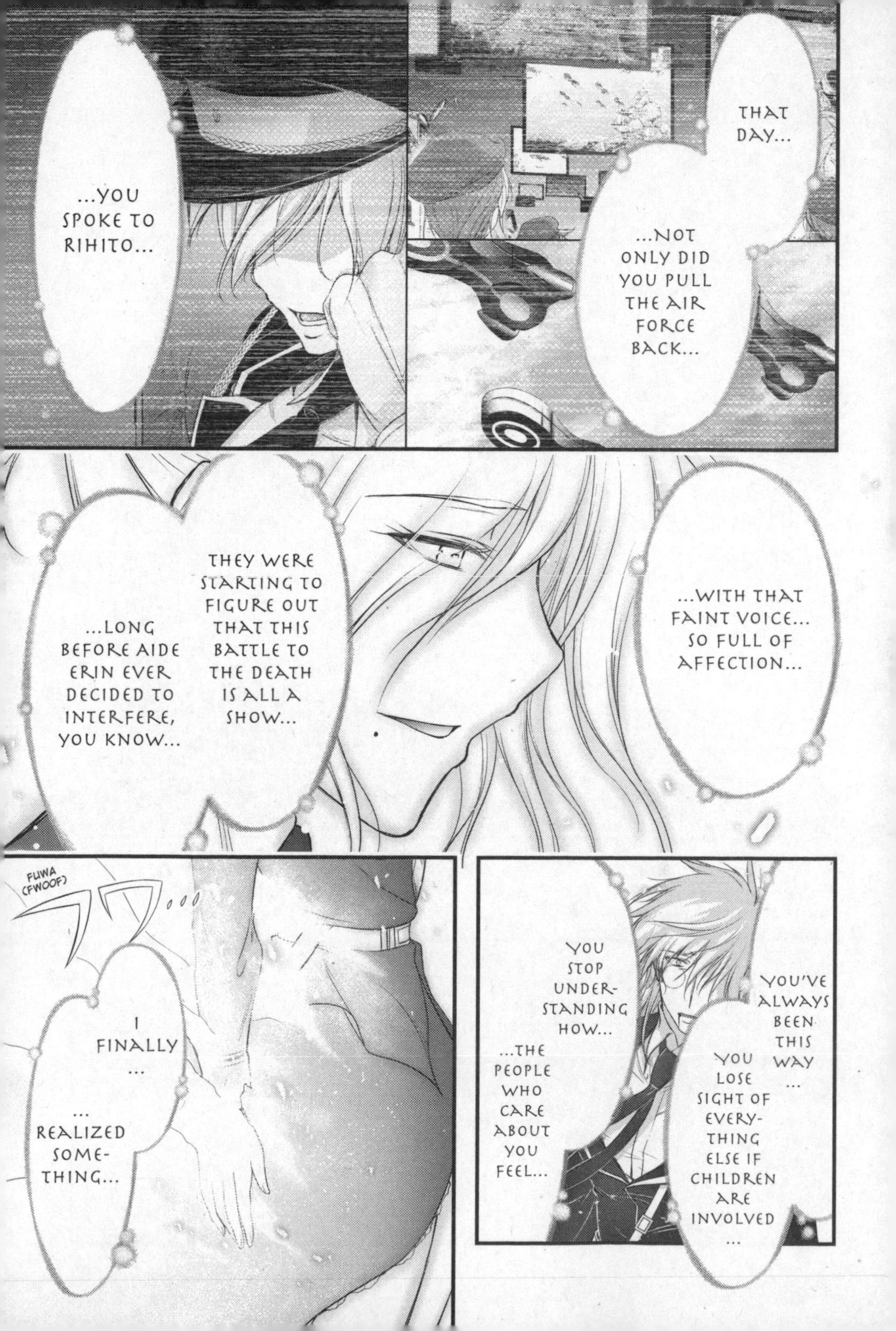
THAT DAY...
...NOT ONLY DID YOU PULL THE AIR FORCE BACK...
...YOU SPOKE TO RIHITO...
...WITH THAT FAINT VOICE... SO FULL OF AFFECTION...
THEY WERE STARTING TO FIGURE OUT THAT THIS BATTLE TO THE DEATH IS ALL A SHOW...
...LONG BEFORE AIDE ERIN EVER DECIDED TO INTERFERE, YOU KNOW...
YOU'VE ALWAYS BEEN THIS WAY...
YOU LOSE SIGHT OF EVERYTHING ELSE IF CHILDREN ARE INVOLVED...
YOU STOP UNDERSTANDING HOW...
...THE PEOPLE WHO CARE ABOUT YOU FEEL...
FUWA (FWOOF)
I FINALLY...
...REALIZED SOMETHING...

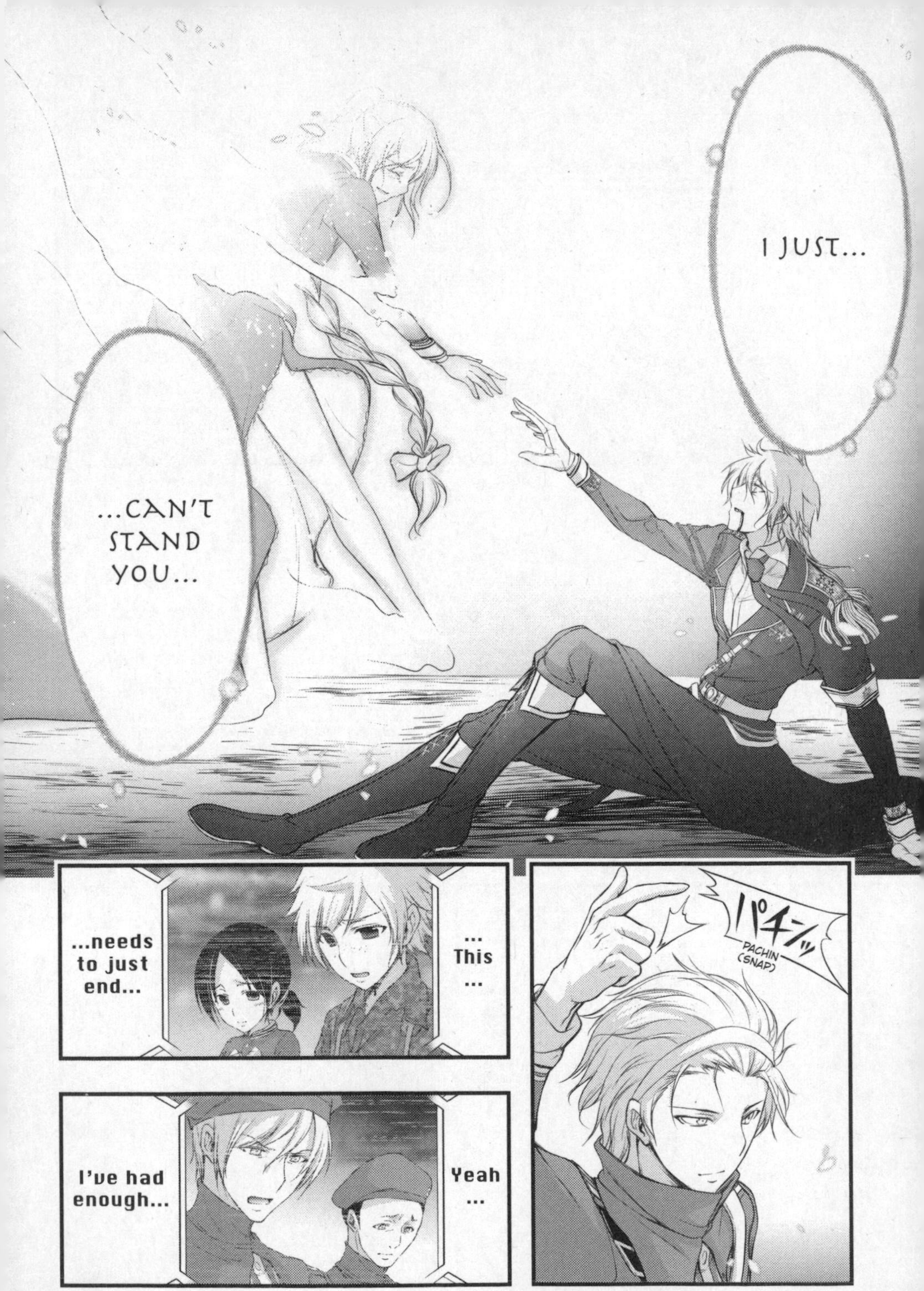
I JUST...
...CAN'T STAND YOU...
パチンッ
PACHIN (SNAP)
... This ...
...needs to just end...
Yeah ...
I've had enough...

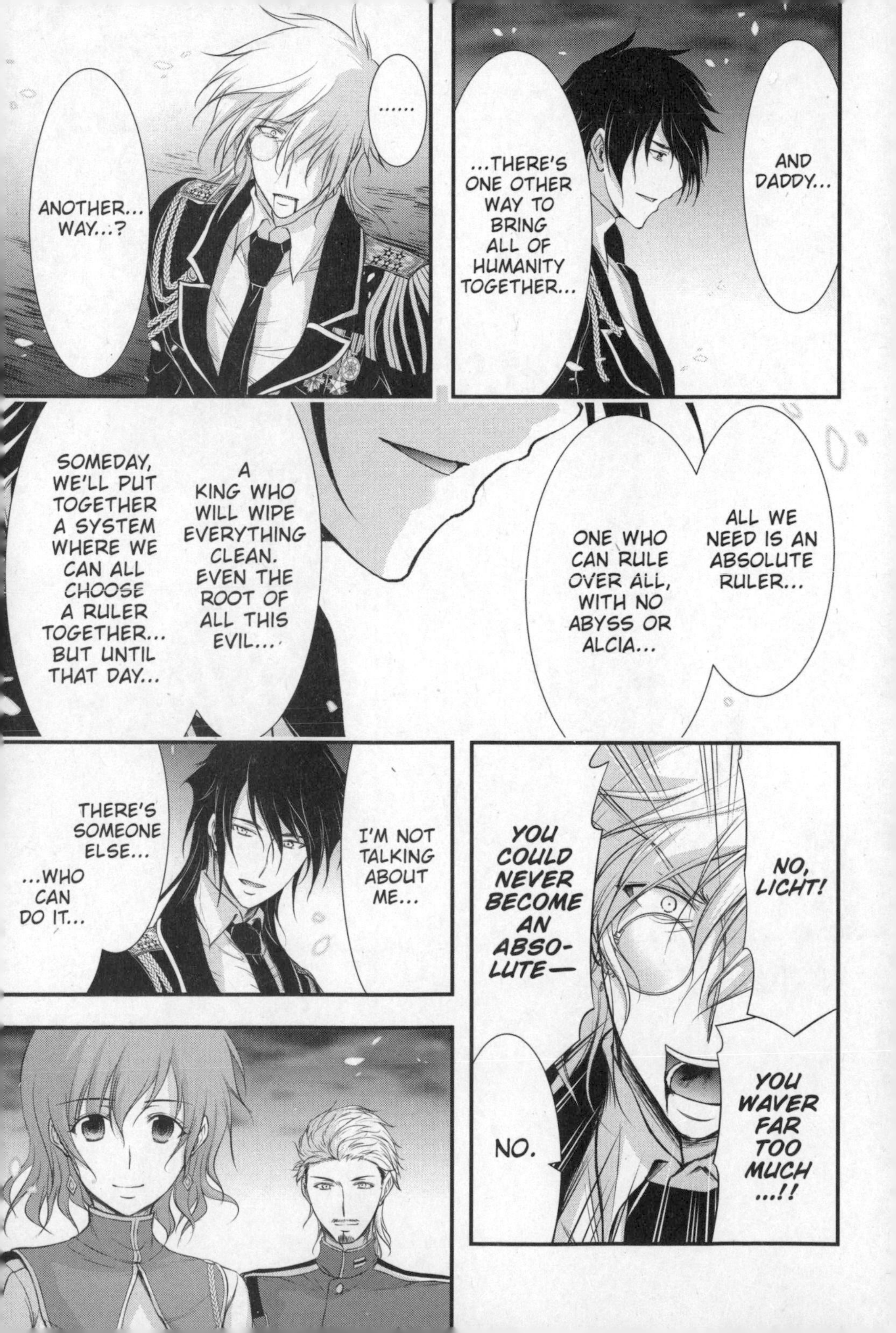
AND DADDY...
...THERE'S ONE OTHER WAY TO BRING ALL OF HUMANITY TOGETHER...
......
ANOTHER... WAY...?
ALL WE NEED IS AN ABSOLUTE RULER...
ONE WHO CAN RULE OVER ALL, WITH NO ABYSS OR ALCIA...
A KING WHO WILL WIPE EVERYTHING CLEAN. EVEN THE ROOT OF ALL THIS EVIL...
SOMEDAY, WE'LL PUT TOGETHER A SYSTEM WHERE WE CAN ALL CHOOSE A RULER TOGETHER... BUT UNTIL THAT DAY...
NO, LICHT!
YOU COULD NEVER BECOME AN ABSO-LUTE—
YOU WAVER FAR TOO MUCH...!!
NO.
I'M NOT TALKING ABOUT ME...
THERE'S SOMEONE ELSE...
...WHO CAN DO IT...

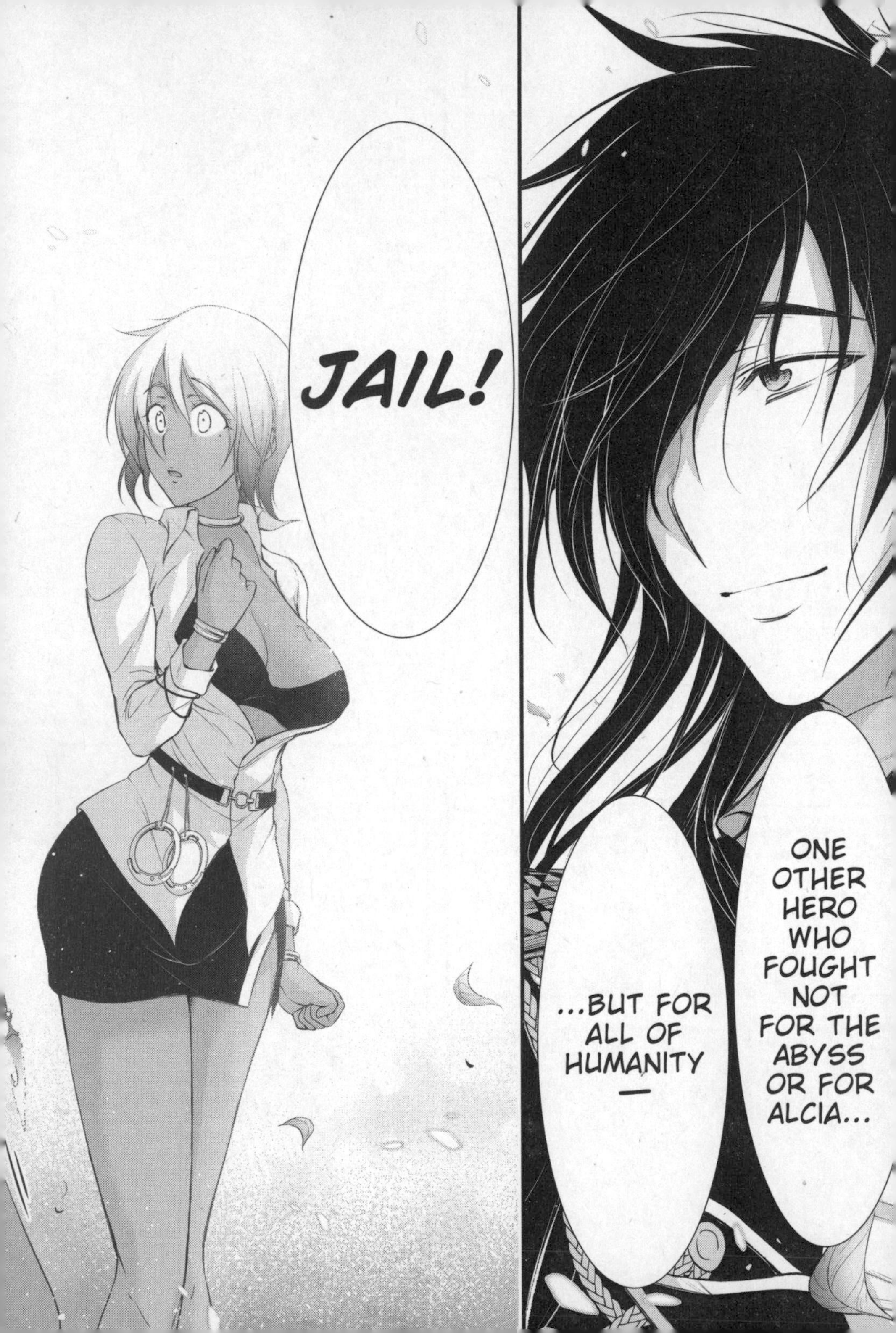
ONE OTHER HERO WHO FOUGHT NOT FOR THE ABYSS OR FOR ALCIA...
...BUT FOR ALL OF HUMANITY —
JAIL!

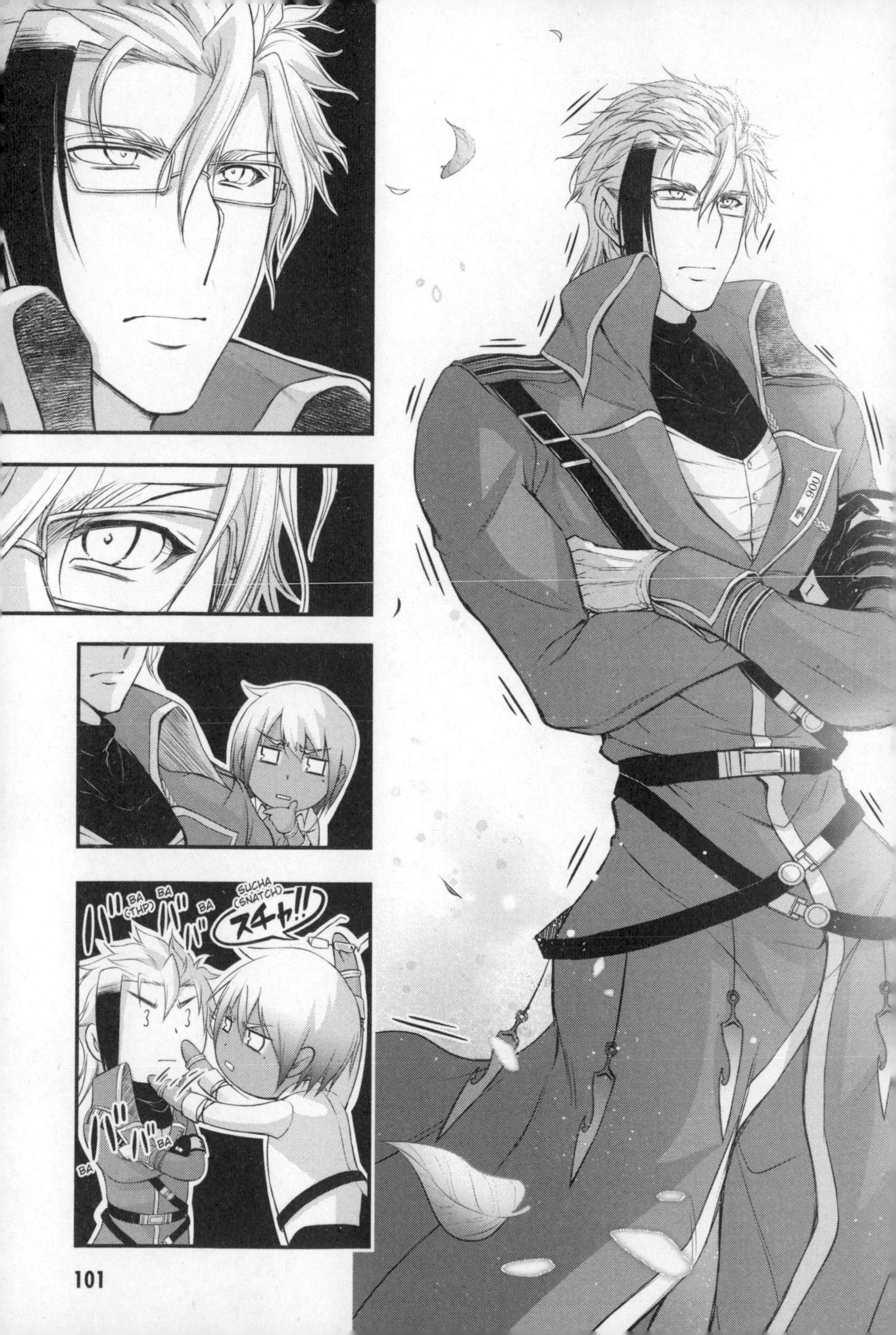
スチャ!!
SUCHA (SNATCH)
BA
BA
BA (THP)
BA
BA

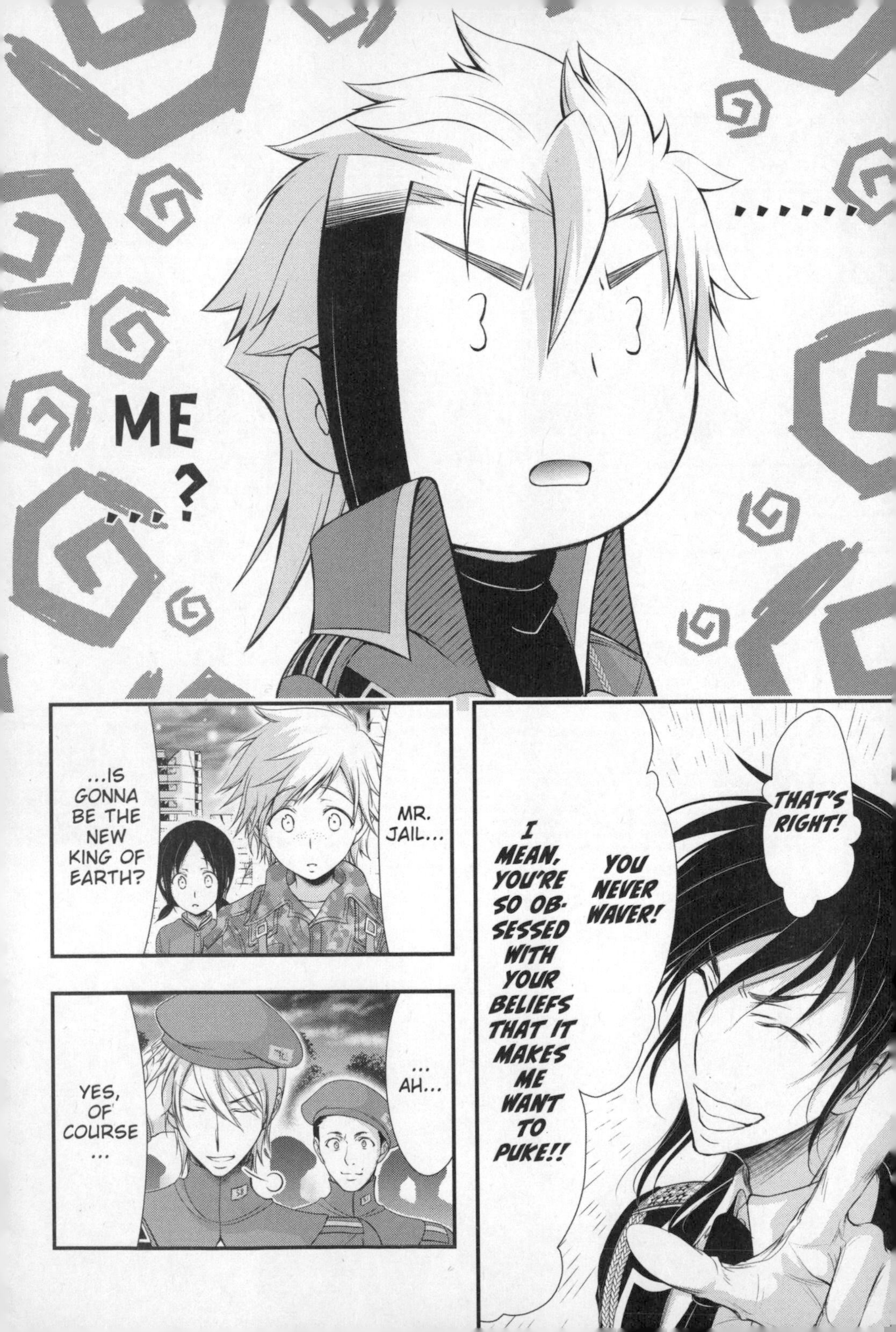
......
ME ...?
THAT'S RIGHT!
YOU NEVER WAVER!
I MEAN, YOU'RE SO OB-SESSED WITH YOUR BELIEFS THAT IT MAKES ME WANT TO PUKE!!
MR. JAIL...
...IS GONNA BE THE NEW KING OF EARTH?
... AH...
YES, OF COURSE ...

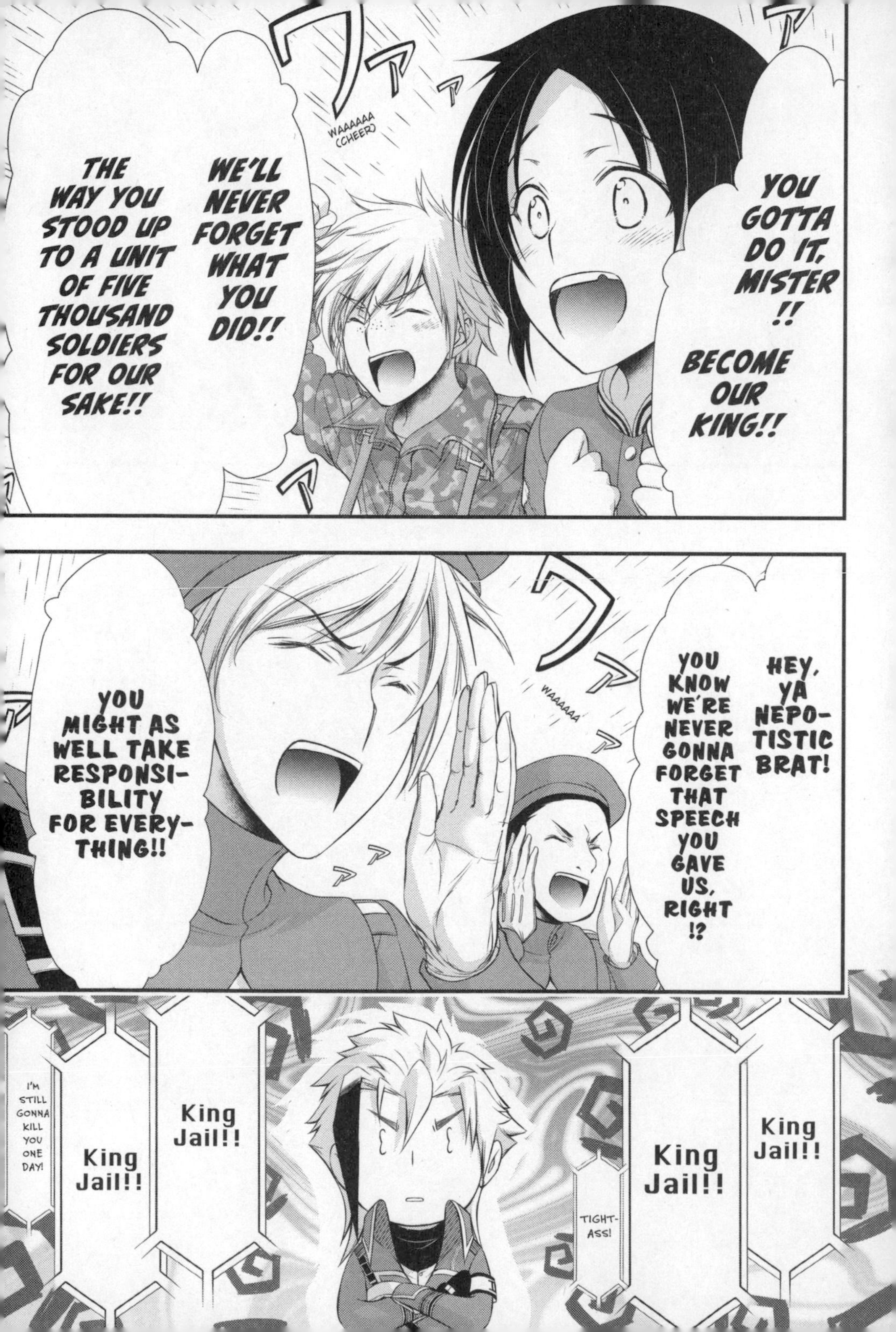
YOU GOTTA DO IT, MISTER!!
BECOME OUR KING!!
WAAAAAA (CHEER)
WE'LL NEVER FORGET WHAT YOU DID!!
THE WAY YOU STOOD UP TO A UNIT OF FIVE THOUSAND SOLDIERS FOR OUR SAKE!!
HEY, YA NEPOTISTIC BRAT!
YOU KNOW WE'RE NEVER GONNA FORGET THAT SPEECH YOU GAVE US, RIGHT!?
WAAAAAA
YOU MIGHT AS WELL TAKE RESPONSIBILITY FOR EVERYTHING!!
King Jail!!
King Jail!!
TIGHT-ASS!
King Jail!!
King Jail!!
I'M STILL GONNA KILL YOU ONE DAY!

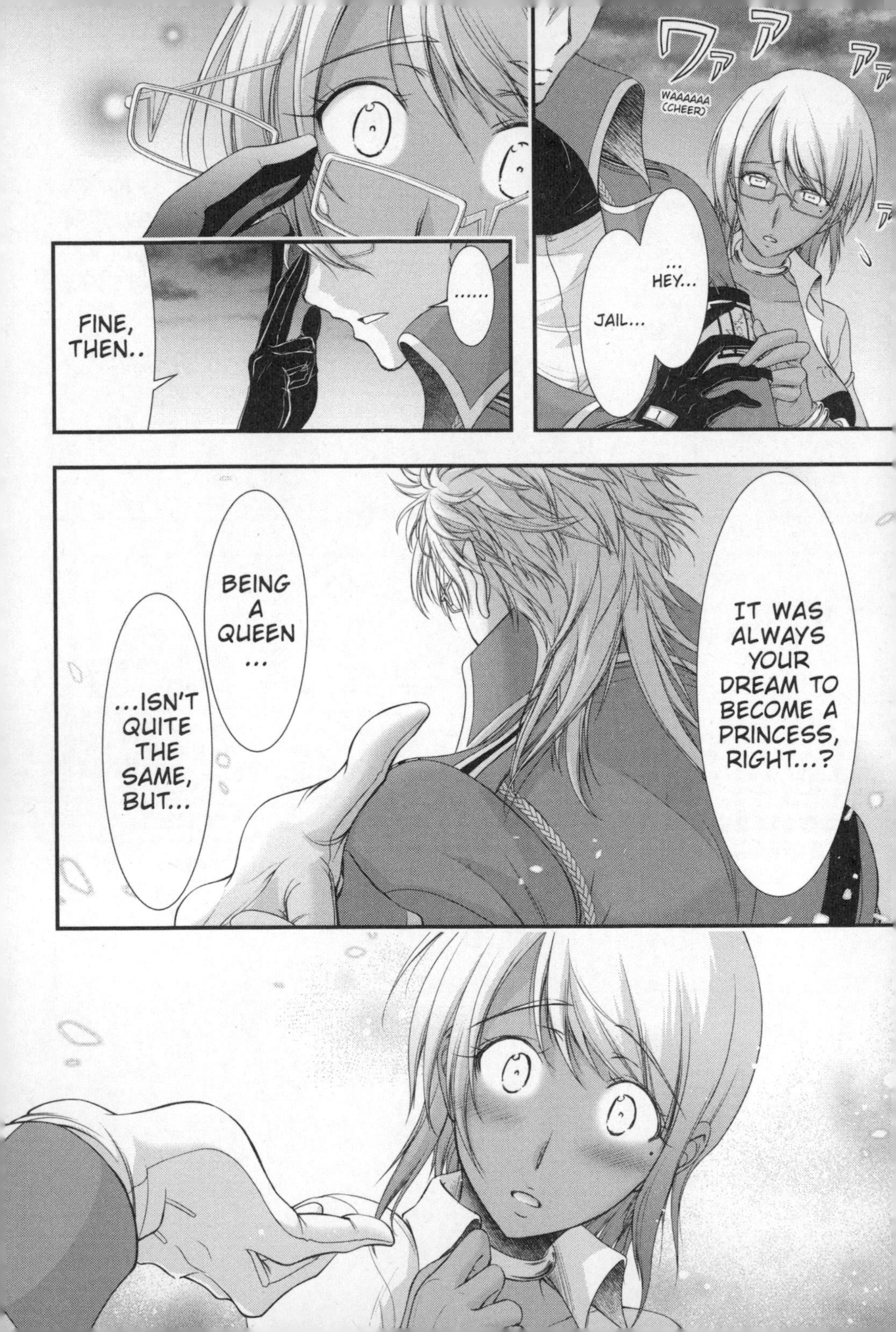
ワァアア
WAAAAAA (CHEER)
... HEY... JAIL...
......
FINE, THEN..
IT WAS ALWAYS YOUR DREAM TO BECOME A PRINCESS, RIGHT...?
BEING A QUEEN ...
...ISN'T QUITE THE SAME, BUT...

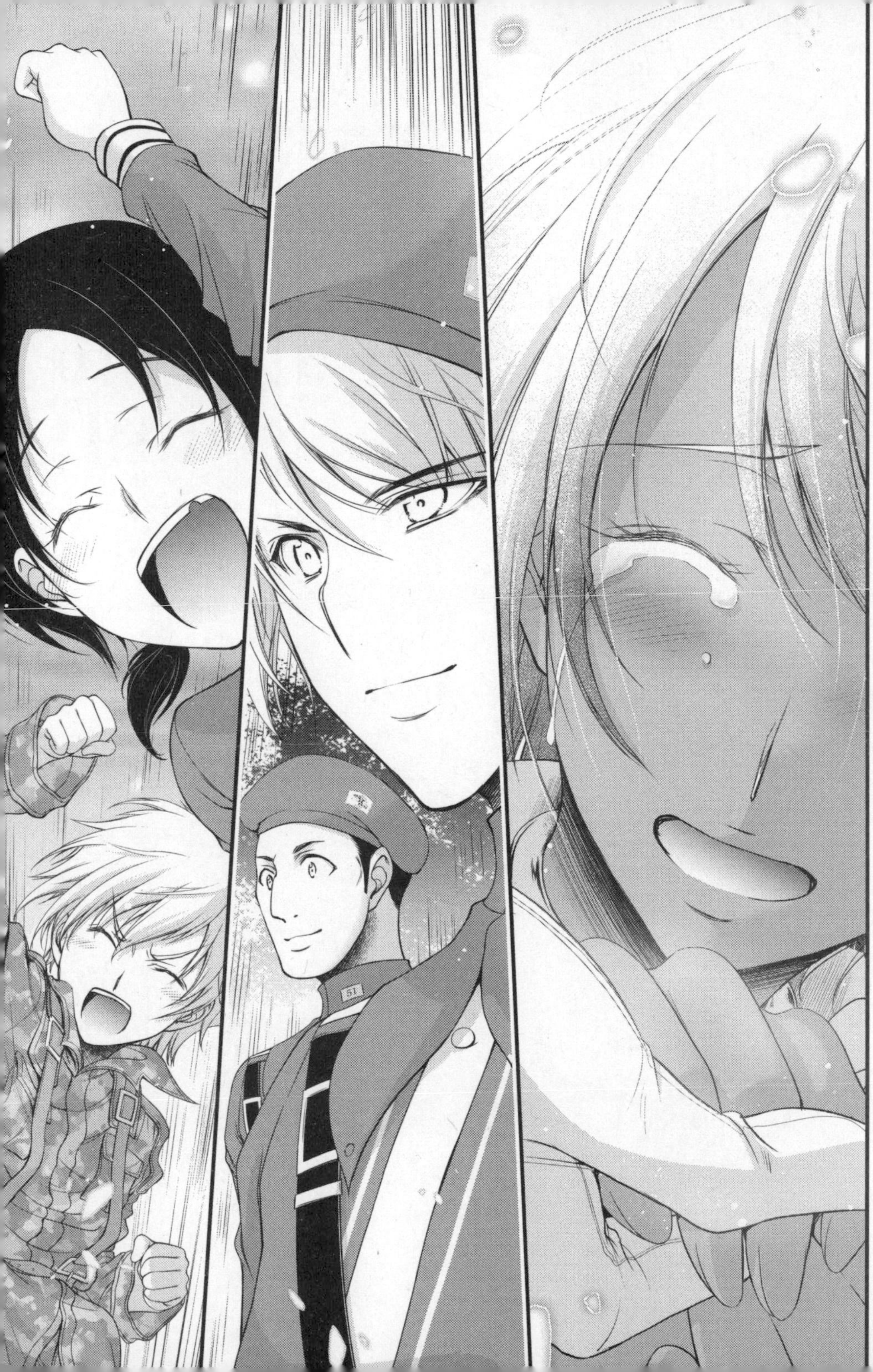

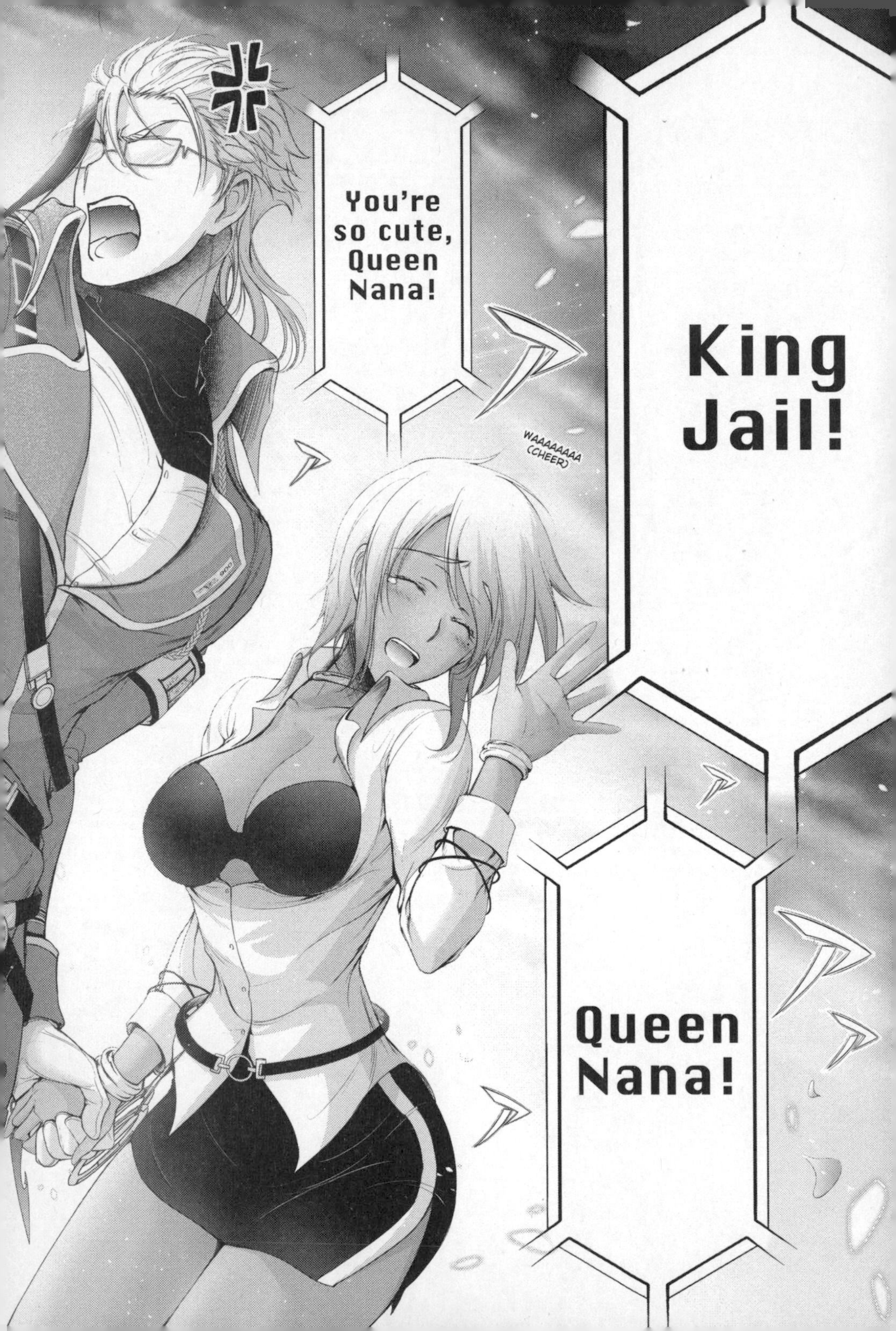
King Jail!
You're so cute, Queen Nana!
WAAAAAAAA (CHEER)
Queen Nana!

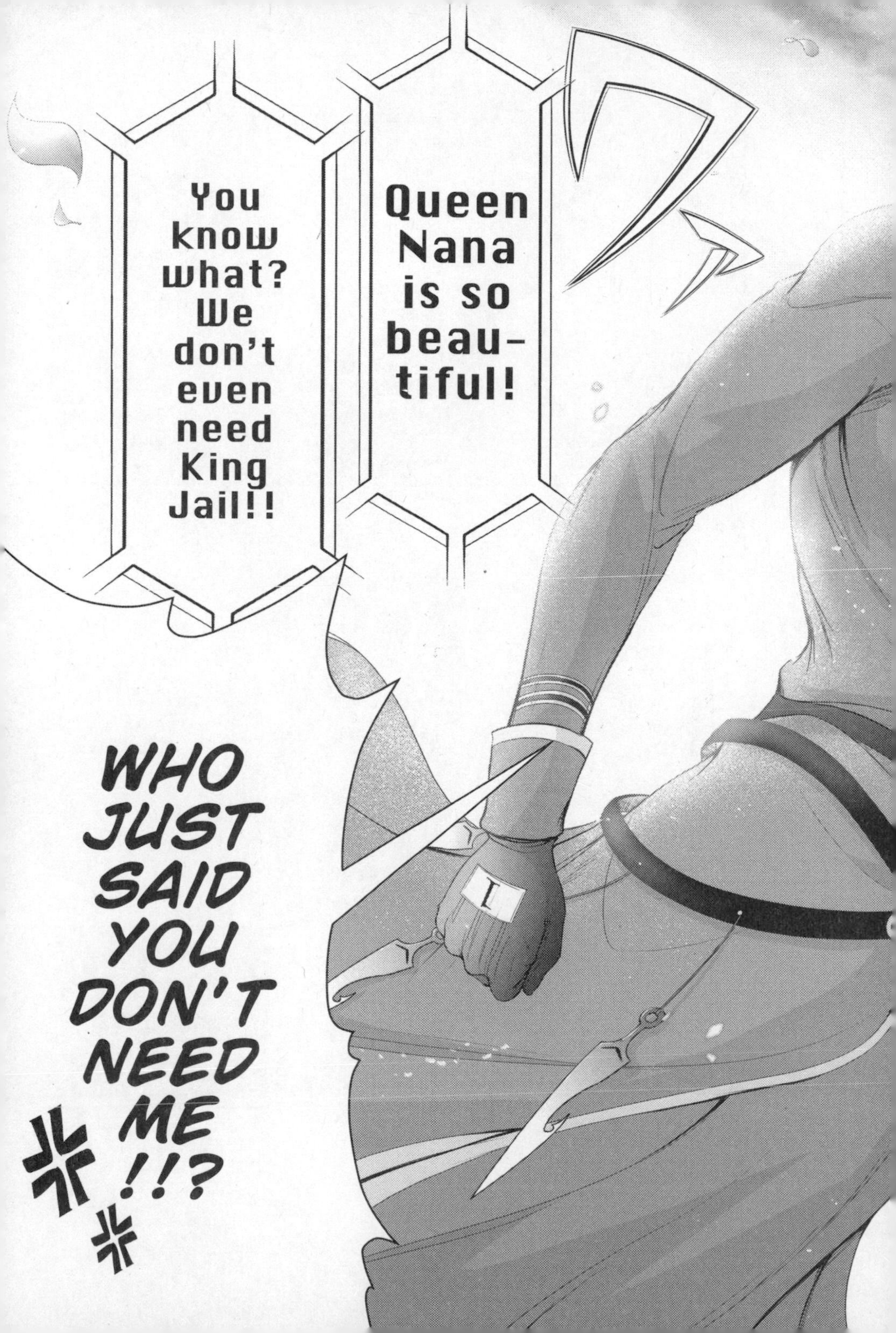
Queen Nana is so beau-tiful!
You know what? We don't even need King Jail!!
WHO JUST SAID YOU DON'T NEED ME!!?

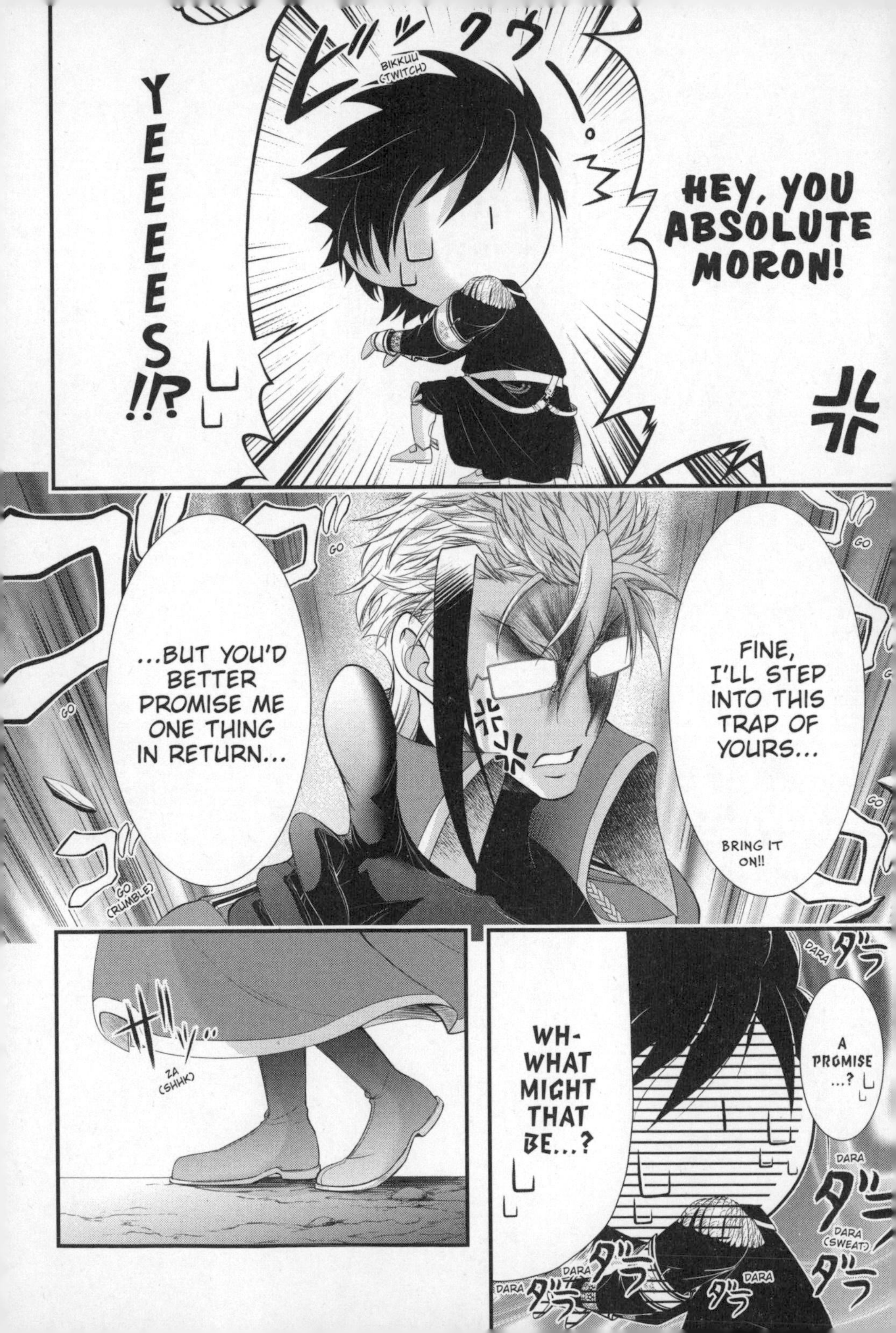
HEY, YOU ABSOLUTE MORON!
BIKKUU (TWITCH)
YEEEEES!?
FINE, I'LL STEP INTO THIS TRAP OF YOURS...
BRING IT ON!!
GO
GO
GO
...BUT YOU'D BETTER PROMISE ME ONE THING IN RETURN...
GO
GO (RUMBLE)
DARA
A PROMISE...?
DARA
DARA (SWEAT)
DARA
DARA
DARA
WH-WHAT MIGHT THAT BE...?
ZA (SHHK)

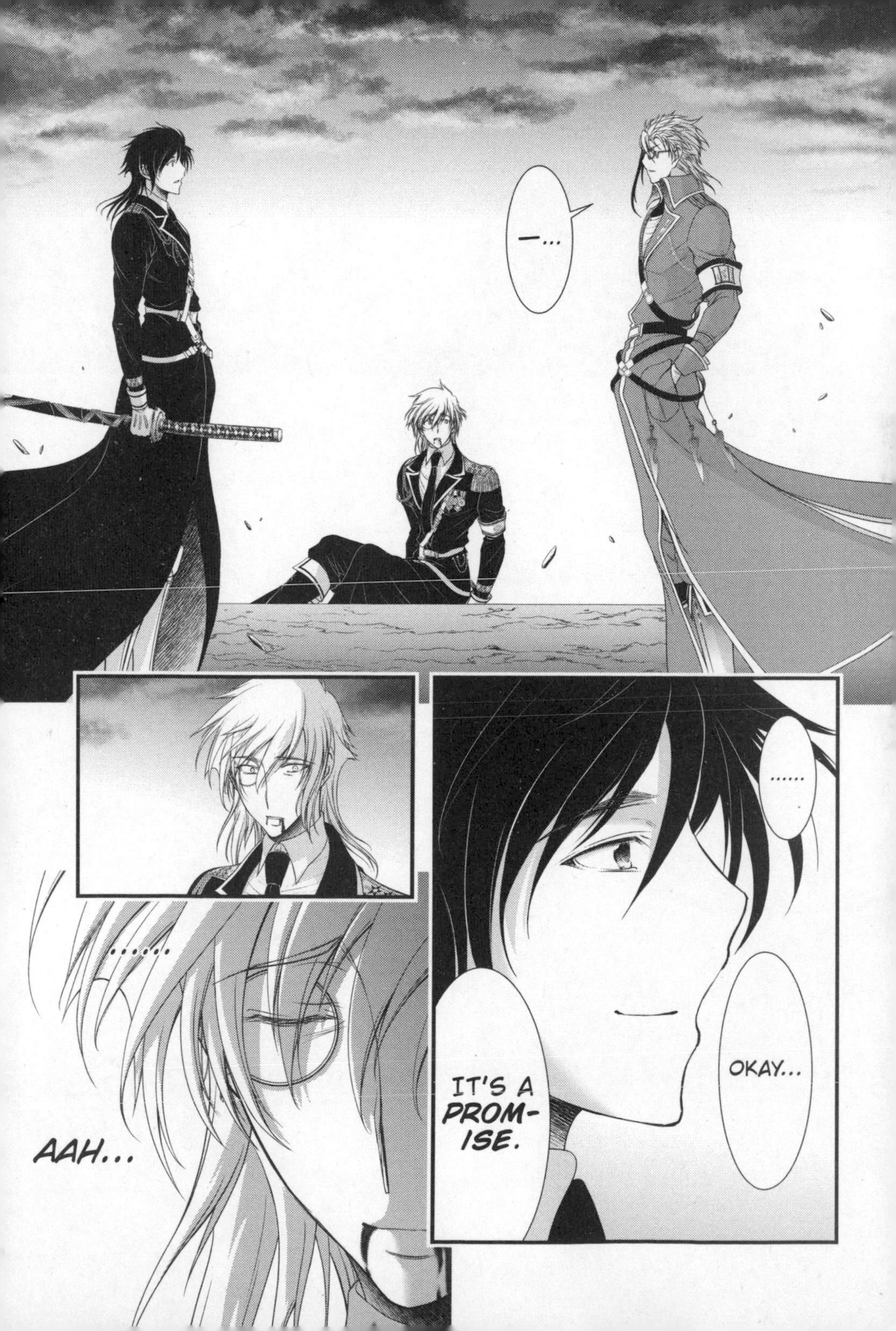
—...
......
OKAY...
IT'S A PROM-
ISE.
......
AAH...

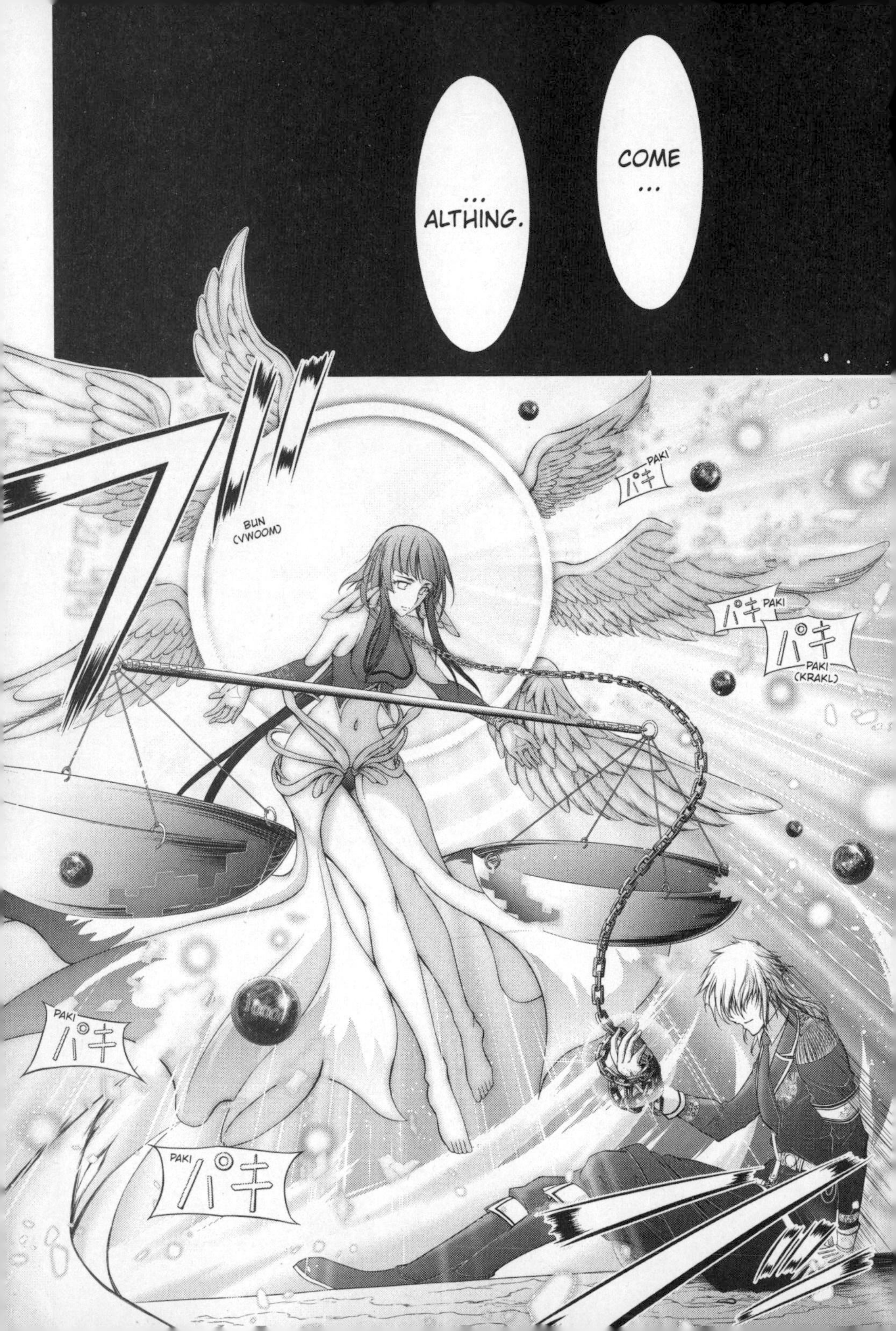
COME ...
... ALTHING.
PAKI パキ
BUN (VWOOM)
パキ PAKI
パキ PAKI (KRAKL)
PAKI パキ
PAKI パキ

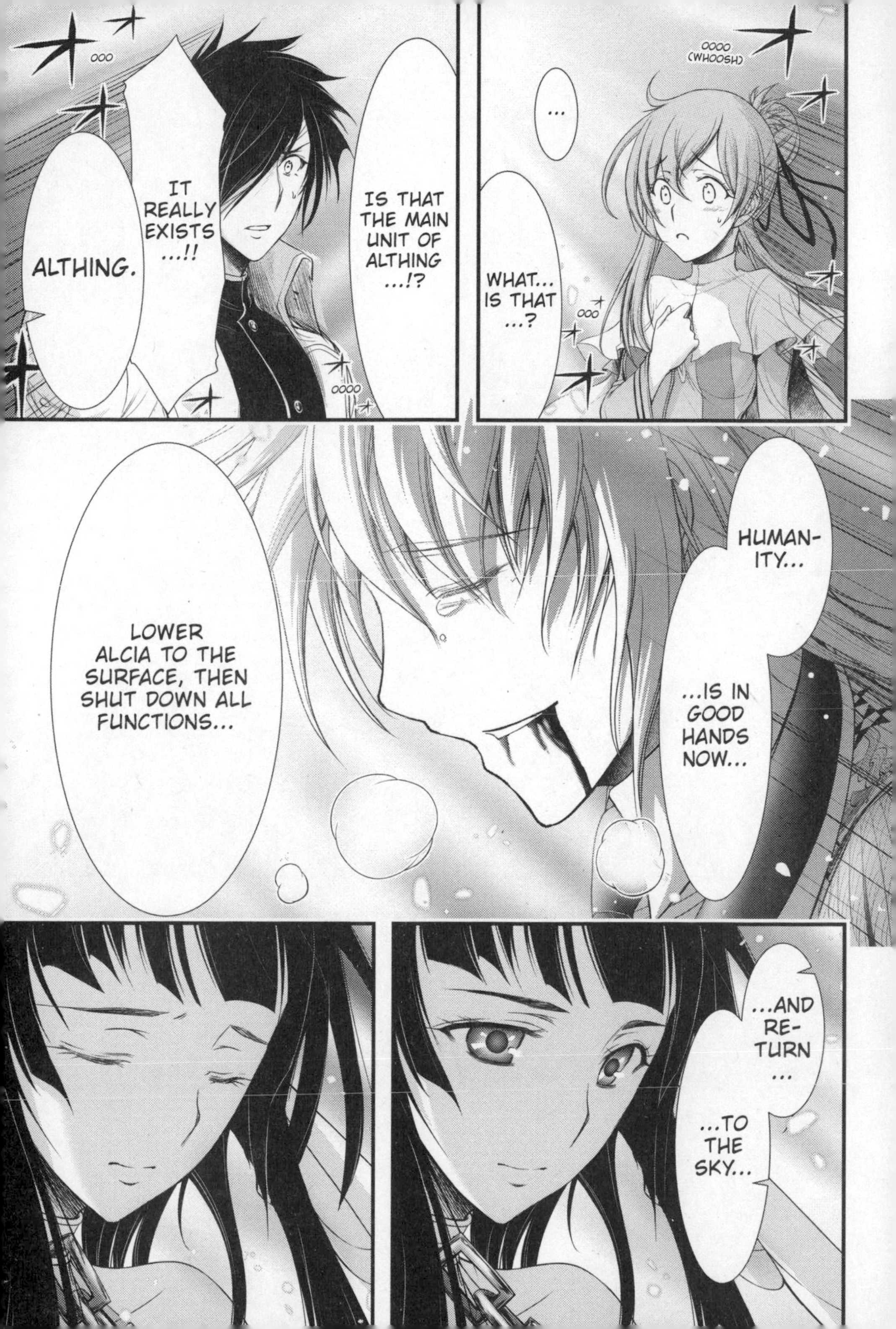
OOOO (WHOOSH)
...
WHAT... IS THAT ...?
OOO
IS THAT THE MAIN UNIT OF ALTHING ...!?
IT REALLY EXISTS ...!!
ALTHING.
OOO
OOOO
HUMAN-ITY...
...IS IN GOOD HANDS NOW...
LOWER ALCIA TO THE SURFACE, THEN SHUT DOWN ALL FUNCTIONS...
...AND RE-TURN ...
...TO THE SKY...

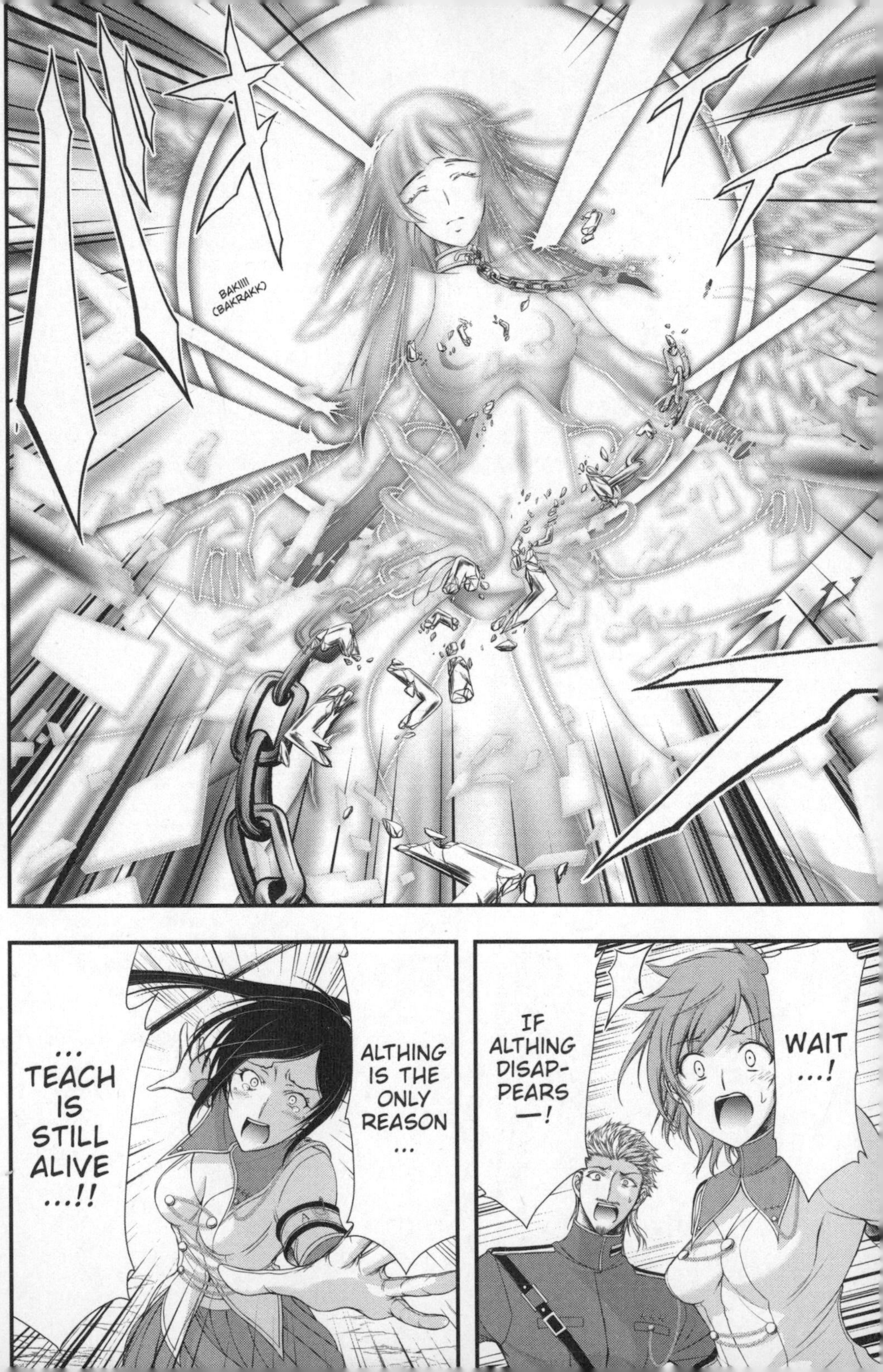
BAKIIII (BAKRAKK)
WAIT ...!
IF ALTHING DISAP-PEARS —!
ALTHING IS THE ONLY REASON ...
... TEACH IS STILL ALIVE ...!!

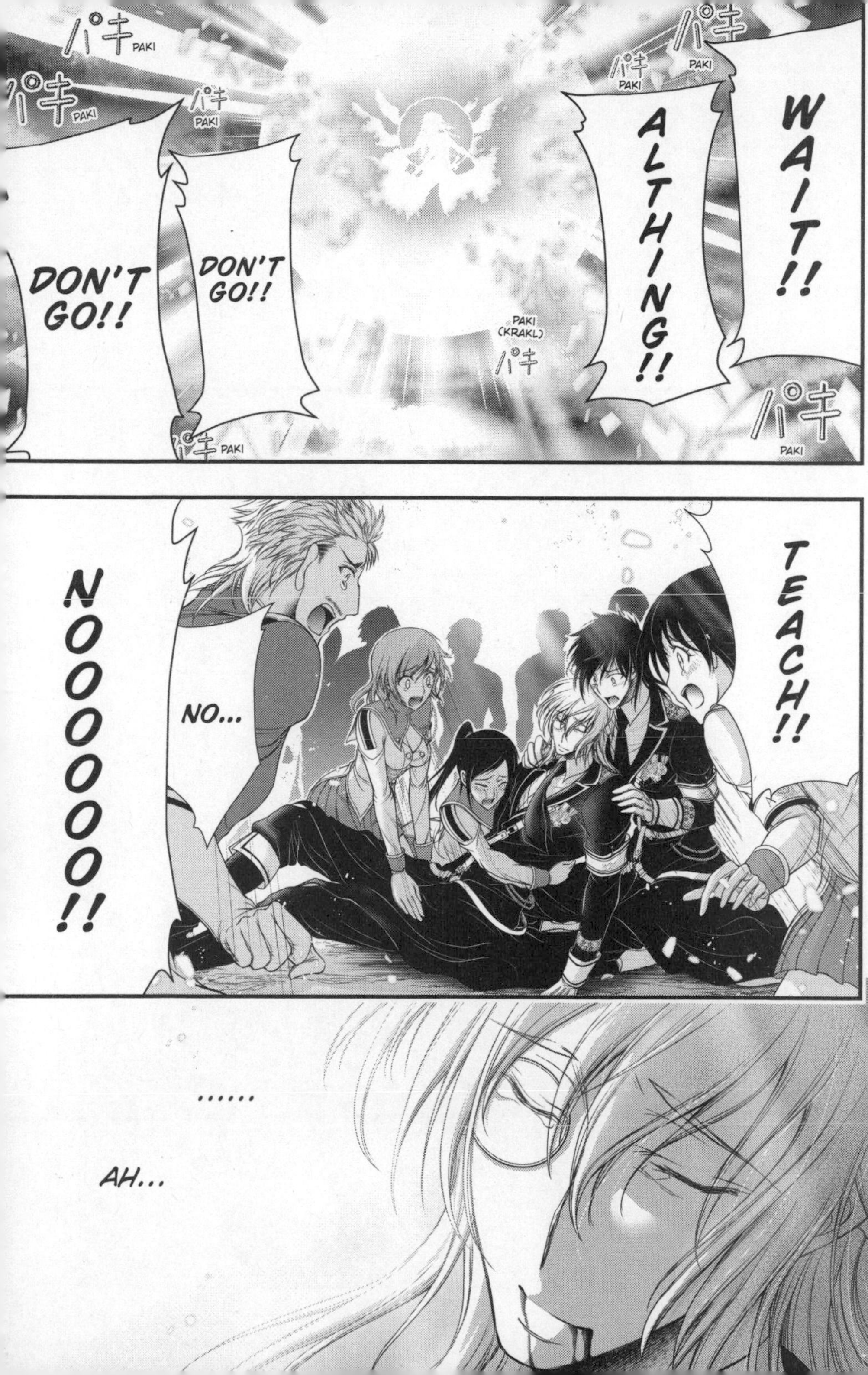
パキ PAKI
パキ PAKI
WAIT!!
ALTHING!!
パキ PAKI
PAKI (KRAKL) パキ
パキ PAKI
DON'T GO!!
DON'T GO!!
パキ PAKI
パキ PAKI
パキ PAKI
TEACH!!
NO...
NOOOOOOOO!!
......
AH...

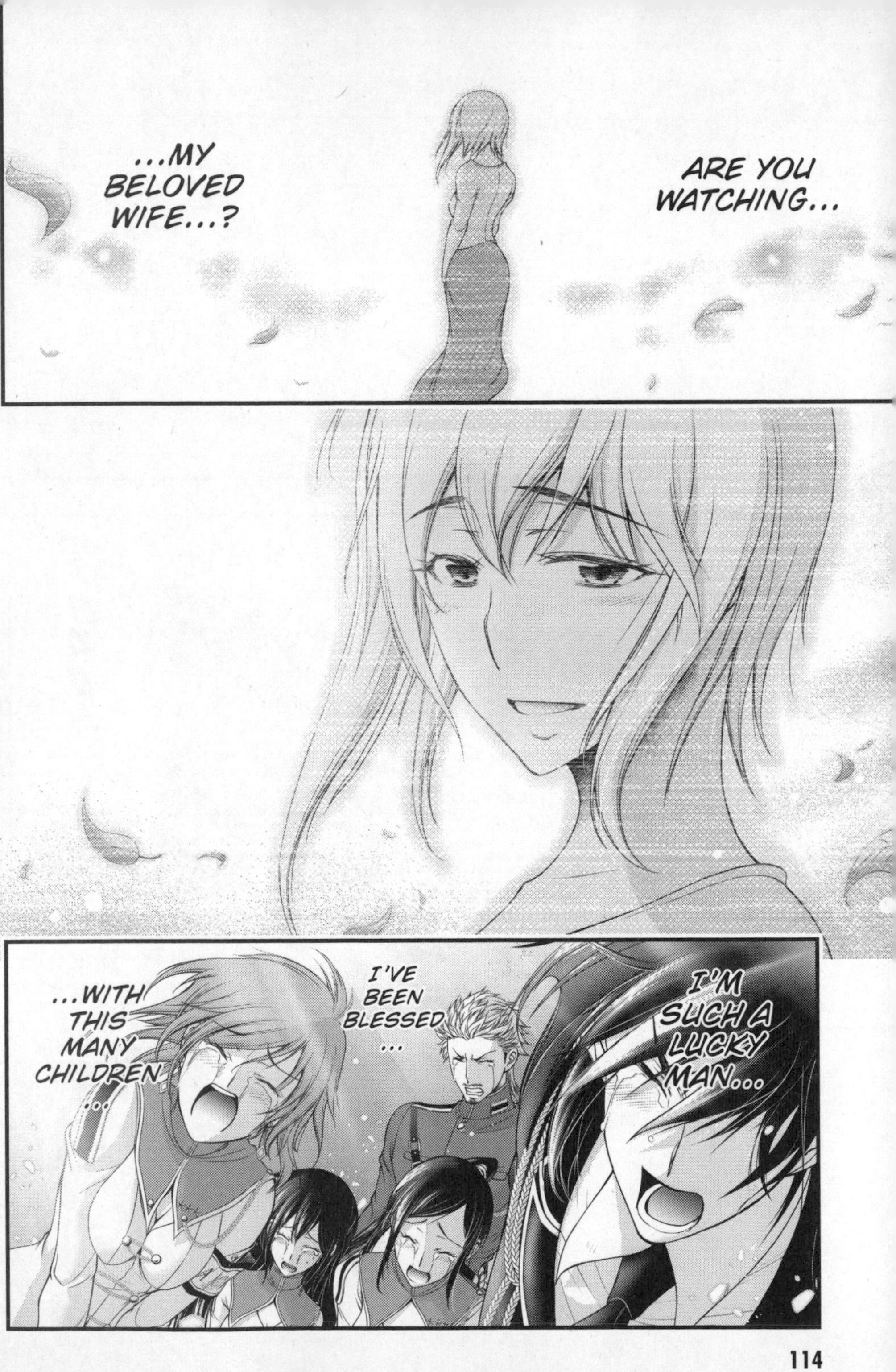
ARE YOU WATCHING...
...MY BELOVED WIFE...?
I'M SUCH A LUCKY MAN...
I'VE BEEN BLESSED...
...WITH THIS MANY CHILDREN...

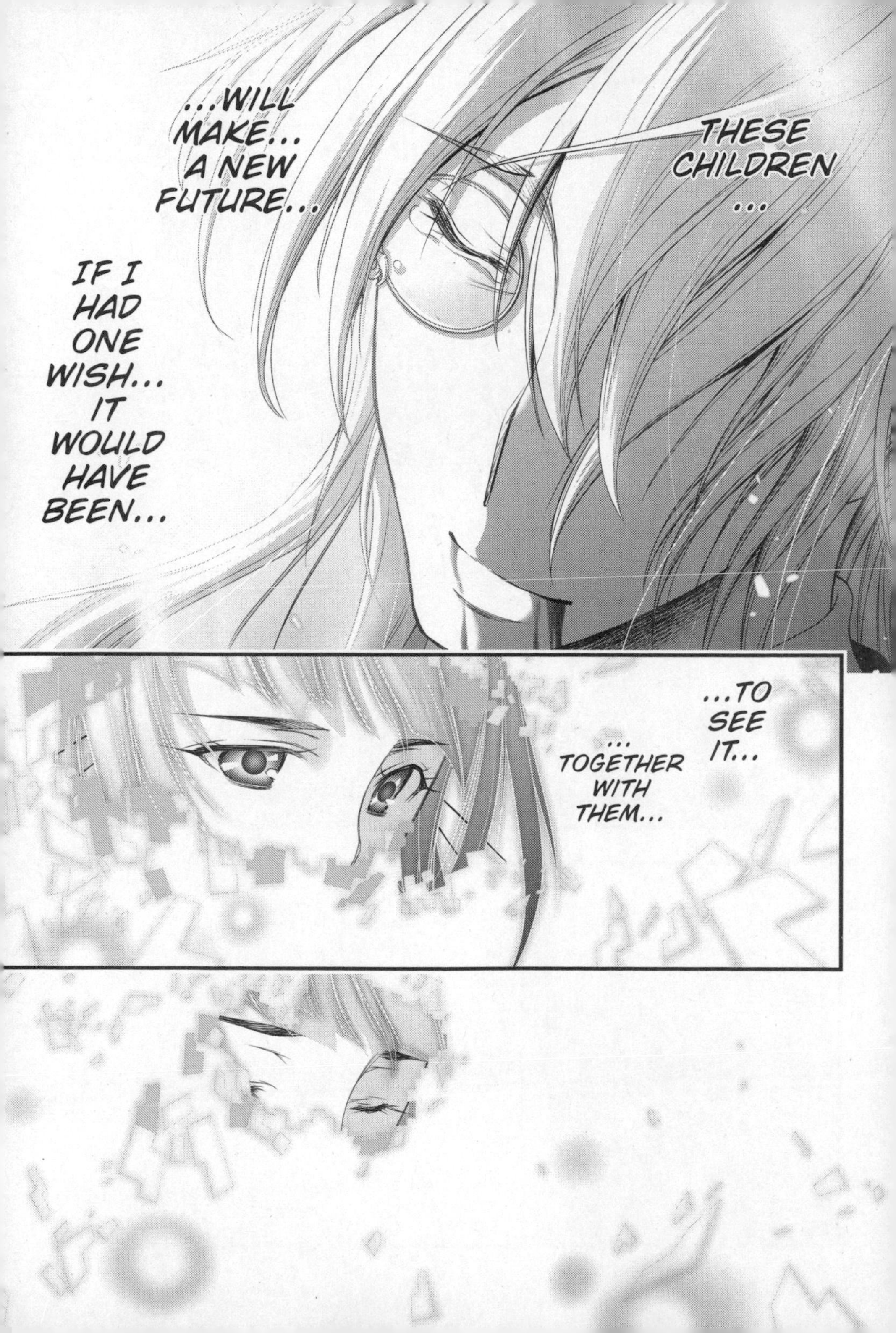
THESE CHILDREN ...
...WILL MAKE... A NEW FUTURE...
IF I HAD ONE WISH... IT WOULD HAVE BEEN...
...TO SEE IT...
... TOGETHER WITH THEM...

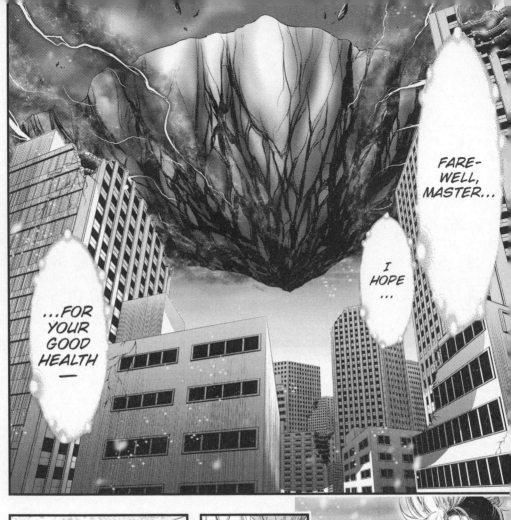

FARE-
WELL,
MASTER...

I
HOPE
...

...FOR
YOUR
GOOD
HEALTH
—

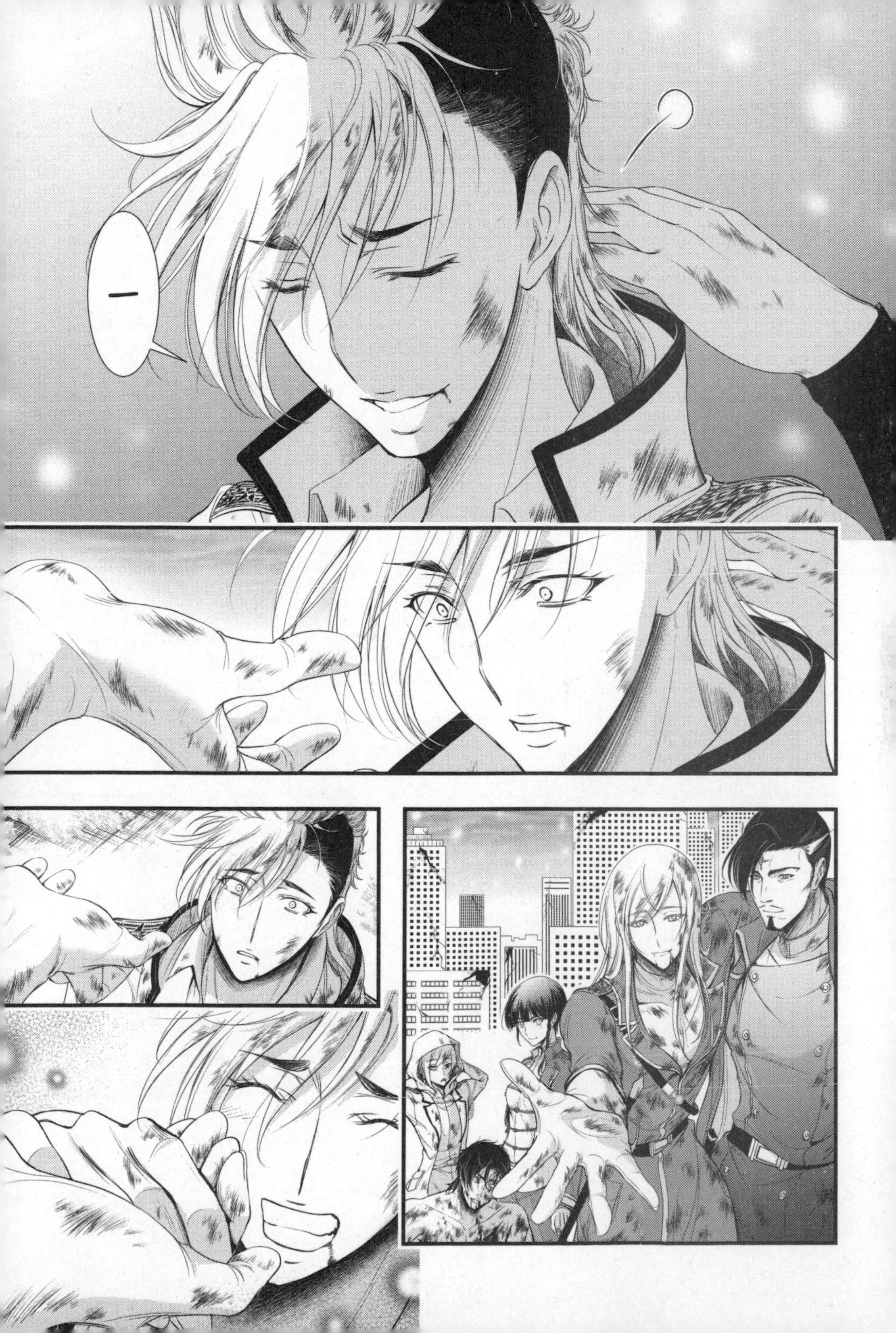
—

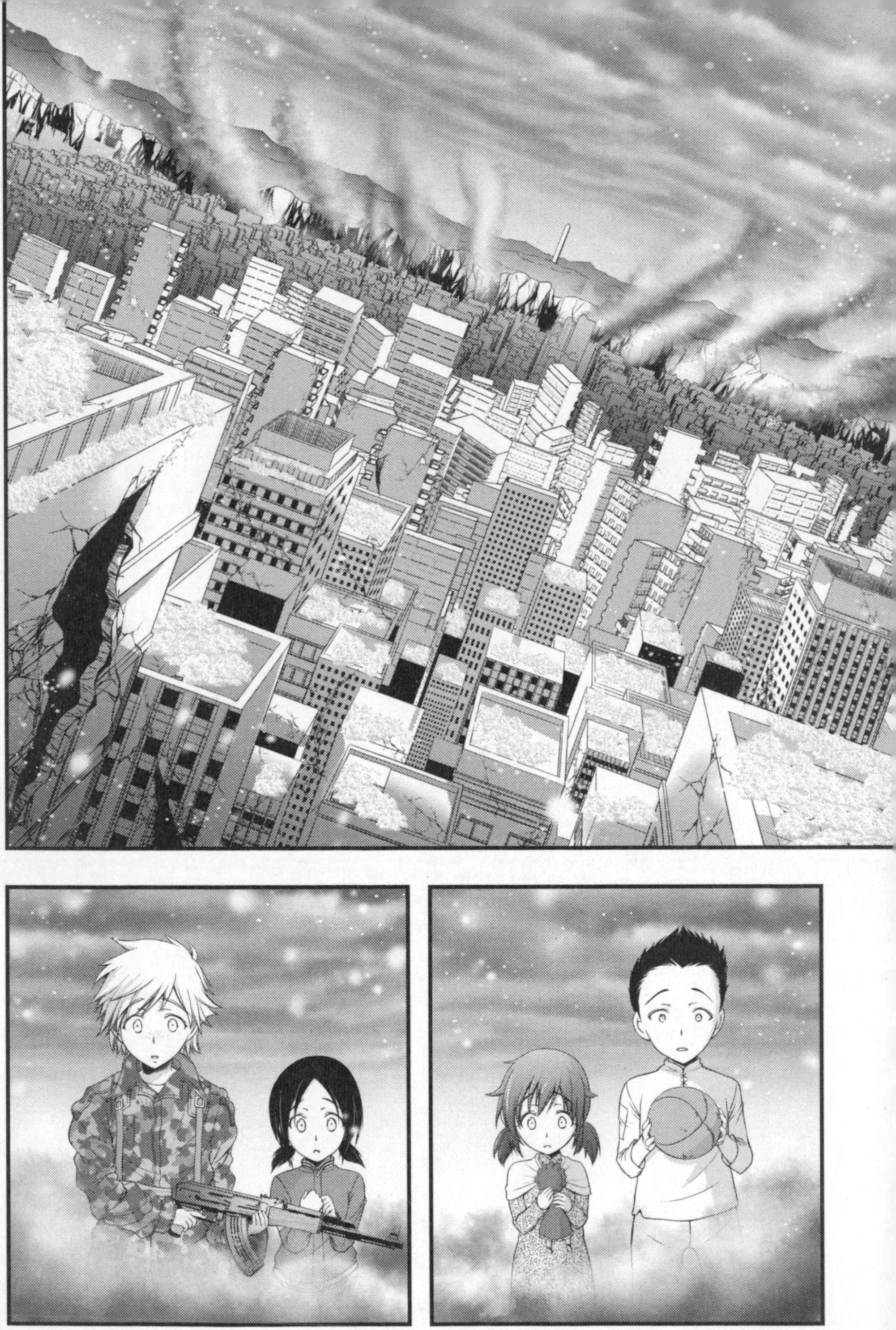

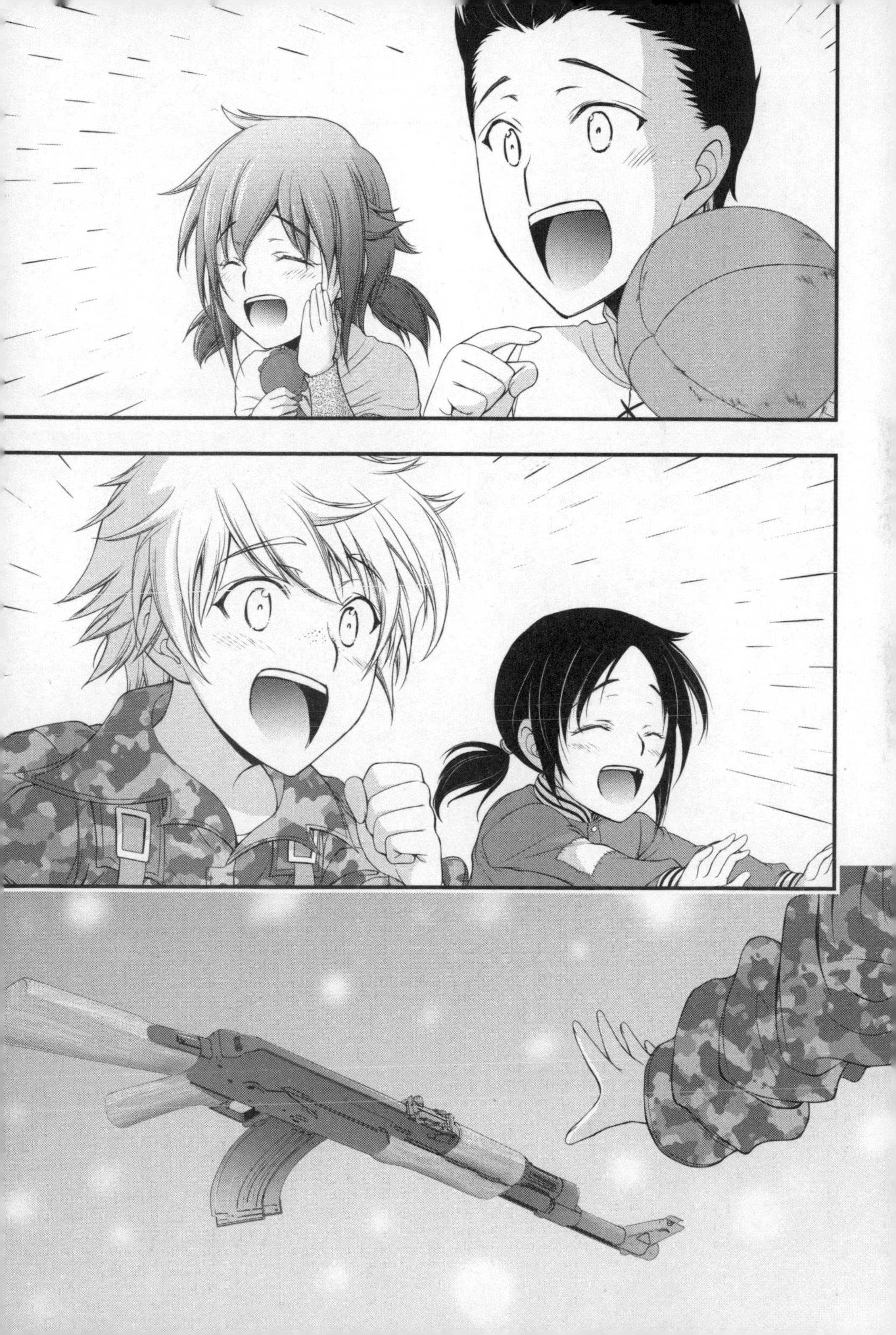

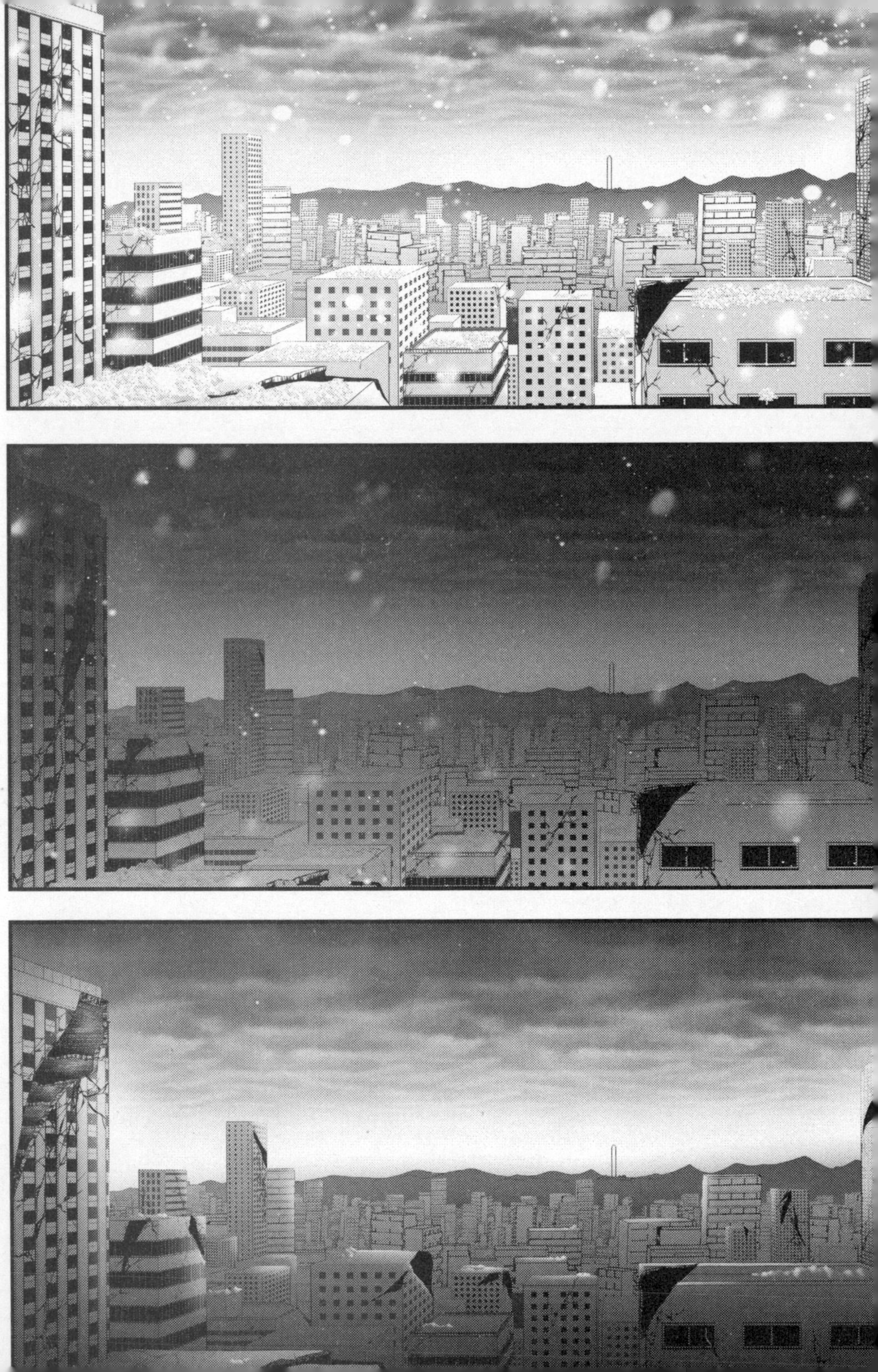

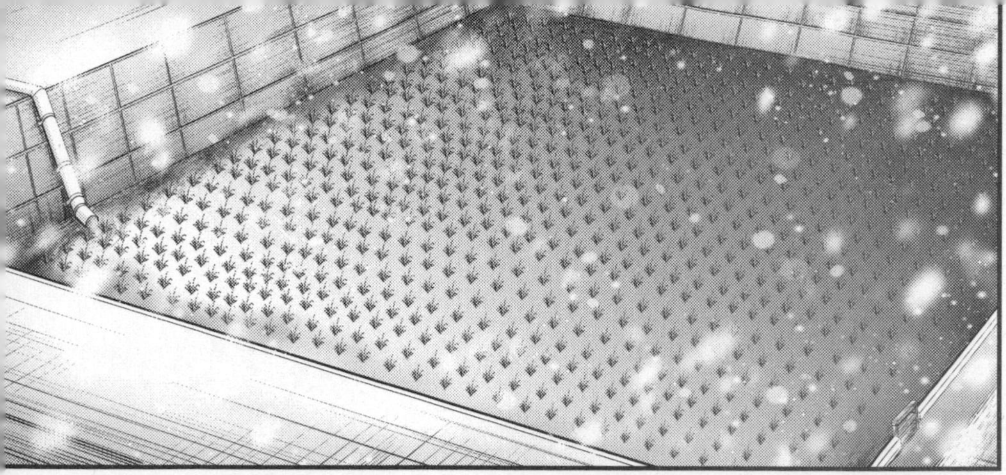
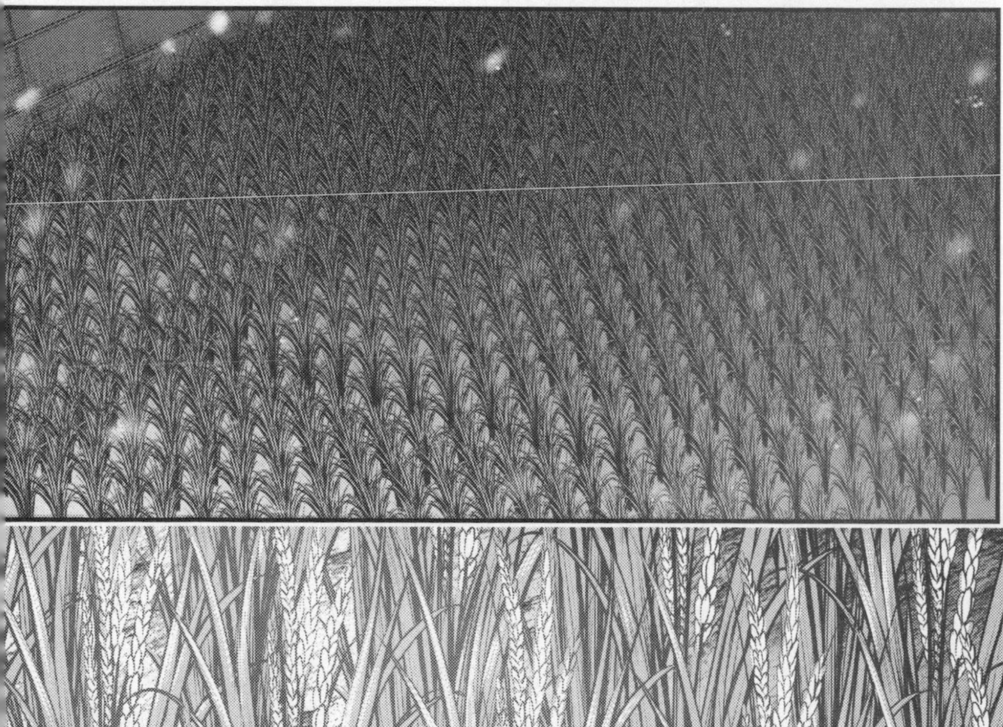
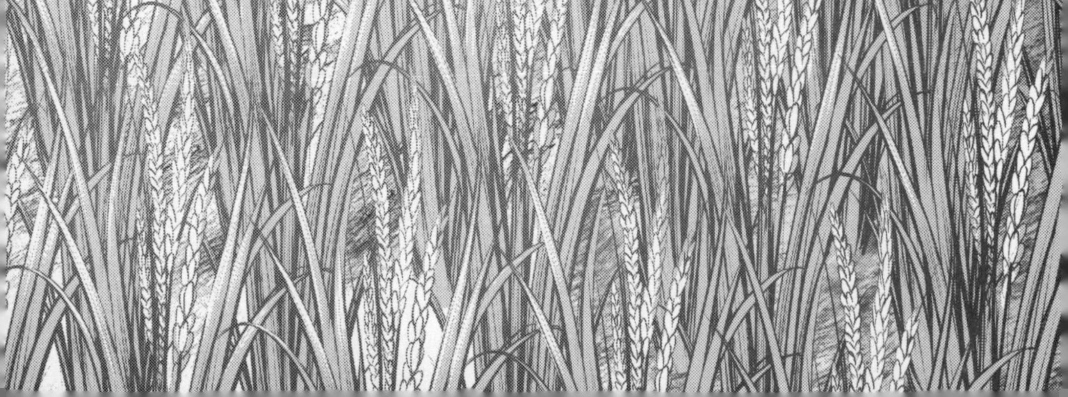

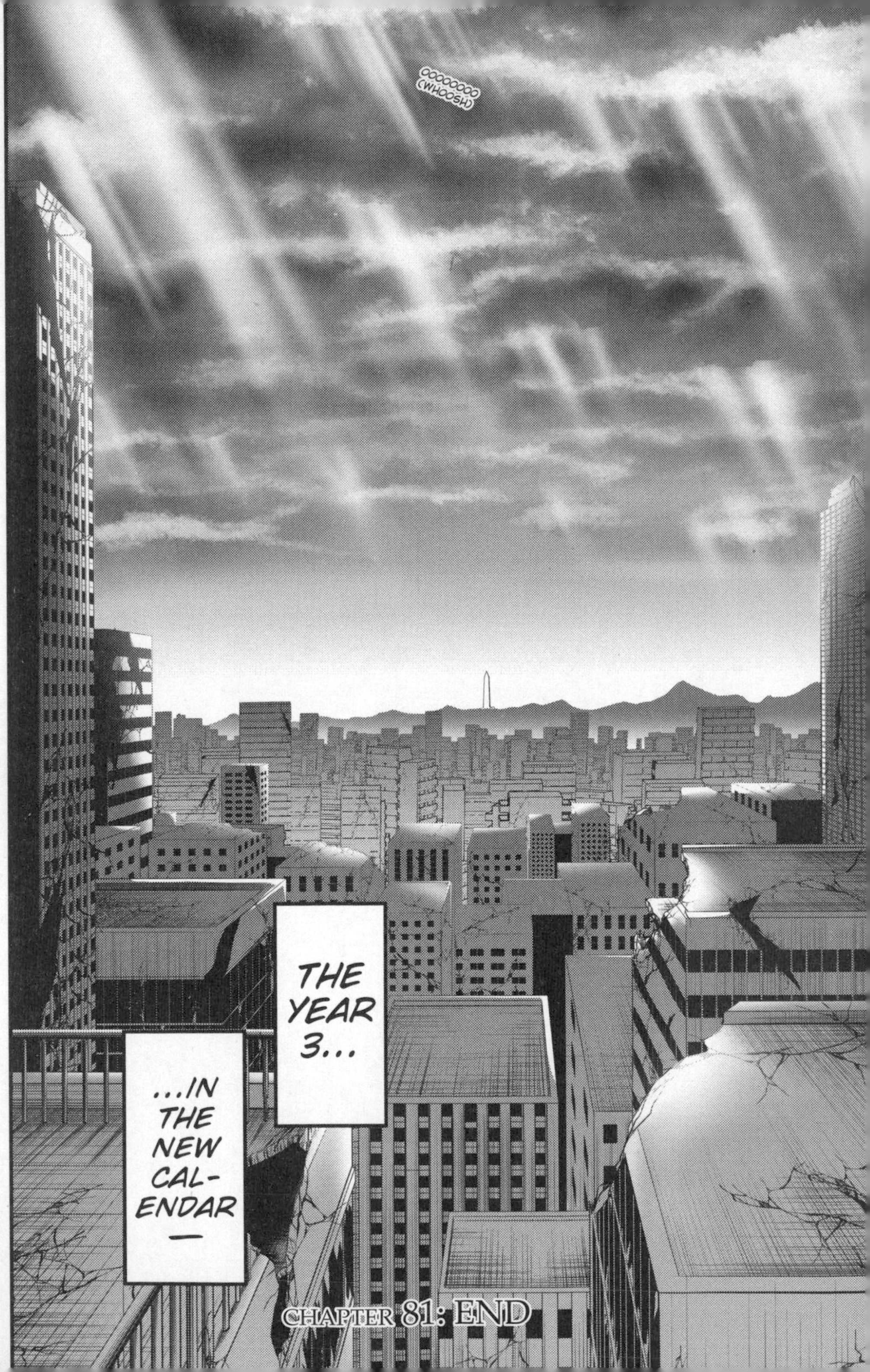
OOOOOOOO
(WHOOSH)
THE YEAR 3...
...IN THE NEW CAL-ENDAR —
CHAPTER 81: END

CHAPTER 82

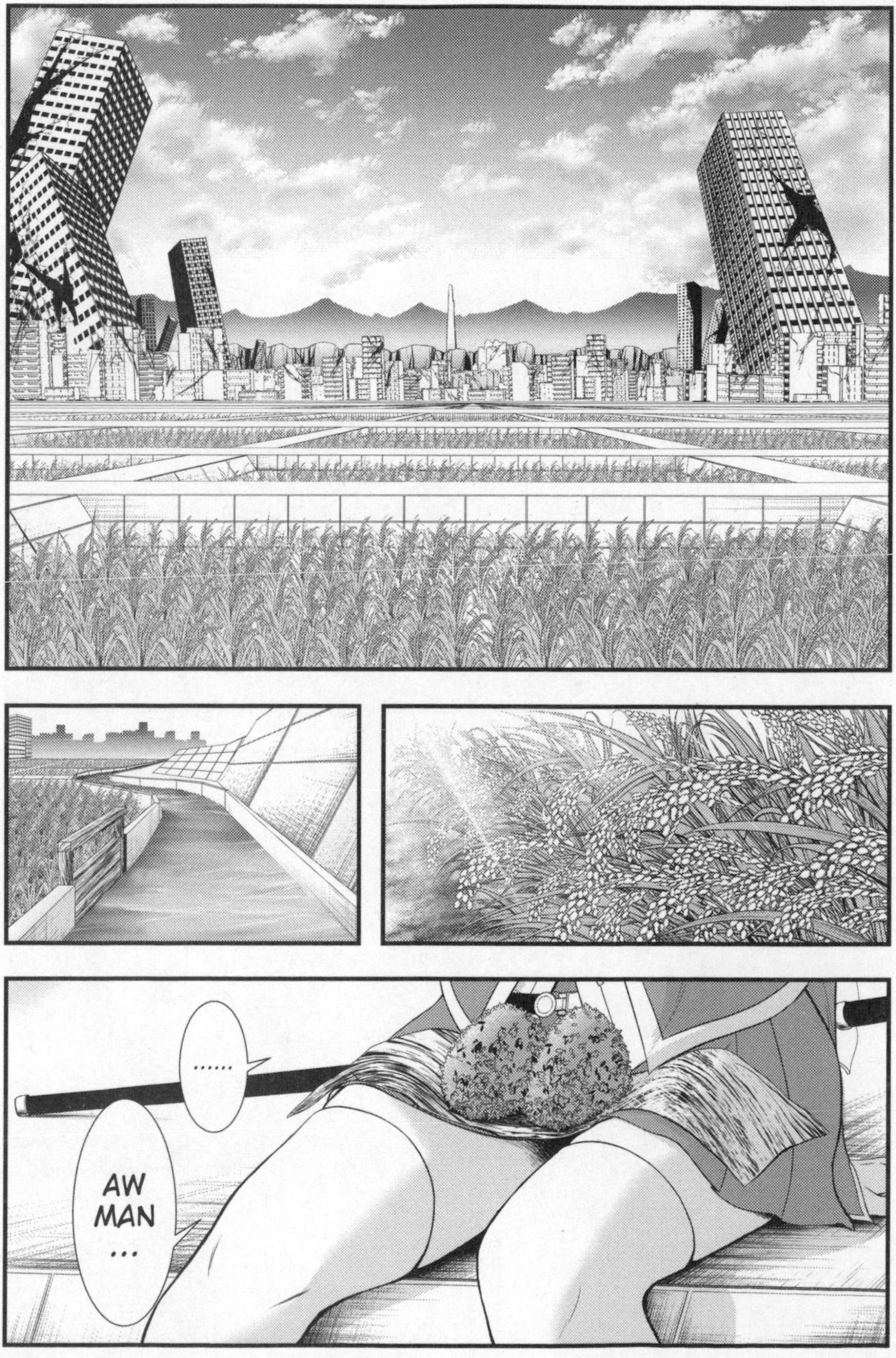
......
AW MAN ...

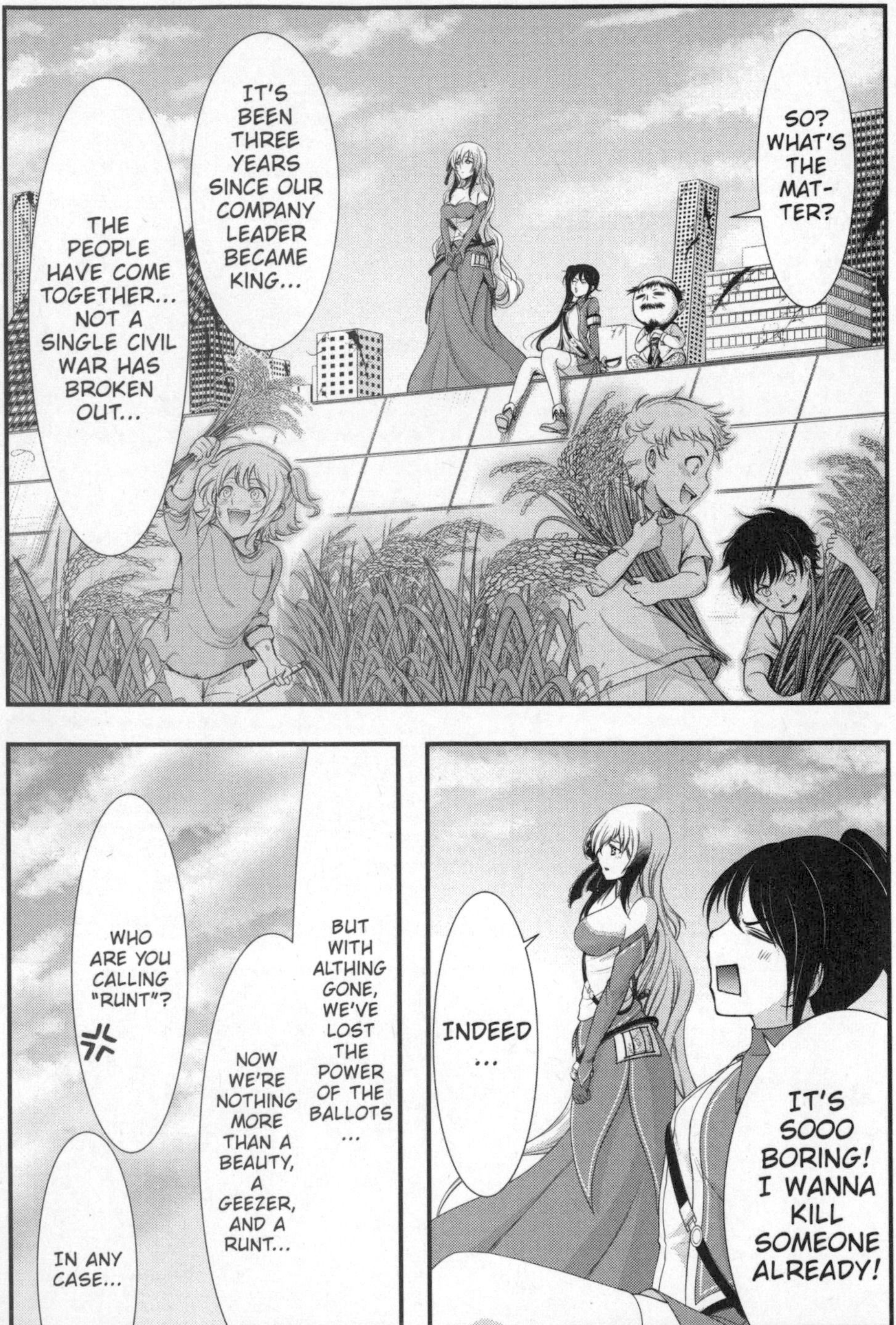
SO? WHAT'S THE MAT-TER?
IT'S BEEN THREE YEARS SINCE OUR COMPANY LEADER BECAME KING...
THE PEOPLE HAVE COME TOGETHER... NOT A SINGLE CIVIL WAR HAS BROKEN OUT...
IT'S SOOO BORING! I WANNA KILL SOMEONE ALREADY!
INDEED...
BUT WITH ALTHING GONE, WE'VE LOST THE POWER OF THE BALLOTS...
NOW WE'RE NOTHING MORE THAN A BEAUTY, A GEEZER, AND A RUNT...
WHO ARE YOU CALLING "RUNT"?
IN ANY CASE...

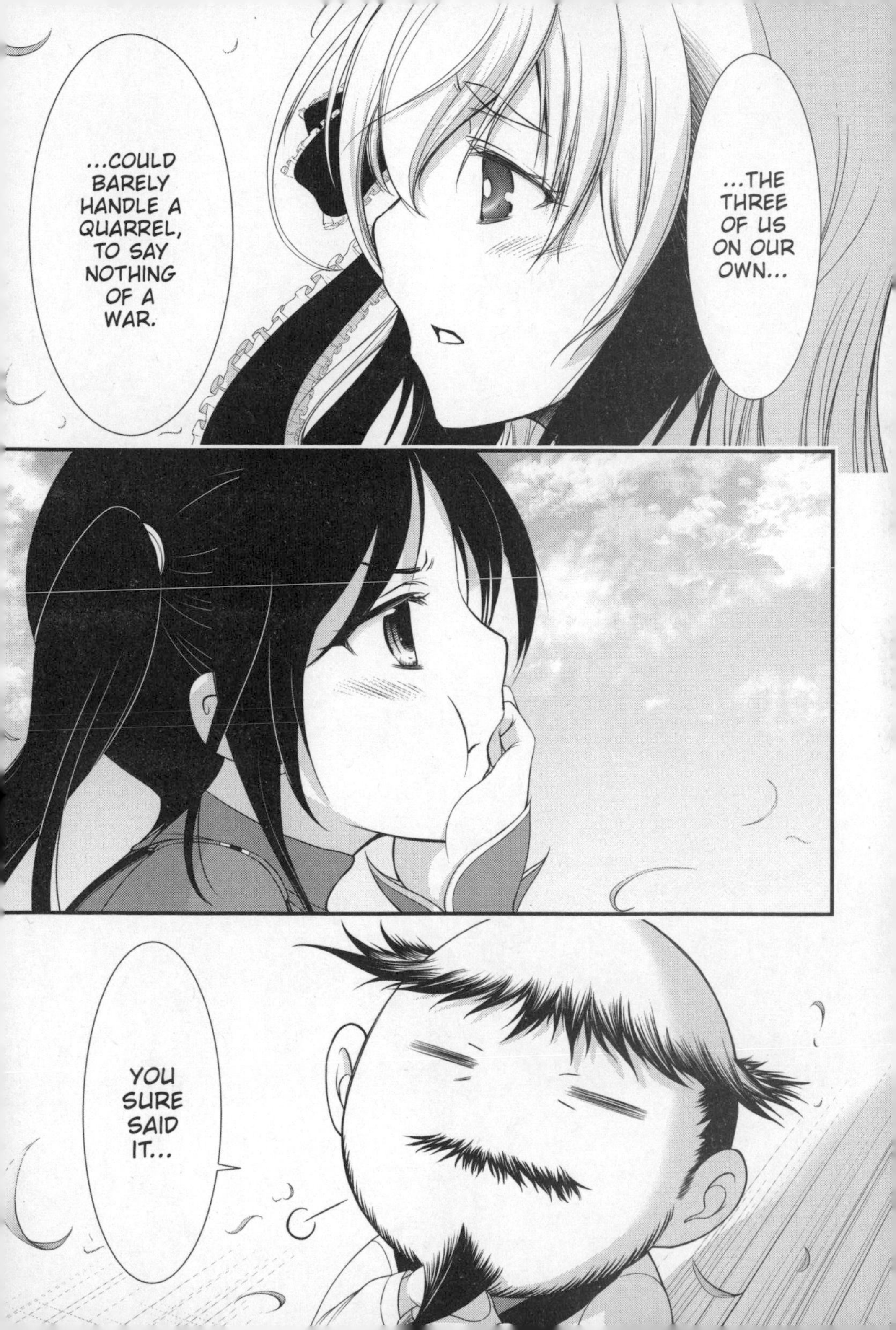
...THE THREE OF US ON OUR OWN...
...COULD BARELY HANDLE A QUARREL, TO SAY NOTHING OF A WAR.
YOU SURE SAID IT...

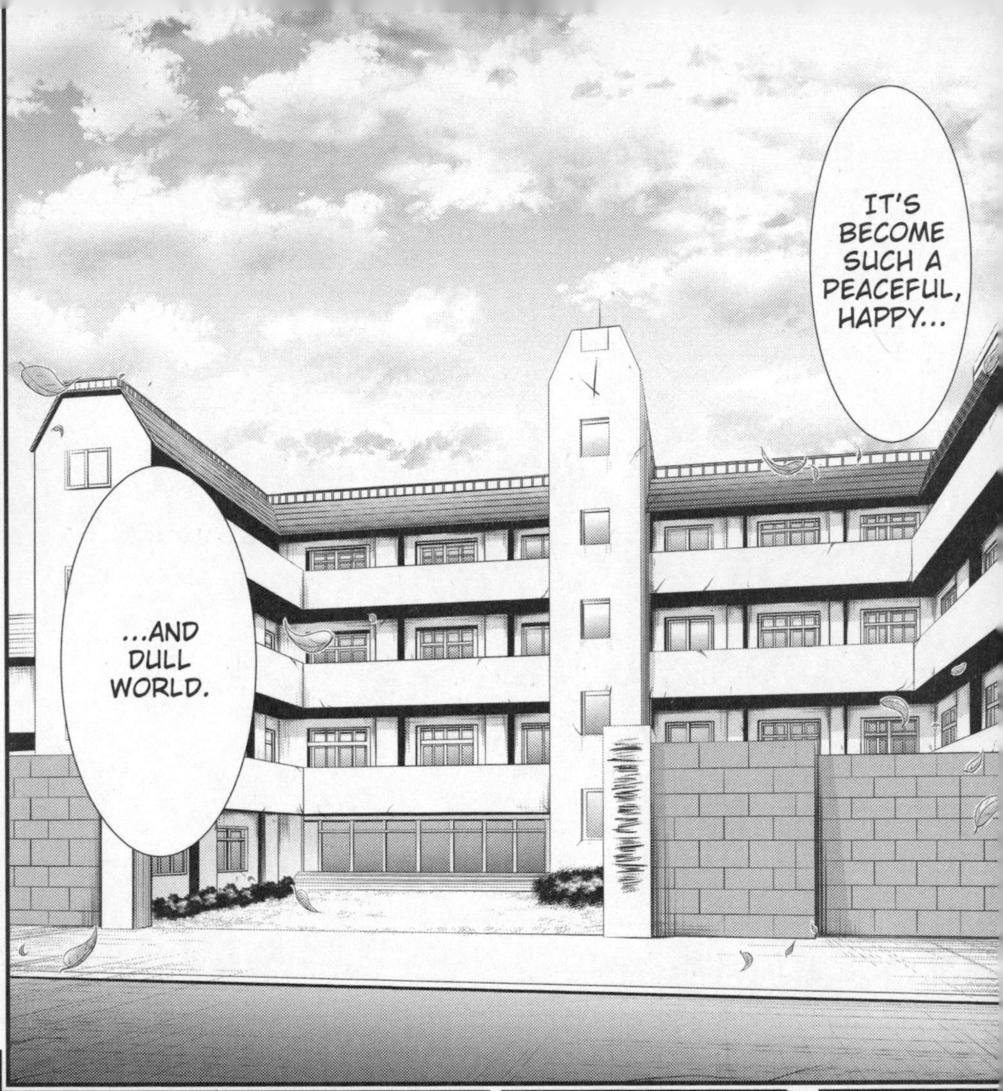
IT'S BECOME SUCH A PEACEFUL, HAPPY...
...AND DULL WORLD.
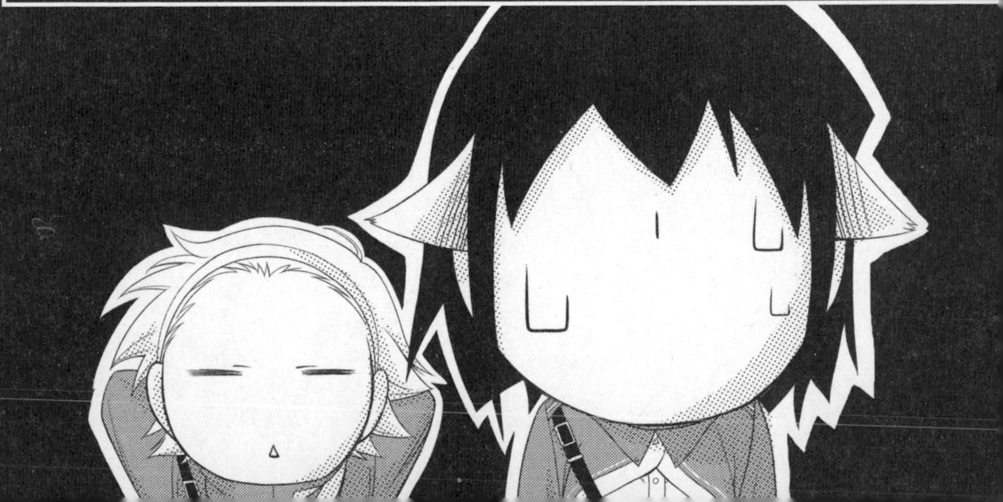

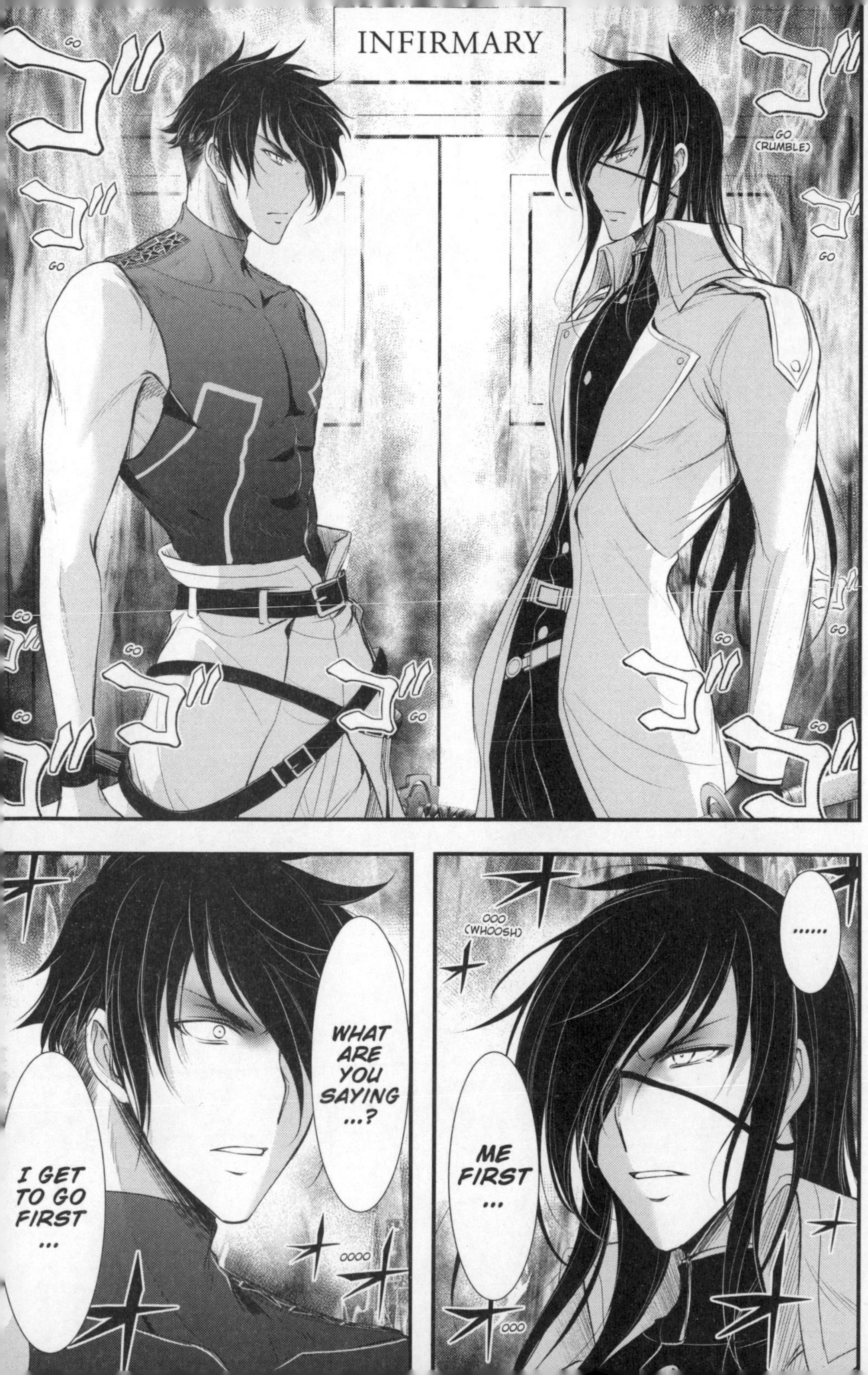
INFIRMARY
GO
GO (RUMBLE)
GO
GO
GO
GO
GO
GO
GO
GO
GO
GO
......
OOO (WHOOSH)
ME FIRST ...
OOO
WHAT ARE YOU SAYING ...?
I GET TO GO FIRST ...
OOOO

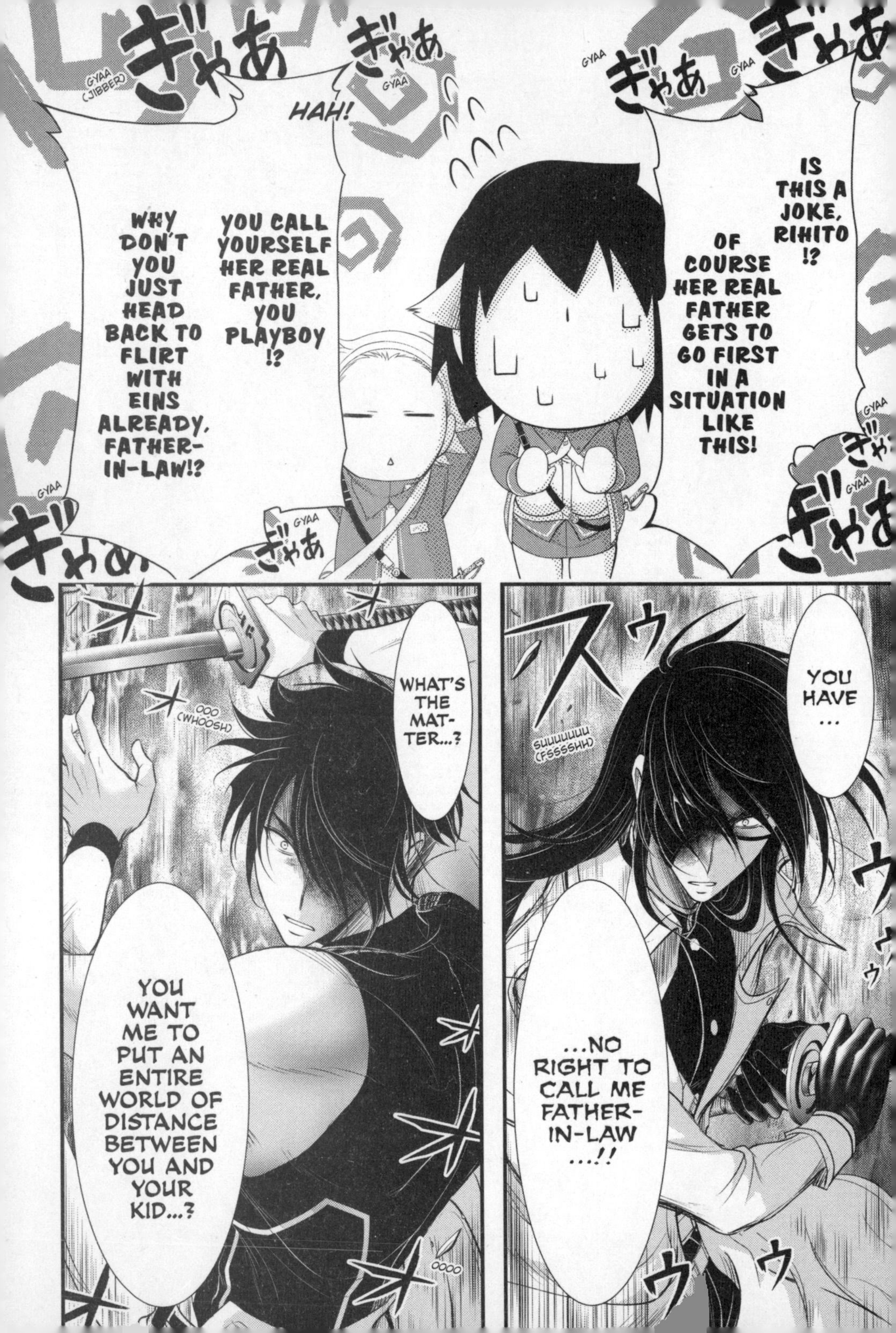
ぎゃあ
GYAA
ぎゃあ
GYAA
IS THIS A JOKE, RIHITO!?
OF COURSE HER REAL FATHER GETS TO GO FIRST IN A SITUATION LIKE THIS!
GYAA
ぎゃあ
GYAA
ぎゃあ
HAH!
ぎゃあ
GYAA
YOU CALL YOURSELF HER REAL FATHER, YOU PLAYBOY!?
ぎゃあ
GYAA (JIBBER)
WHY DON'T YOU JUST HEAD BACK TO FLIRT WITH EINS ALREADY, FATHER-IN-LAW!?
GYAA
ぎゃあ
GYAA
ぎゃあ
スウ
SUUUUUUU (FSSSSHH)
YOU HAVE ...
...NO RIGHT TO CALL ME FATHER-IN-LAW ...!!
ウウウウ
OOO (WHOOSH)
WHAT'S THE MAT-TER...?
YOU WANT ME TO PUT AN ENTIRE WORLD OF DISTANCE BETWEEN YOU AND YOUR KID...?
OOOO

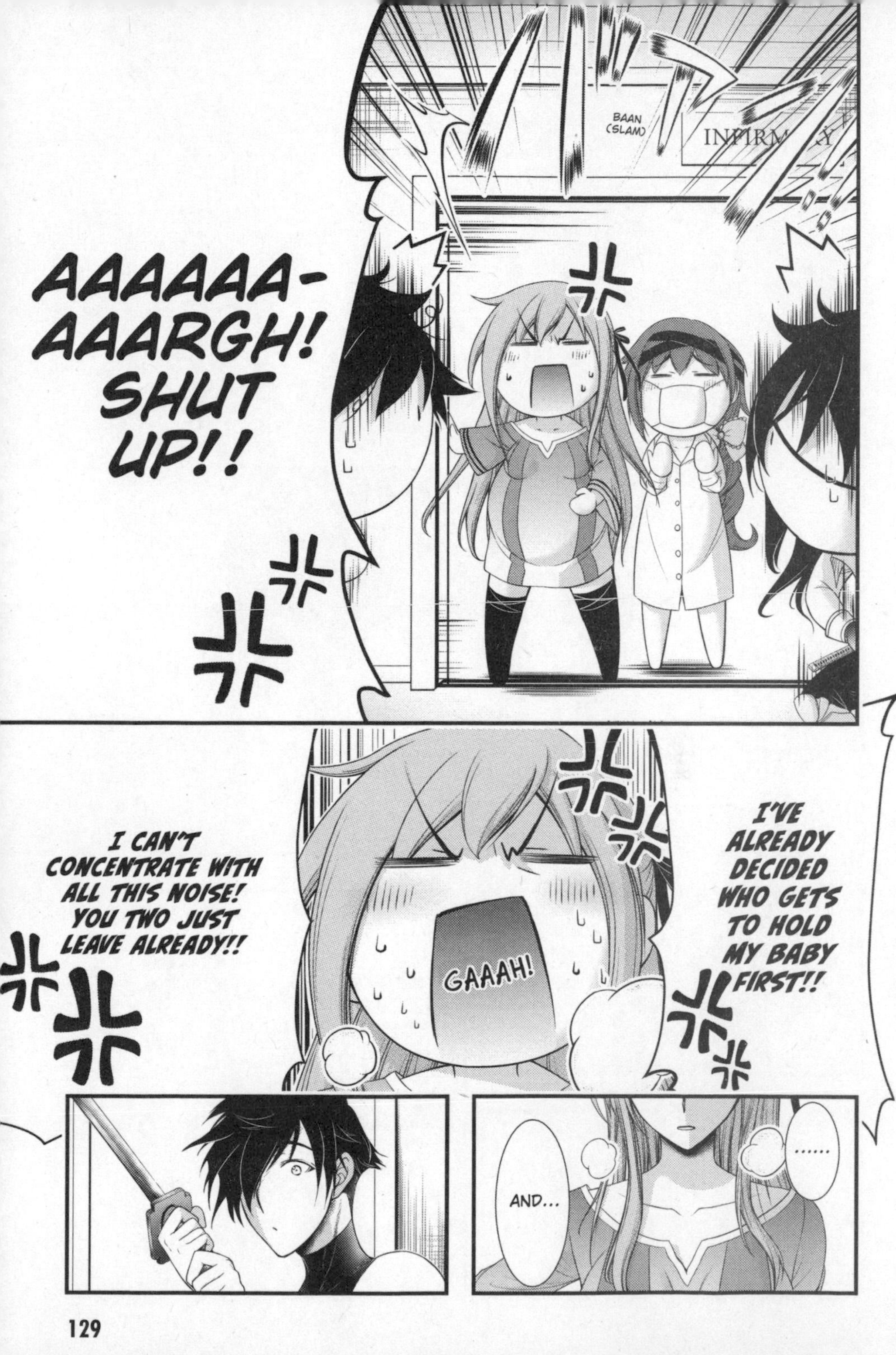
BAAN (SLAM)
AAAAAA-AAARGH! SHUT UP!!
I'VE ALREADY DECIDED WHO GETS TO HOLD MY BABY FIRST!!
GAAAH!
I CAN'T CONCENTRATE WITH ALL THIS NOISE! YOU TWO JUST LEAVE ALREADY!!
......
AND...

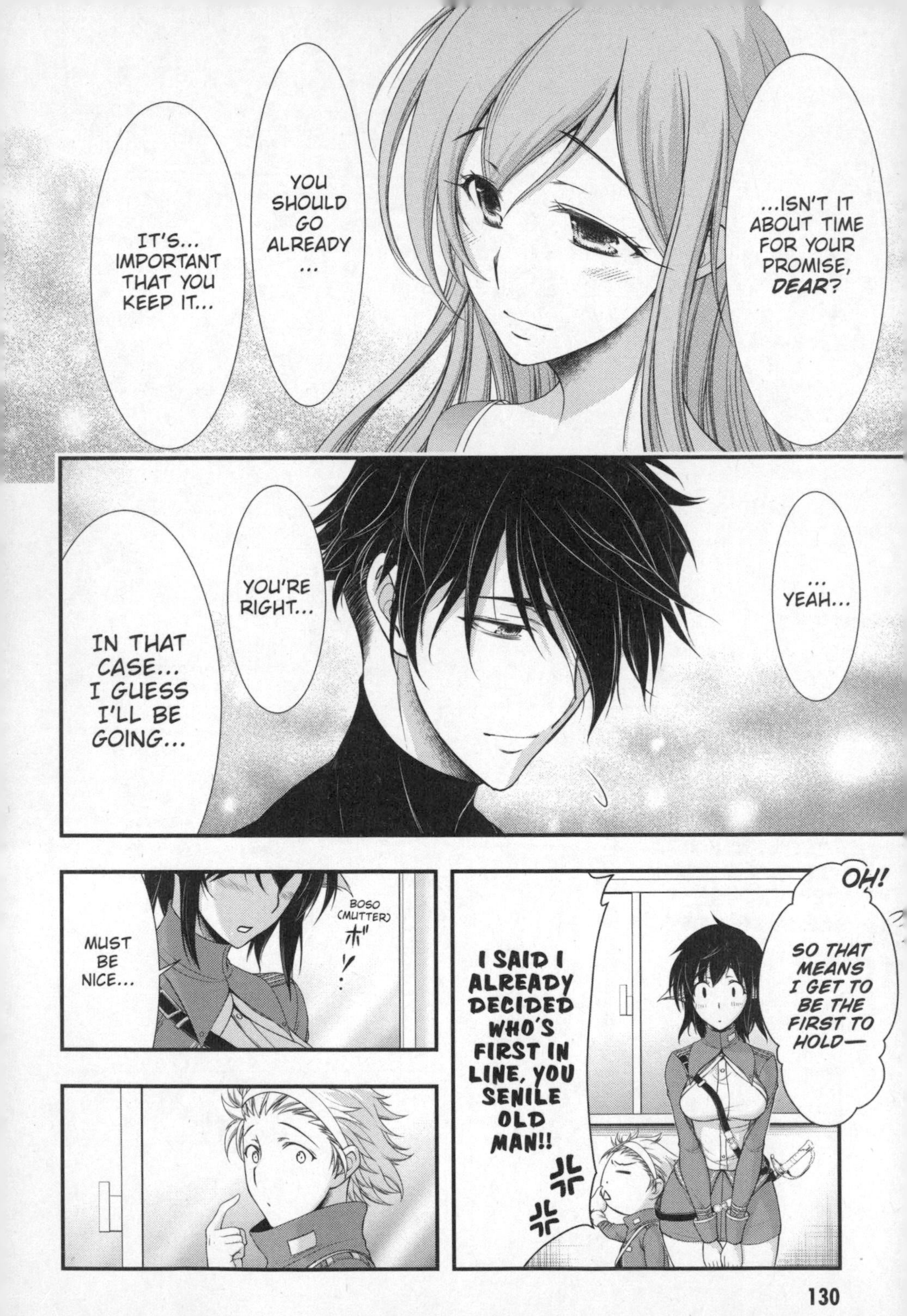

...ISN'T IT ABOUT TIME FOR YOUR PROMISE, DEAR?
YOU SHOULD GO ALREADY ...
IT'S... IMPORTANT THAT YOU KEEP IT...
... YEAH...
YOU'RE RIGHT...
IN THAT CASE... I GUESS I'LL BE GOING...
OH!
SO THAT MEANS I GET TO BE THE FIRST TO HOLD—
I SAID I ALREADY DECIDED WHO'S FIRST IN LINE, YOU SENILE OLD MAN!!
BOSO (MUTTER)
ボソ
MUST BE NICE...

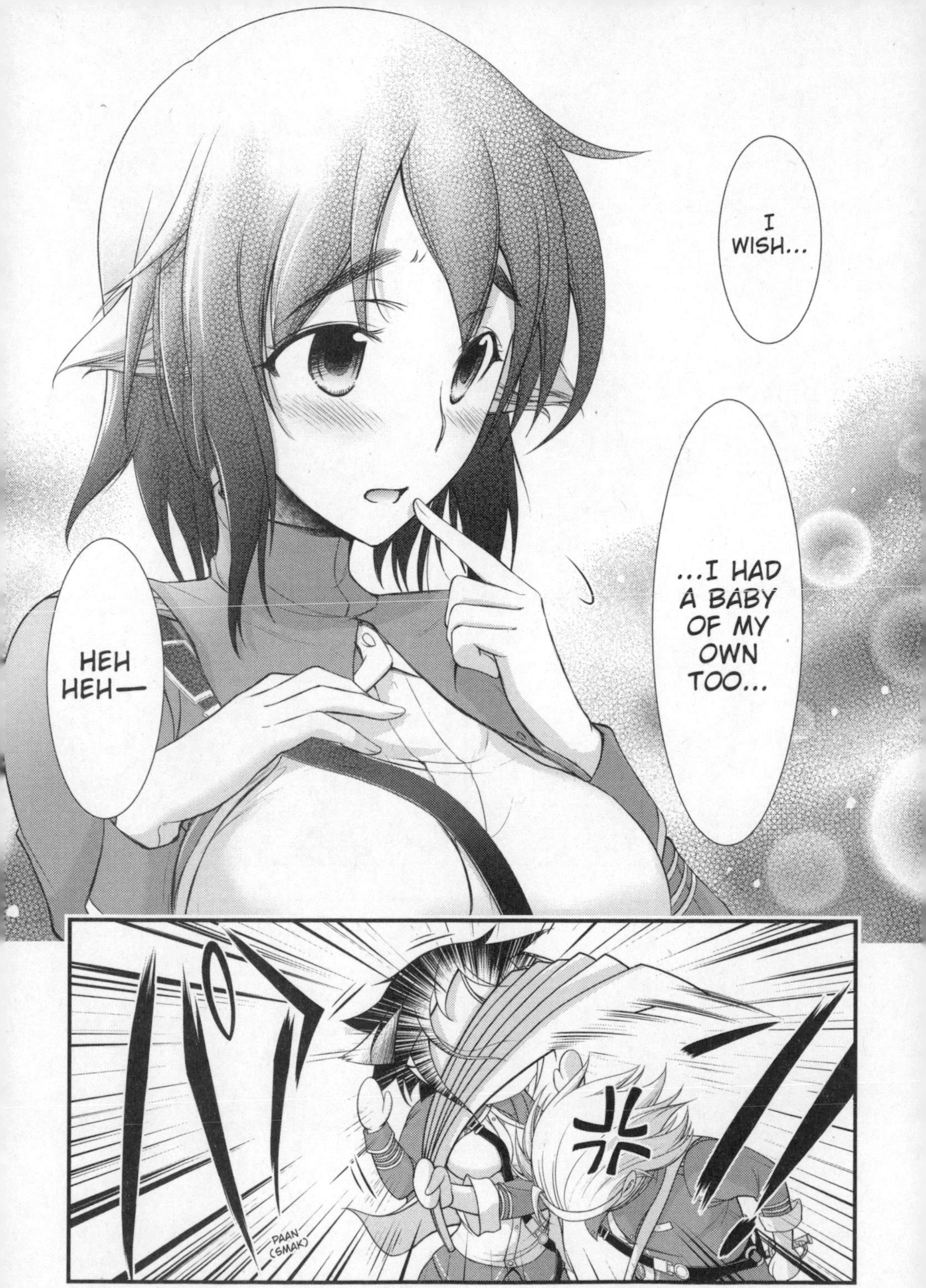
I WISH...
...I HAD A BABY OF MY OWN TOO...
HEH HEH—
パ
PAAN (SMAK)

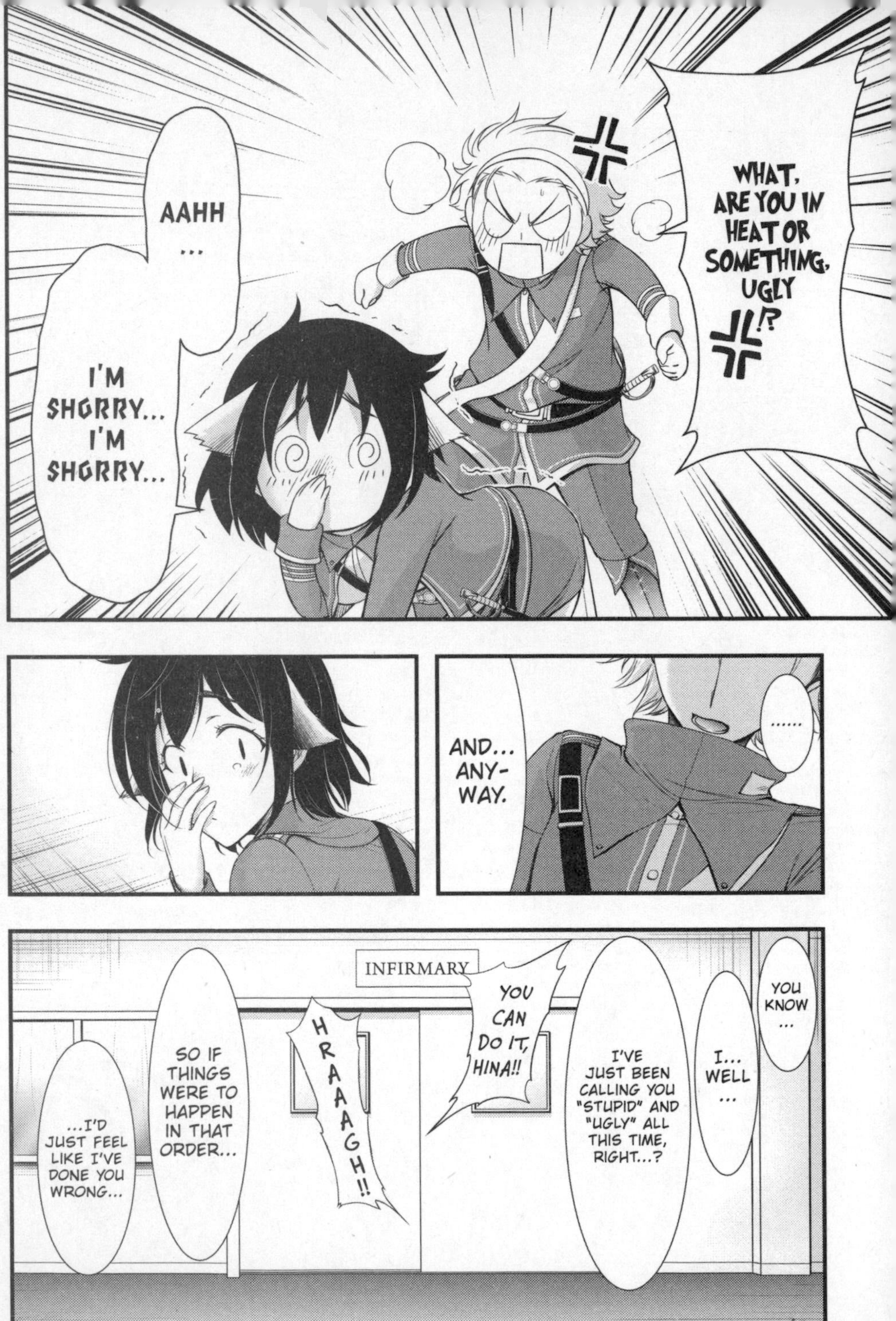
WHAT, ARE YOU IN HEAT OR SOMETHING, UGLY!?
AAHH ...
I'M SHGRRY... I'M SHGRRY...
......
AND... ANY-WAY.
YOU KNOW ...
I... WELL ...
I'VE JUST BEEN CALLING YOU "STUPID" AND "UGLY" ALL THIS TIME, RIGHT...?
YOU CAN DO IT, HINA!!
INFIRMARY
HRAAAGH!!
SO IF THINGS WERE TO HAPPEN IN THAT ORDER...
...I'D JUST FEEL LIKE I'VE DONE YOU WRONG...

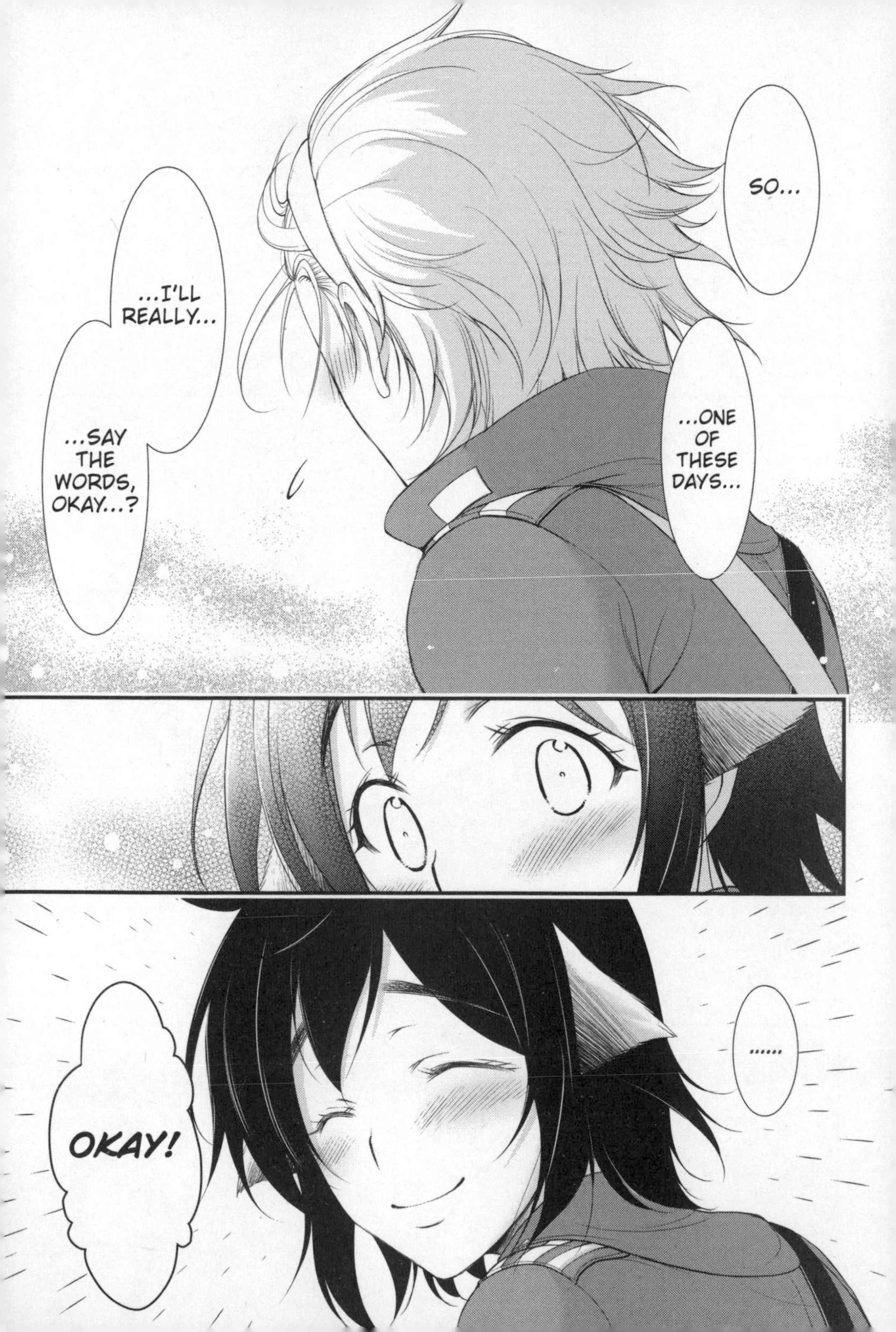
SO...
...ONE OF THESE DAYS...
...I'LL REALLY...
...SAY THE WORDS, OKAY...?
......
OKAY!

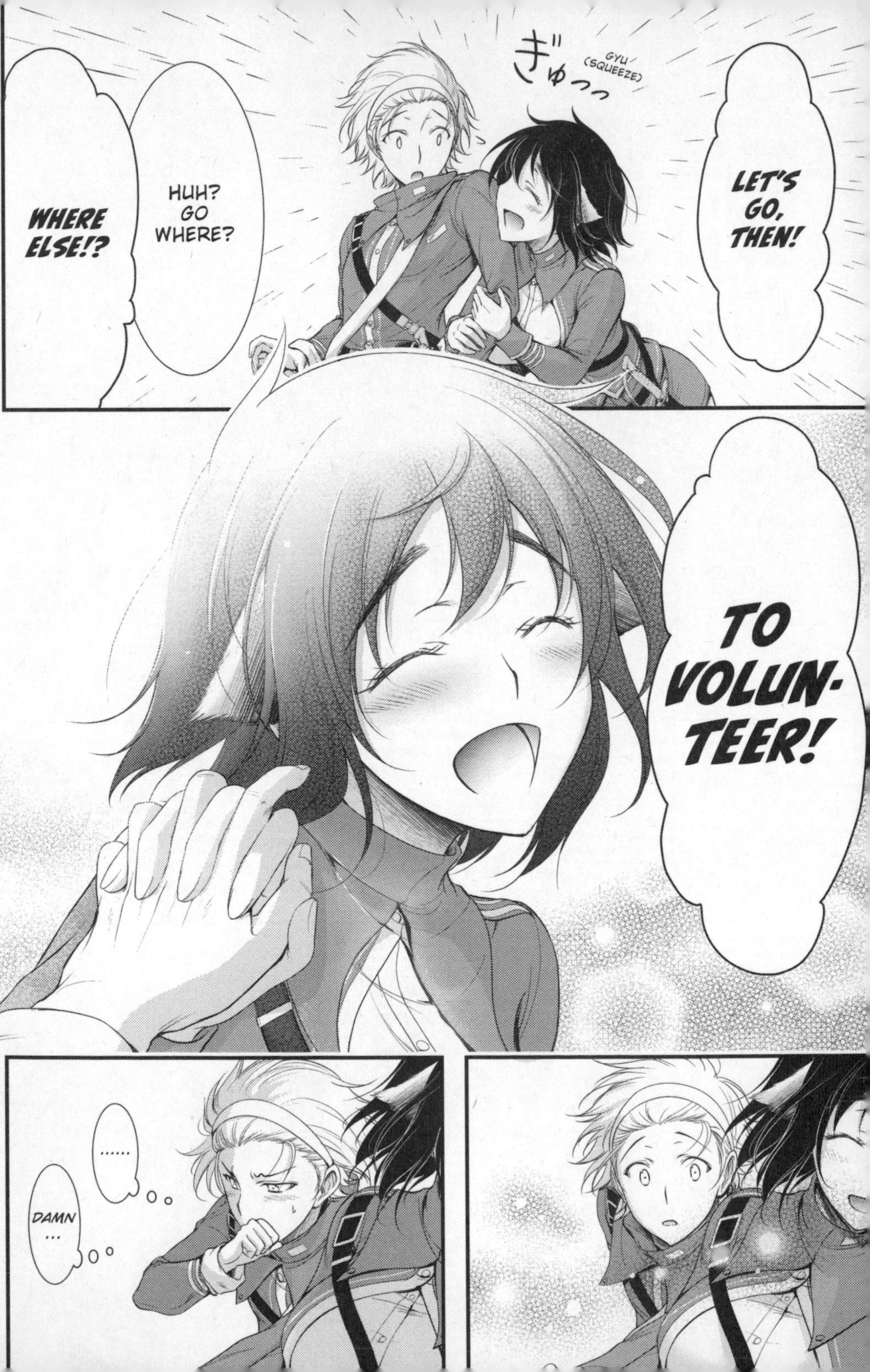
LET'S GO, THEN!
ぎゅっっ
GYU (SQUEEZE)
HUH? GO WHERE?
WHERE ELSE!?
TO VOLUN-TEER!
......
DAMN...

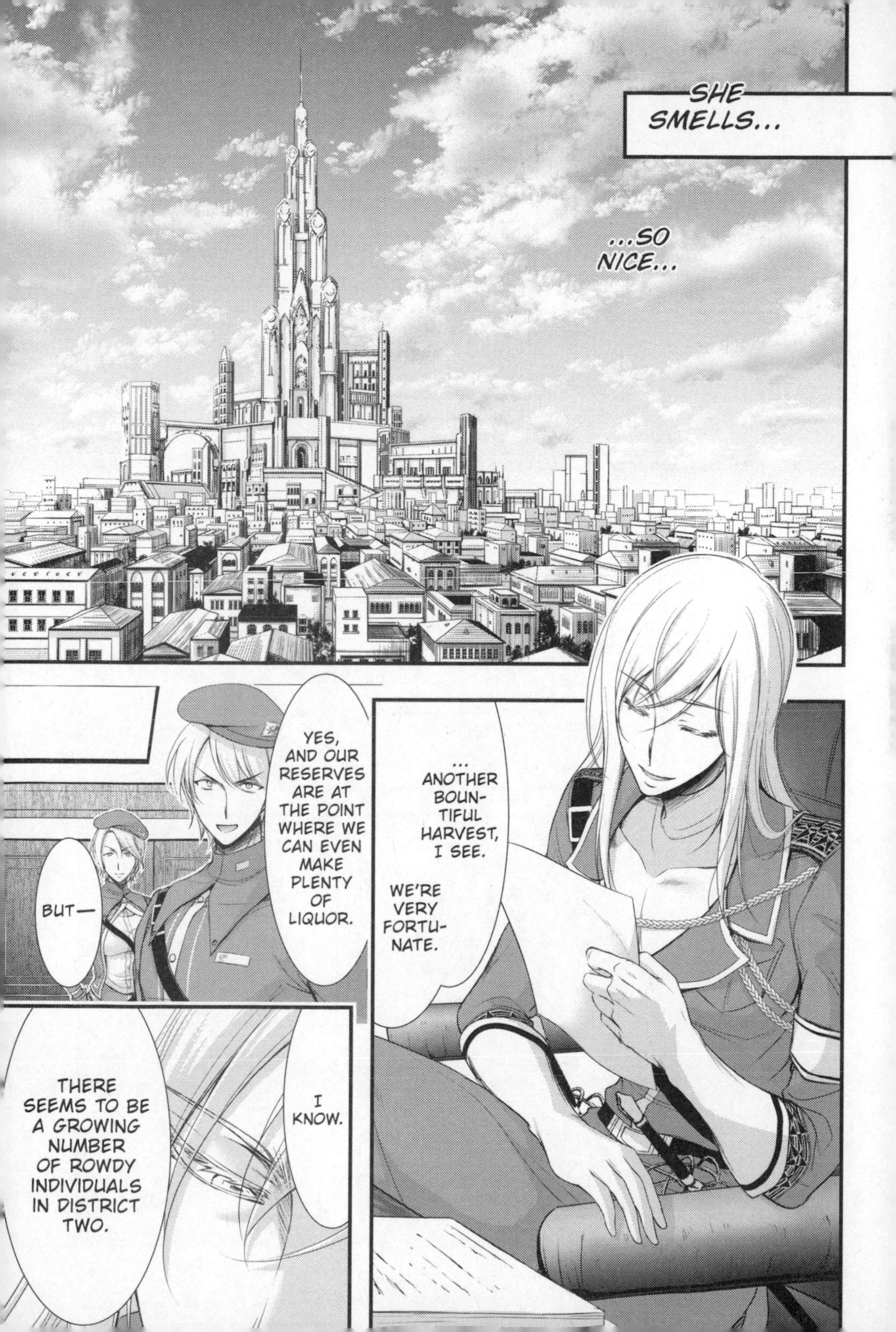
SHE SMELLS...
...SO NICE...
... ANOTHER BOUNTIFUL HARVEST, I SEE.
WE'RE VERY FORTUNATE.
YES, AND OUR RESERVES ARE AT THE POINT WHERE WE CAN EVEN MAKE PLENTY OF LIQUOR.
BUT—
THERE SEEMS TO BE A GROWING NUMBER OF ROWDY INDIVIDUALS IN DISTRICT TWO.
I KNOW.

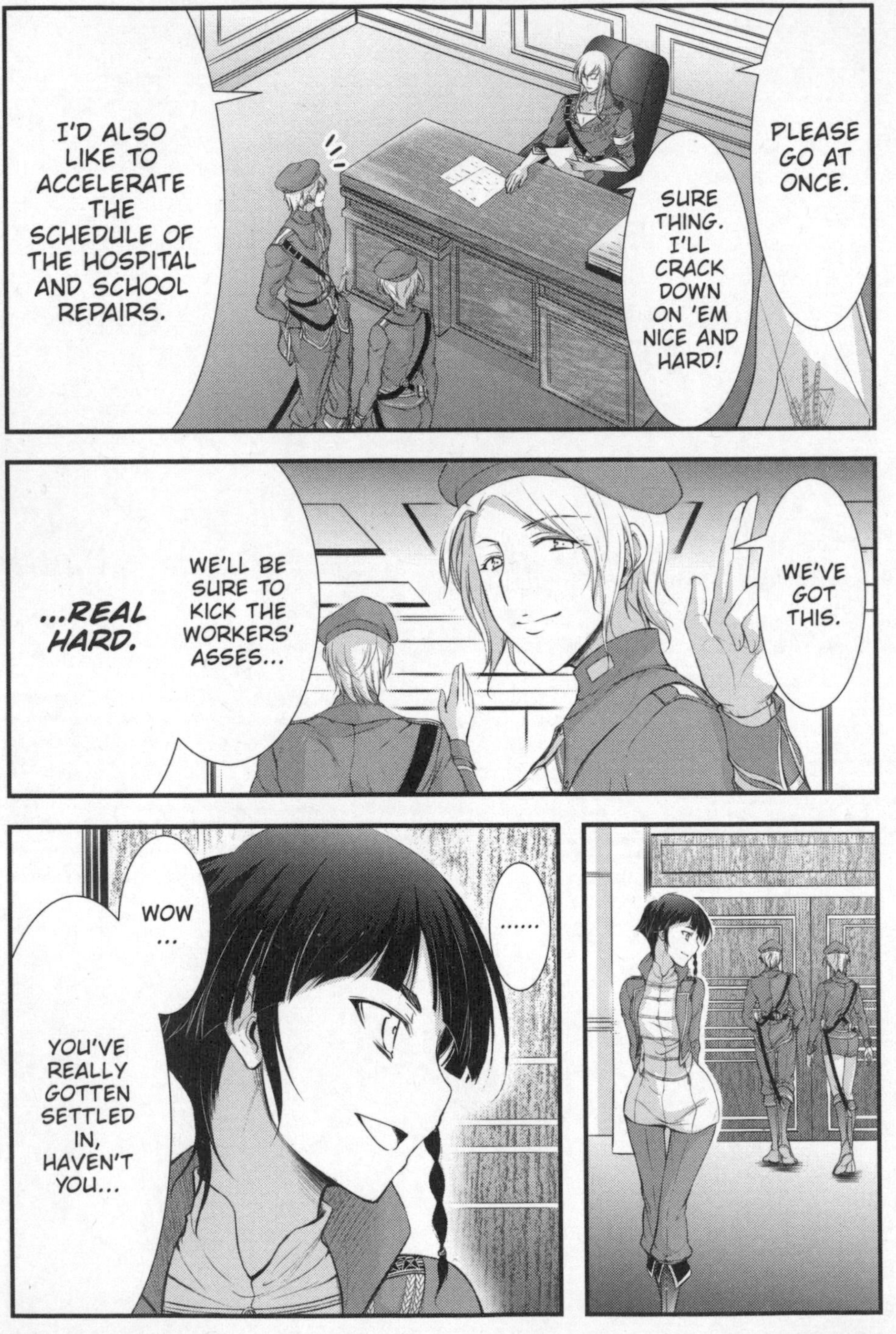
PLEASE GO AT ONCE.
SURE THING. I'LL CRACK DOWN ON 'EM NICE AND HARD!
I'D ALSO LIKE TO ACCELERATE THE SCHEDULE OF THE HOSPITAL AND SCHOOL REPAIRS.
WE'VE GOT THIS.
WE'LL BE SURE TO KICK THE WORKERS' ASSES...
...REAL HARD.
......
WOW...
YOU'VE REALLY GOTTEN SETTLED IN, HAVEN'T YOU...

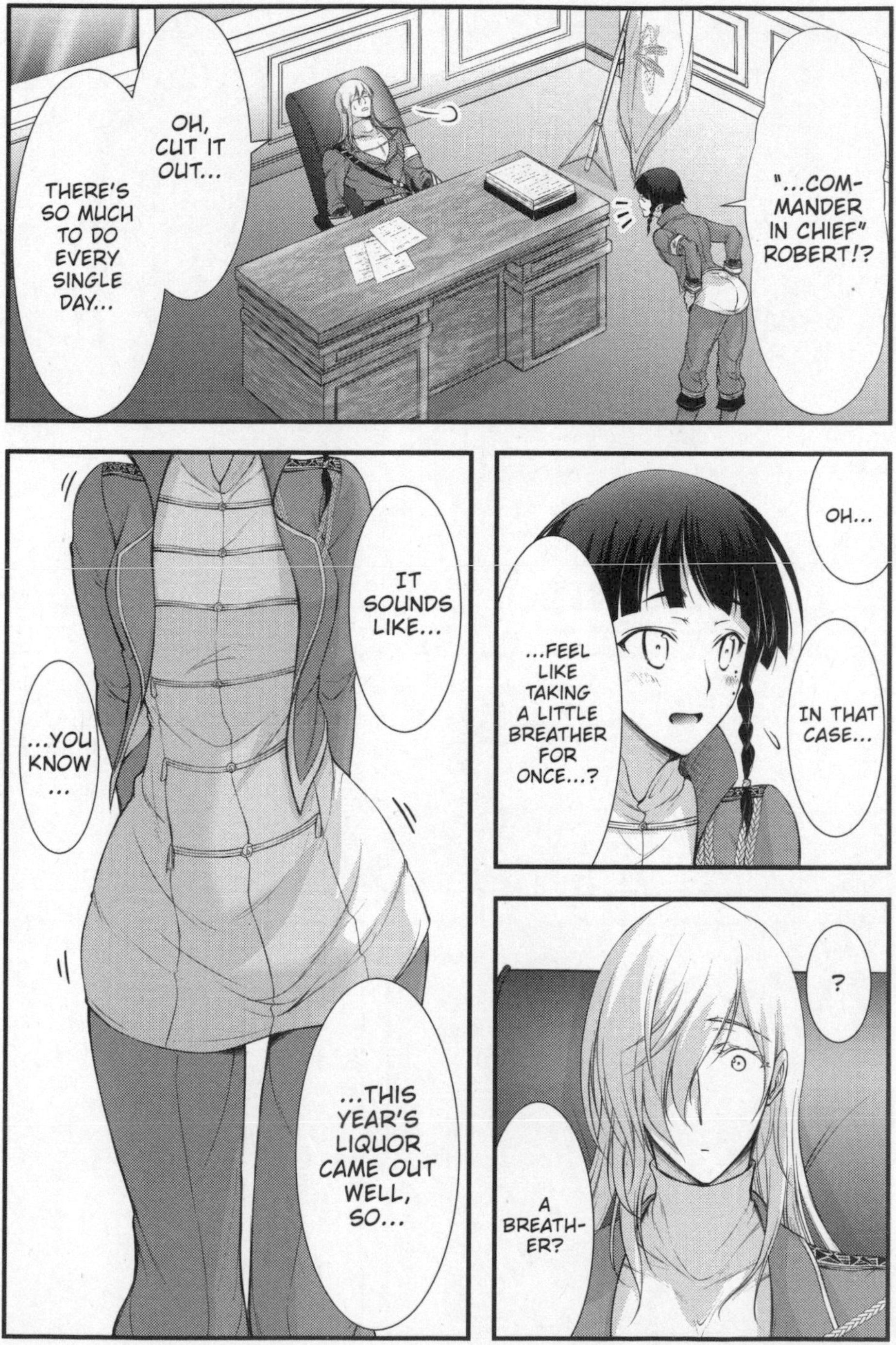
"...COM-MANDER IN CHIEF" ROBERT!?
OH, CUT IT OUT...
THERE'S SO MUCH TO DO EVERY SINGLE DAY...
OH...
IN THAT CASE...
...FEEL LIKE TAKING A LITTLE BREATHER FOR ONCE...?
?
A BREATH-ER?
IT SOUNDS LIKE...
...YOU KNOW...
...THIS YEAR'S LIQUOR CAME OUT WELL, SO...

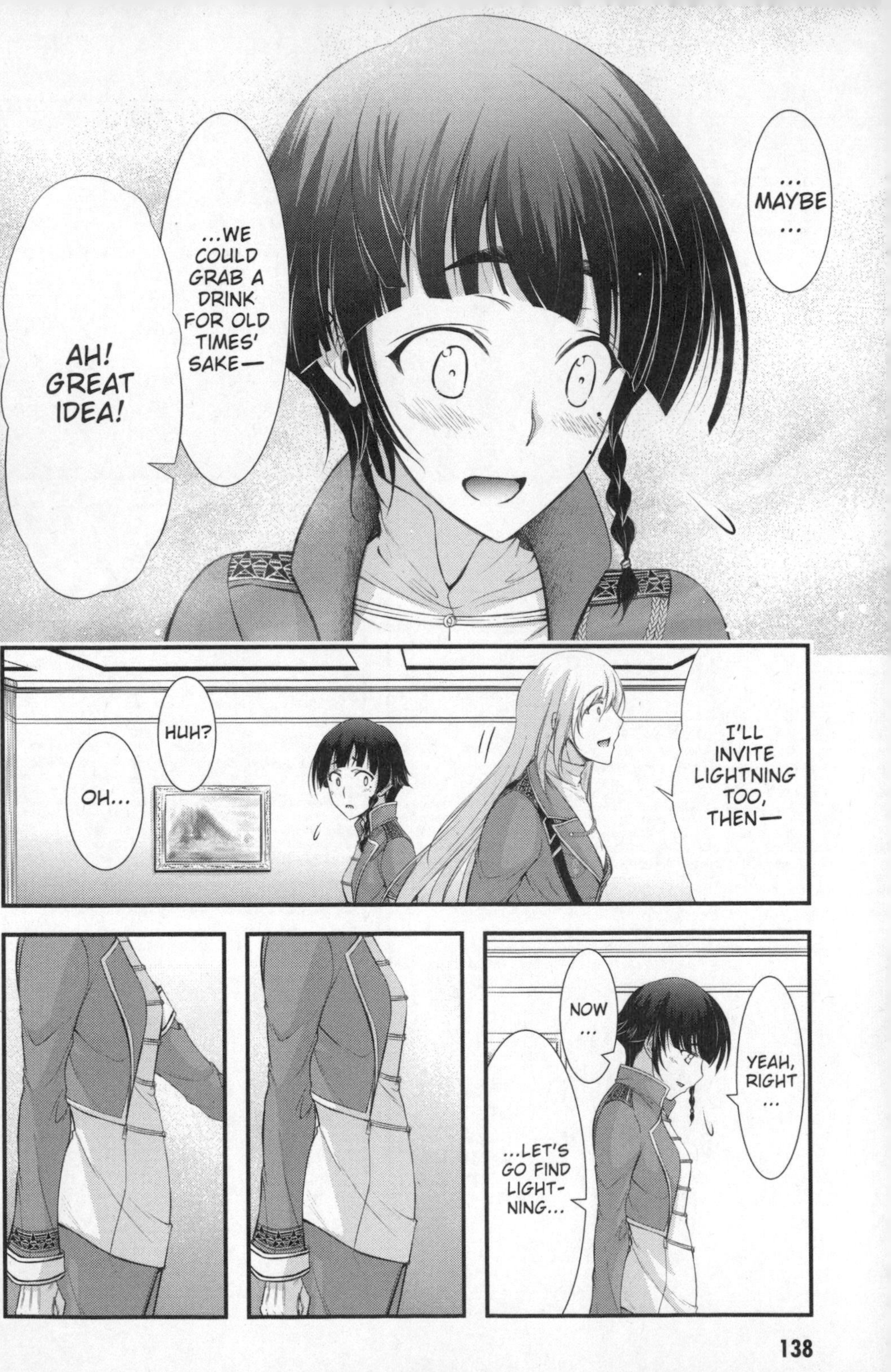
...MAYBE...
...WE COULD GRAB A DRINK FOR OLD TIMES' SAKE—
AH! GREAT IDEA!
I'LL INVITE LIGHTNING TOO, THEN—
HUH?
OH...
YEAH, RIGHT...
NOW...
...LET'S GO FIND LIGHT-NING...

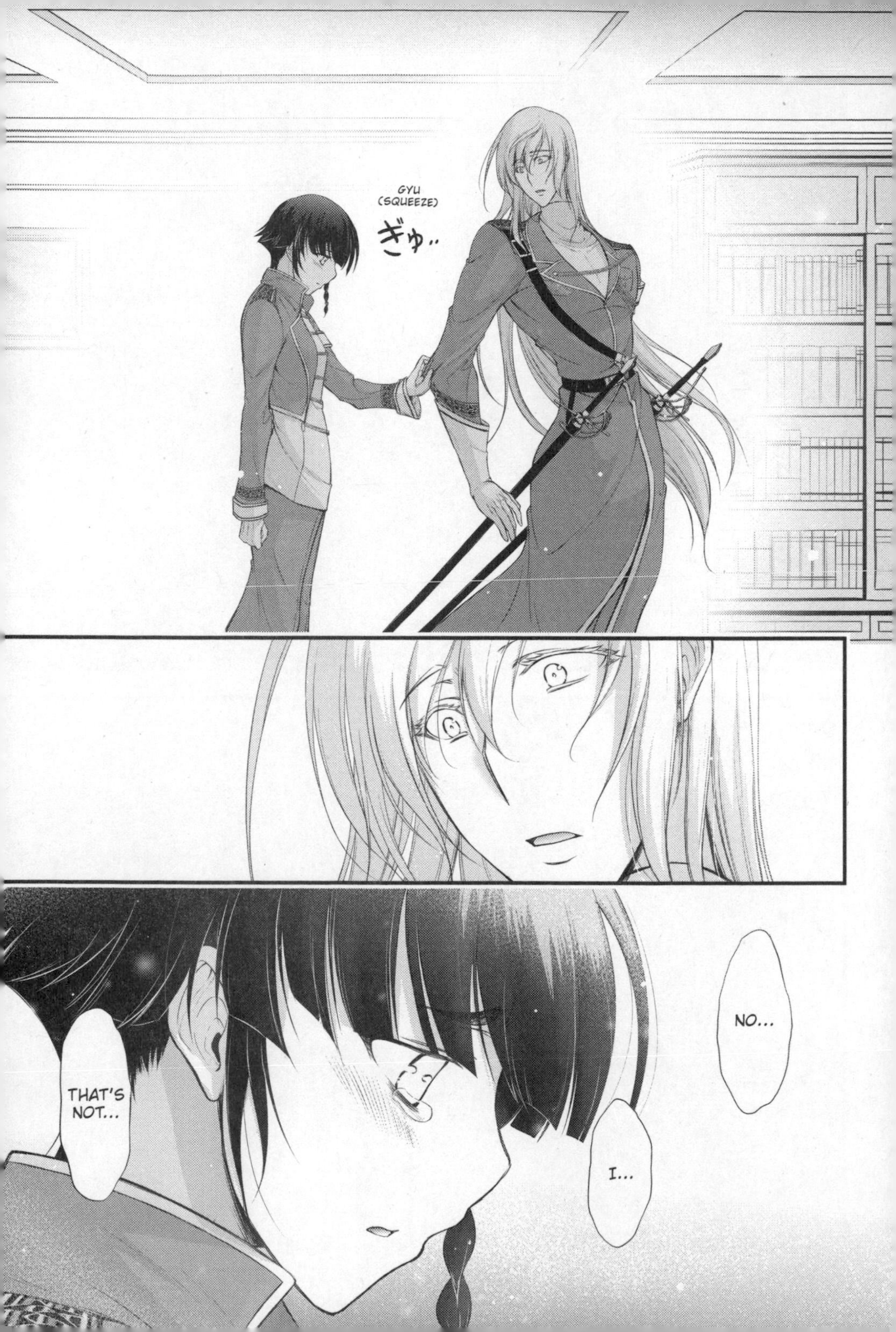
GYU (SQUEEZE)
ぎゅ‥
NO...
I...
THAT'S NOT...

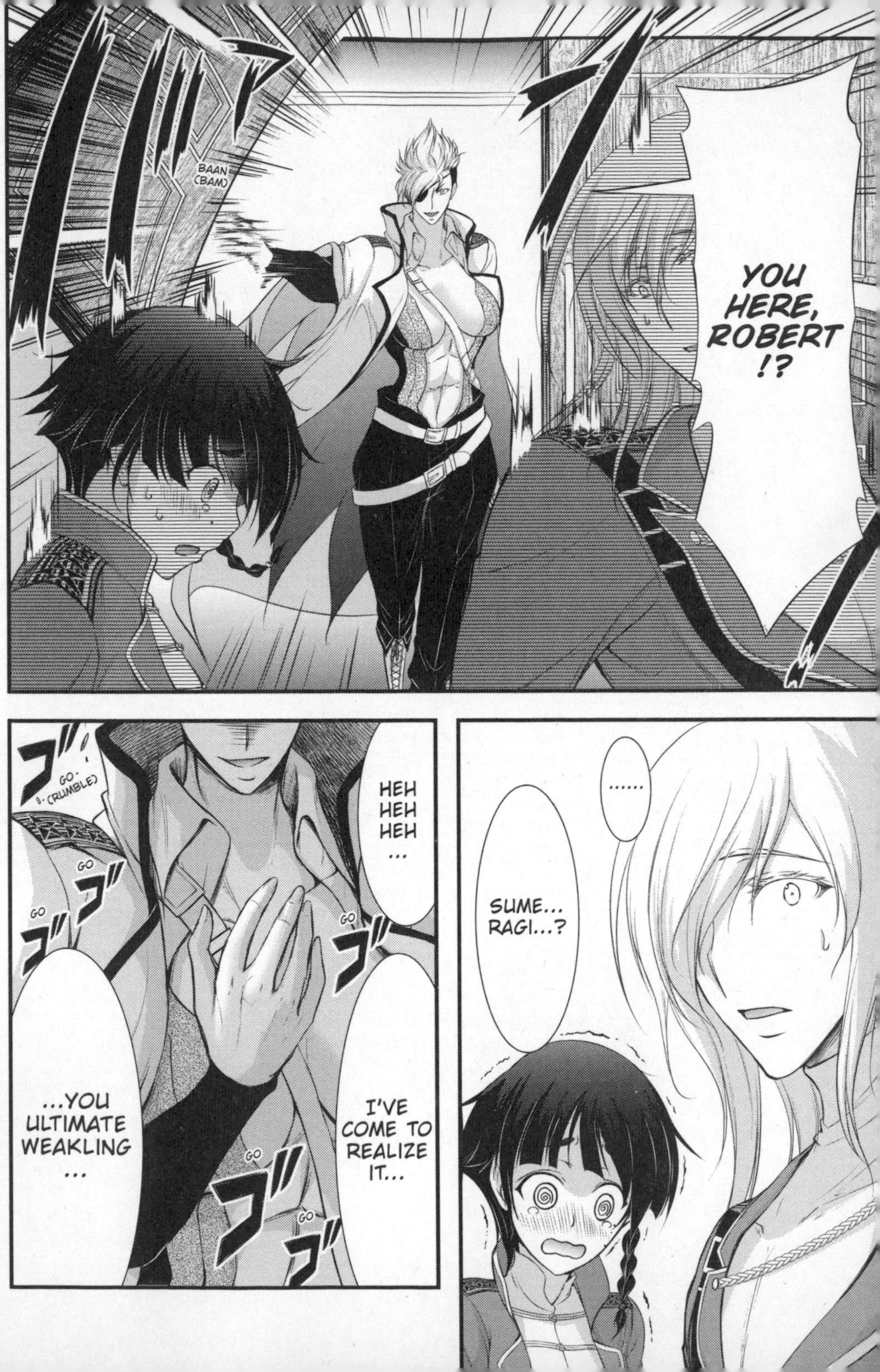
YOU HERE, ROBERT!?
BAAN (BAM)
......
SUME... RAGI...?
GO (RUMBLE)
HEH HEH HEH...
I'VE COME TO REALIZE IT...
...YOU ULTIMATE WEAKLING...
GO
GO
GO
GO
GO

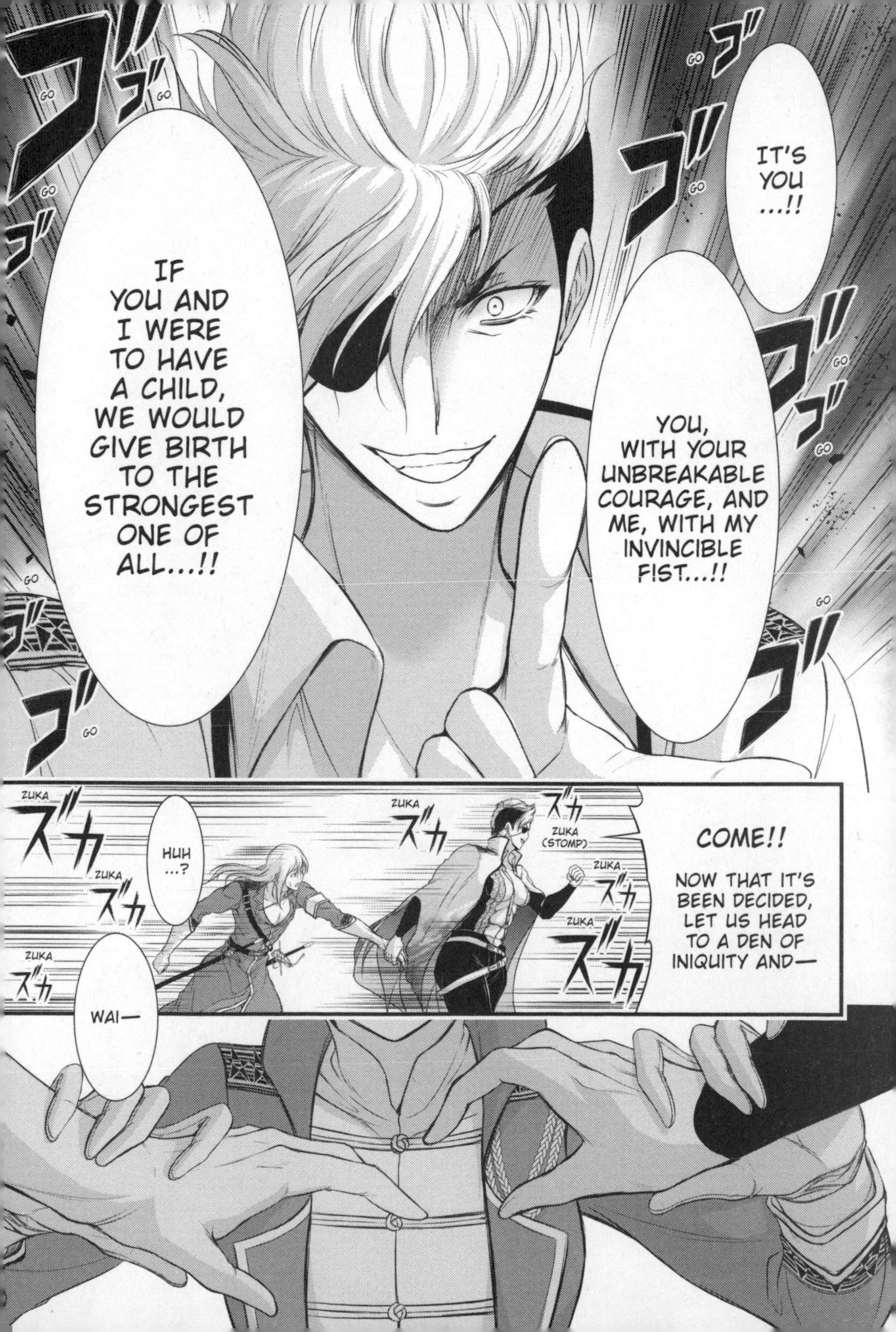
GO GO GO GO GO GO
IT'S YOU ...!!
YOU, WITH YOUR UNBREAKABLE COURAGE, AND ME, WITH MY INVINCIBLE FIST...!!
IF YOU AND I WERE TO HAVE A CHILD, WE WOULD GIVE BIRTH TO THE STRONGEST ONE OF ALL...!!
GO GO GO GO
COME!!
NOW THAT IT'S BEEN DECIDED, LET US HEAD TO A DEN OF INIQUITY AND—
ZUKA (STOMP)
ZUKA ZUKA ZUKA ZUKA ZUKA ZUKA
HUH ...?
WAI—

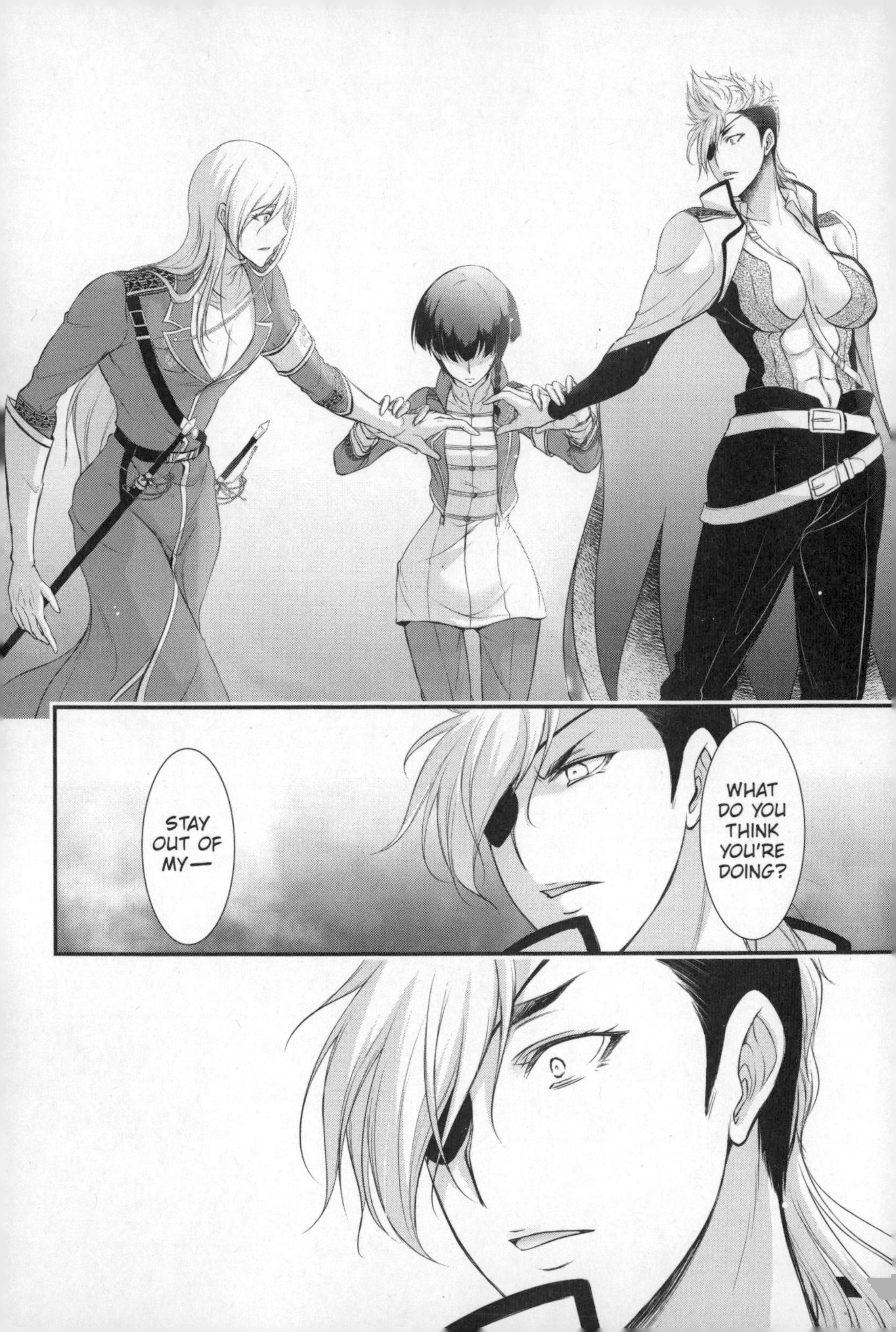
WHAT DO YOU THINK YOU'RE DOING?
STAY OUT OF MY—

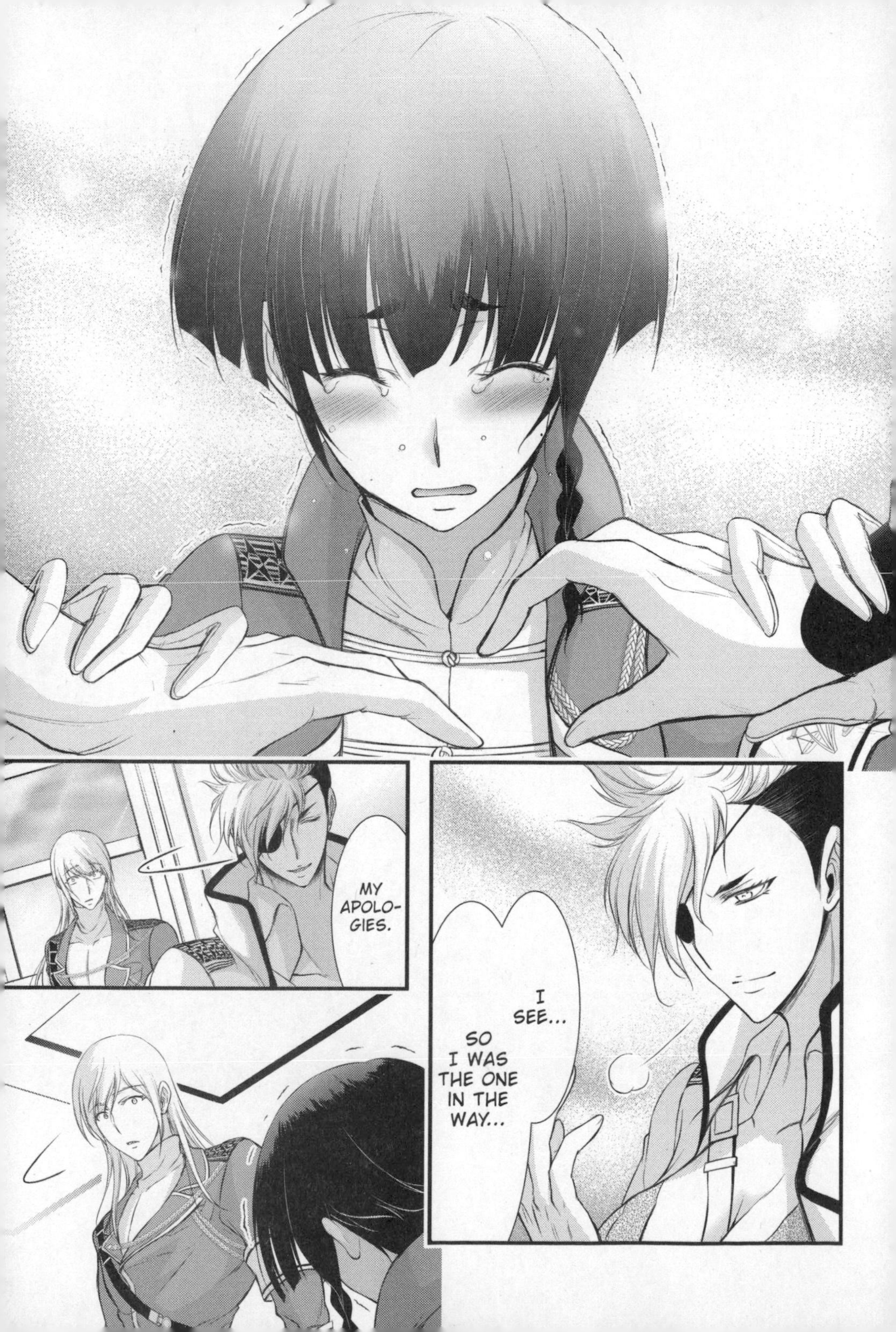
I SEE... SO I WAS THE ONE IN THE WAY...
MY APOLO-GIES.

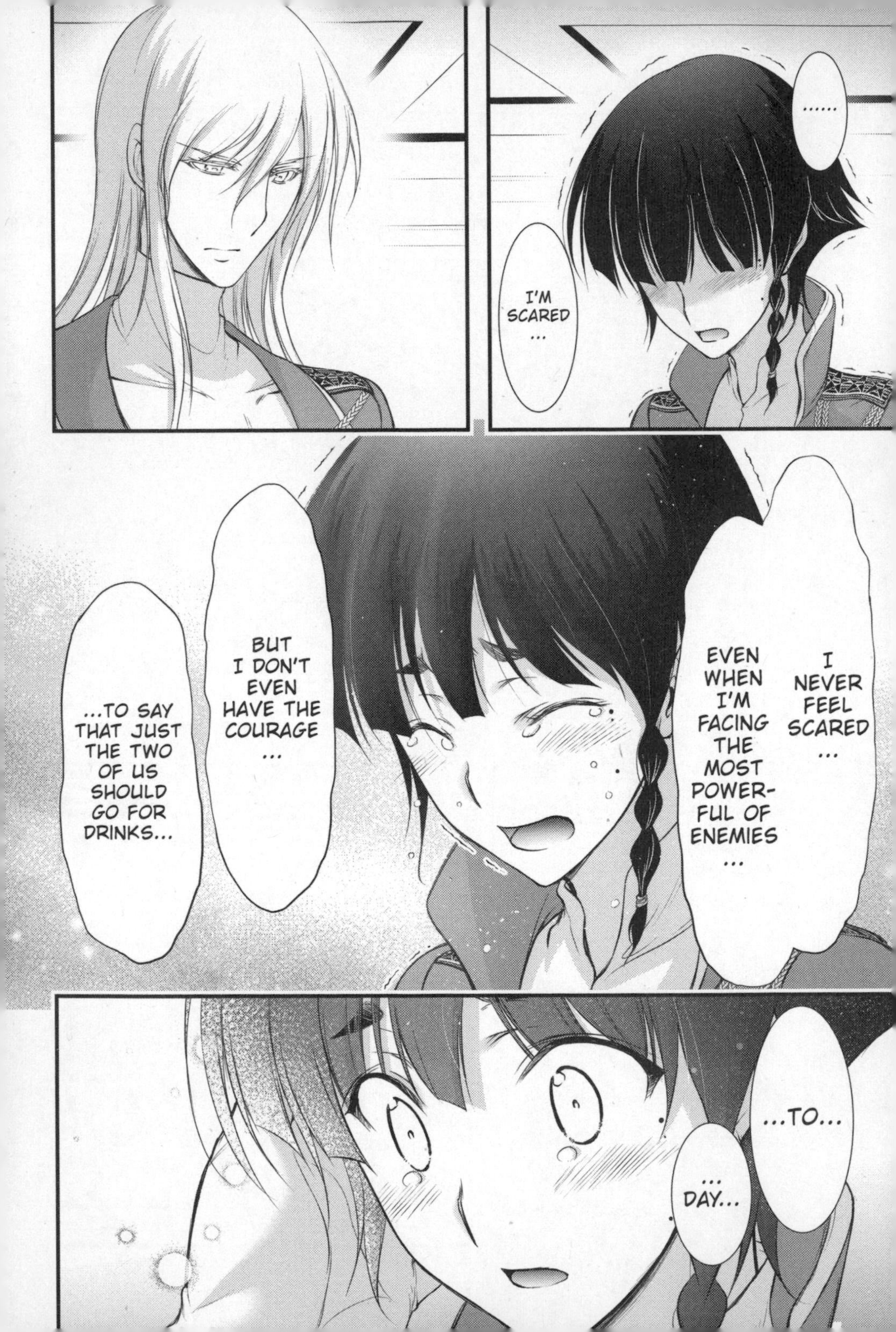
......
I'M SCARED ...
I NEVER FEEL SCARED ...
EVEN WHEN I'M FACING THE MOST POWER-FUL OF ENEMIES ...
BUT I DON'T EVEN HAVE THE COURAGE ...
...TO SAY THAT JUST THE TWO OF US SHOULD GO FOR DRINKS...
...TO...
... DAY...

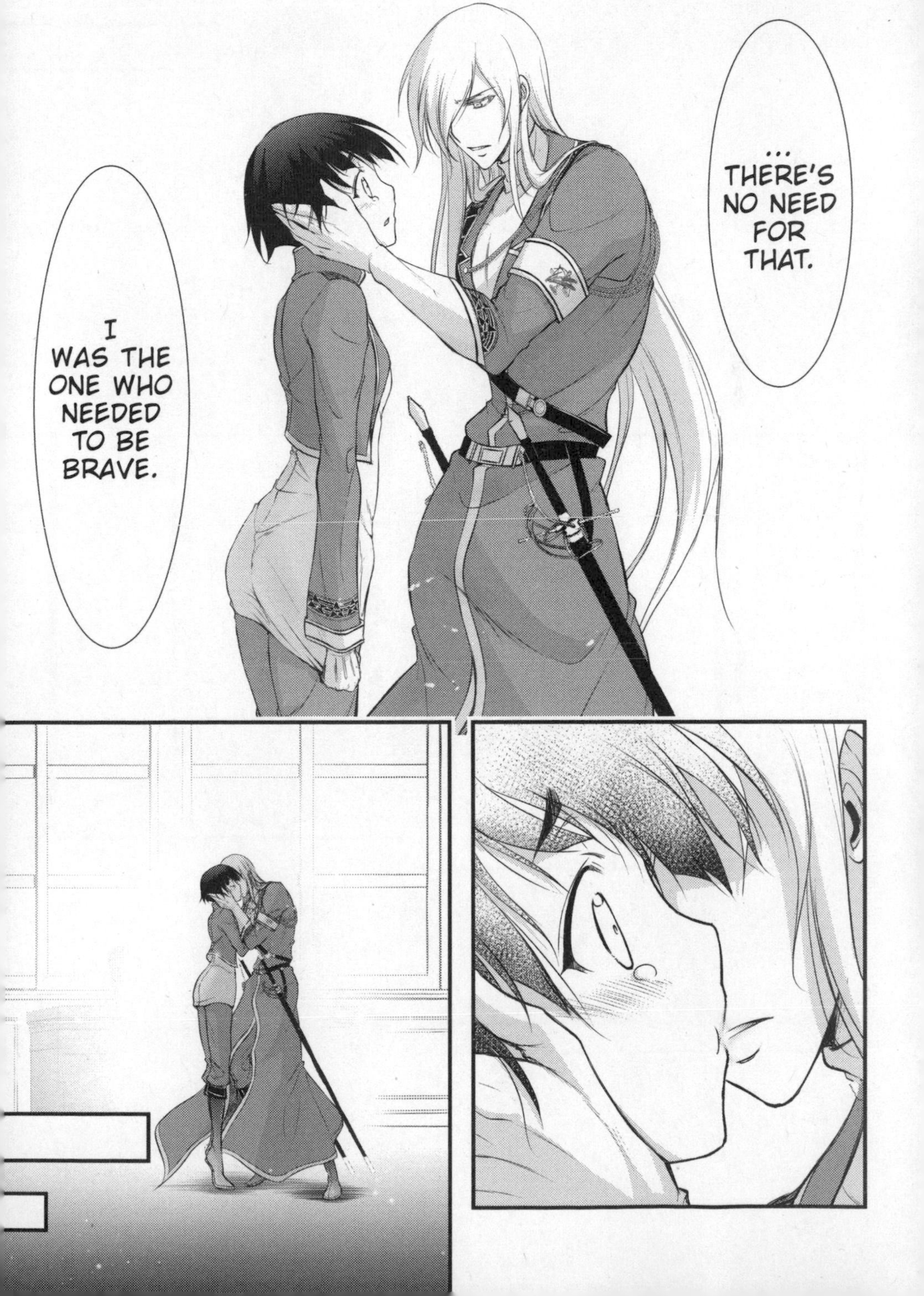
...THERE'S NO NEED FOR THAT.
I WAS THE ONE WHO NEEDED TO BE BRAVE.

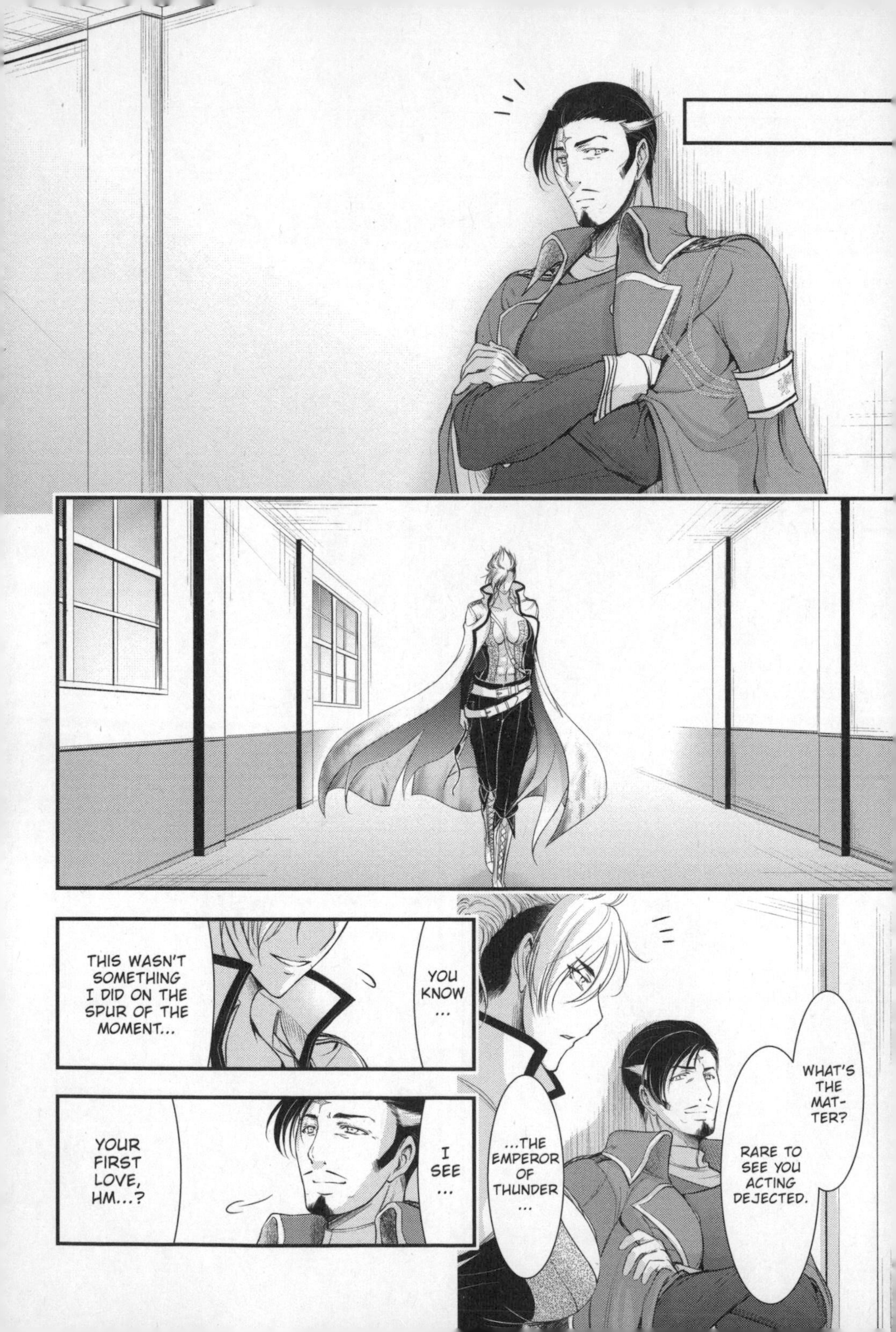
WHAT'S THE MAT-TER?
RARE TO SEE YOU ACTING DEJECTED.
...THE EMPEROR OF THUNDER...
YOU KNOW...
THIS WASN'T SOMETHING I DID ON THE SPUR OF THE MOMENT...
I SEE...
YOUR FIRST LOVE, HM...?

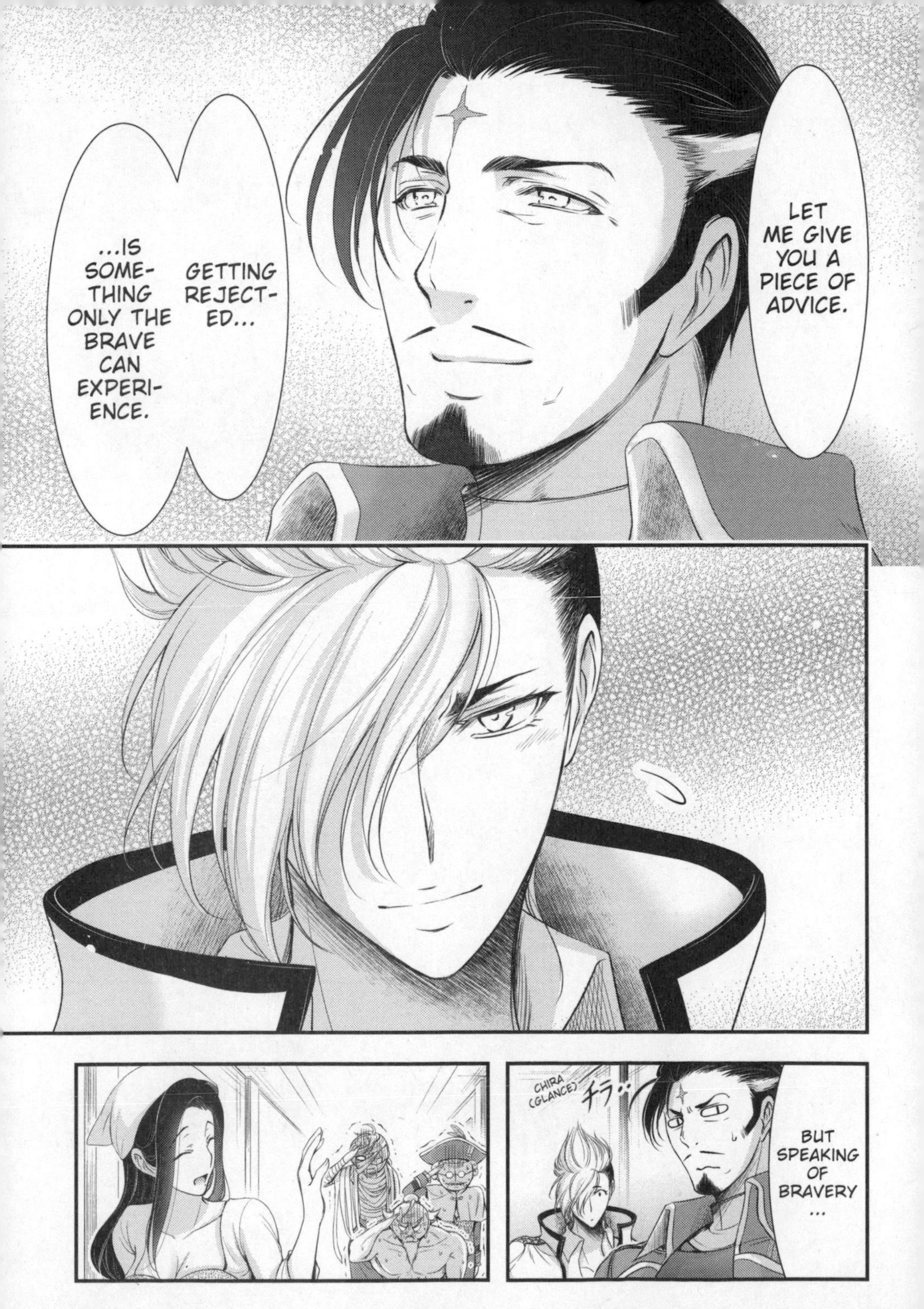
LET ME GIVE YOU A PIECE OF ADVICE.
GETTING REJECT-ED...
...IS SOME-THING ONLY THE BRAVE CAN EXPERI-ENCE.
CHIRA (GLANCE) チラ
BUT SPEAKING OF BRAVERY ...

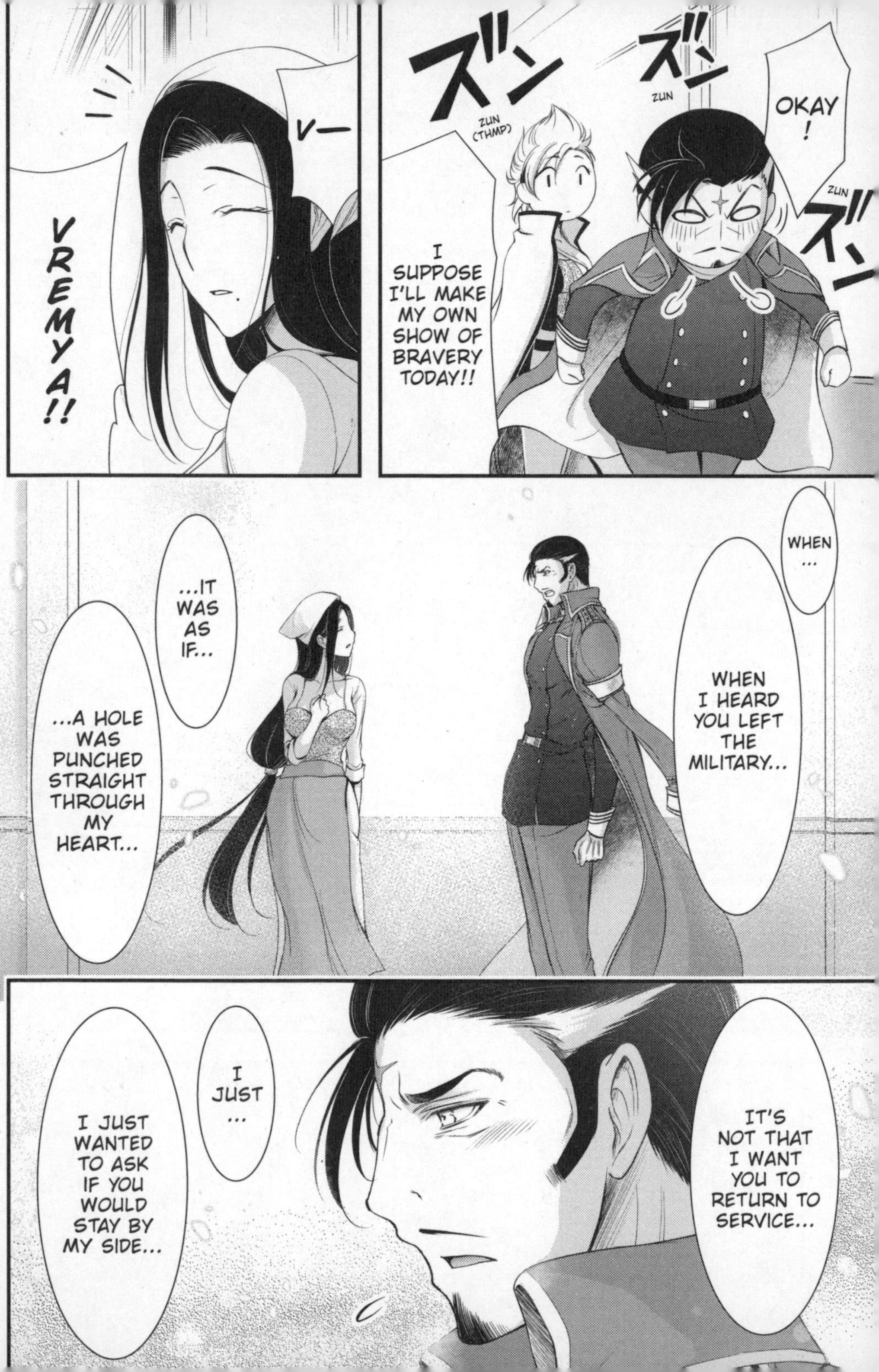
OKAY!
ズン
ZUN
ズン
ZUN
ズン
ZUN (THMP)
I SUPPOSE I'LL MAKE MY OWN SHOW OF BRAVERY TODAY!!
VREMYA!!
WHEN...
WHEN I HEARD YOU LEFT THE MILITARY...
...IT WAS AS IF...
...A HOLE WAS PUNCHED STRAIGHT THROUGH MY HEART...
IT'S NOT THAT I WANT YOU TO RETURN TO SERVICE...
I JUST...
I JUST WANTED TO ASK IF YOU WOULD STAY BY MY SIDE...

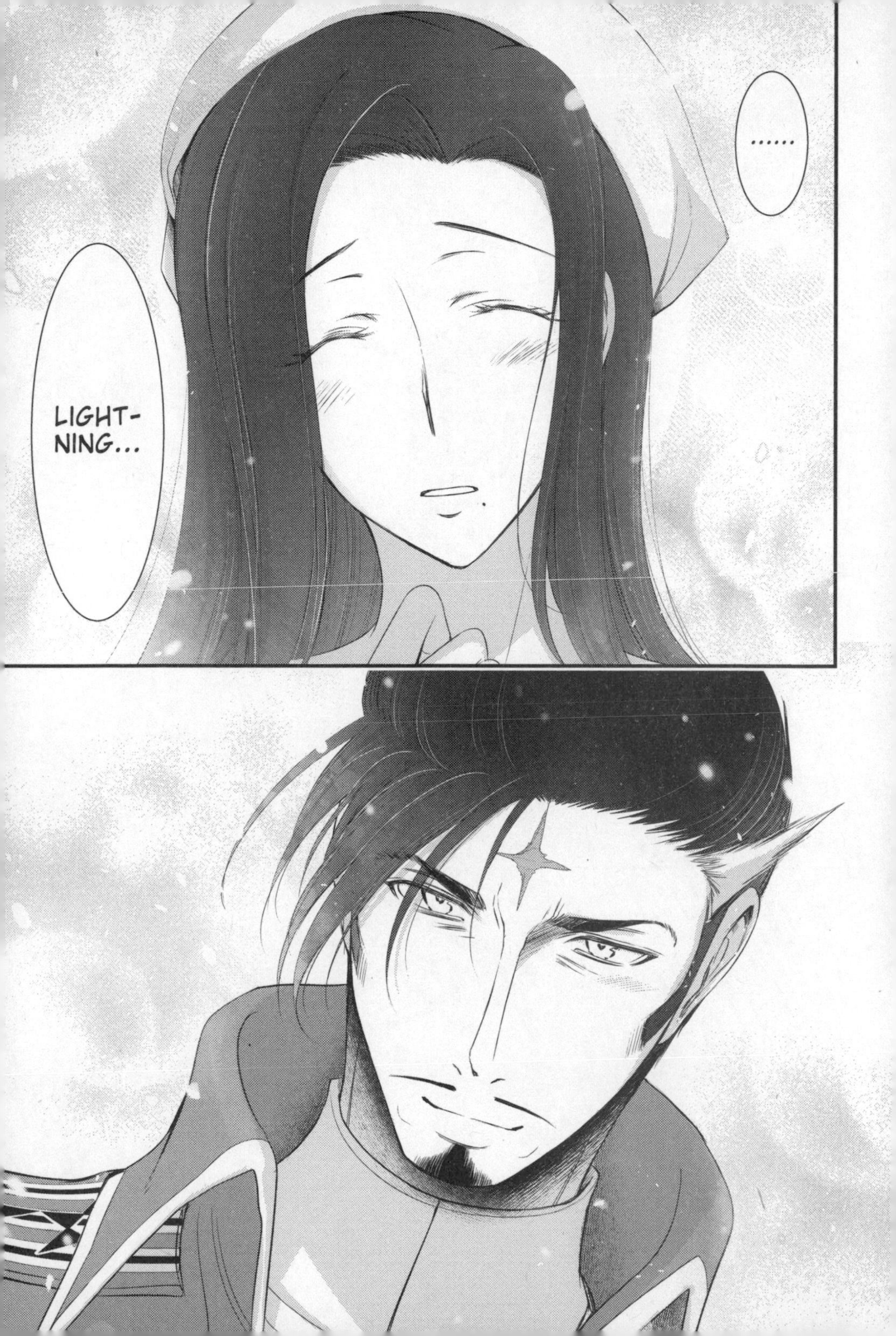
......
LIGHT-NING...

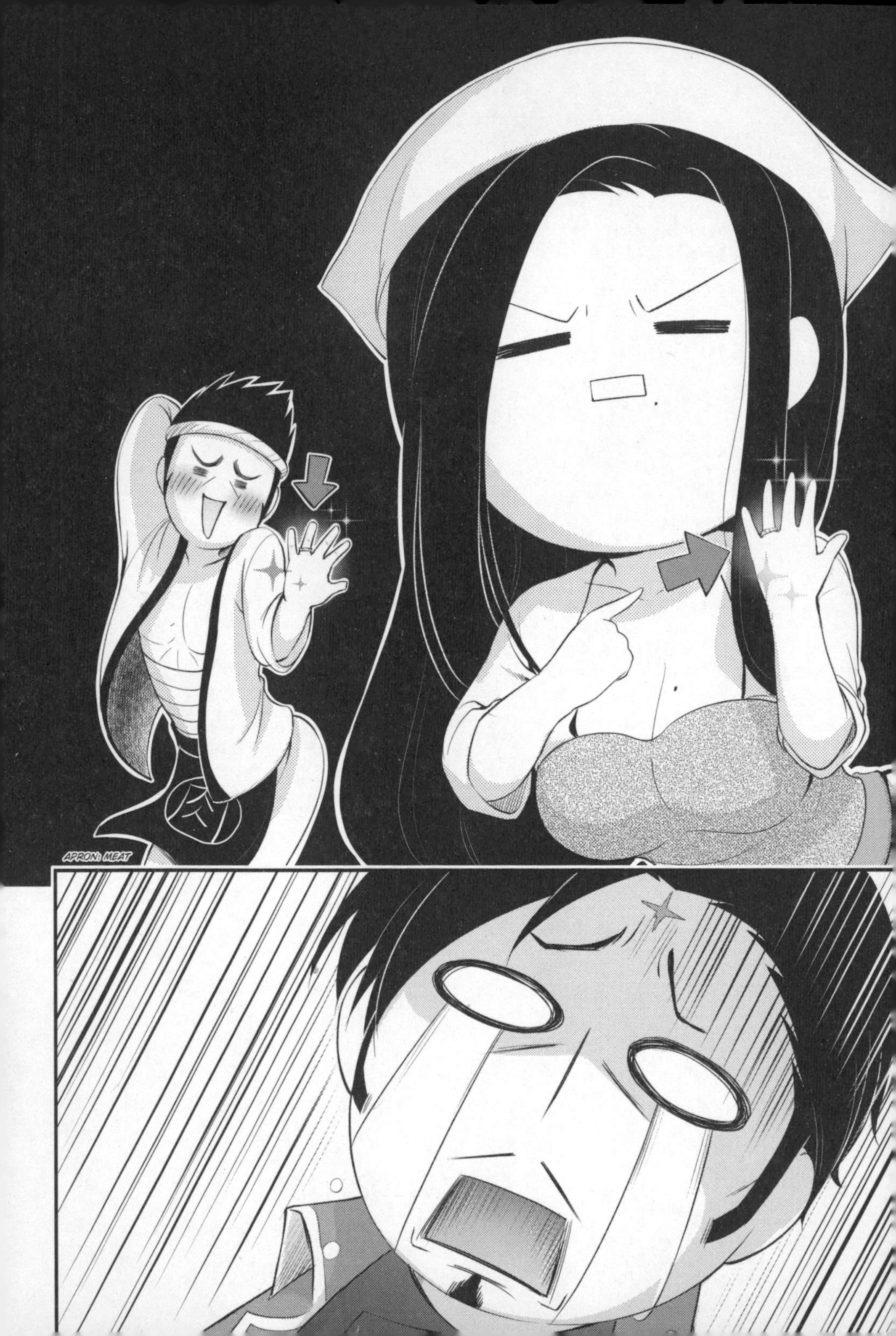
APRON: MEAT

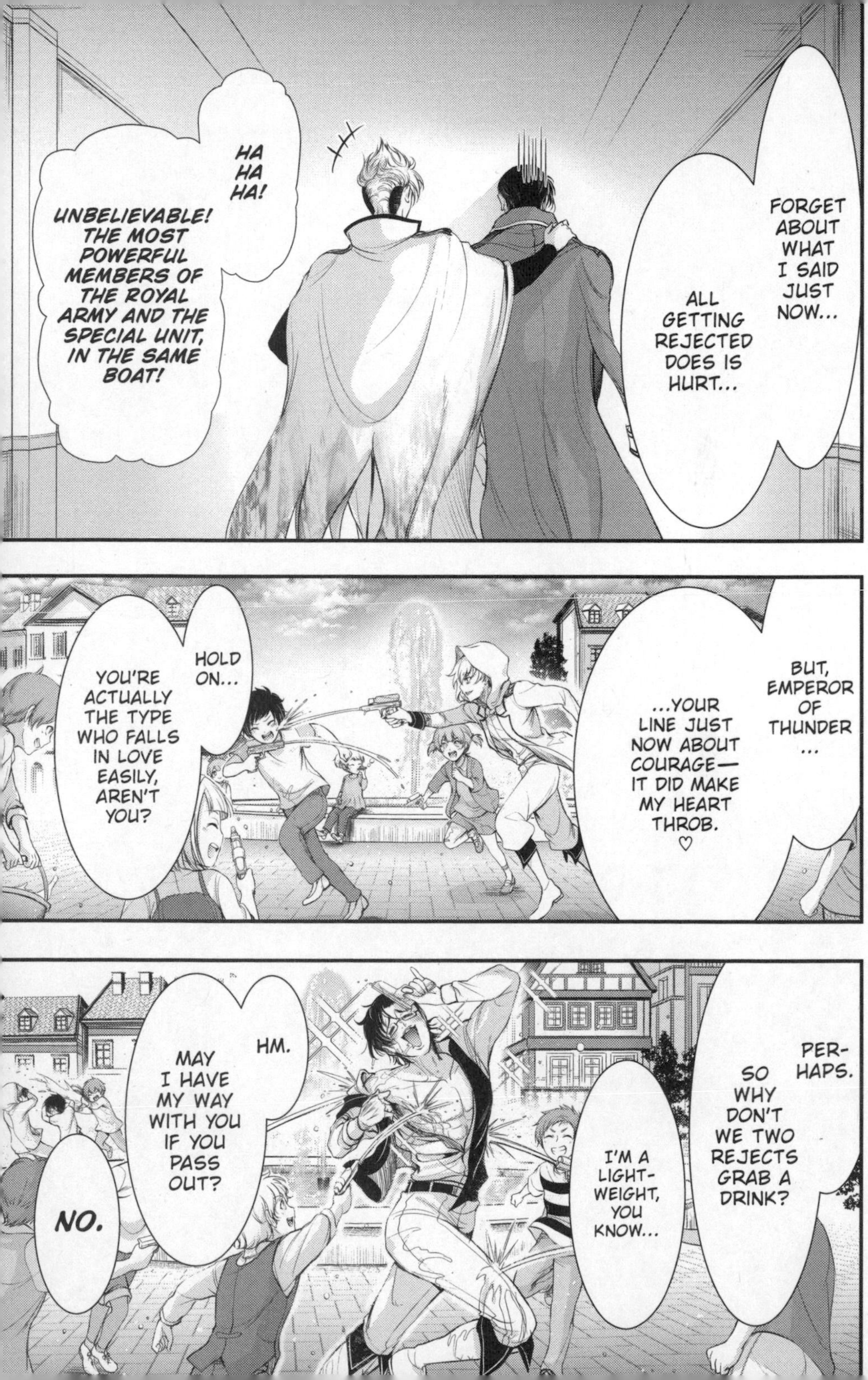
FORGET ABOUT WHAT I SAID JUST NOW...
ALL GETTING REJECTED DOES IS HURT...
HA HA HA!
UNBELIEVABLE! THE MOST POWERFUL MEMBERS OF THE ROYAL ARMY AND THE SPECIAL UNIT, IN THE SAME BOAT!
BUT, EMPEROR OF THUNDER...
...YOUR LINE JUST NOW ABOUT COURAGE—IT DID MAKE MY HEART THROB. ♡
HOLD ON...
YOU'RE ACTUALLY THE TYPE WHO FALLS IN LOVE EASILY, AREN'T YOU?
PER-HAPS.
SO WHY DON'T WE TWO REJECTS GRAB A DRINK?
I'M A LIGHT-WEIGHT, YOU KNOW...
HM.
MAY I HAVE MY WAY WITH YOU IF YOU PASS OUT?
NO.

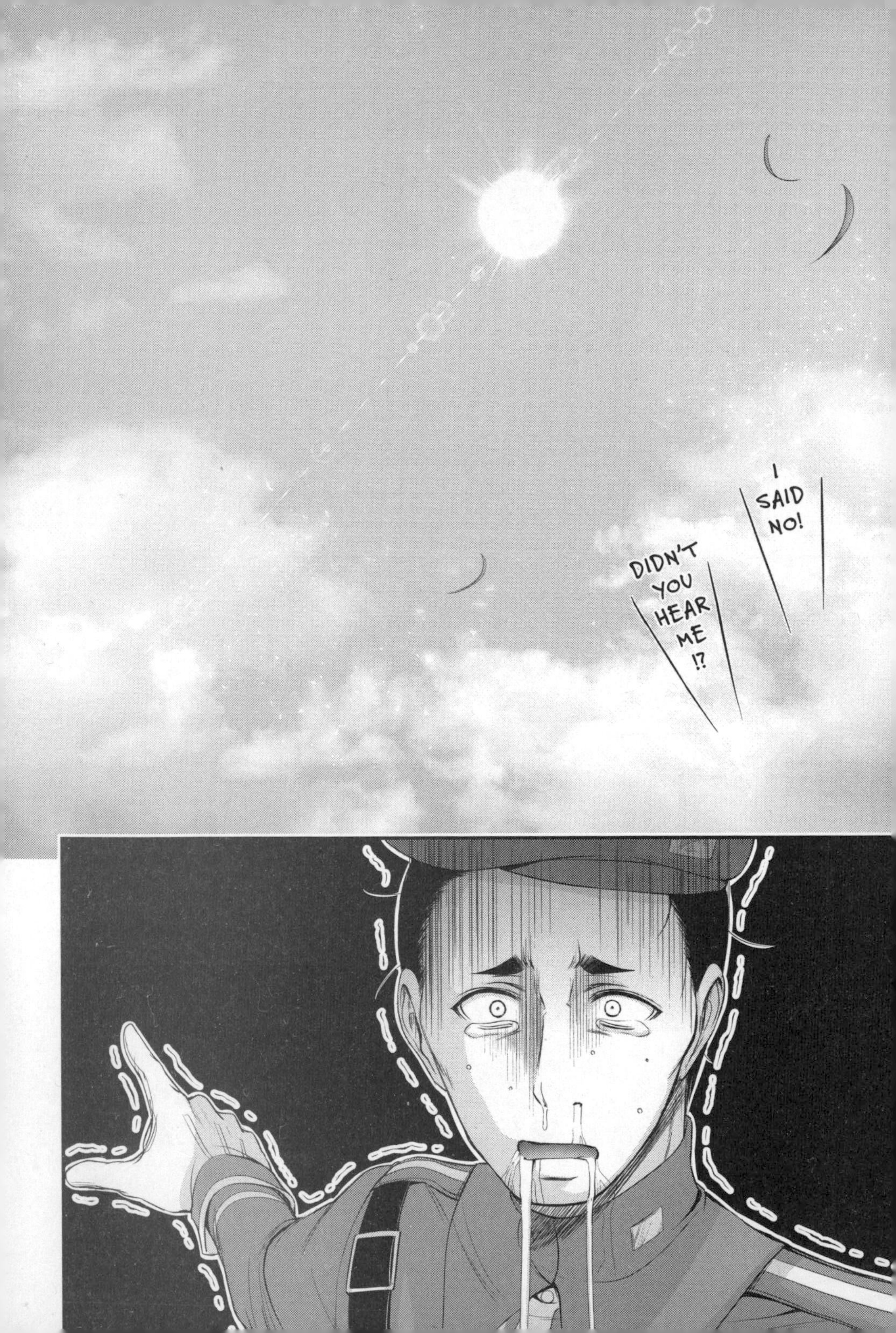
I SAID NO!
DIDN'T YOU HEAR ME!?

CHAPTER 82: A PEACEFUL, HAPPY, DULL WORLD

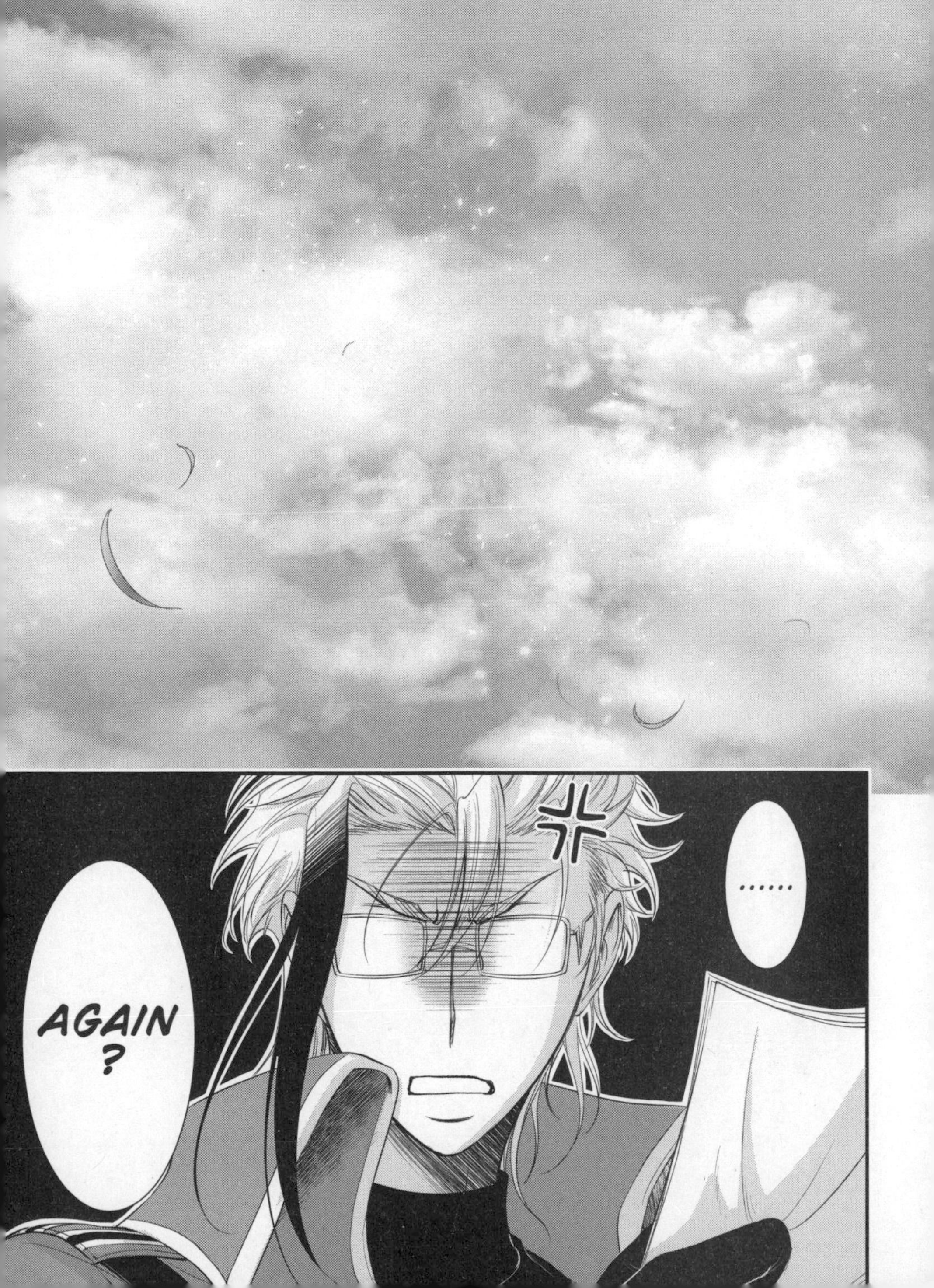

......
AGAIN?

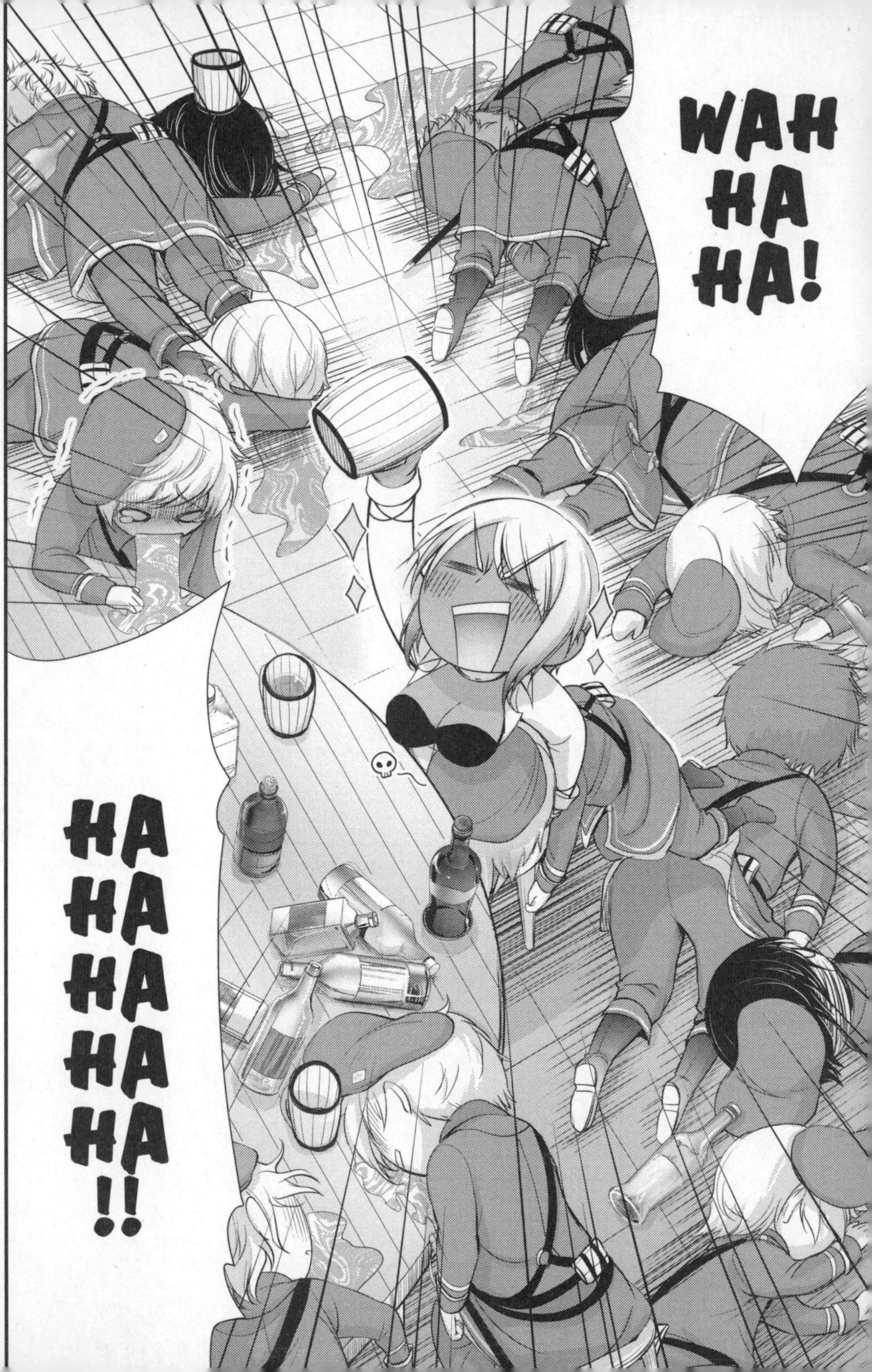
WAH HA HA HA!
HA HA HA HA HA HA HA!!

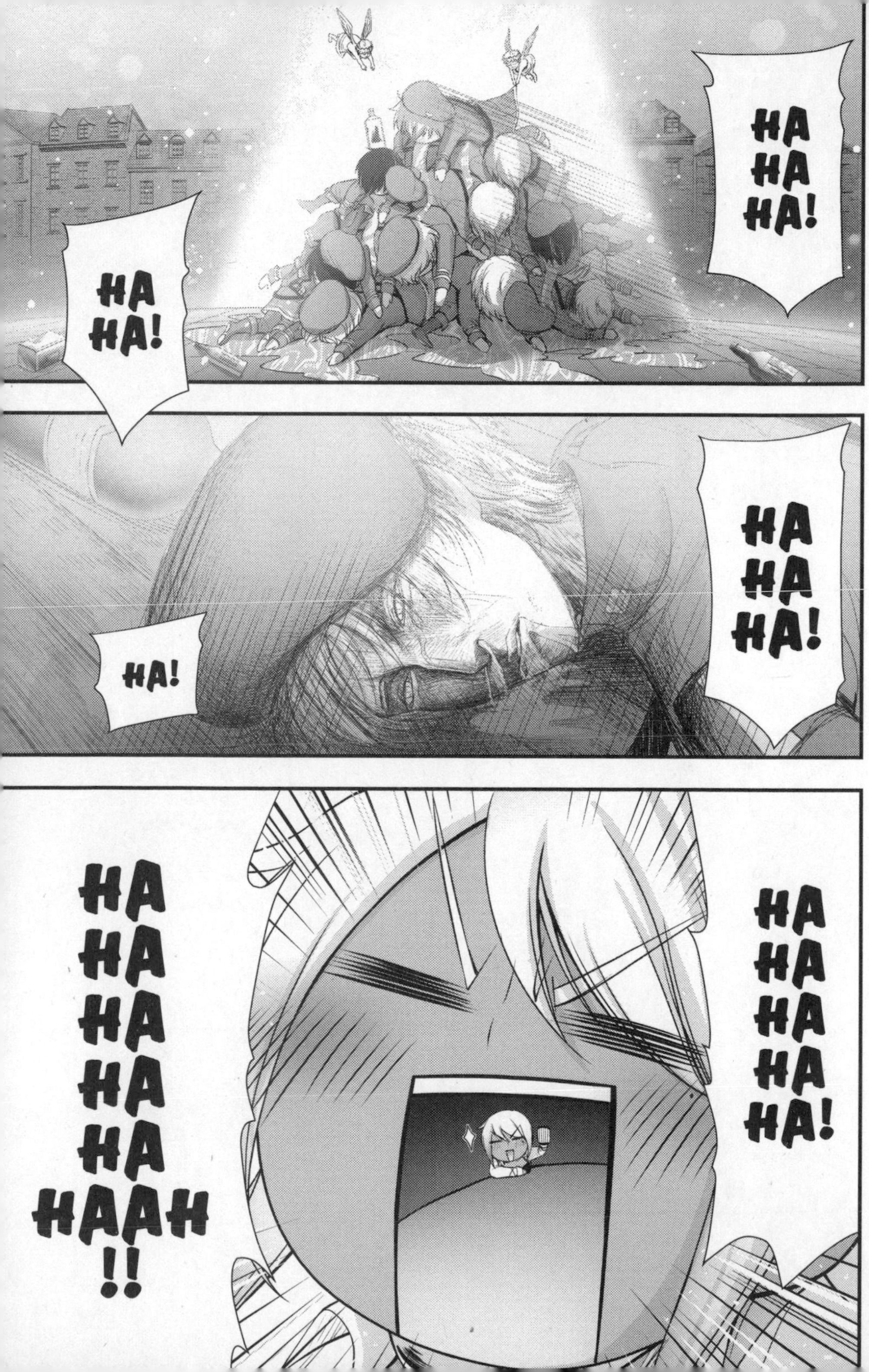
HA HA HA!
HA HA!
HA HA HA!
HA!
HA HA HA HA HA!
HA HA HA HA HA HAAH!!

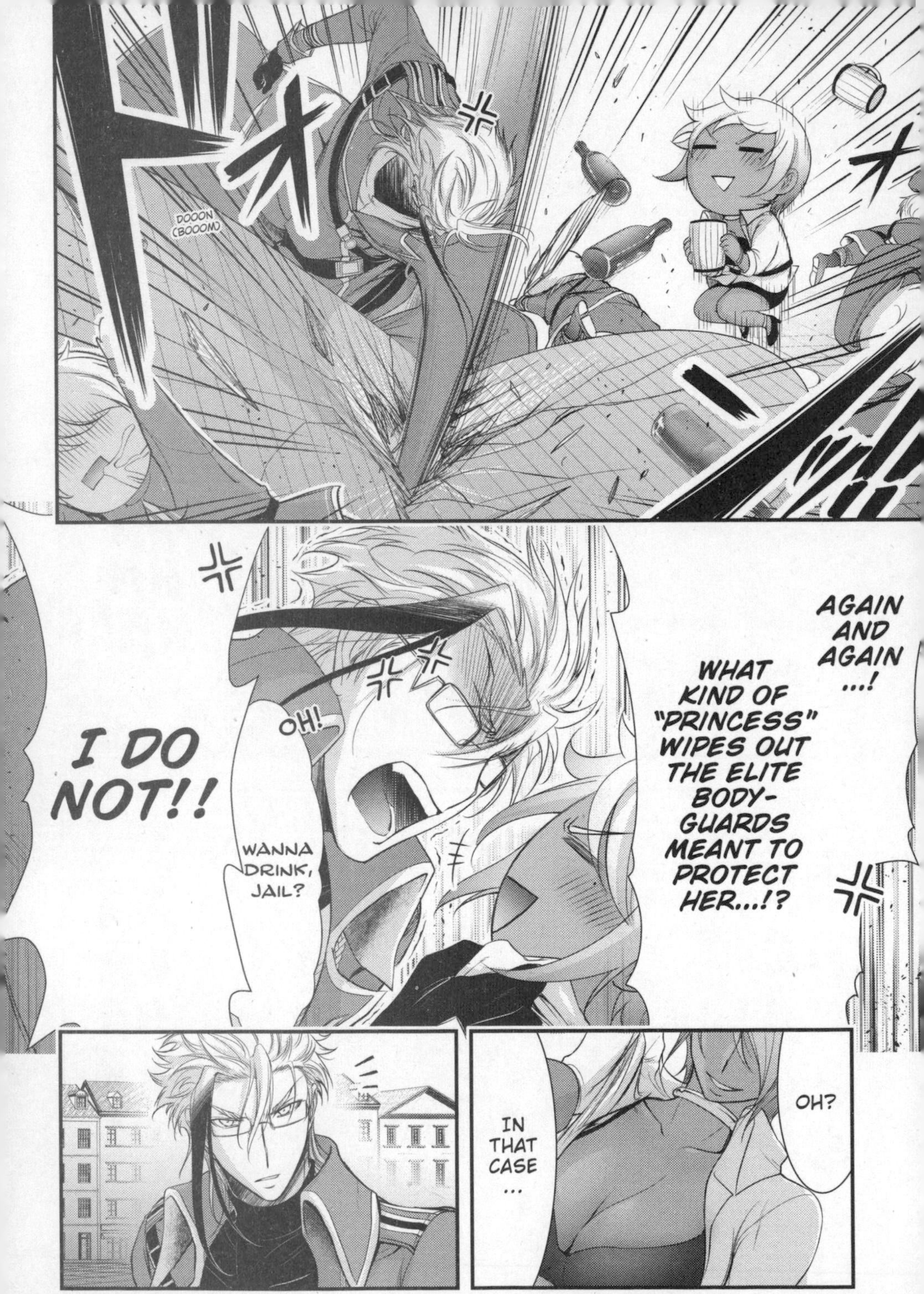
DOOON
(BOOOM)
AGAIN AND AGAIN ...!
WHAT KIND OF "PRINCESS" WIPES OUT THE ELITE BODY-GUARDS MEANT TO PROTECT HER...!?
OH!
WANNA DRINK, JAIL?
I DO NOT!!
OH?
IN THAT CASE ...

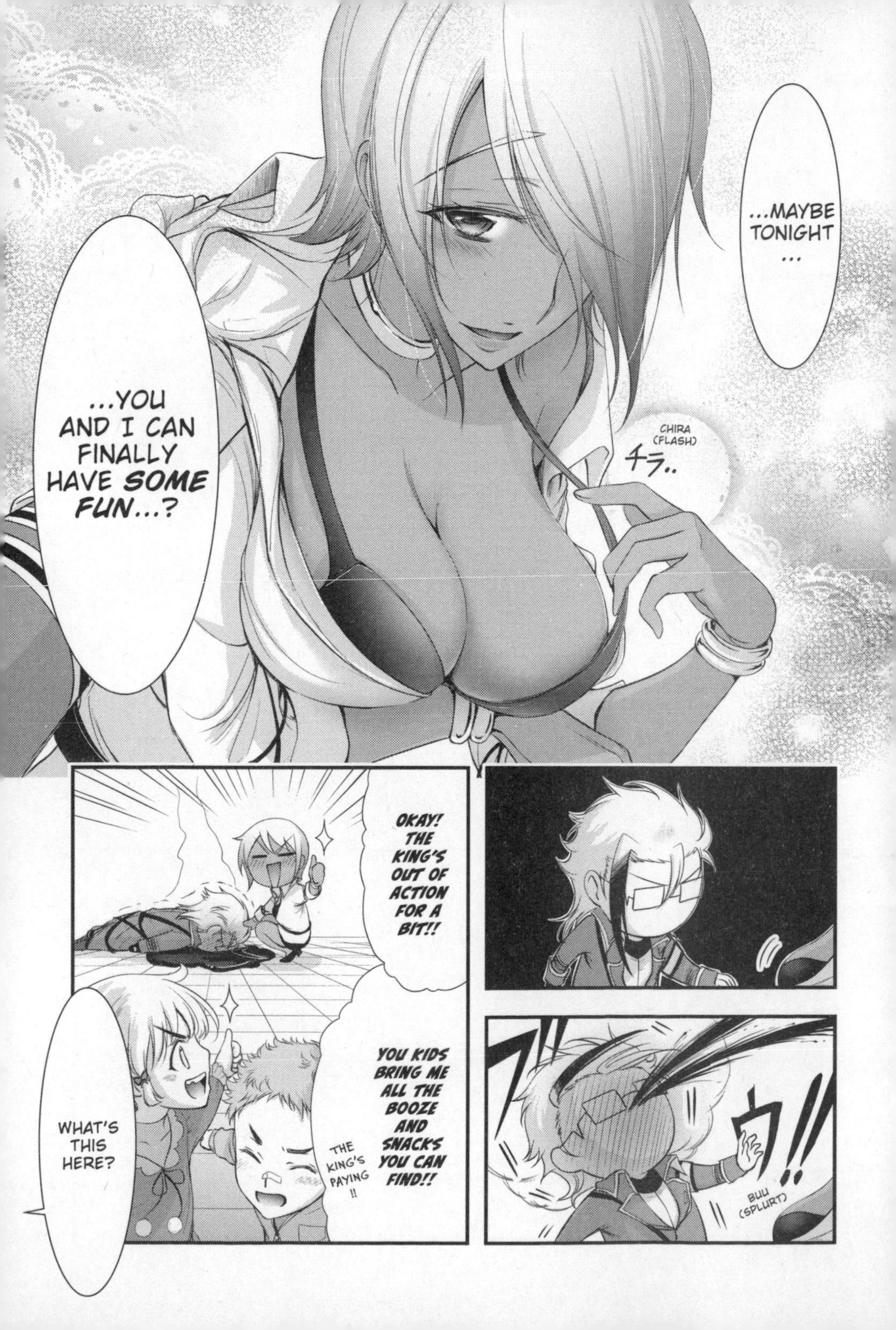
...MAYBE TONIGHT ...
...YOU AND I CAN FINALLY HAVE **SOME FUN**...?
CHIRA (FLASH)
チラ..
OKAY! THE KING'S OUT OF ACTION FOR A BIT!!
ブウ!!
BUU (SPLURT)
YOU KIDS BRING ME ALL THE BOOZE AND SNACKS YOU CAN FIND!!
THE KING'S PAYING !!
WHAT'S THIS HERE?

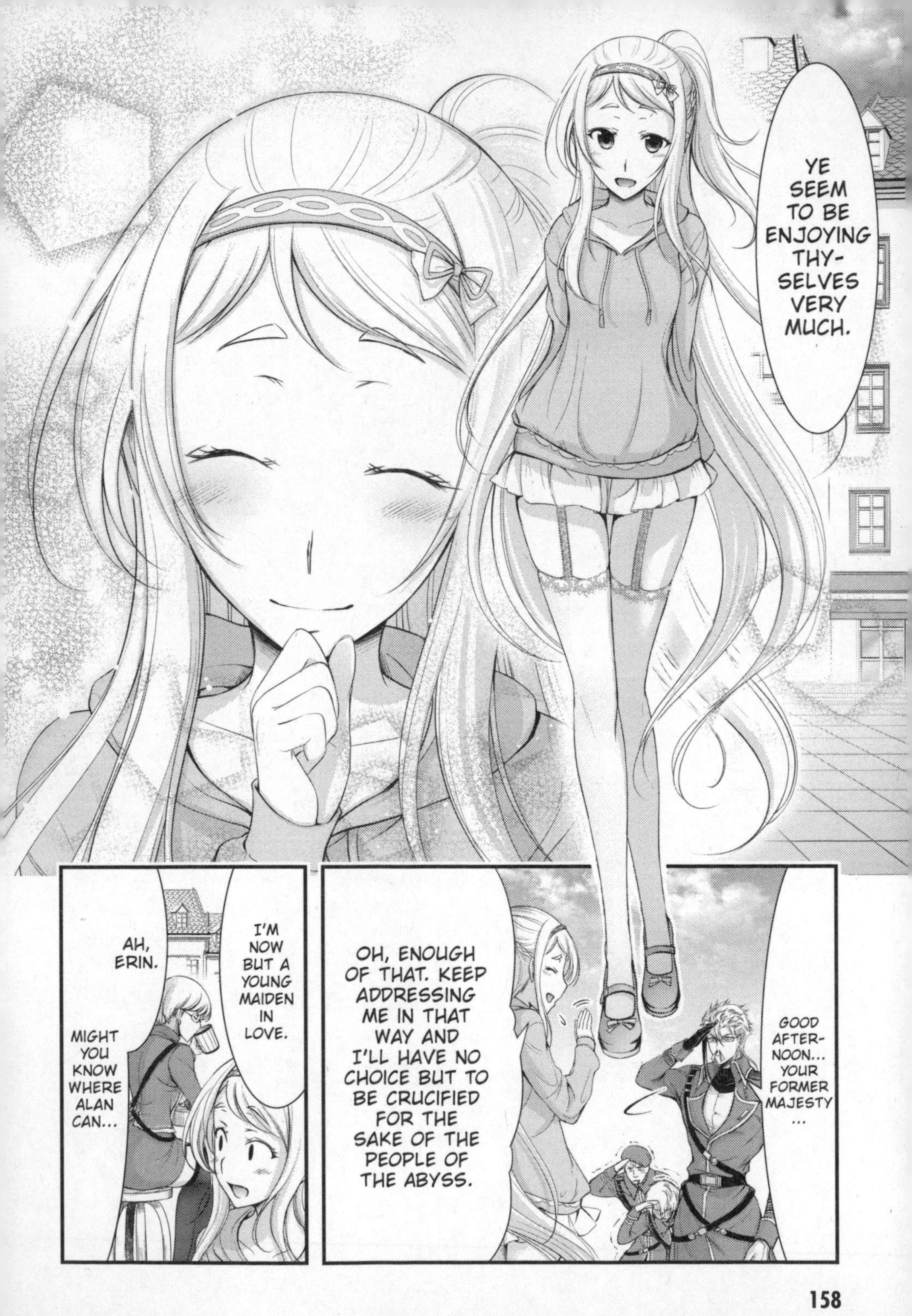
YE SEEM TO BE ENJOYING THY-SELVES VERY MUCH.
GOOD AFTER-NOON... YOUR FORMER MAJESTY ...
OH, ENOUGH OF THAT. KEEP ADDRESSING ME IN THAT WAY AND I'LL HAVE NO CHOICE BUT TO BE CRUCIFIED FOR THE SAKE OF THE PEOPLE OF THE ABYSS.
I'M NOW BUT A YOUNG MAIDEN IN LOVE.
AH, ERIN.
MIGHT YOU KNOW WHERE ALAN CAN...

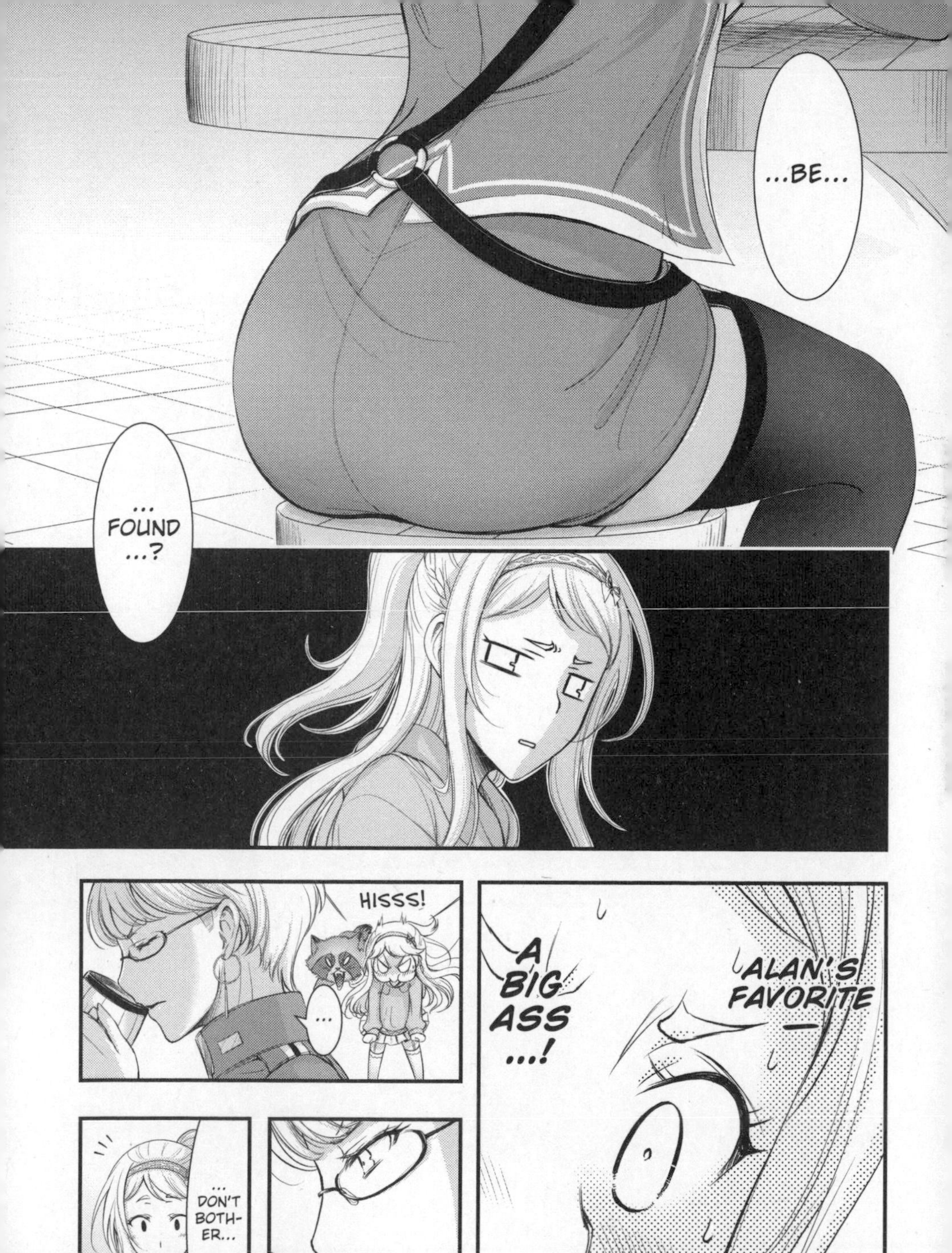
...BE...
...FOUND...?
ALAN'S FAVORITE—
A BIG ASS...!
HISSS!
...
...DON'T BOTHER...

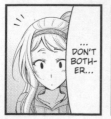

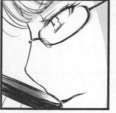

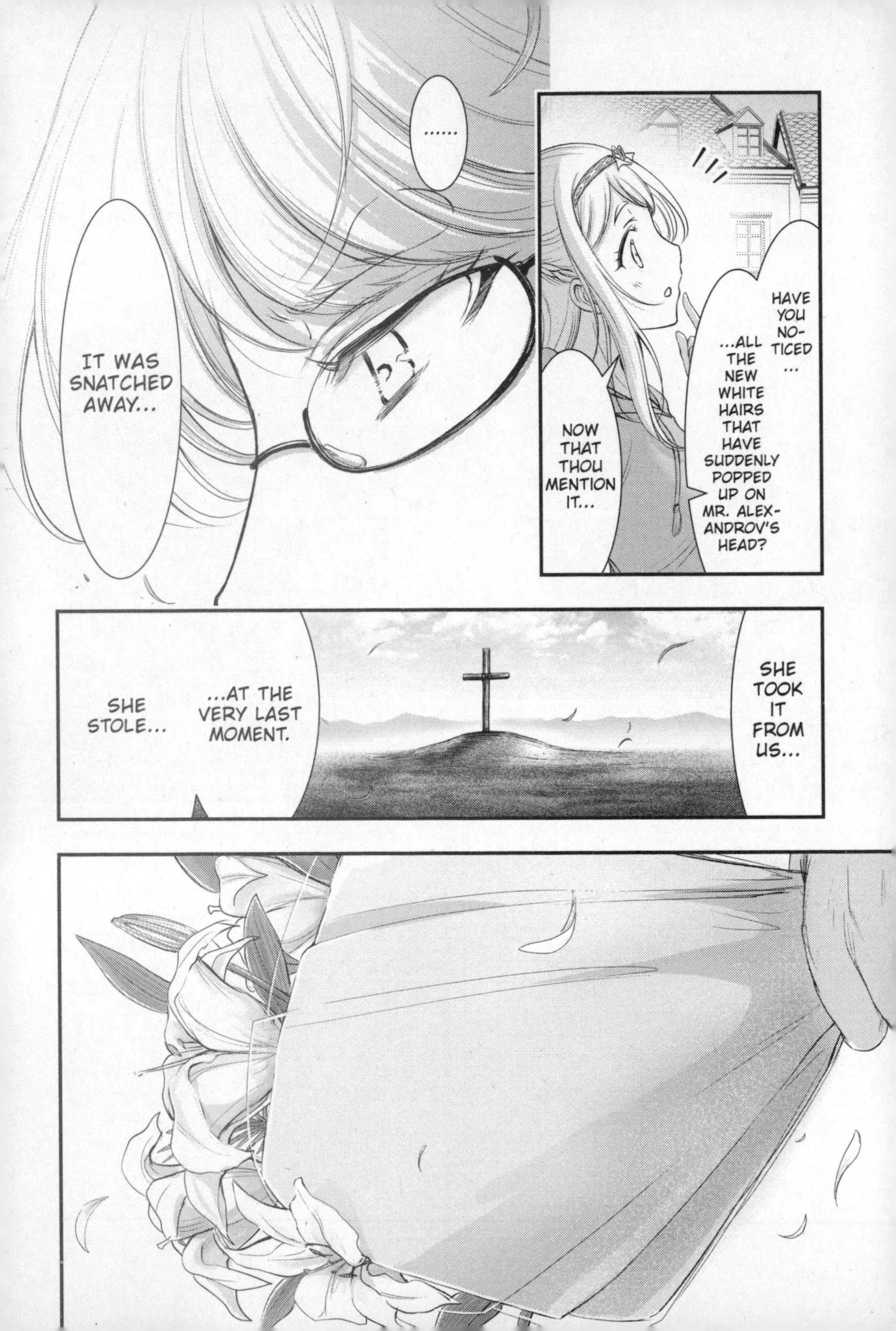
HAVE YOU NO-TICED...
...ALL THE NEW WHITE HAIRS THAT HAVE SUDDENLY POPPED UP ON MR. ALEX-ANDROV'S HEAD?
NOW THAT THOU MENTION IT...
......
IT WAS SNATCHED AWAY...
SHE TOOK IT FROM US...
...AT THE VERY LAST MOMENT.
SHE STOLE...

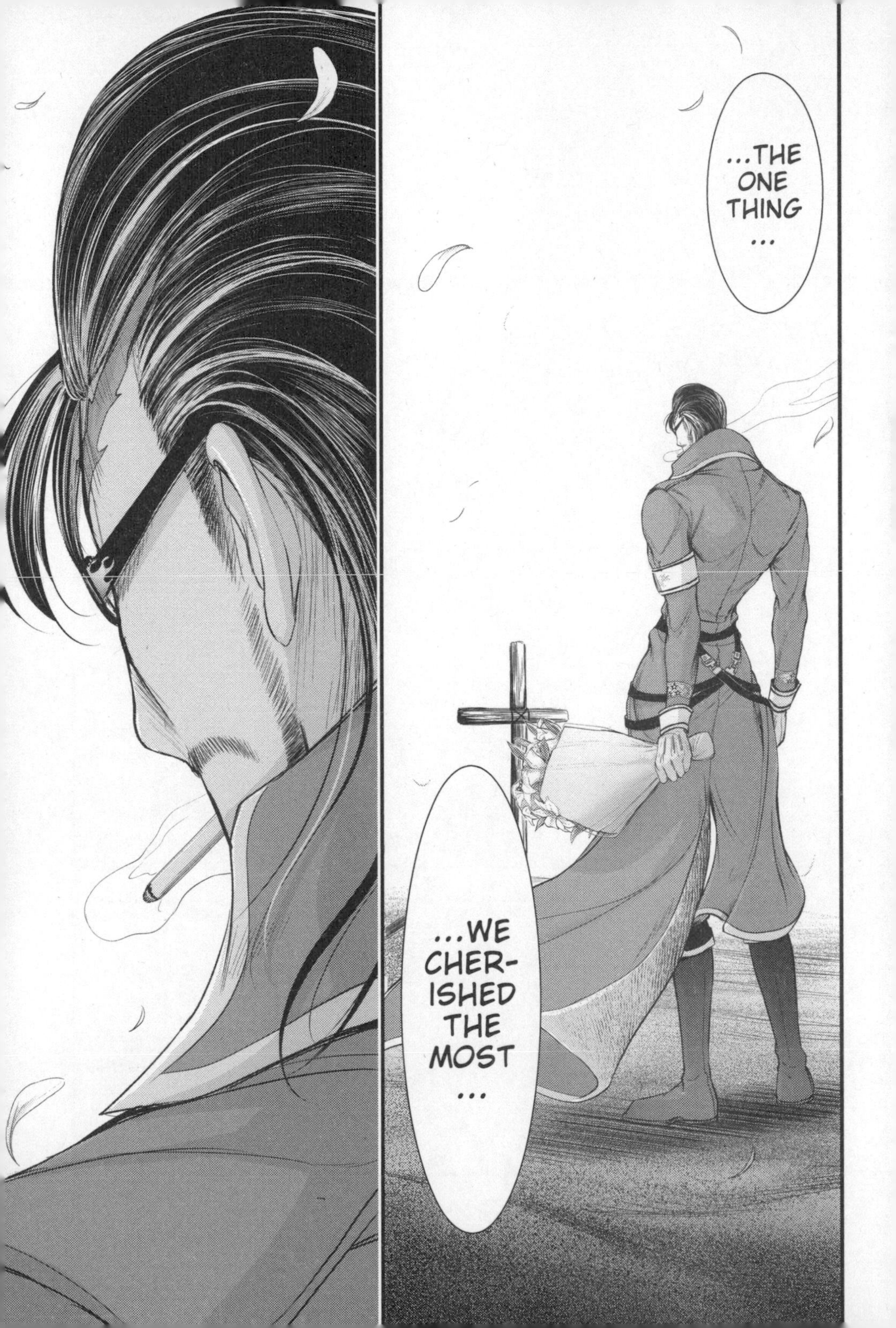
...THE ONE THING ...
...WE CHER-ISHED THE MOST ...

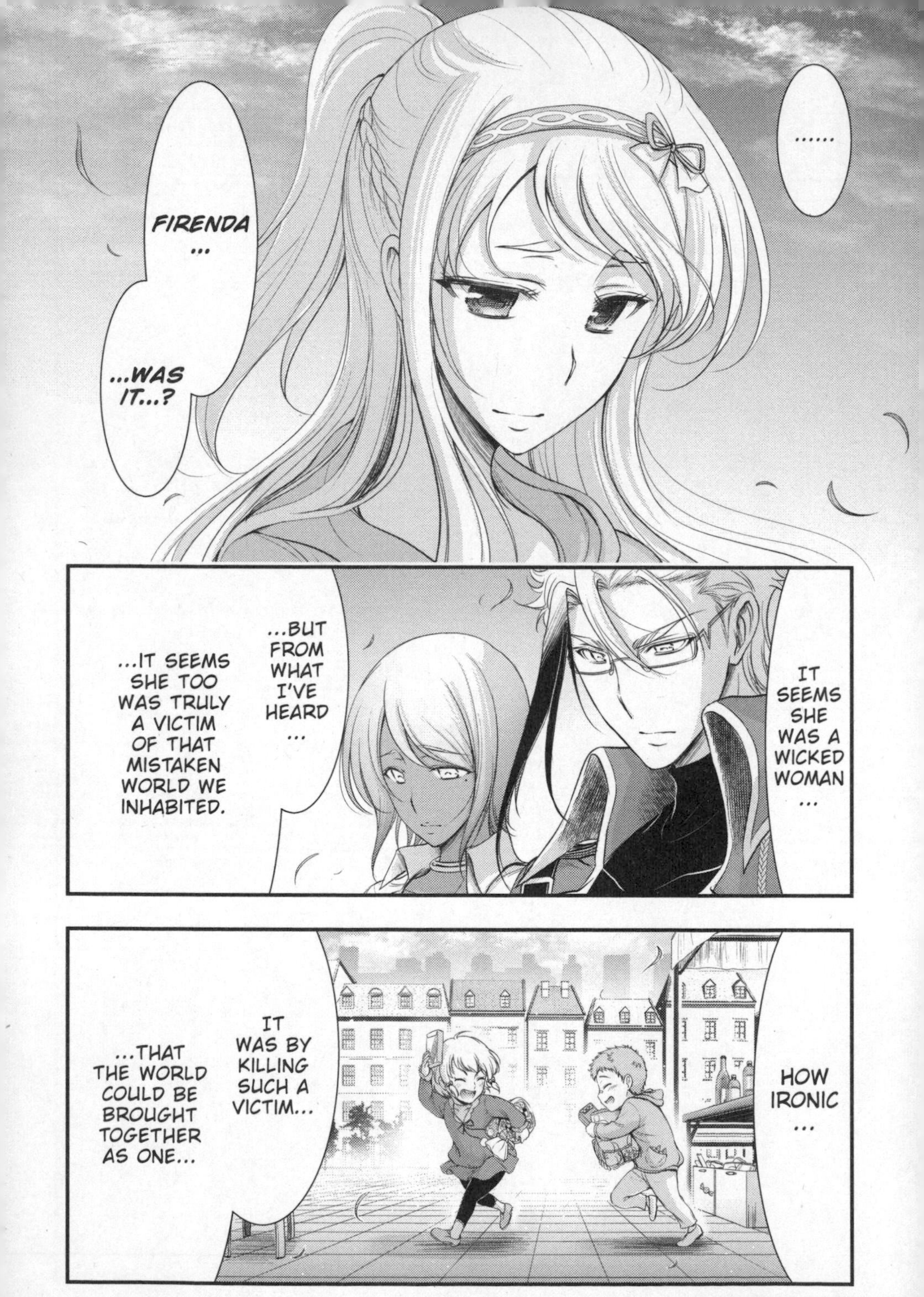
......
FIRENDA...
...WAS IT...?
IT SEEMS SHE WAS A WICKED WOMAN...
...BUT FROM WHAT I'VE HEARD...
...IT SEEMS SHE TOO WAS TRULY A VICTIM OF THAT MISTAKEN WORLD WE INHABITED.
HOW IRONIC...
IT WAS BY KILLING SUCH A VICTIM...
...THAT THE WORLD COULD BE BROUGHT TOGETHER AS ONE...

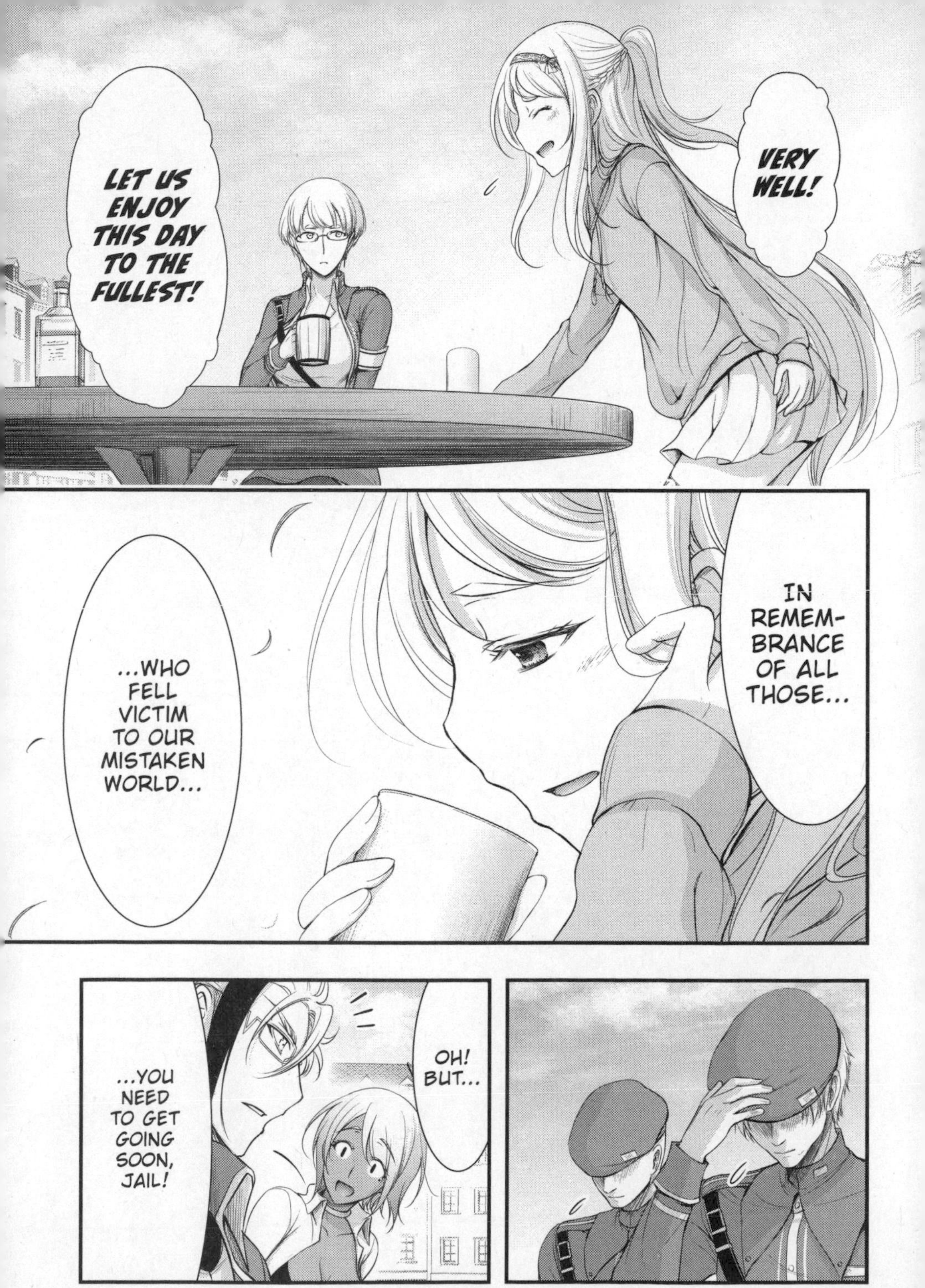
VERY WELL!
LET US ENJOY THIS DAY TO THE FULLEST!
IN REMEMBRANCE OF ALL THOSE...
...WHO FELL VICTIM TO OUR MISTAKEN WORLD...
OH! BUT...
...YOU NEED TO GET GOING SOON, JAIL!

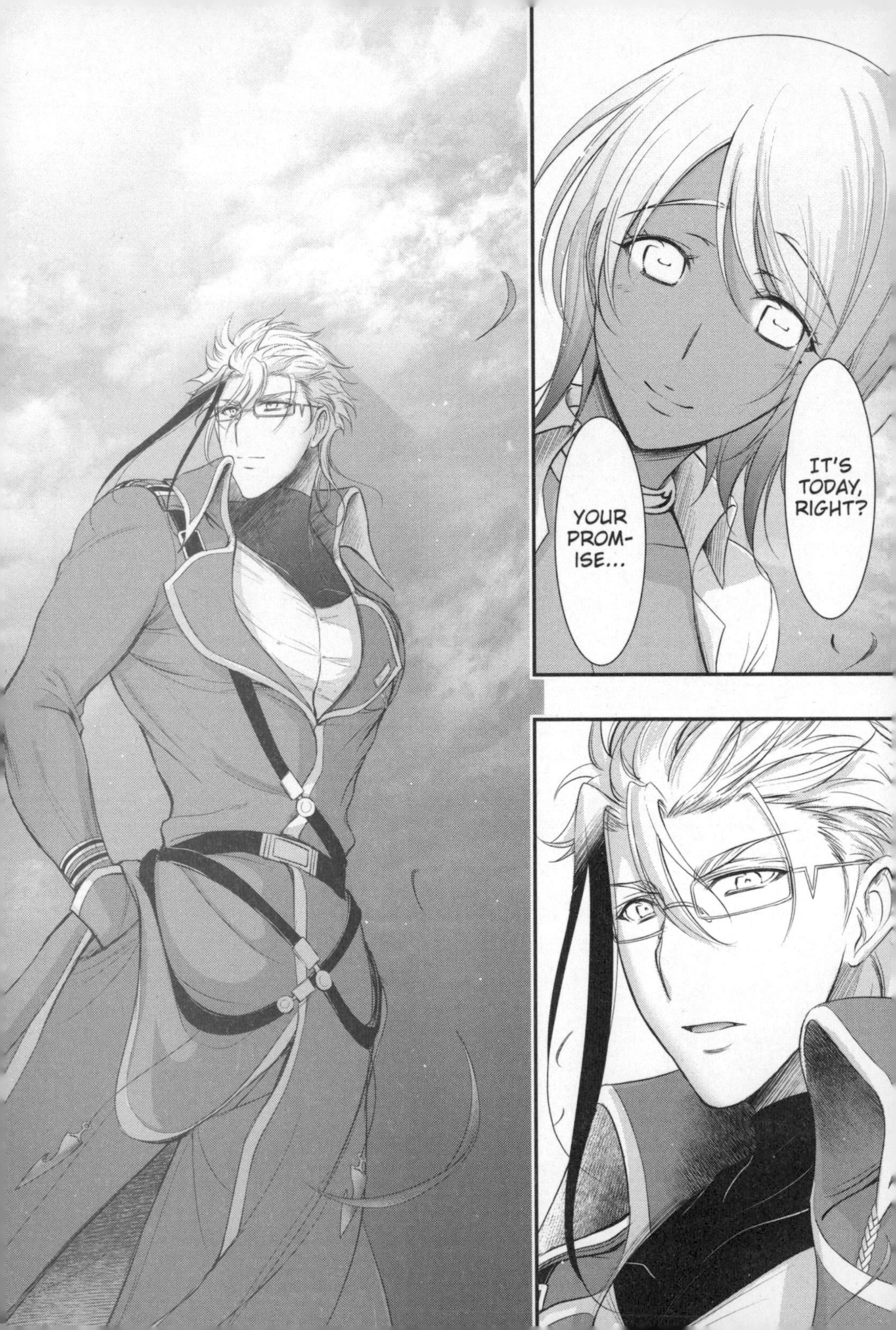
IT'S TODAY, RIGHT?
YOUR PROMISE…

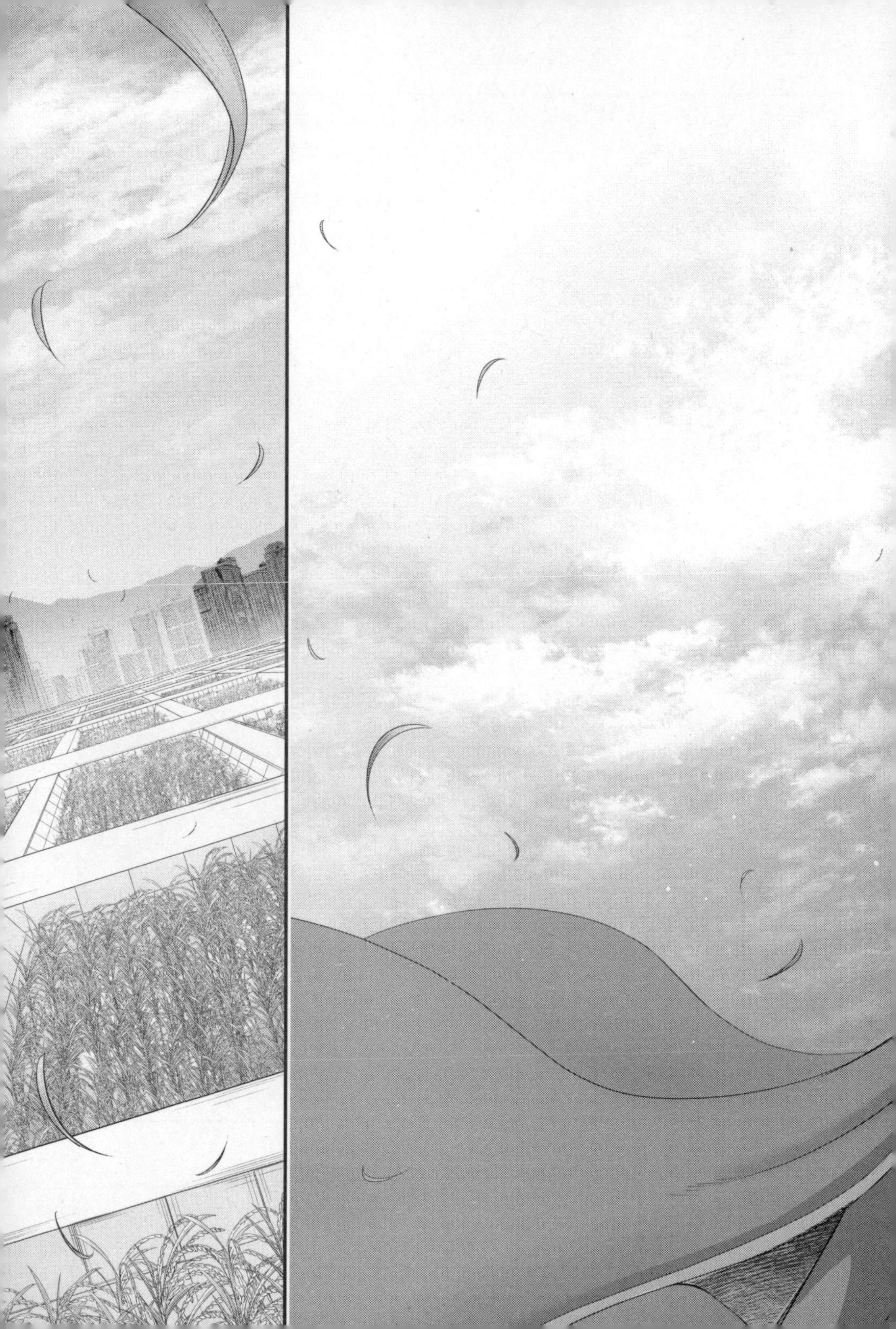

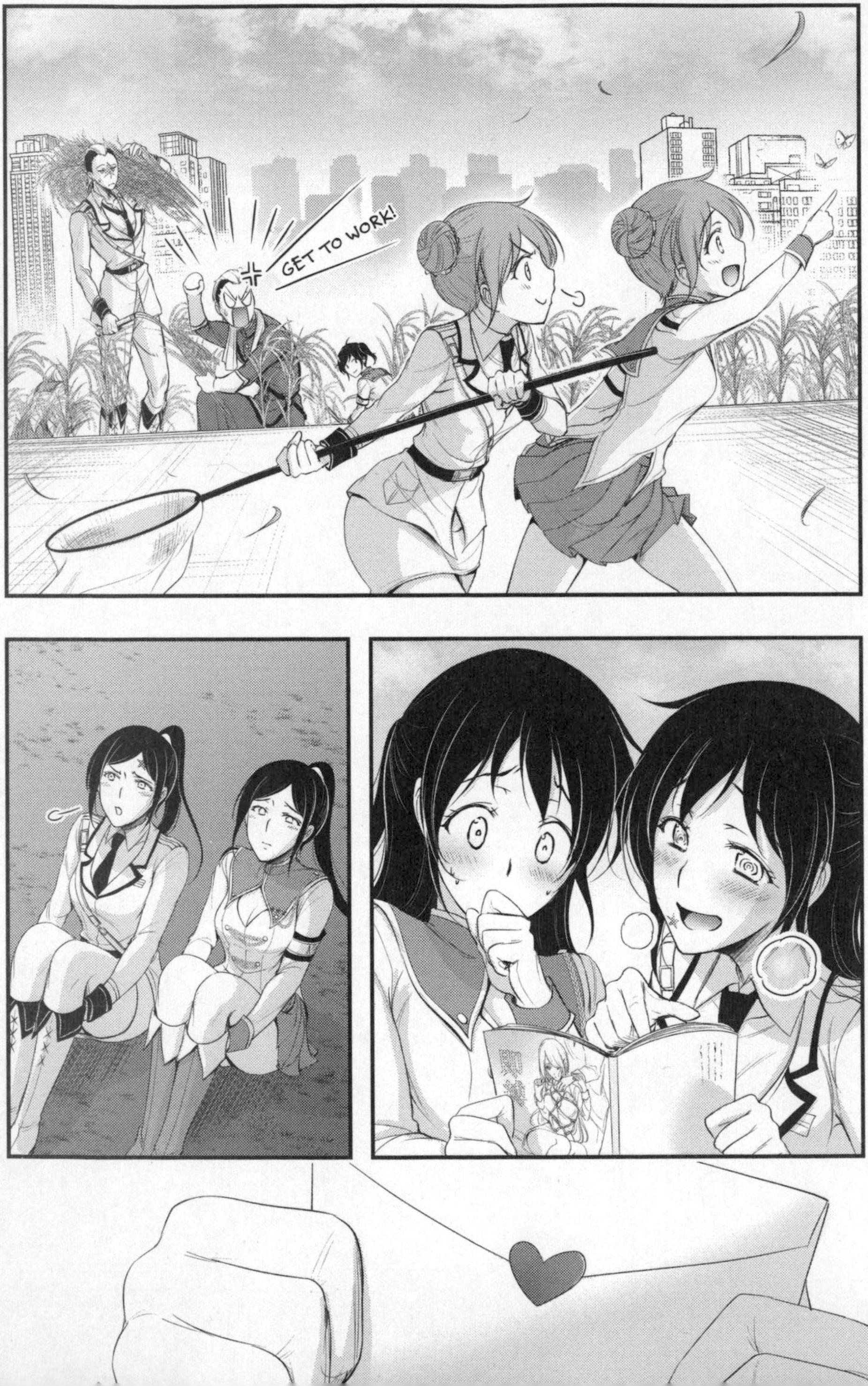
GET TO WORK!

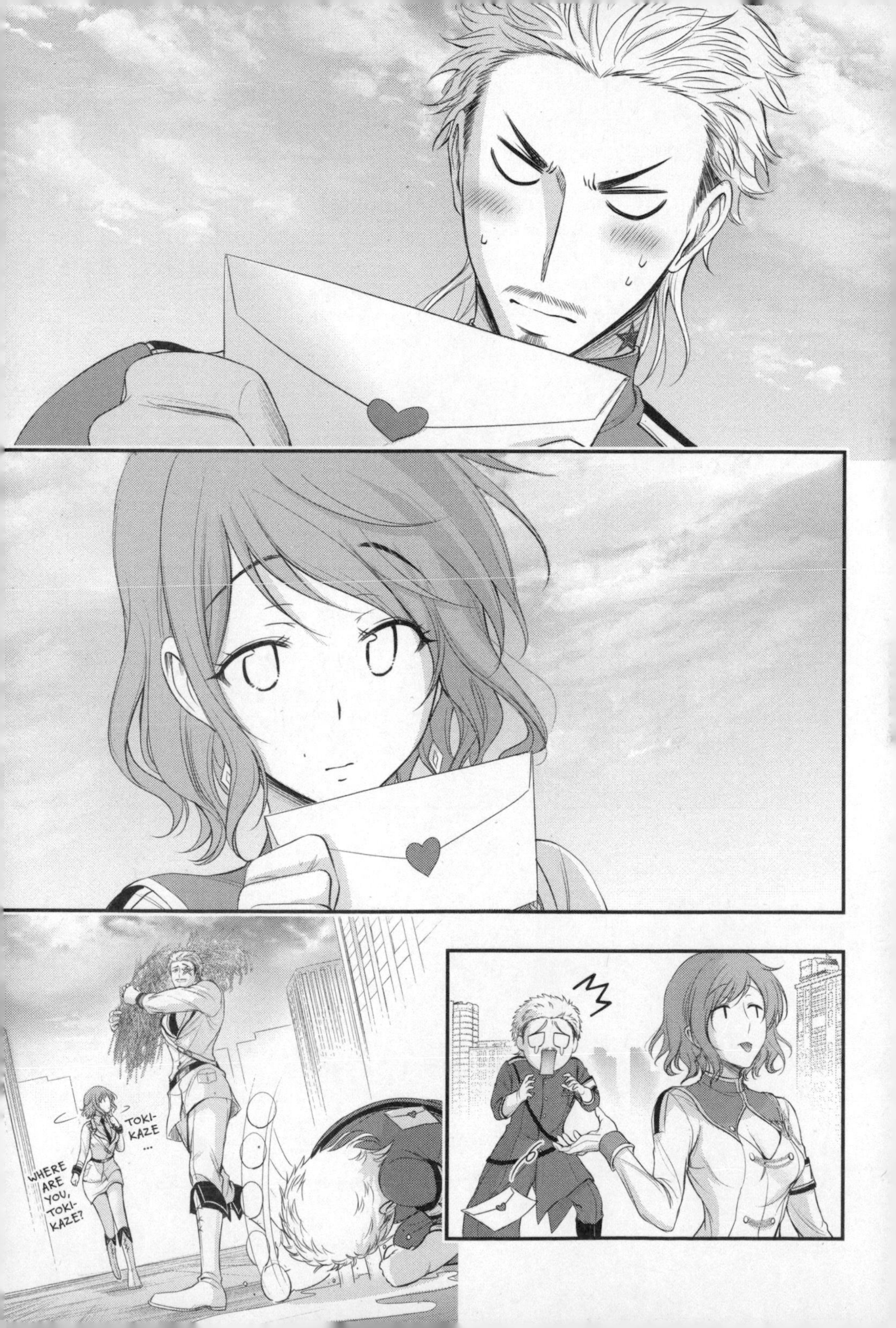
TOKI-KAZE ...
WHERE ARE YOU, TOKI-KAZE?

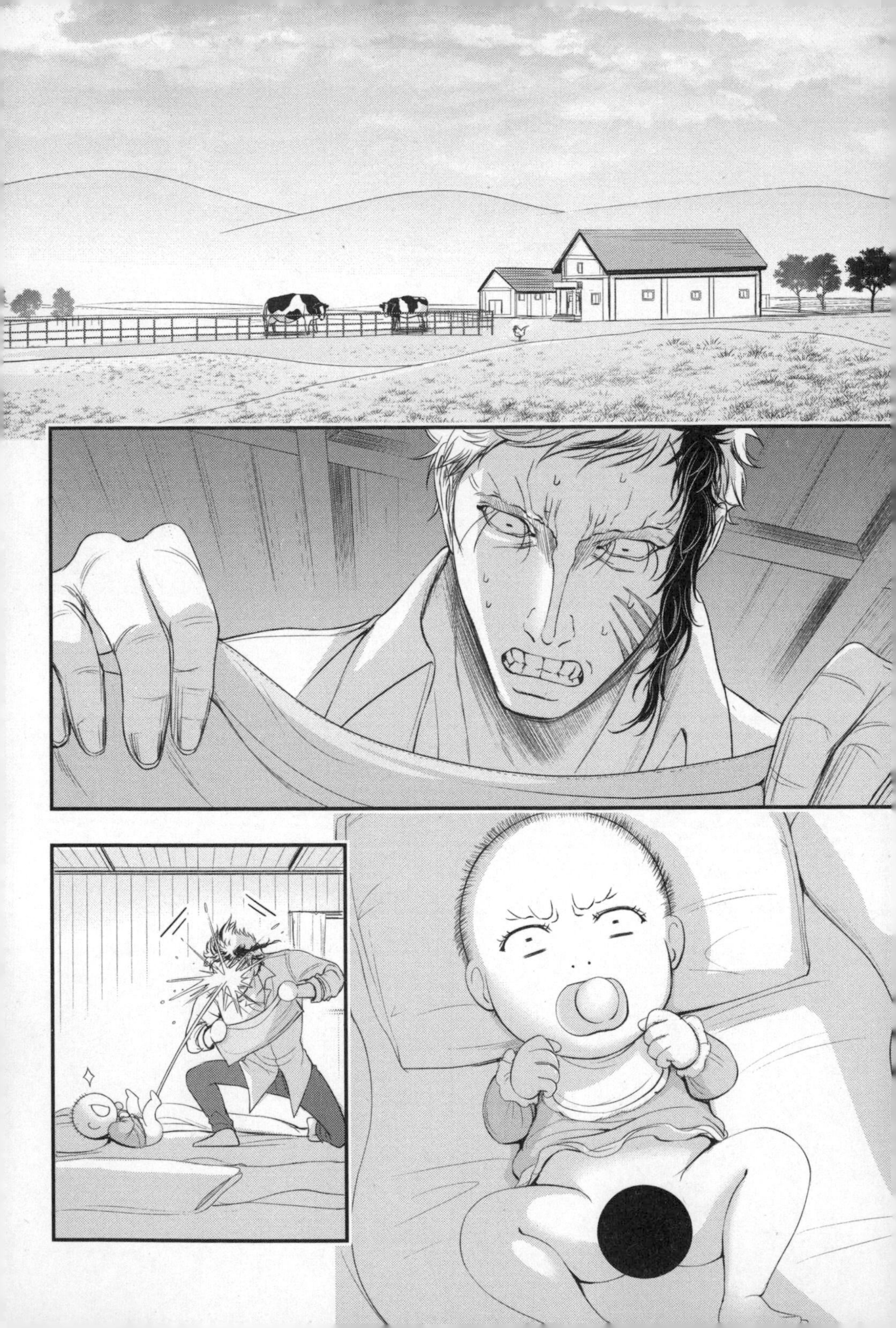

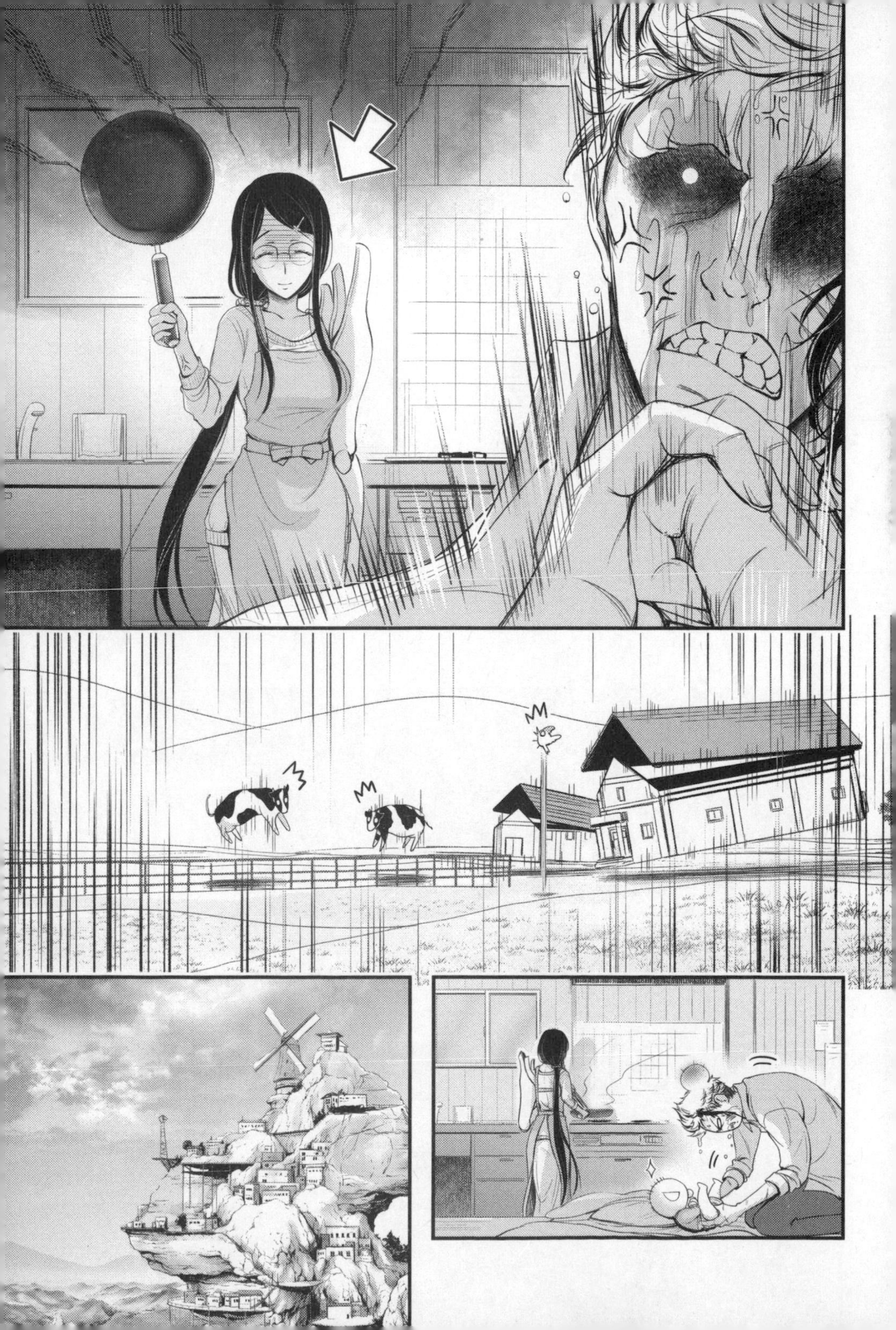

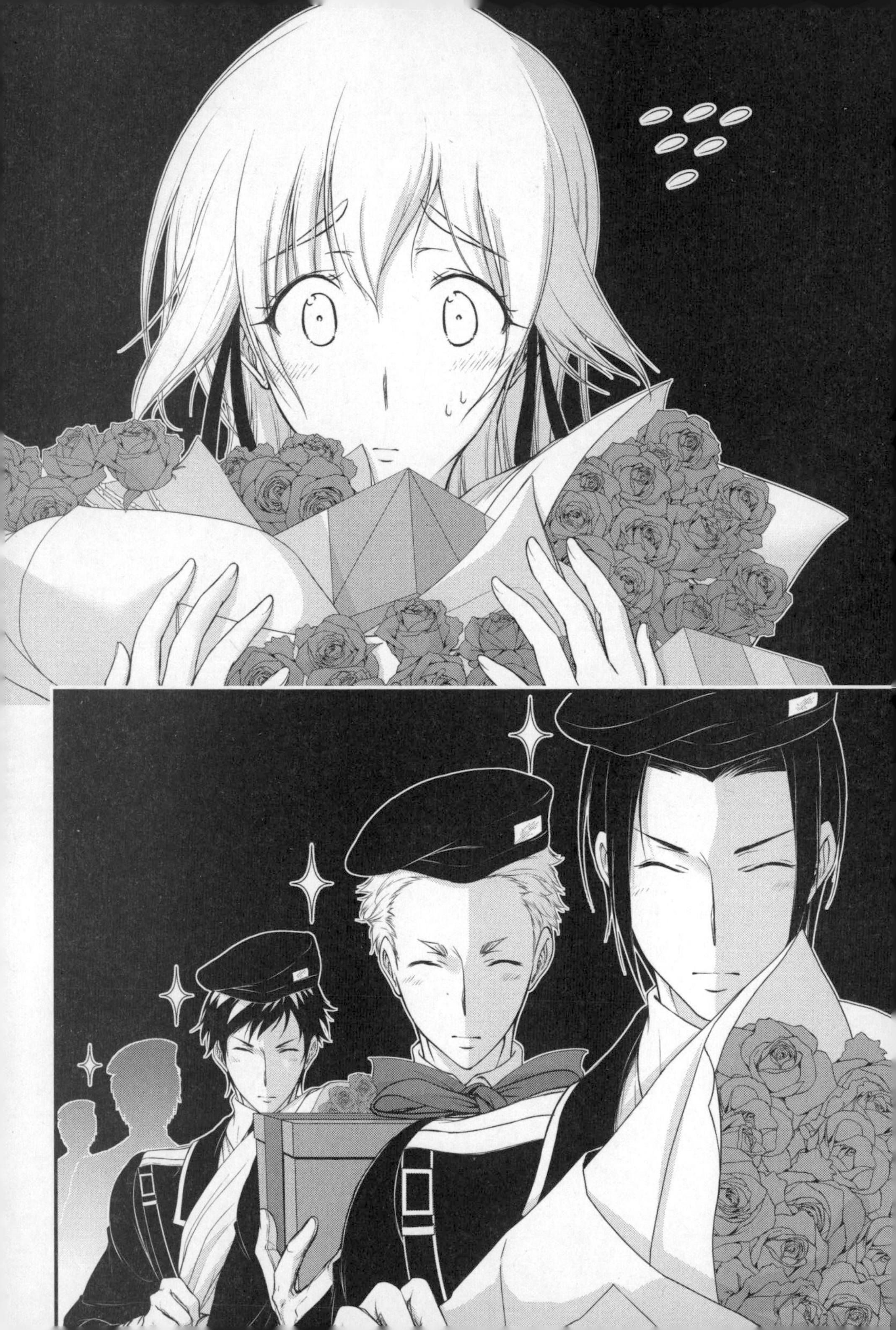

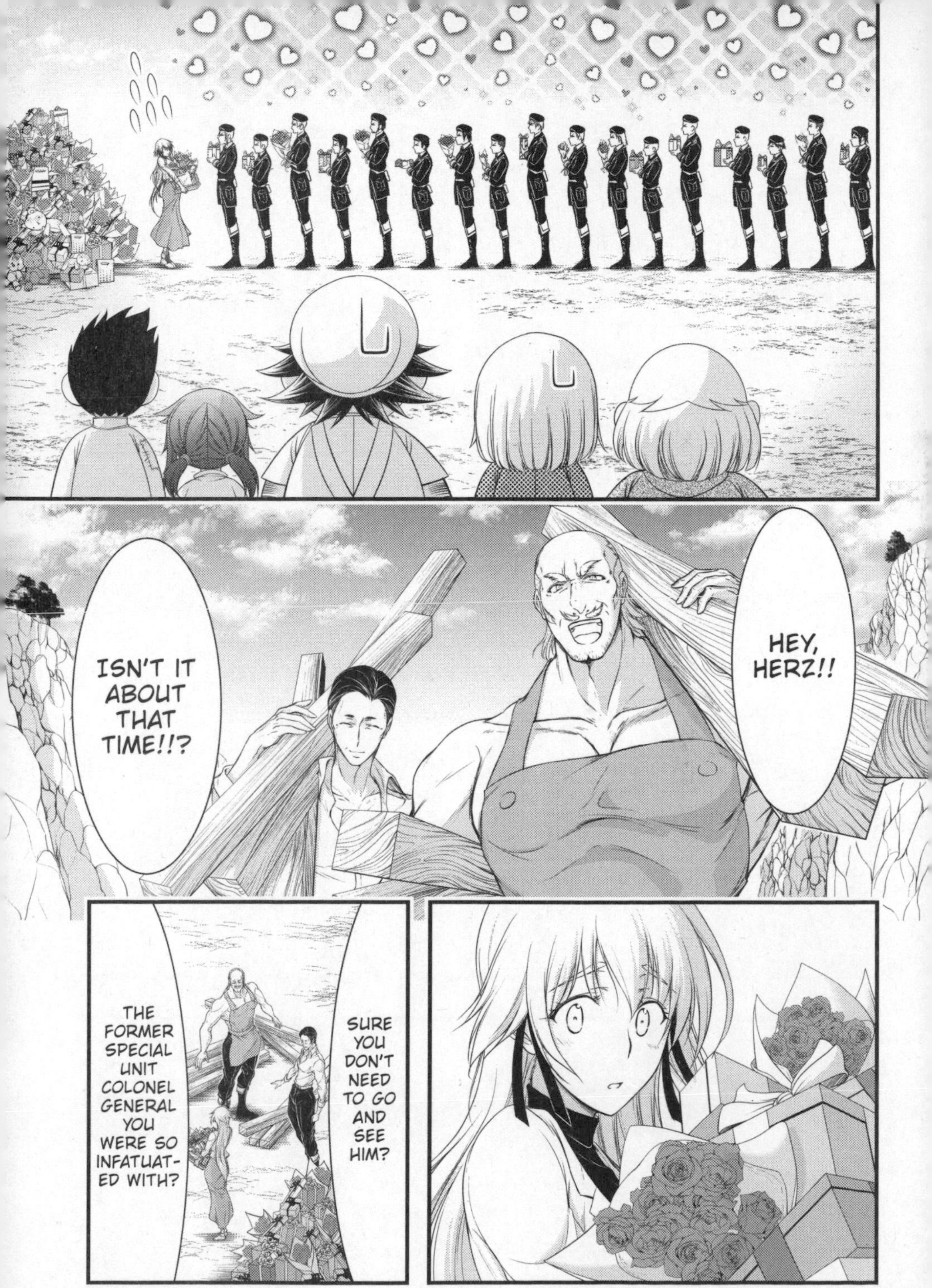
HEY, HERZ!!
ISN'T IT ABOUT THAT TIME!!?
SURE YOU DON'T NEED TO GO AND SEE HIM?
THE FORMER SPECIAL UNIT COLONEL GENERAL YOU WERE SO INFATUAT-ED WITH?

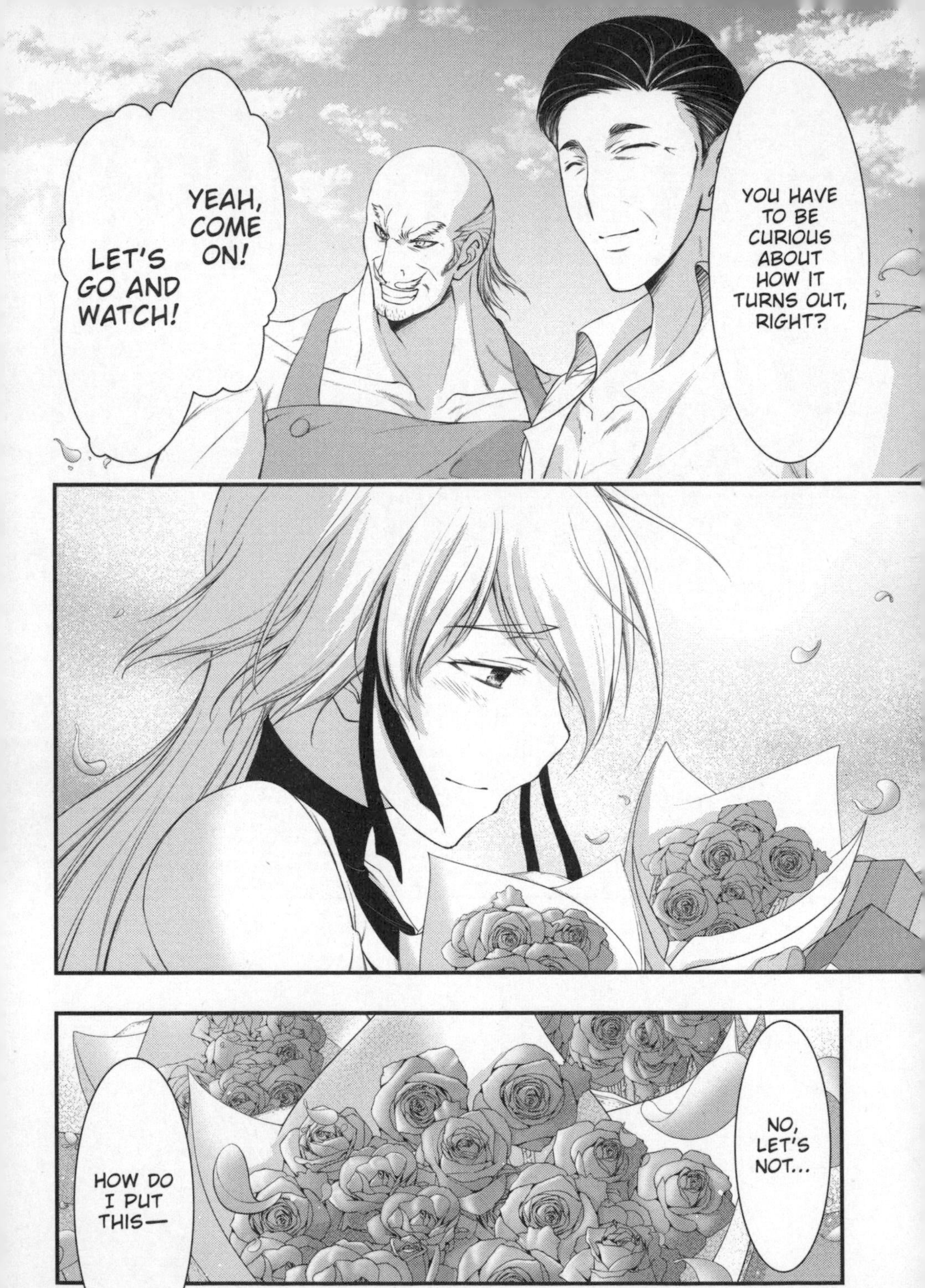
YOU HAVE TO BE CURIOUS ABOUT HOW IT TURNS OUT, RIGHT?
YEAH, COME ON!
LET'S GO AND WATCH!
NO, LET'S NOT...
HOW DO I PUT THIS—

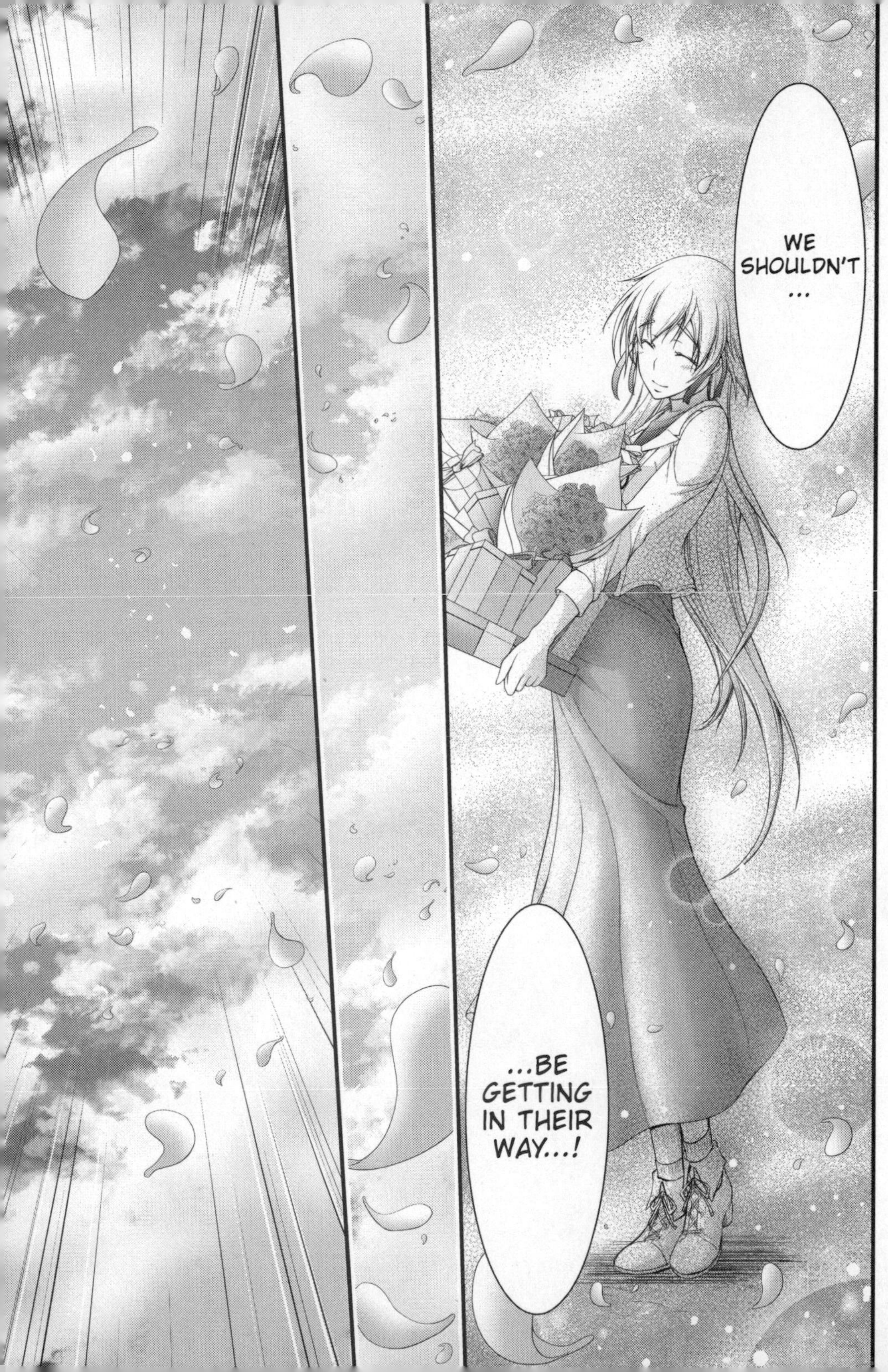
WE SHOULDN'T ...
...BE GETTING IN THEIR WAY...!

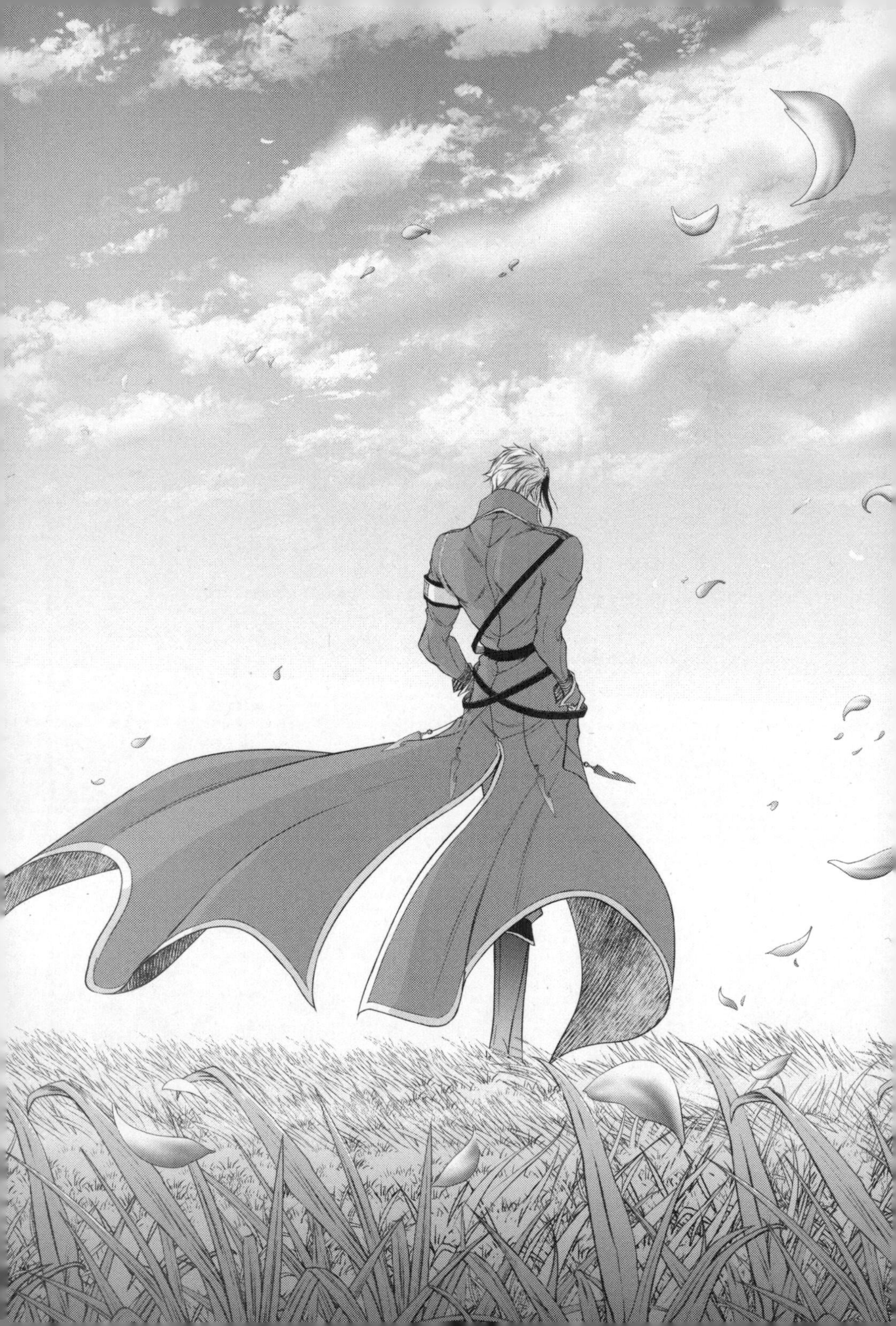

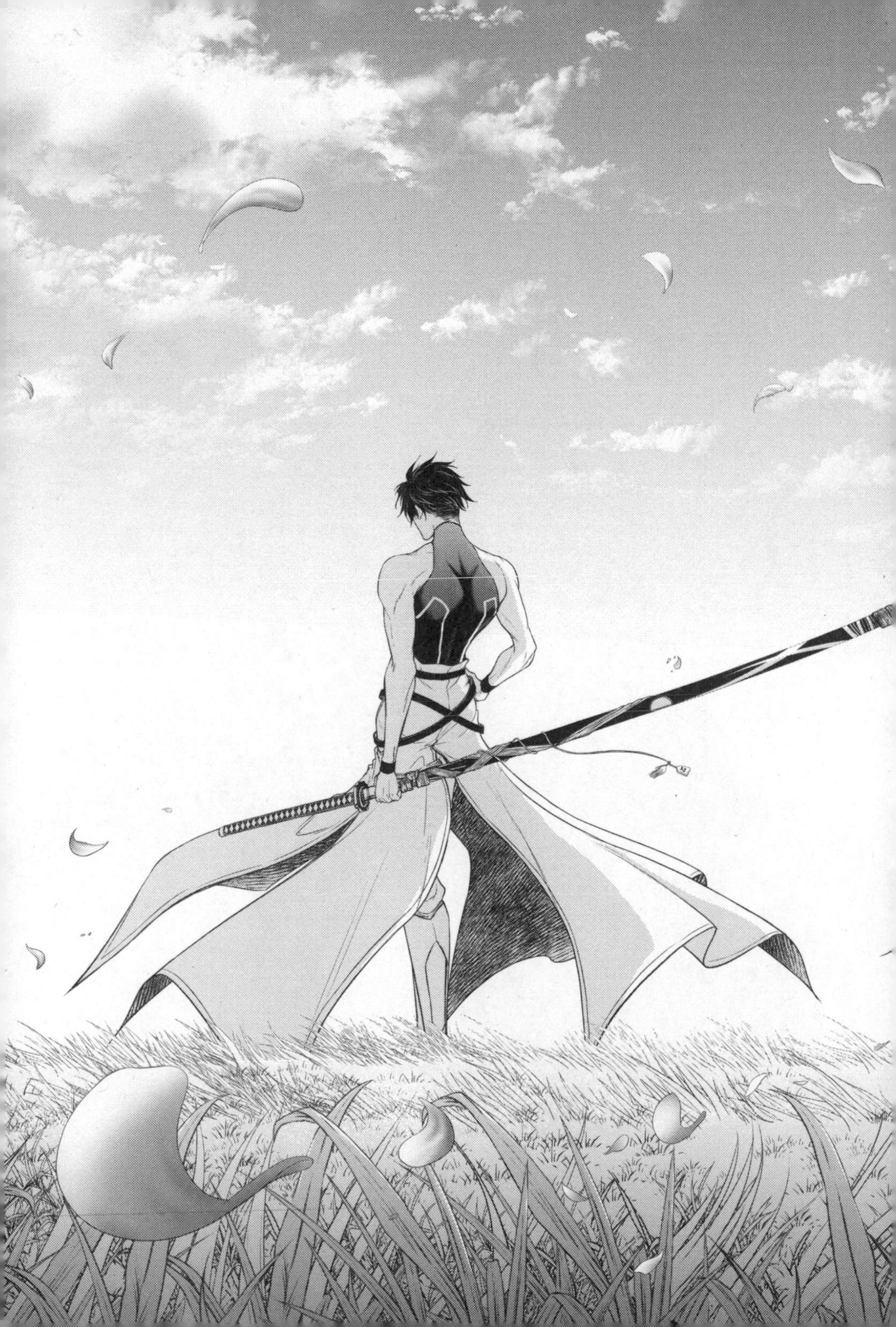

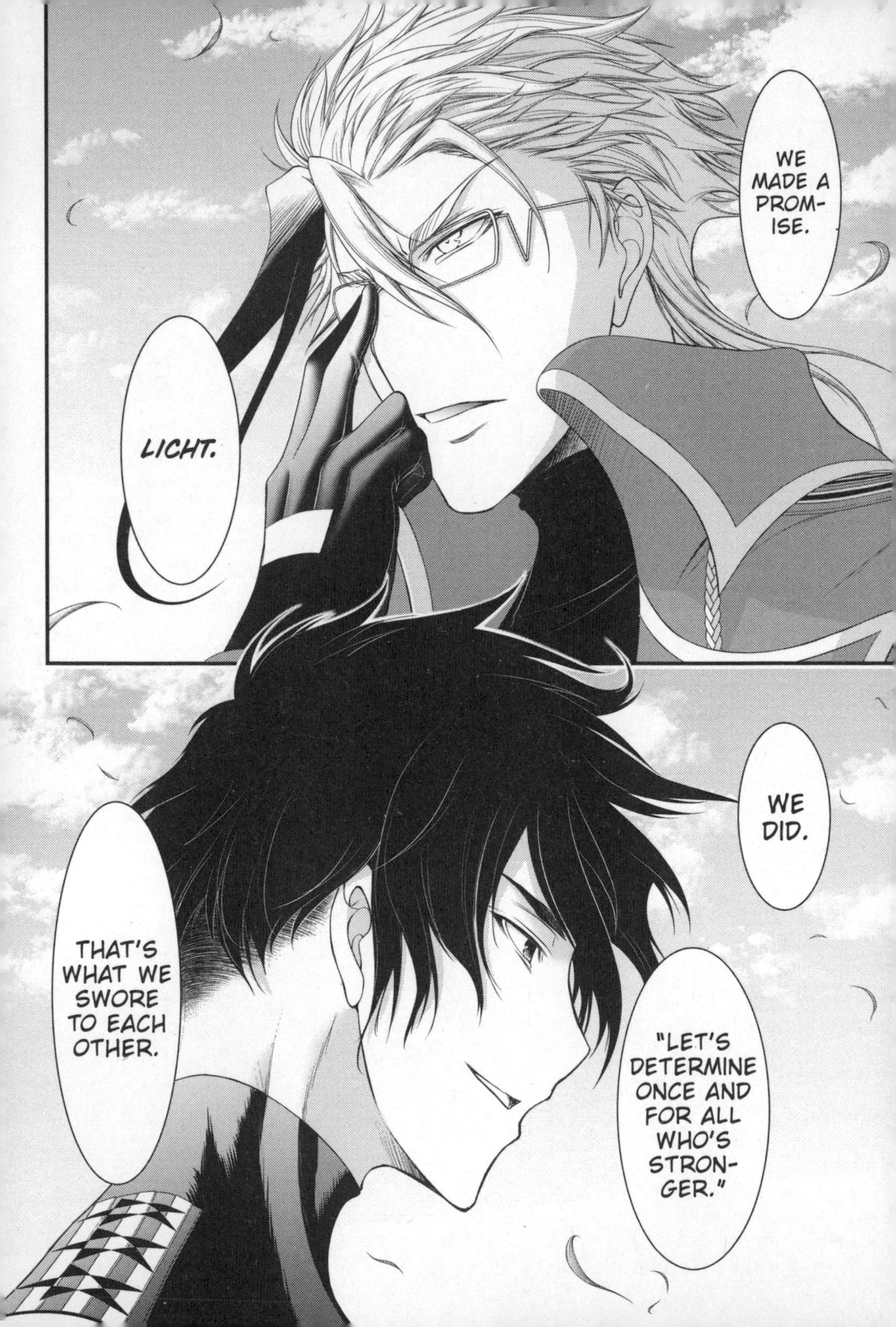
WE MADE A PROMISE.
LICHT.
WE DID.
"LET'S DETERMINE ONCE AND FOR ALL WHO'S STRONGER."
THAT'S WHAT WE SWORE TO EACH OTHER.

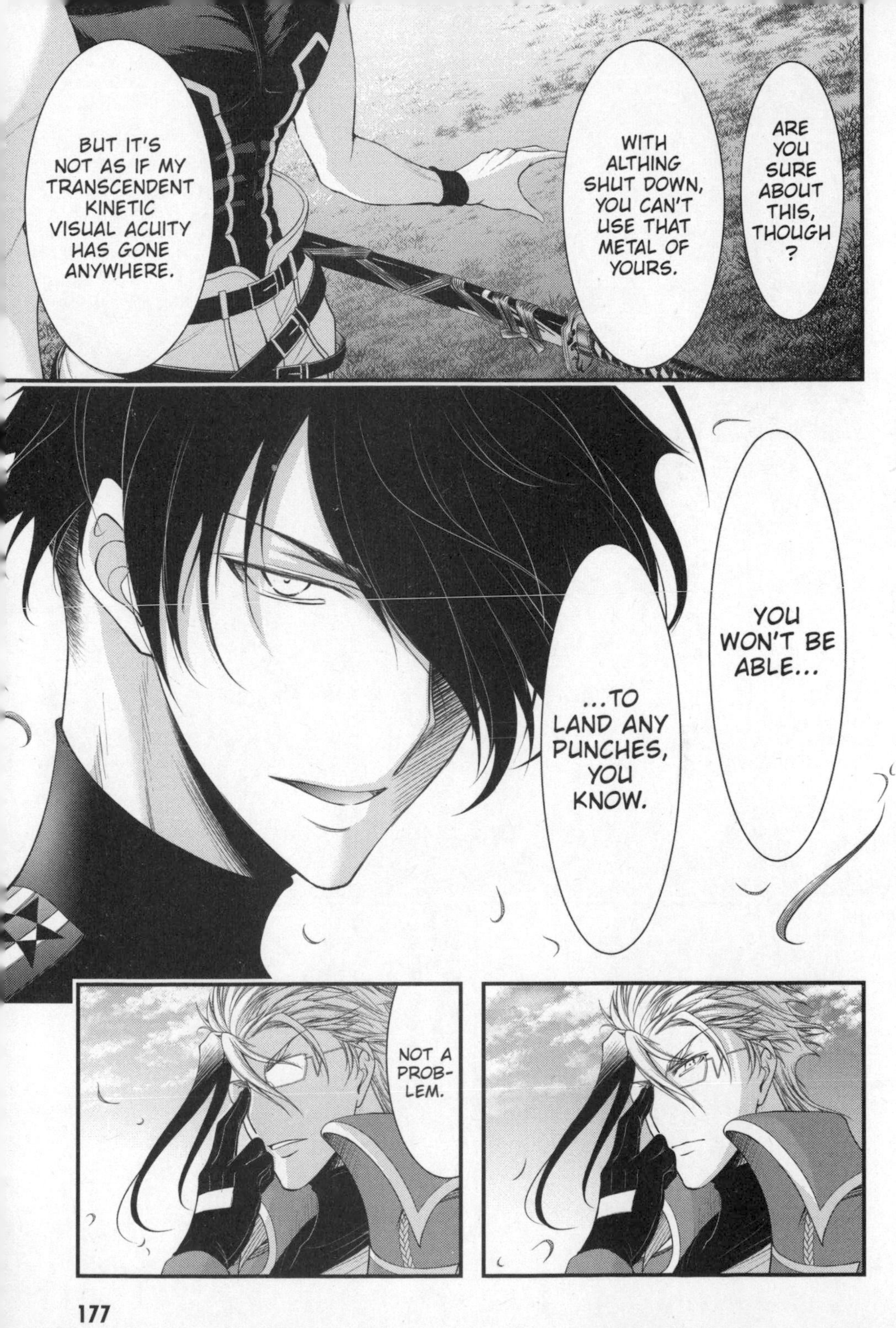
ARE YOU SURE ABOUT THIS, THOUGH?
WITH ALTHING SHUT DOWN, YOU CAN'T USE THAT METAL OF YOURS.
BUT IT'S NOT AS IF MY TRANSCENDENT KINETIC VISUAL ACUITY HAS GONE ANYWHERE.
YOU WON'T BE ABLE...
...TO LAND ANY PUNCHES, YOU KNOW.
NOT A PROB-LEM.

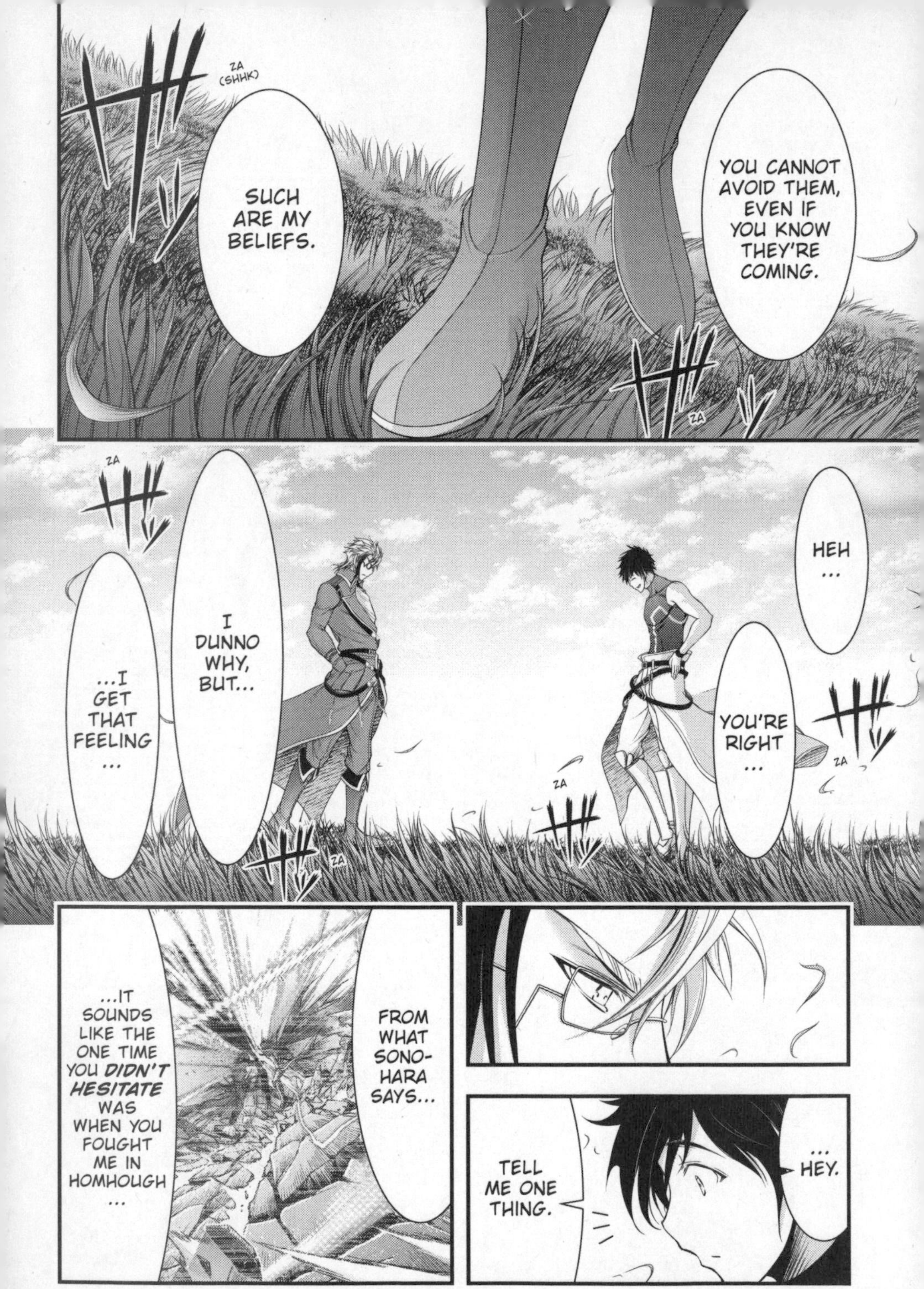
YOU CANNOT AVOID THEM, EVEN IF YOU KNOW THEY'RE COMING.
ZA (SHHK)
SUCH ARE MY BELIEFS.
ZA
HEH...
YOU'RE RIGHT...
ZA
ZA
I DUNNO WHY, BUT...
...I GET THAT FEELING...
ZA
ZA
...HEY.
TELL ME ONE THING.
FROM WHAT SONO-HARA SAYS...
...IT SOUNDS LIKE THE ONE TIME YOU ***DIDN'T HESITATE*** WAS WHEN YOU FOUGHT ME IN HOMHOUGH...

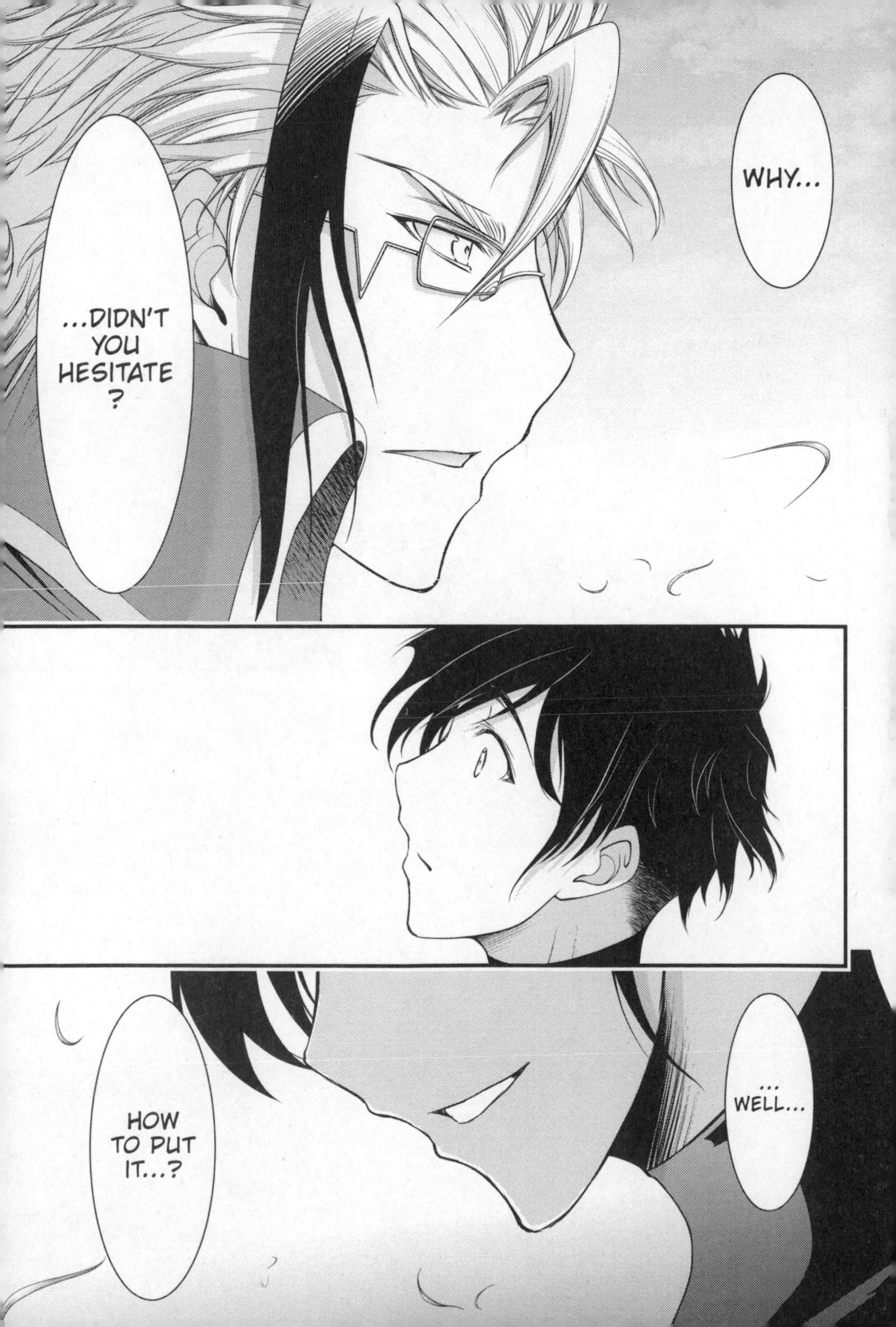
WHY...
...DIDN'T YOU HESITATE?
...WELL...
HOW TO PUT IT...?

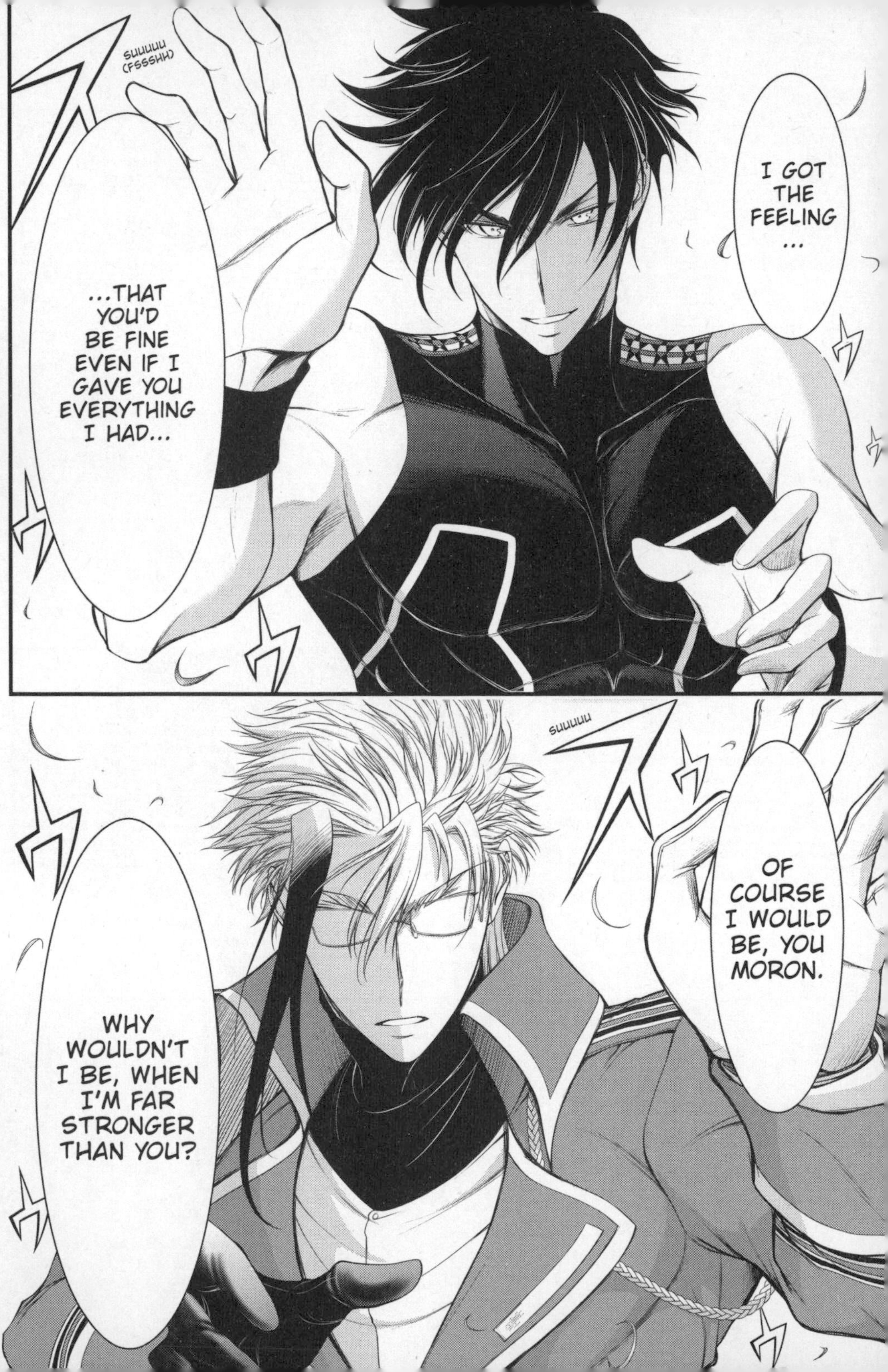

SUUUUU (FSSSHH)
I GOT THE FEELING...
...THAT YOU'D BE FINE EVEN IF I GAVE YOU EVERYTHING I HAD...
SUUUUU
OF COURSE I WOULD BE, YOU MORON.
WHY WOULDN'T I BE, WHEN I'M FAR STRONGER THAN YOU?

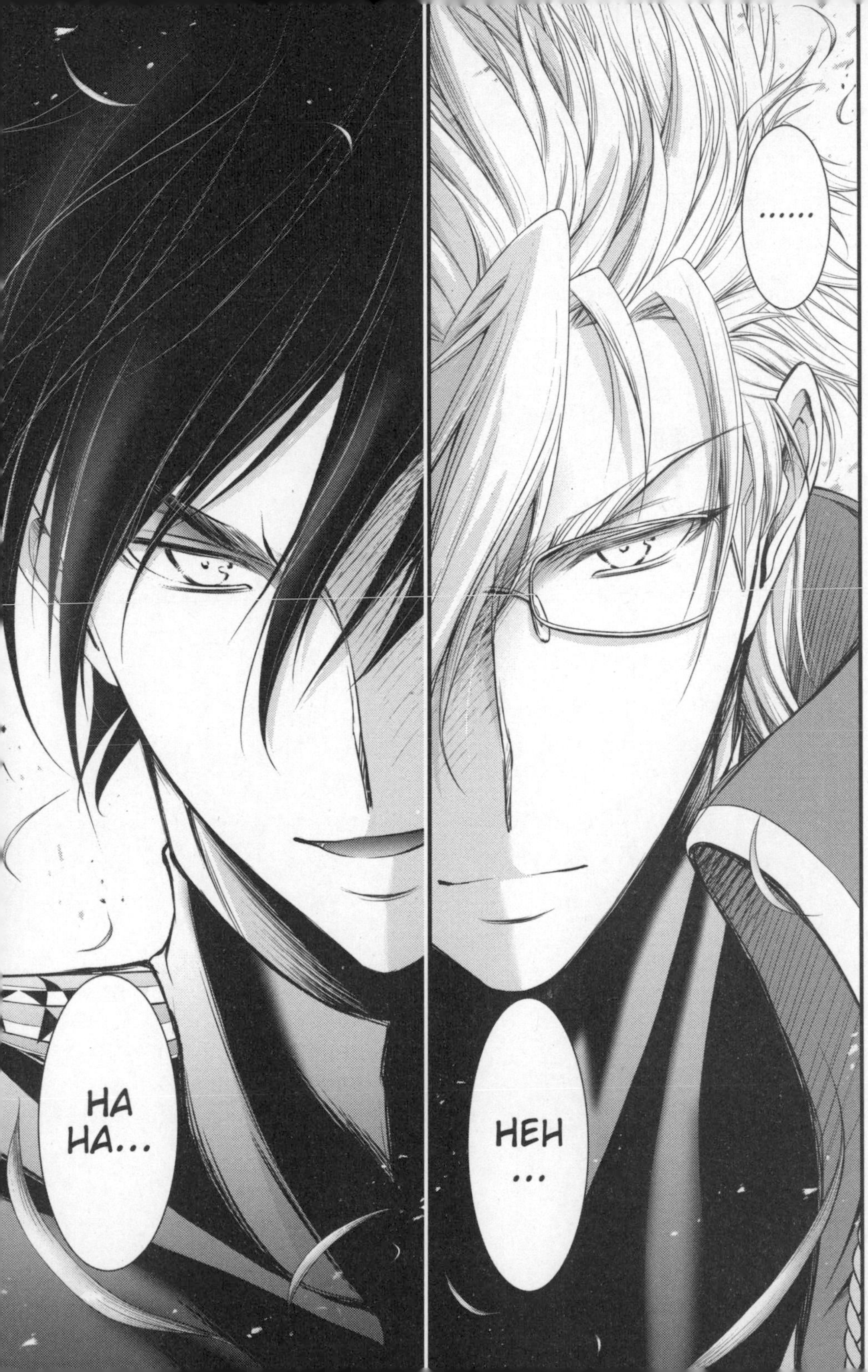
......
HEH ...
HA HA...

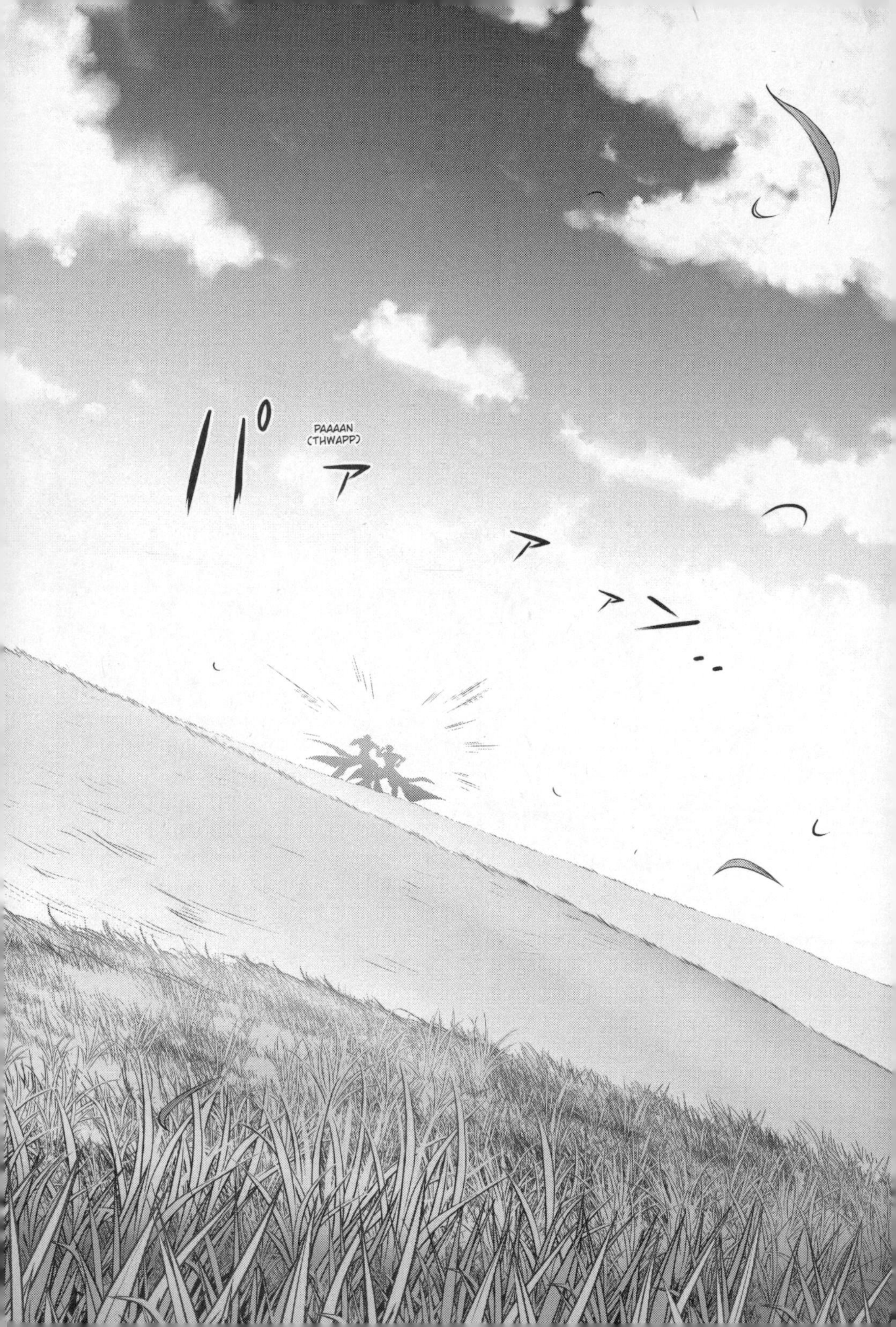
パァァァン…
PAAAAN (THWAPP)

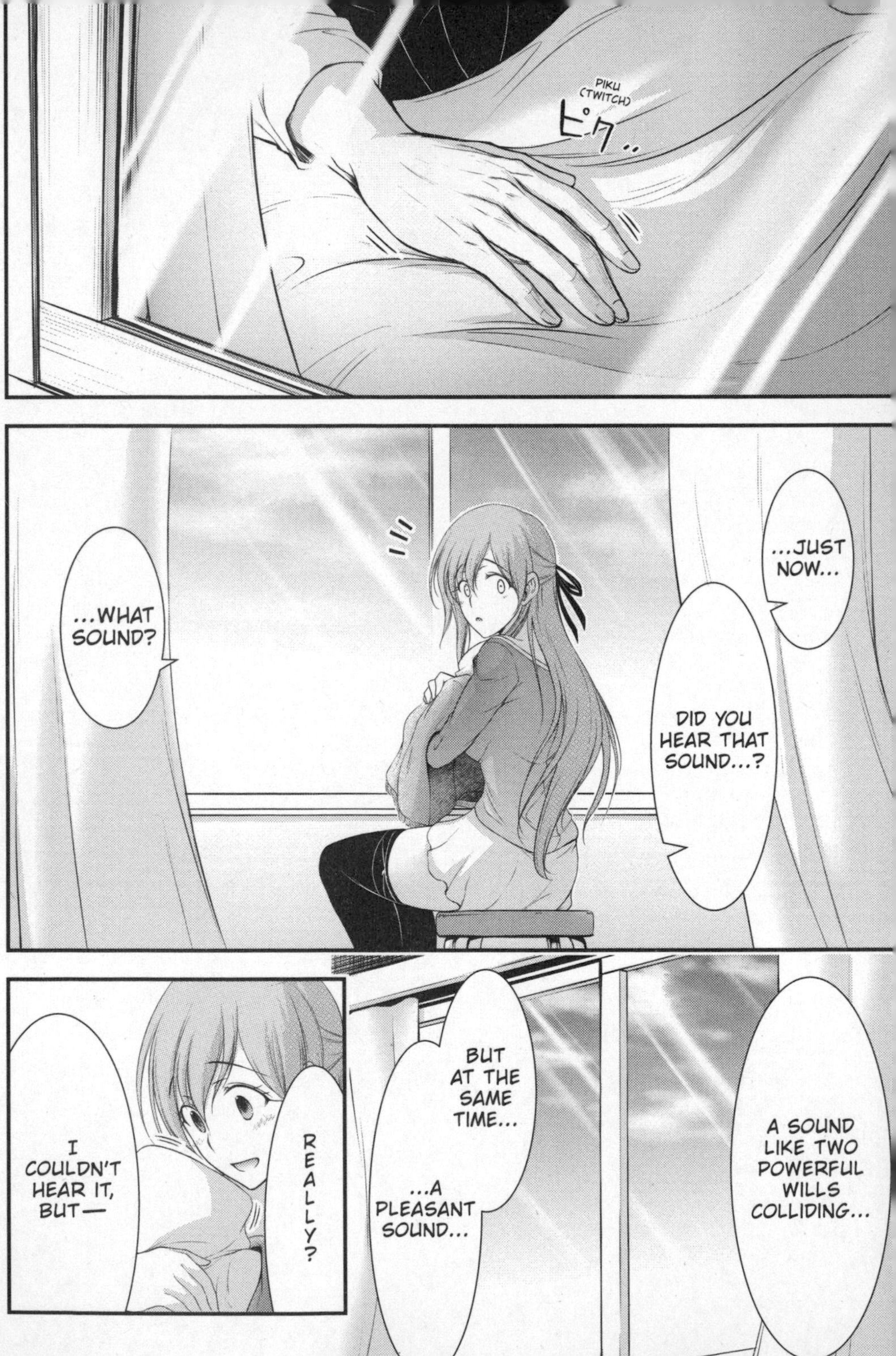
PIKU (TWITCH)
ピク
...JUST NOW...
DID YOU HEAR THAT SOUND...?
...WHAT SOUND?
A SOUND LIKE TWO POWERFUL WILLS COLLIDING...
BUT AT THE SAME TIME...
...A PLEASANT SOUND...
REALLY?
I COULDN'T HEAR IT, BUT—

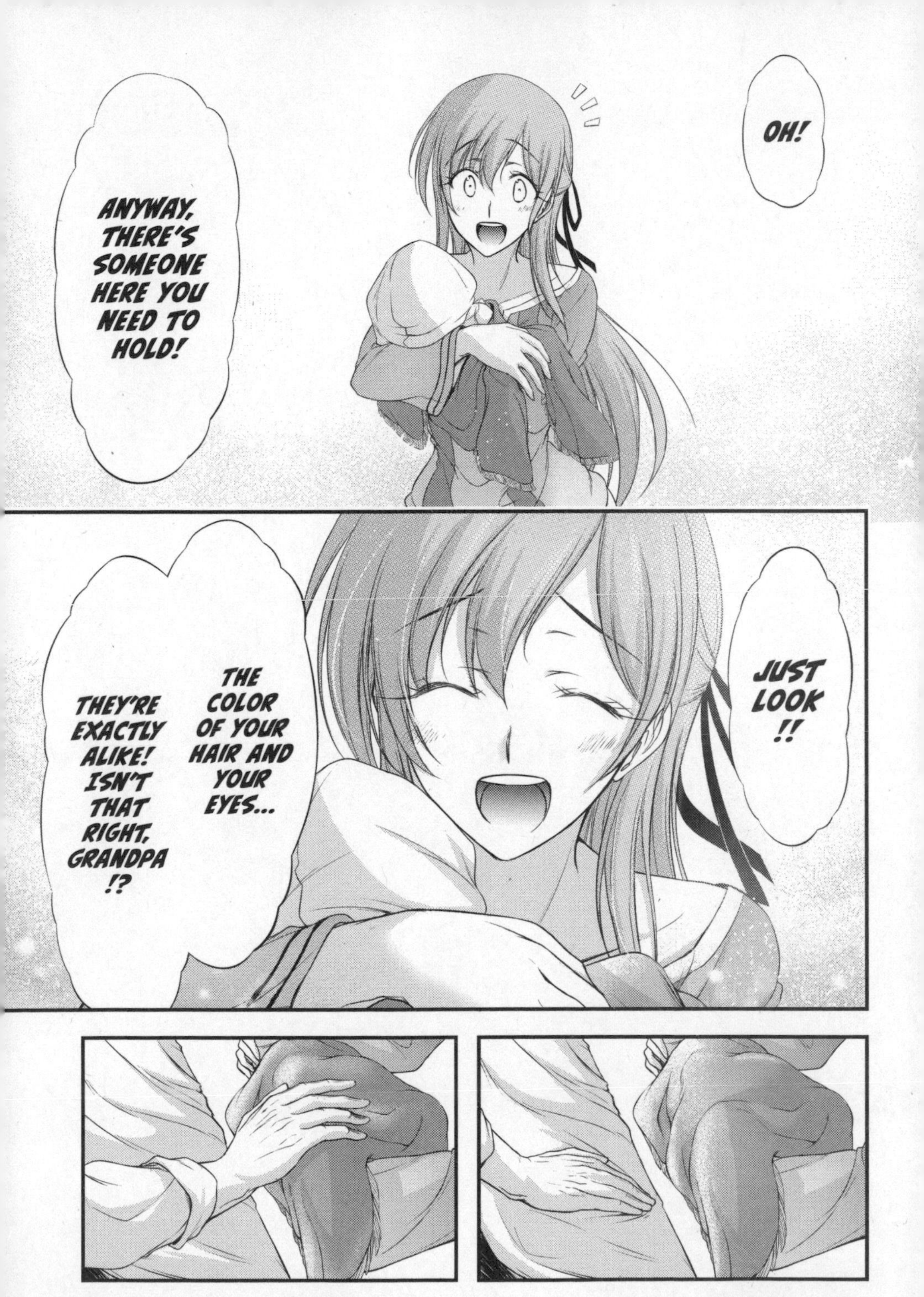
OH!
ANYWAY, THERE'S SOMEONE HERE YOU NEED TO HOLD!
JUST LOOK!!
THE COLOR OF YOUR HAIR AND YOUR EYES...
THEY'RE EXACTLY ALIKE! ISN'T THAT RIGHT, GRANDPA!?

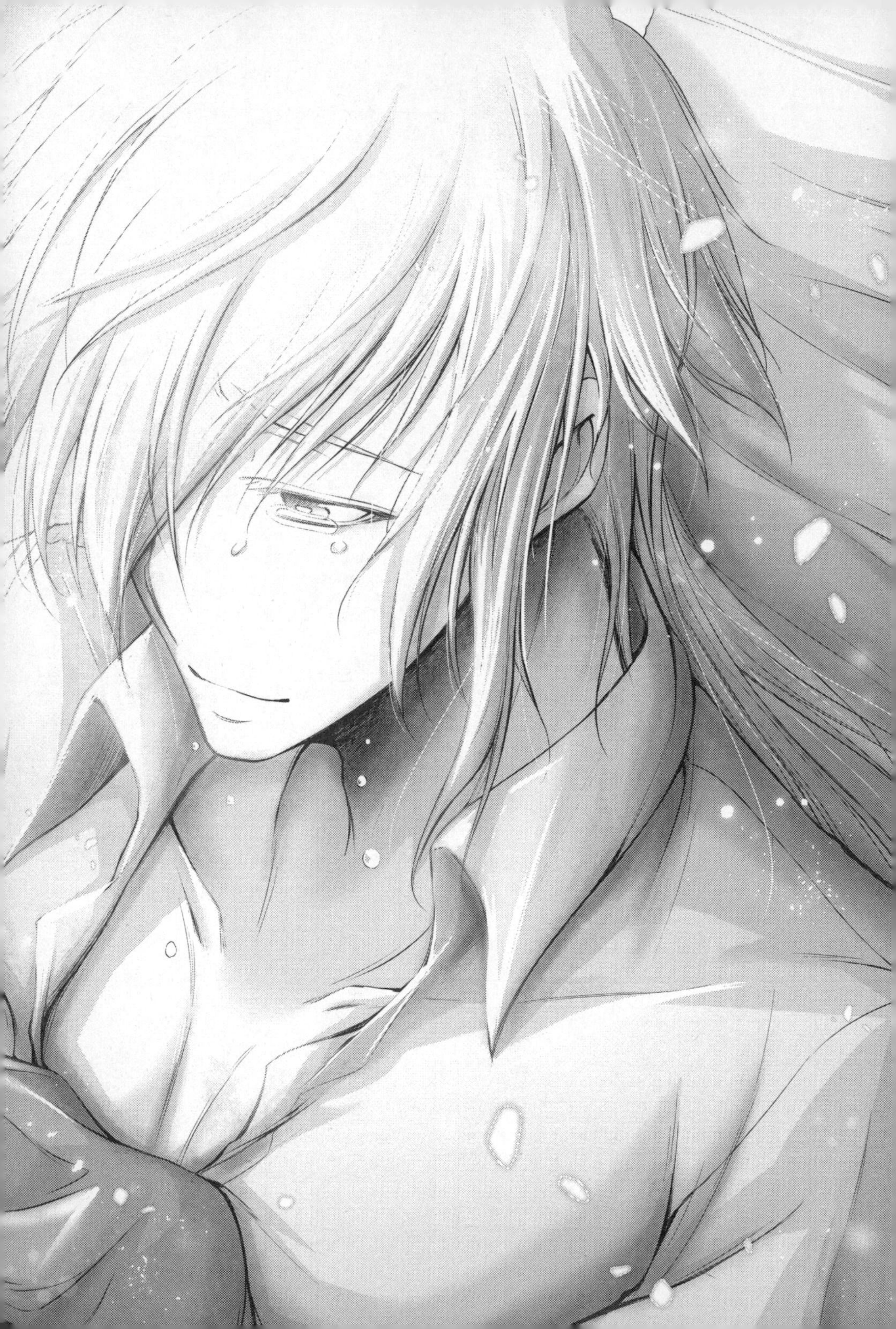

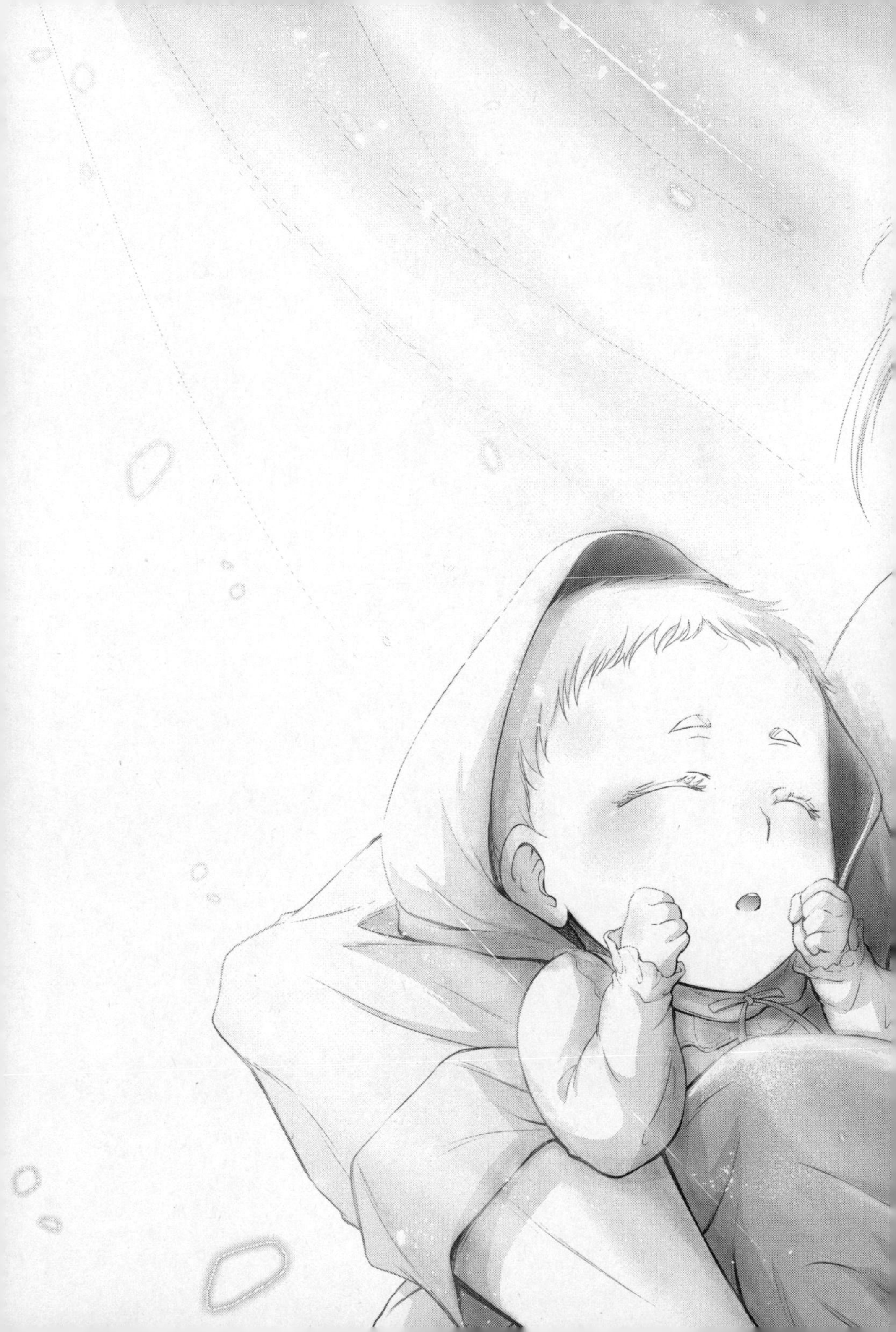

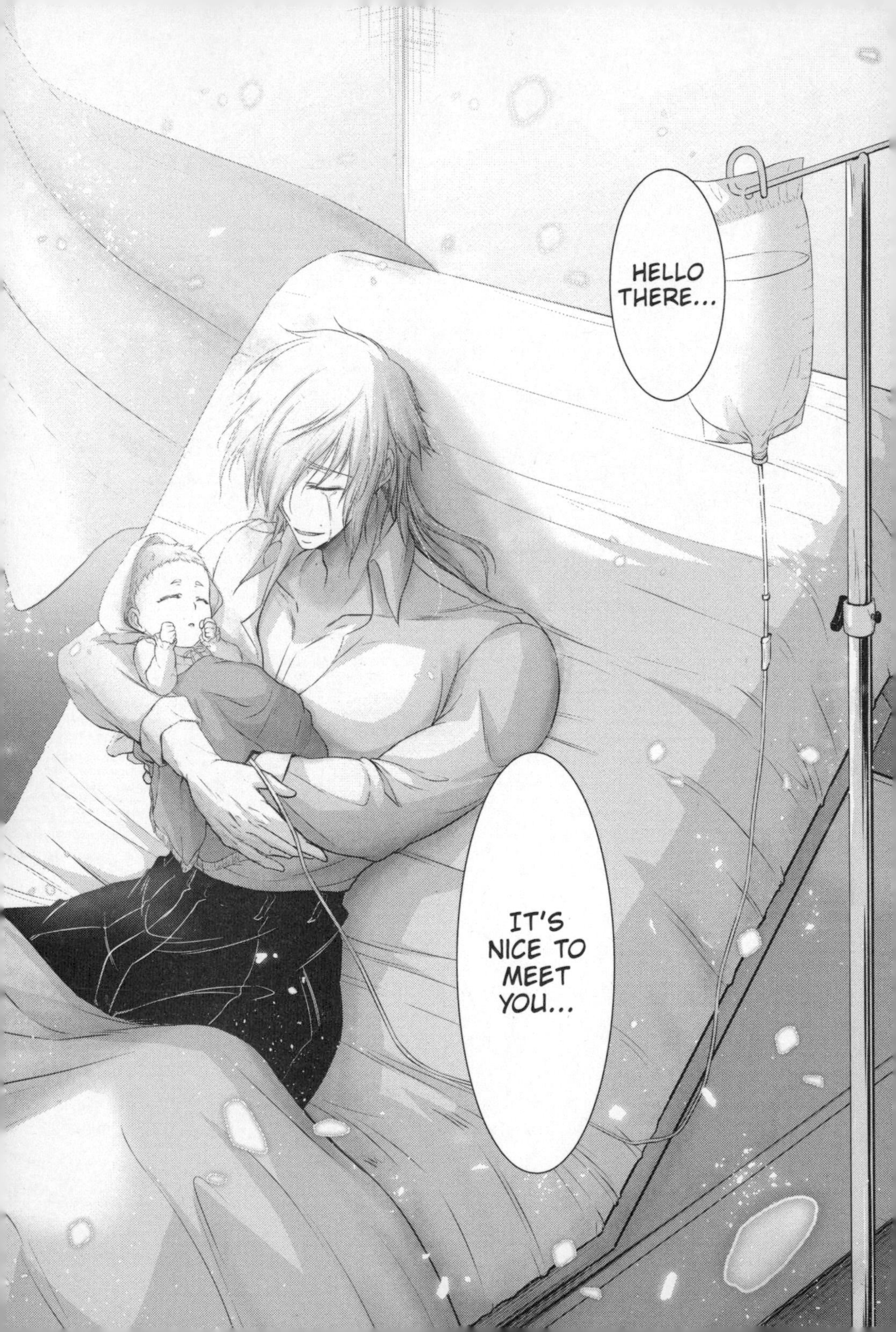
HELLO THERE...
IT'S NICE TO MEET YOU...

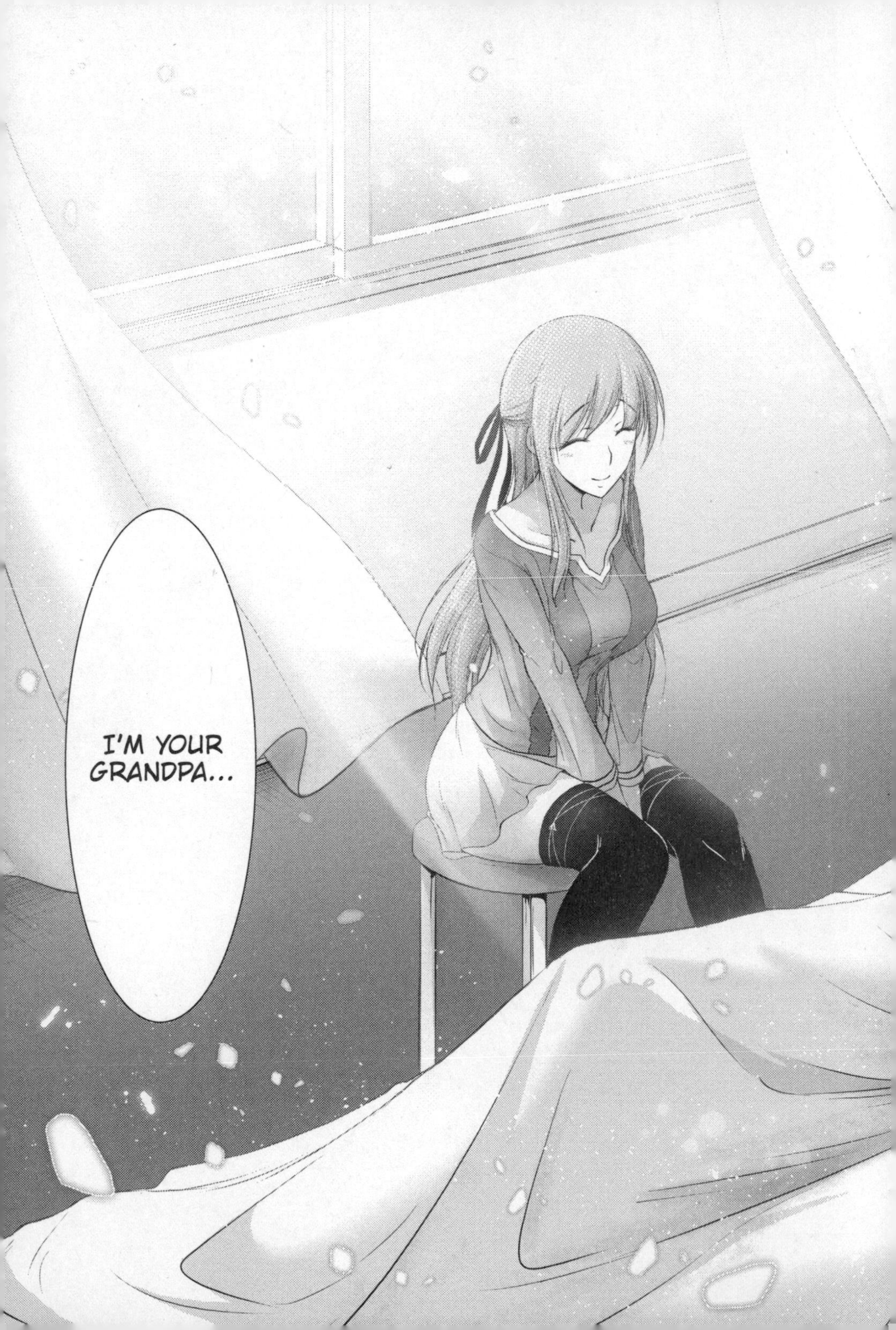
I'M YOUR GRANDPA...

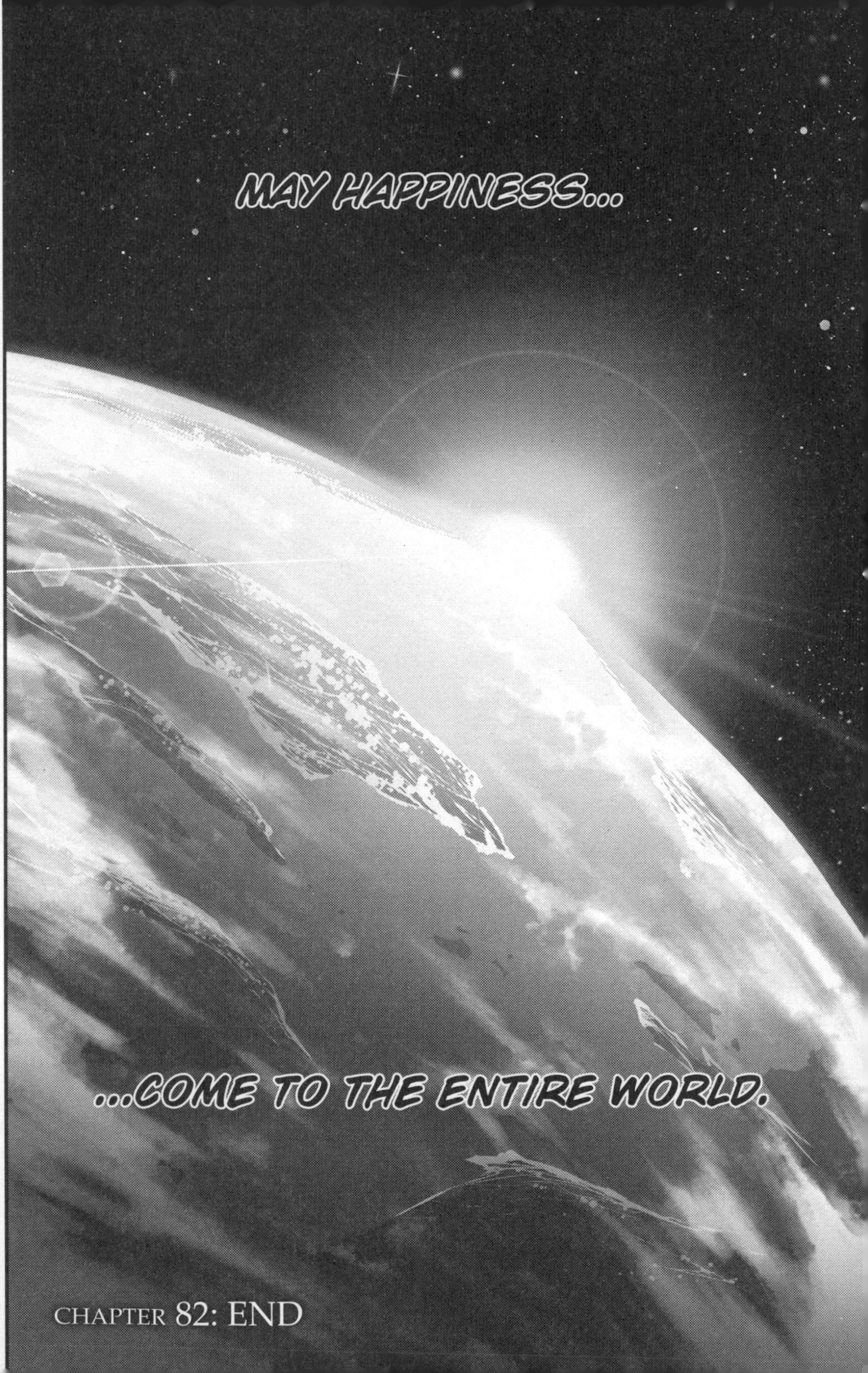
MAY HAPPINESS...
...COME TO THE ENTIRE WORLD.

CHAPTER 82: END

Plunderer

Extra Episode

ORIGINAL CHAPTERS CREATED FOR THE
PLUNDERER TV ANIME BLU-RAY BOX SETS

Extra

plunderer

1

ORIGINAL BOOKLET #1 INCLUDED IN BLU-RAY
BOX #1 OF THE PLUNDERER TV ANIME

Special Episode

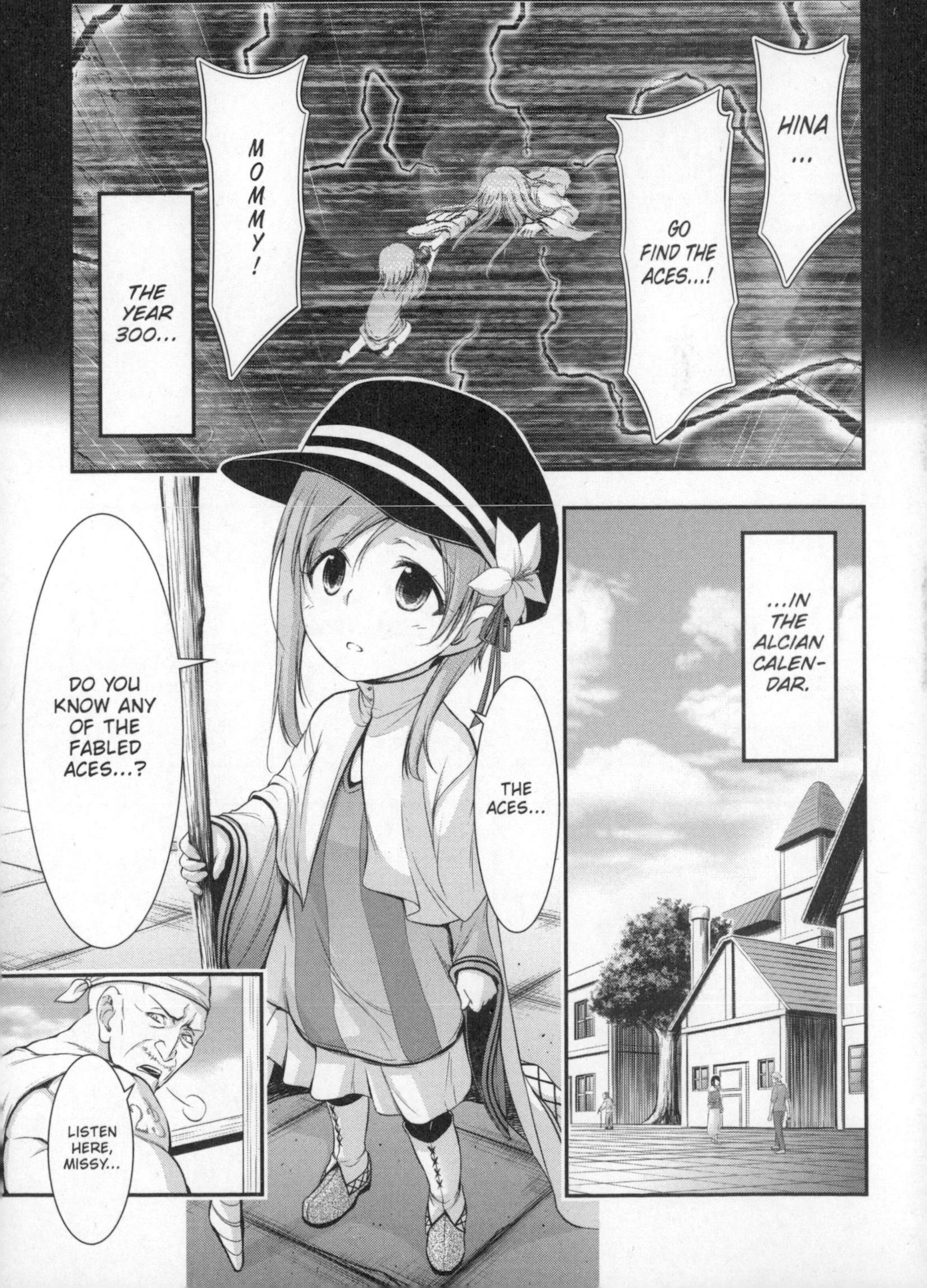
HINA ...
GO FIND THE ACES...!
MOMMY!
THE YEAR 300...
...IN THE ALCIAN CALEN-DAR.
THE ACES...
DO YOU KNOW ANY OF THE FABLED ACES...?
LISTEN HERE, MISSY...

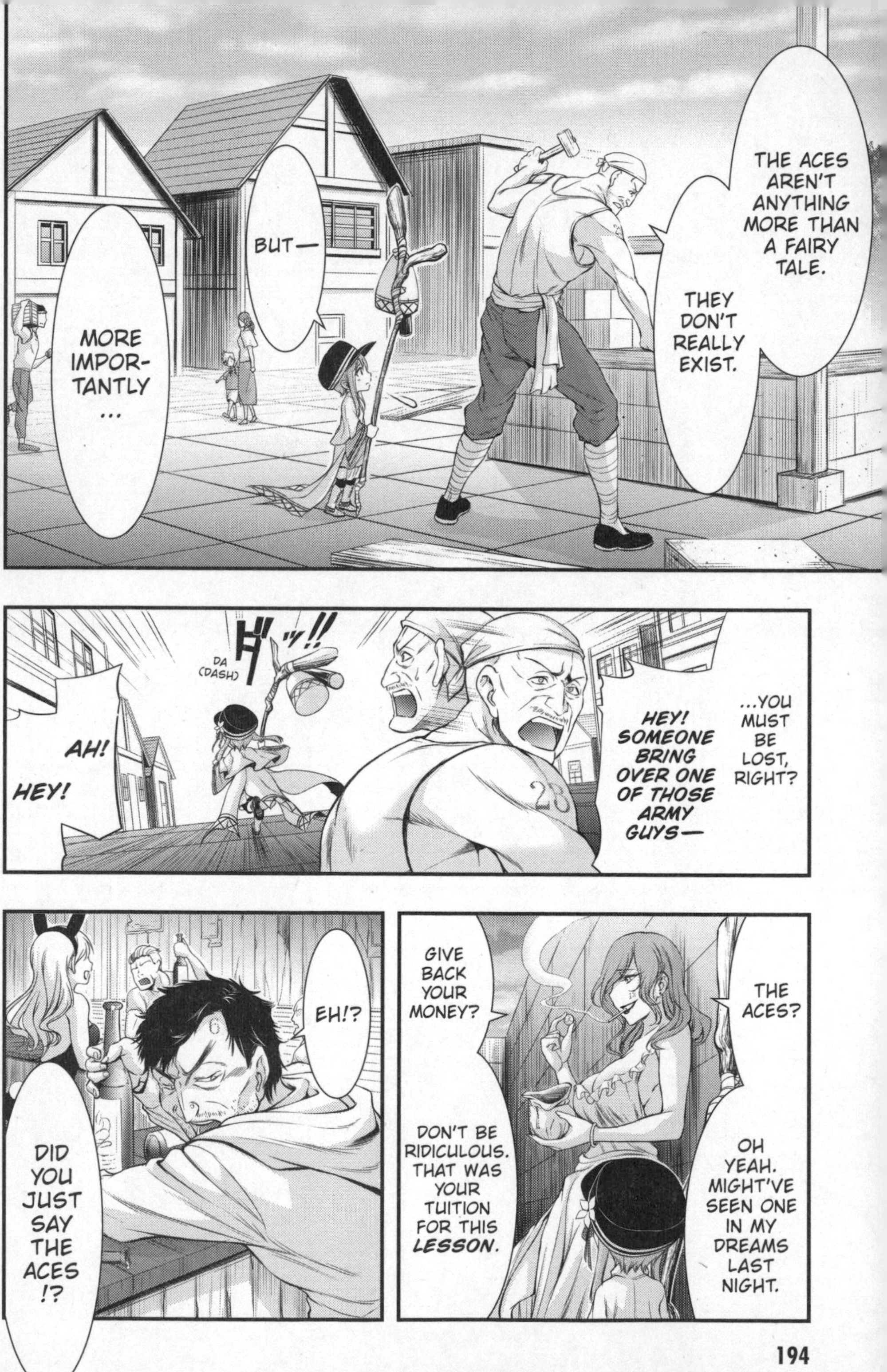
THE ACES AREN'T ANYTHING MORE THAN A FAIRY TALE.
THEY DON'T REALLY EXIST.
BUT—
MORE IMPOR-TANTLY ...
...YOU MUST BE LOST, RIGHT?
HEY! SOMEONE BRING OVER ONE OF THOSE ARMY GUYS—
ダッ!!
DA (DASH)
AH!
HEY!
THE ACES?
OH YEAH. MIGHT'VE SEEN ONE IN MY DREAMS LAST NIGHT.
GIVE BACK YOUR MONEY?
DON'T BE RIDICULOUS. THAT WAS YOUR TUITION FOR THIS LESSON.
EH!?
DID YOU JUST SAY THE ACES !?

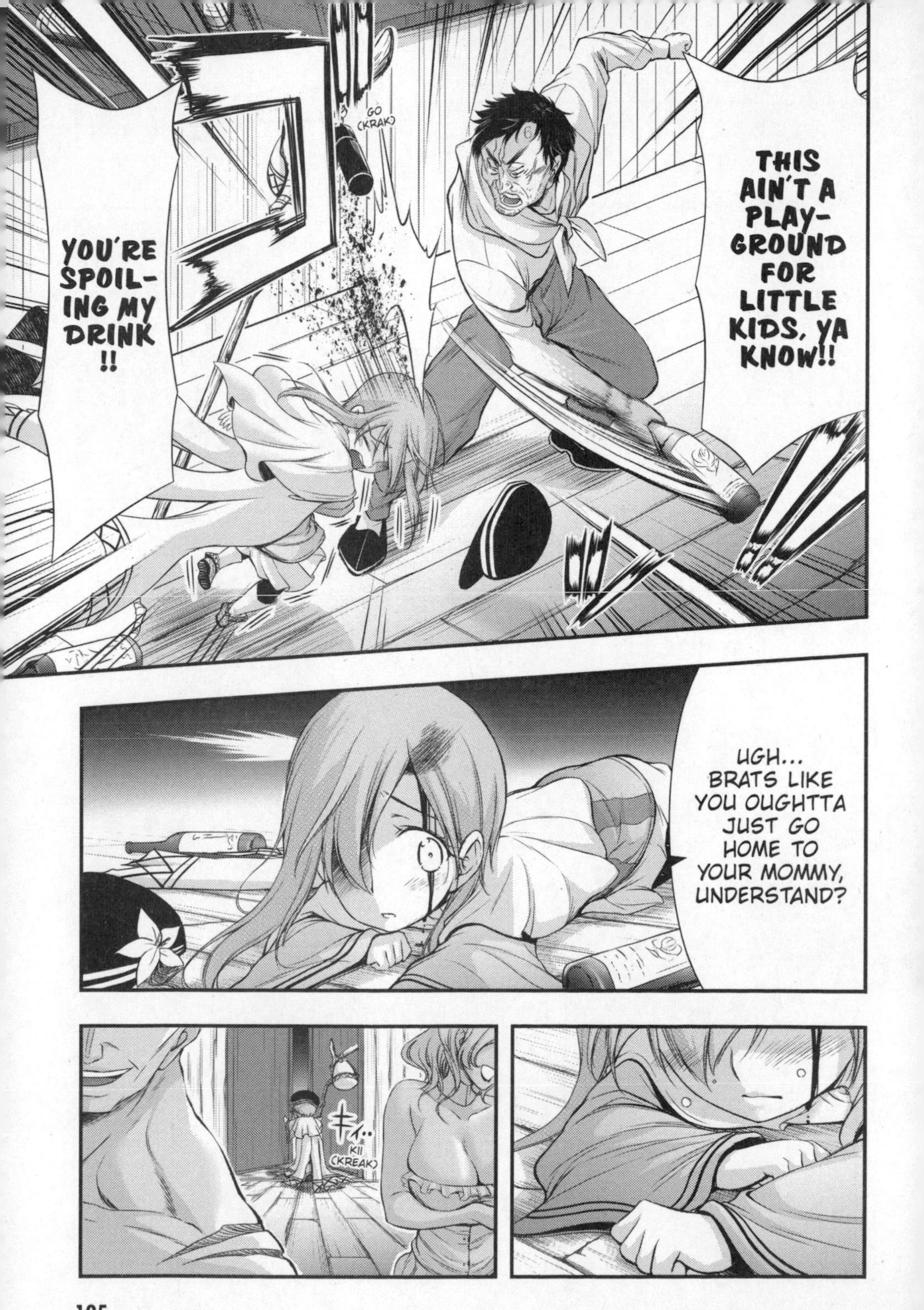
THIS AIN'T A PLAY-GROUND FOR LITTLE KIDS, YA KNOW!!
GO (KRAK)
YOU'RE SPOIL-ING MY DRINK!!
UGH... BRATS LIKE YOU OUGHTTA JUST GO HOME TO YOUR MOMMY, UNDERSTAND?
KII (KREAK)

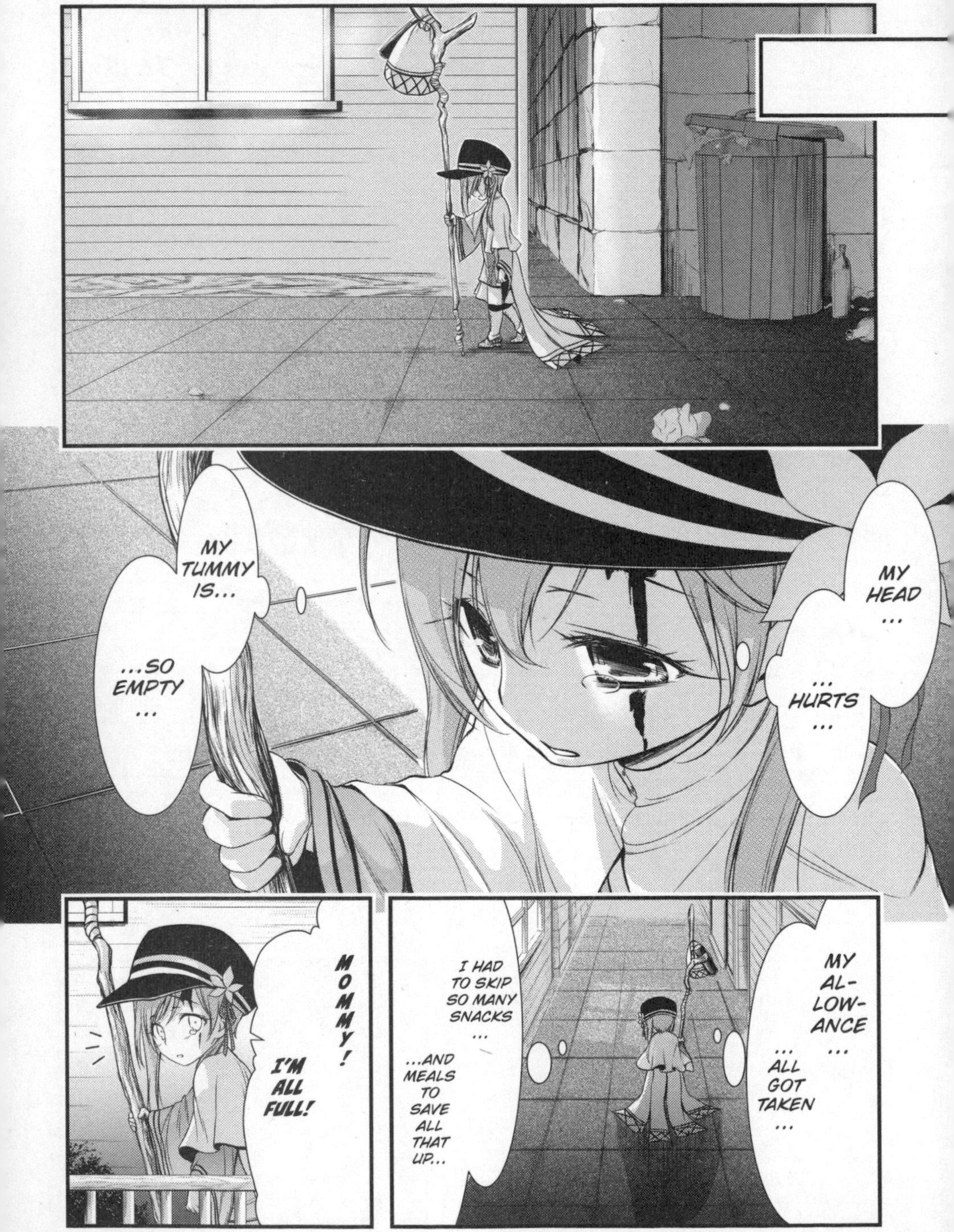
MY HEAD ...
... HURTS ...
MY TUMMY IS...
...SO EMPTY ...
MY AL-LOW-ANCE ...
... ALL GOT TAKEN ...
I HAD TO SKIP SO MANY SNACKS ...
...AND MEALS TO SAVE ALL THAT UP...
MOMMY!
I'M ALL FULL!

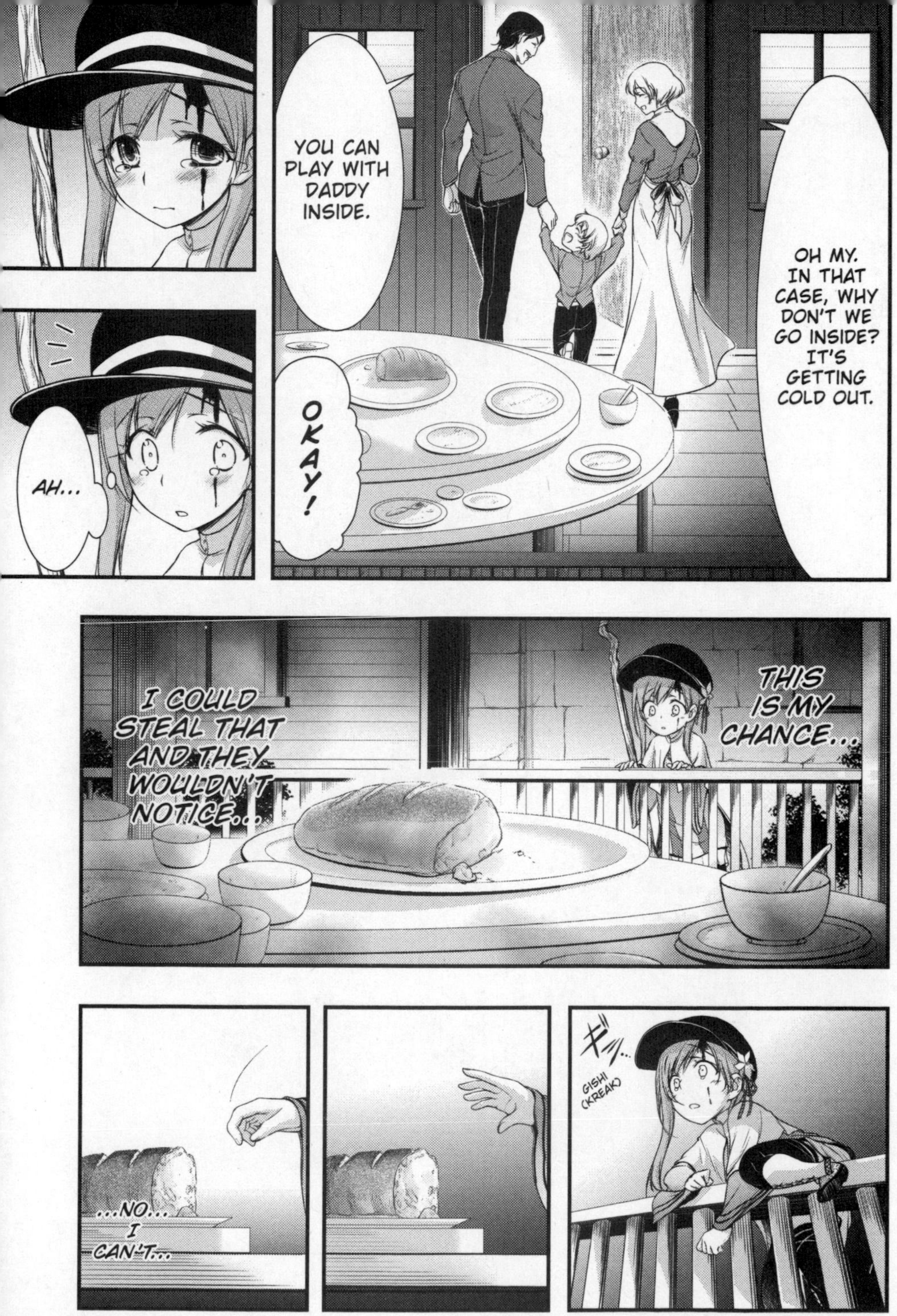
OH MY. IN THAT CASE, WHY DON'T WE GO INSIDE? IT'S GETTING COLD OUT.
YOU CAN PLAY WITH DADDY INSIDE.
OKAY!
AH...
THIS IS MY CHANCE...
I COULD STEAL THAT AND THEY WOULDN'T NOTICE...
ギシ...
GISHI (KREAK)
...NO... I CAN'T...

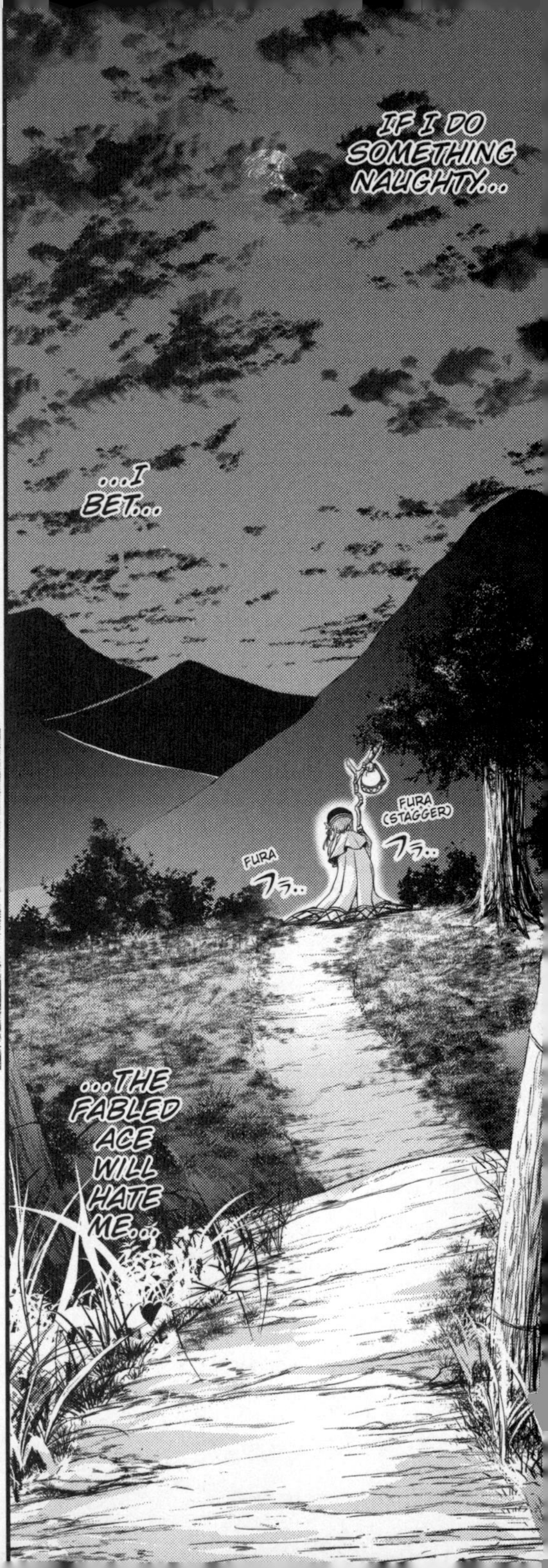
IF I DO SOMETHING NAUGHTY...
...I BET...
FURA (STAGGER) フラ..
FURA フラ..
...THE FABLED ACE WILL HATE ME...

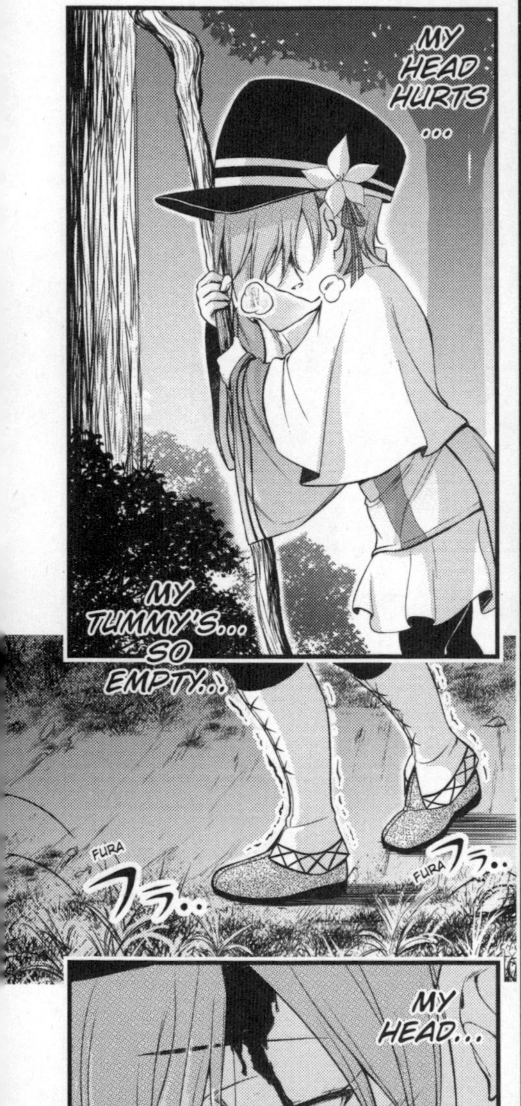
MY HEAD HURTS ...
MY TUMMY'S... SO EMPTY...
FURA フラ..
FURA フラ..
MY HEAD...
...HURTS...
MY TUMMY'S...

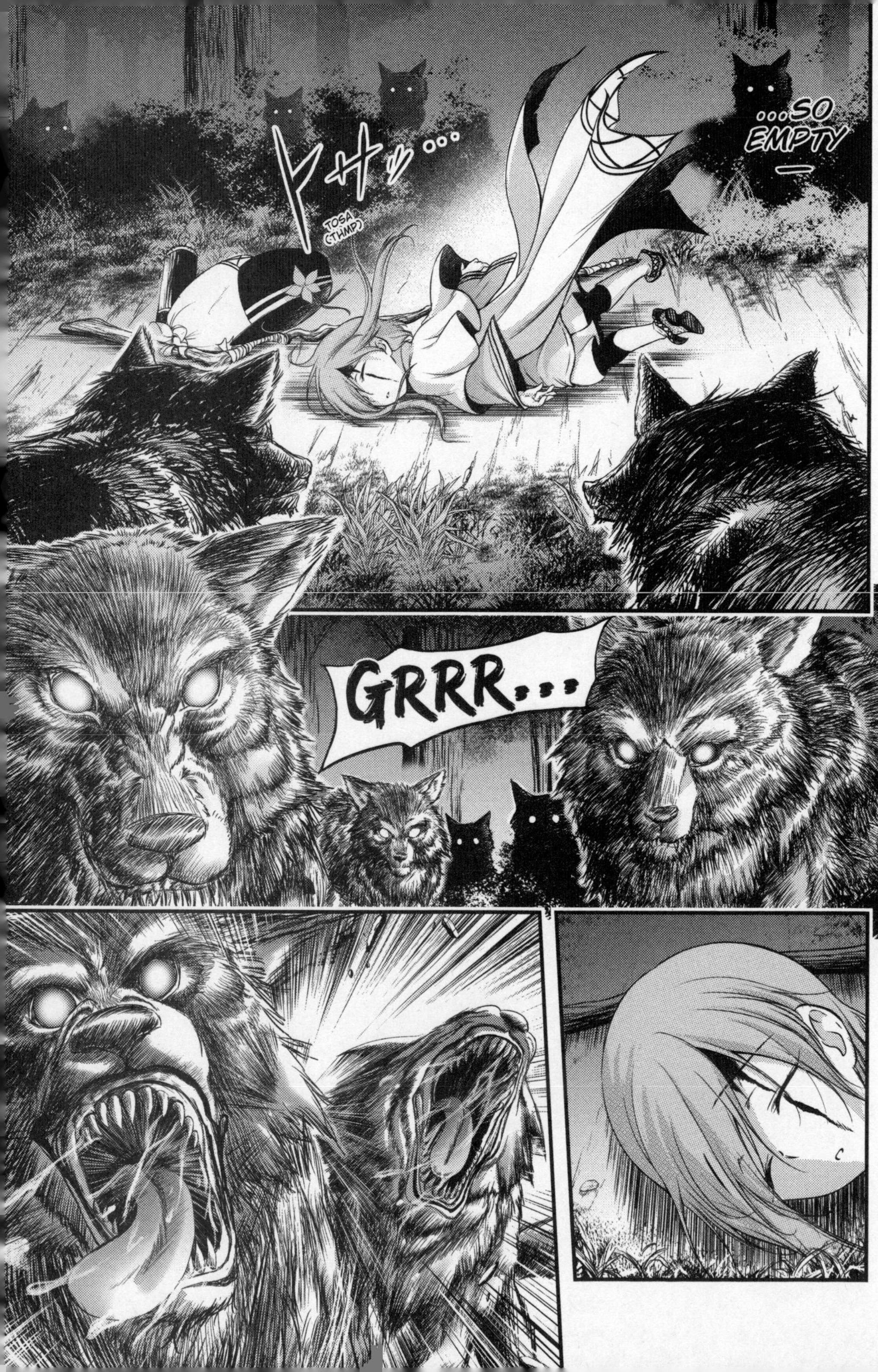
...SO EMPTY —
ドサッ…
TOSA (THMP)
GRRR...

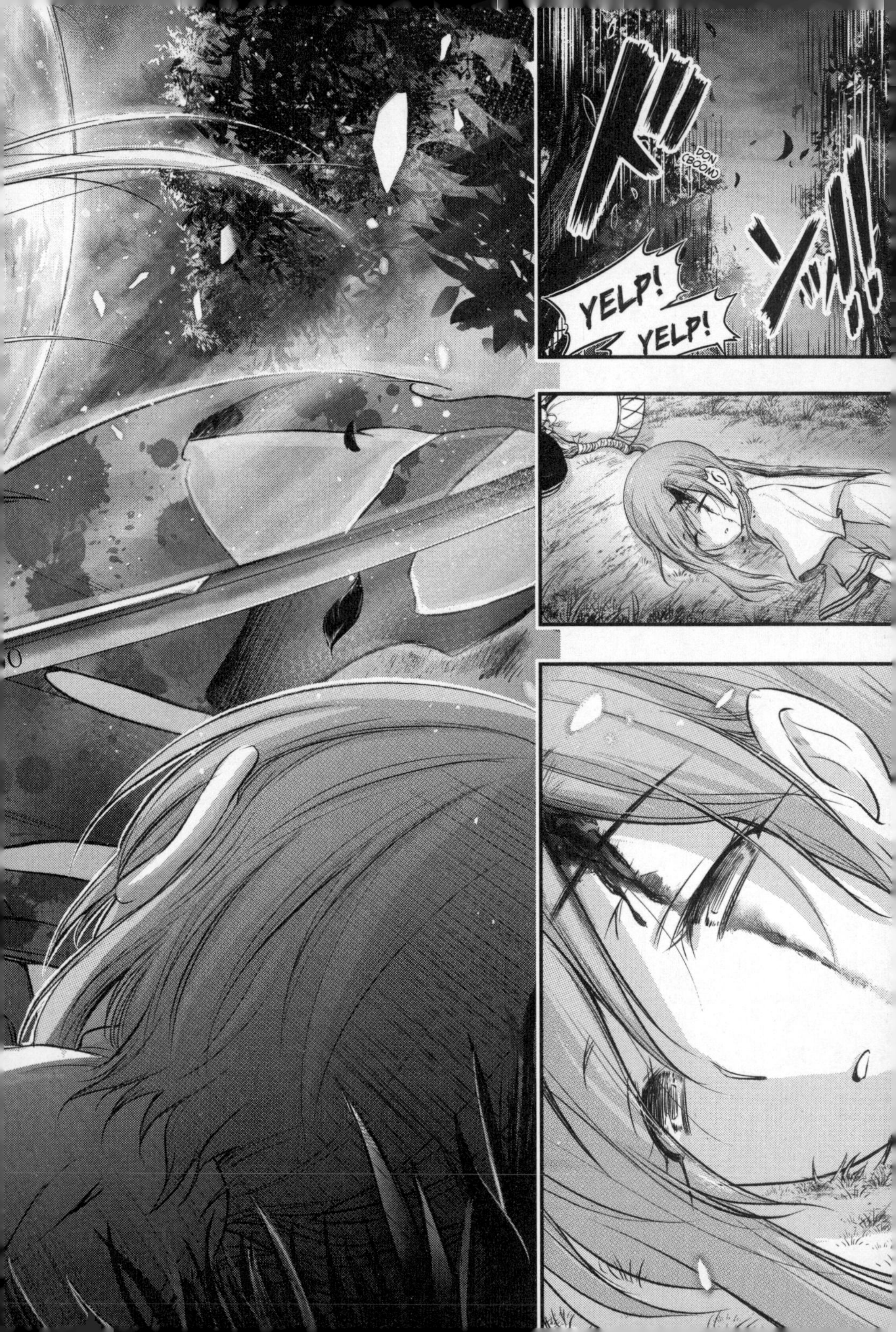
DON (BOOM)
YELP!
YELP!

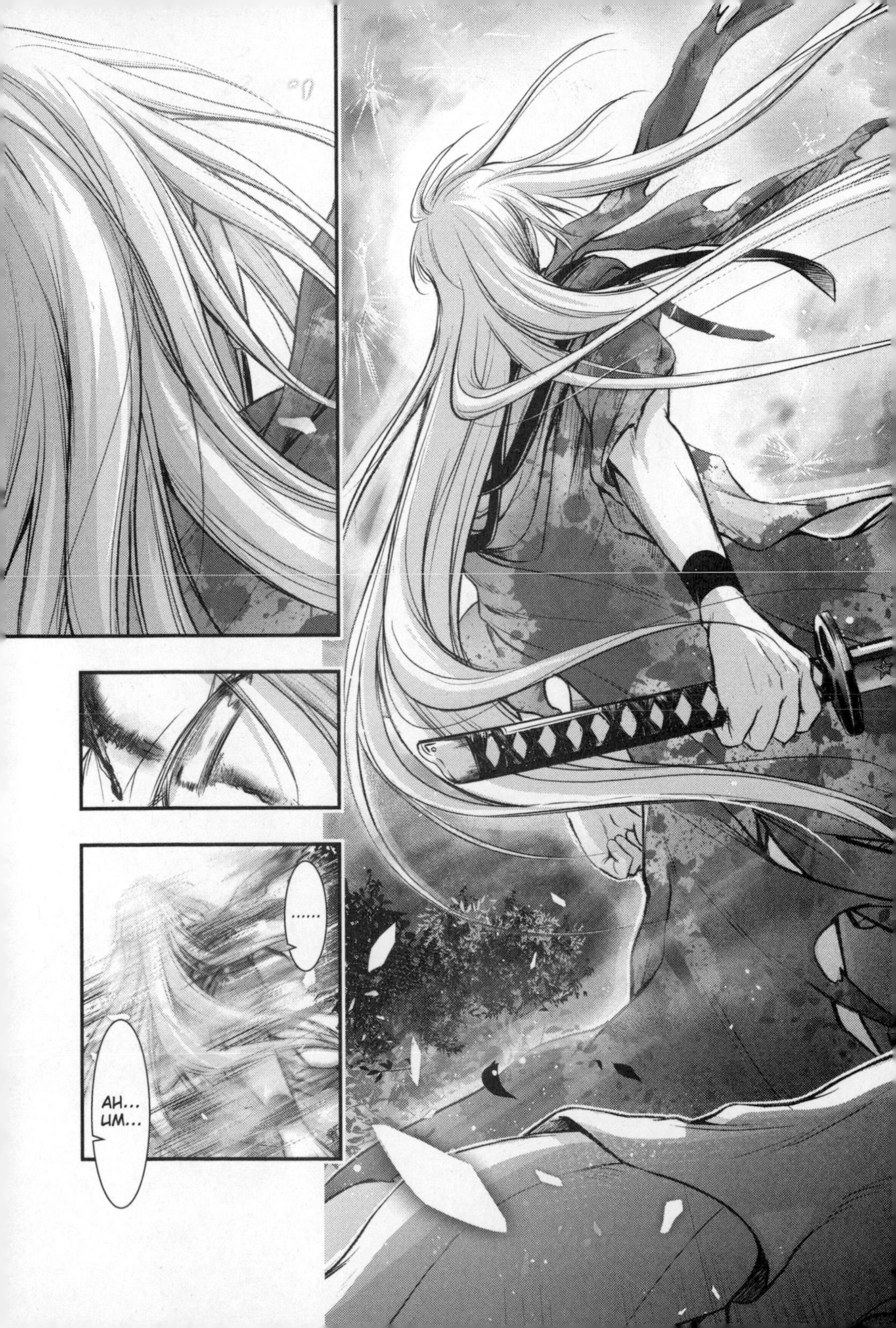
……
AH… UM…

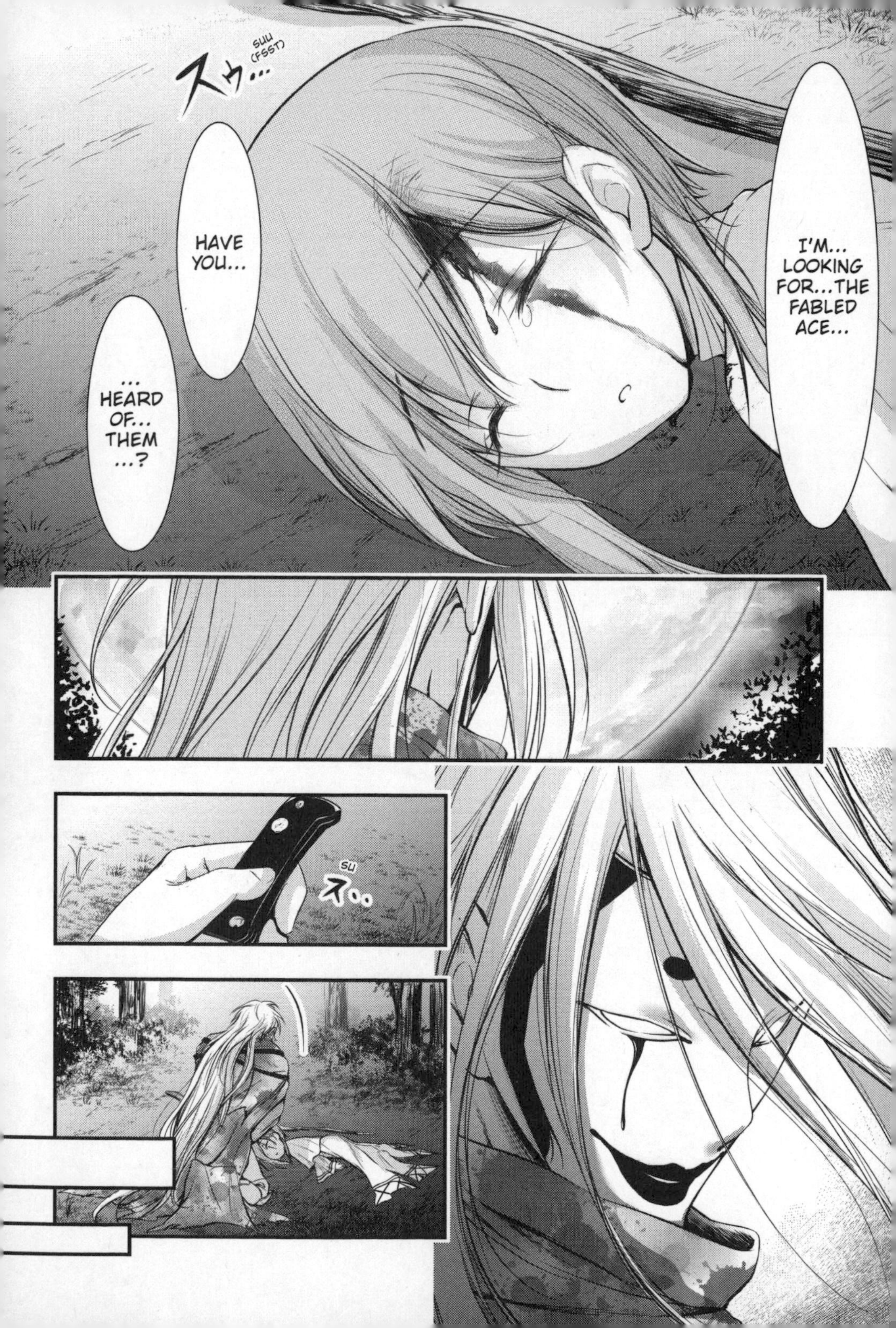
I'M... LOOKING FOR...THE FABLED ACE...
スゥ...
SUU (FSST)
HAVE YOU...
...HEARD OF... THEM ...?
SU

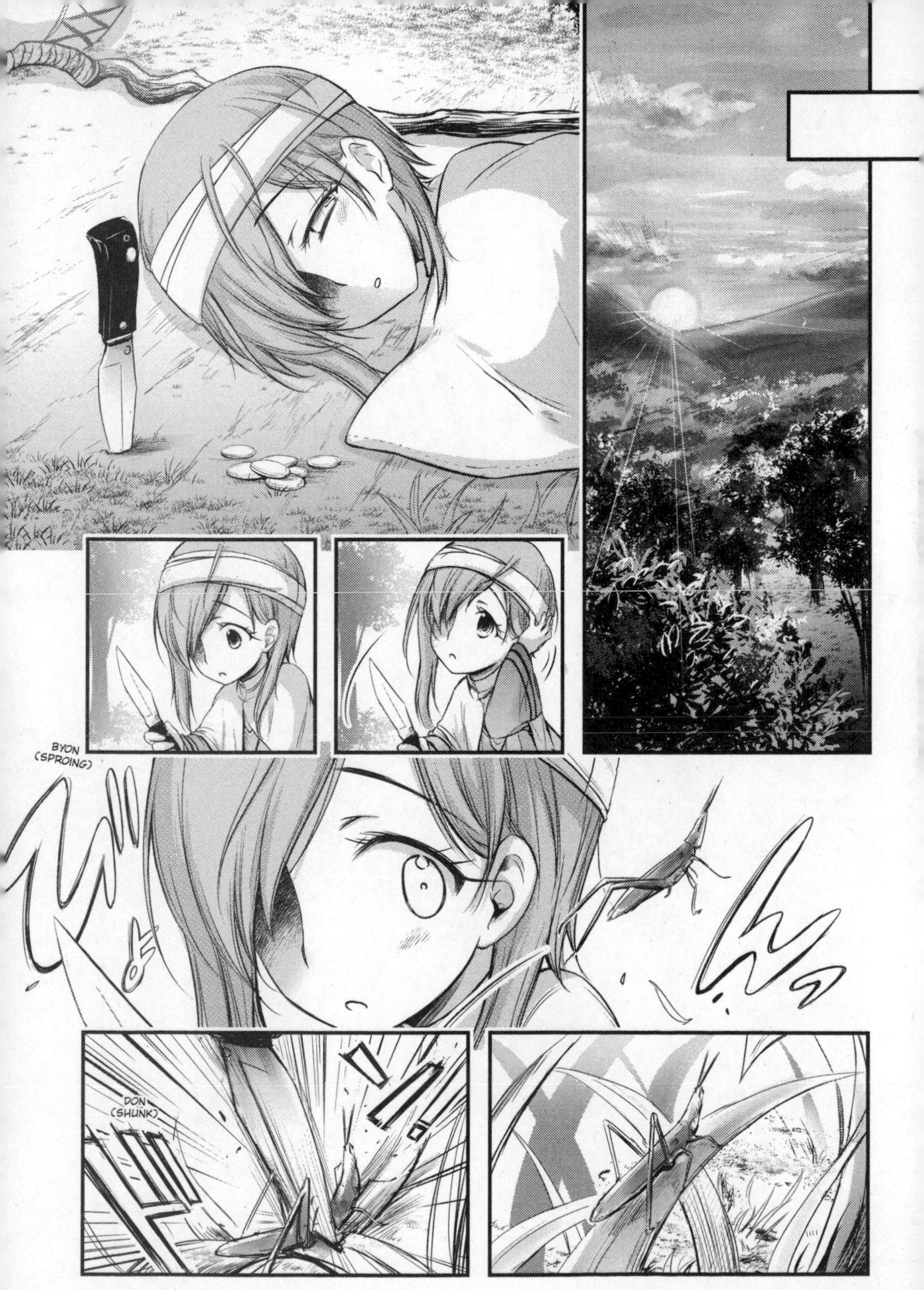
BYON
(SPROING)
DON
(SHUNK)

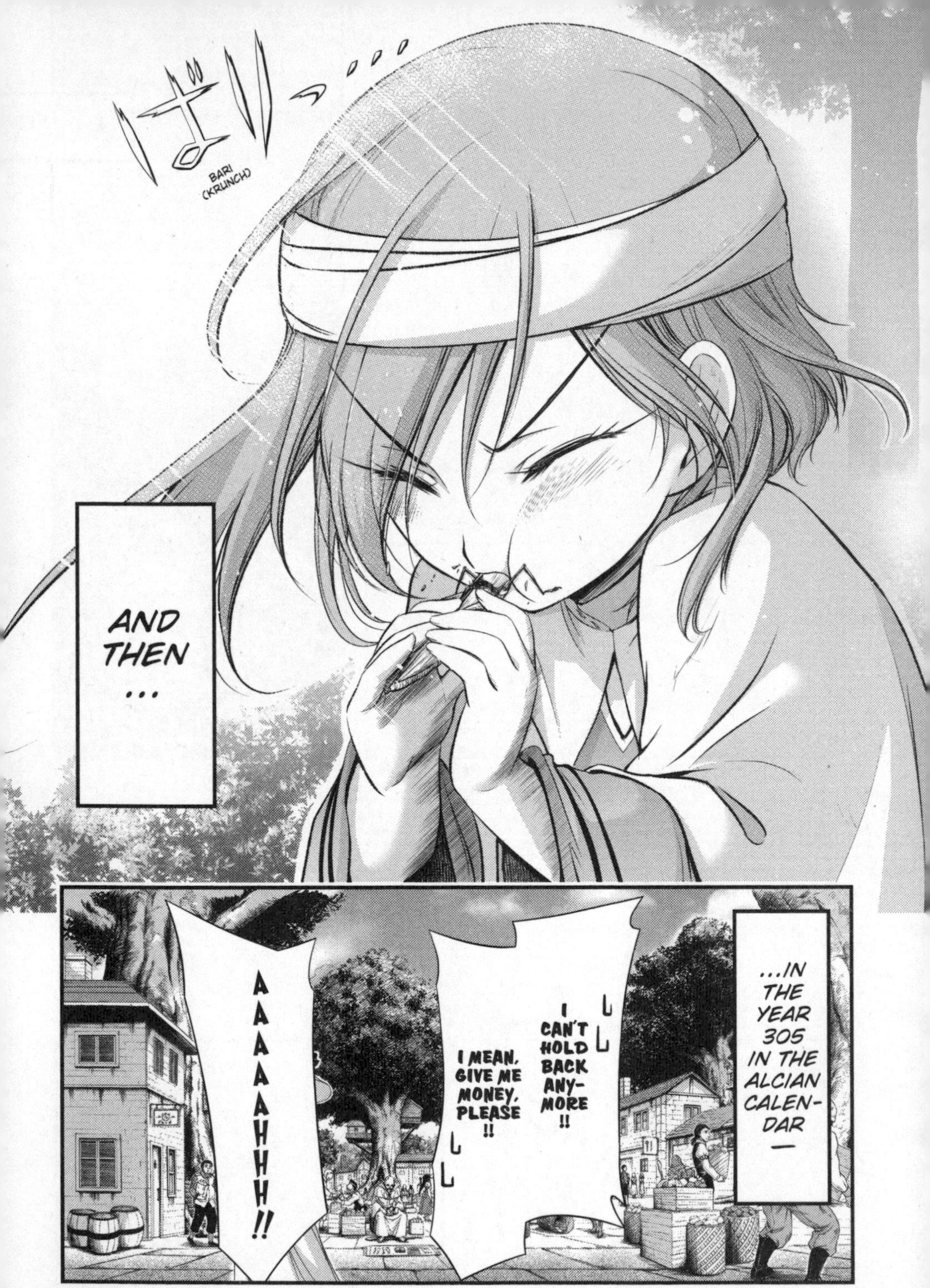
ばりっ
BARI (KRUNCH)
AND THEN ...
...IN THE YEAR 305 IN THE ALCIAN CALEN-DAR —
I CAN'T HOLD BACK ANY-MORE !!
I MEAN, GIVE ME MONEY, PLEASE !!
AAAAAAHHH!!

END

Plunderer

≪ E X T R A ★ ≫

Extra

plunderer

ORIGINAL BOOKLET #2 INCLUDED IN BLU-RAY
BOX #2 OF THE PLUNDERER TV ANIME

Special Episode

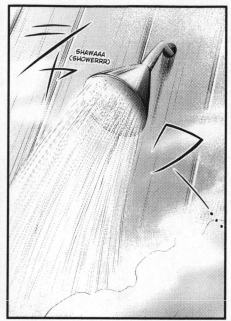

SHAWAAA
(SHOWERRR)

SU
(FSST)

BA
(BAM)

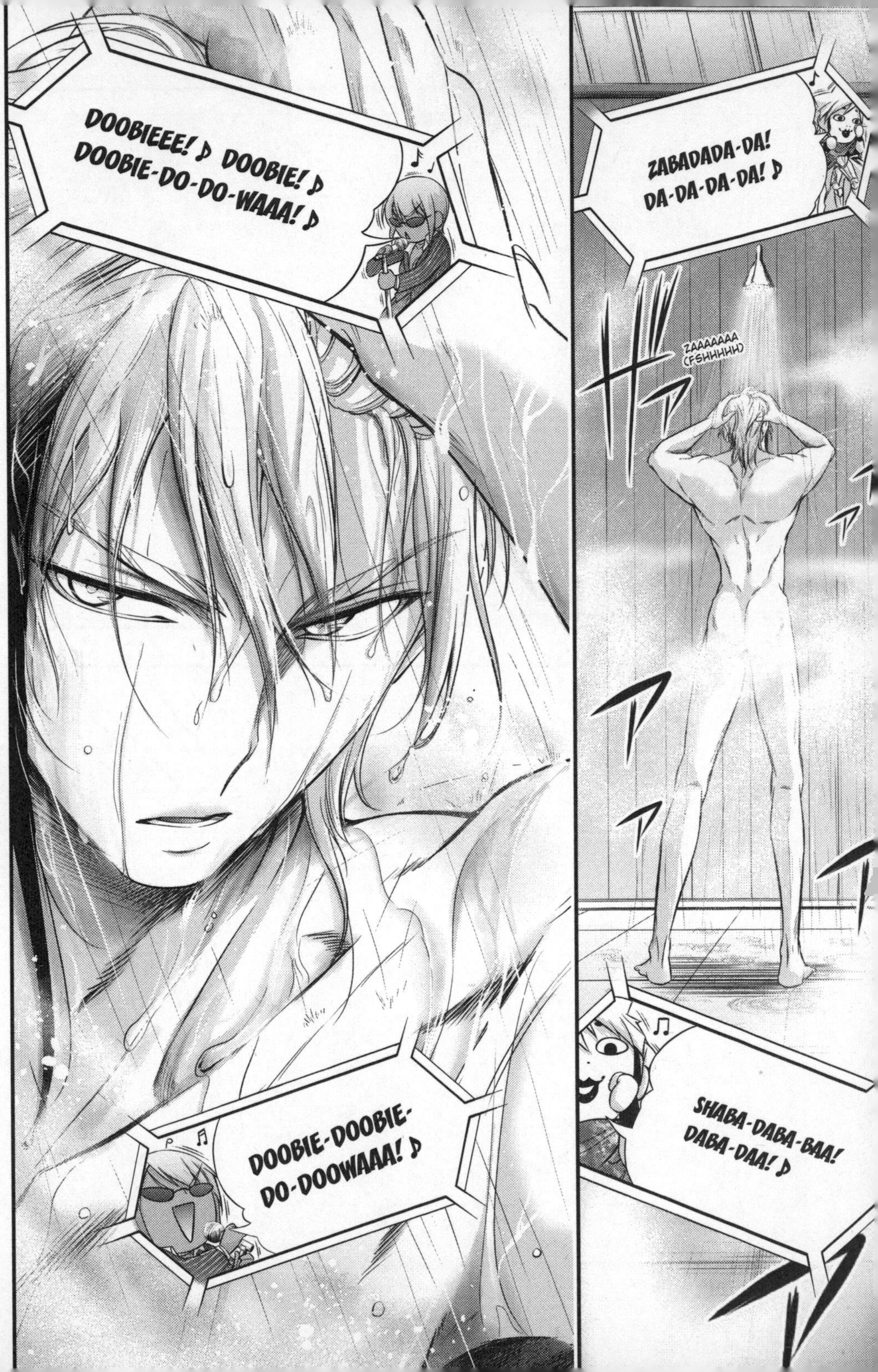
ZABADADA-DA! DA-DA-DA-DA! ♪
ZAAAAAAA (FSHHHHH)
SHABA-DABA-BAA! DABA-DAA! ♪
DOOBIEEE! ♪ DOOBIE! ♪ DOOBIE-DO-DO-WAAA! ♪
DOOBIE-DOOBIE-DO-DOOWAAA! ♪

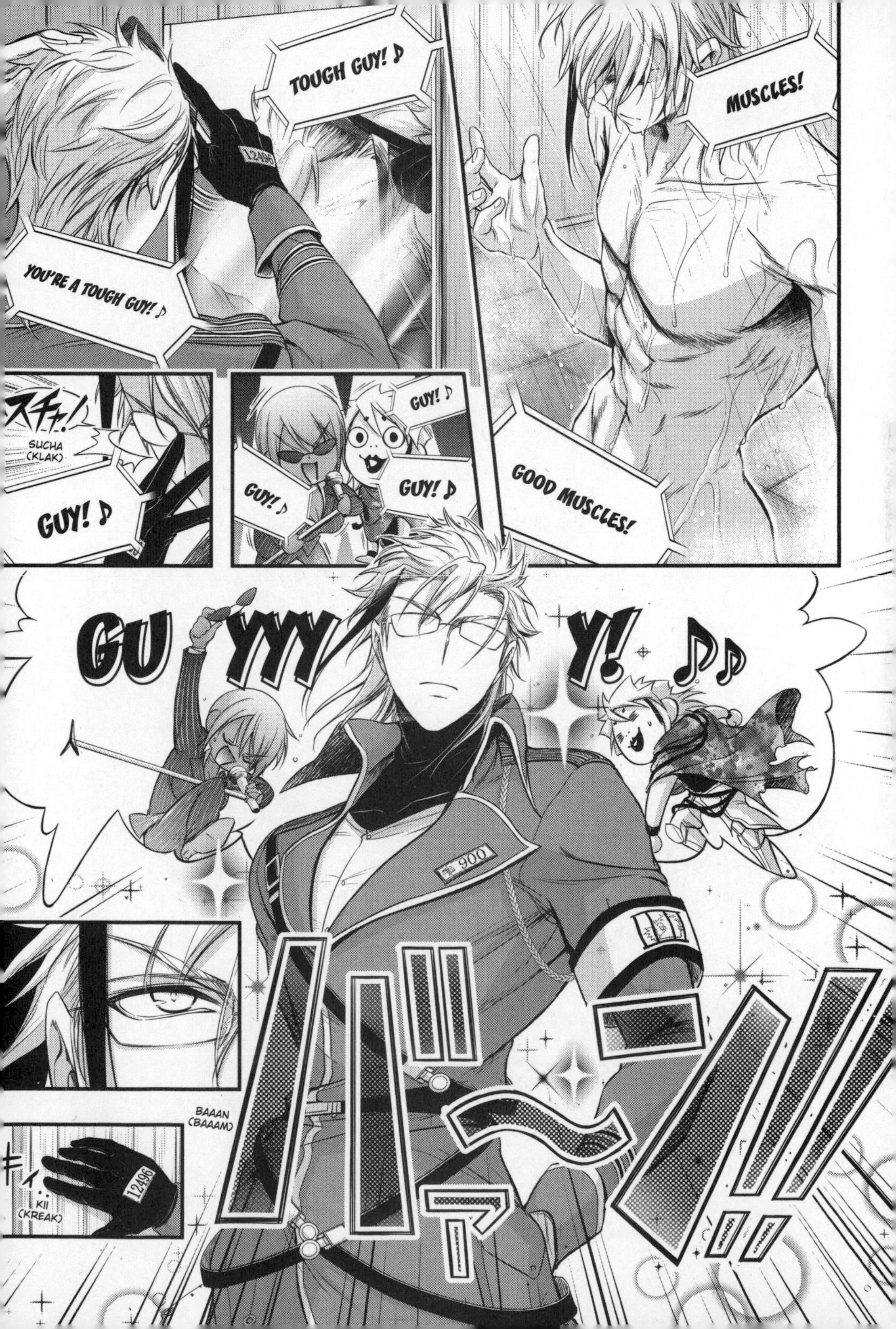

MUSCLES!
GOOD MUSCLES!
TOUGH GUY! ♪
YOU'RE A TOUGH GUY! ♪
GUY! ♪
GUY! ♪
GUY! ♪
スチャ!
SUCHA (KLAK)
GUY! ♪
GU YYY Y! ♪♪
バァ～ン!!
BAAAN (BAAAM)
キィ
KII (KREAK)

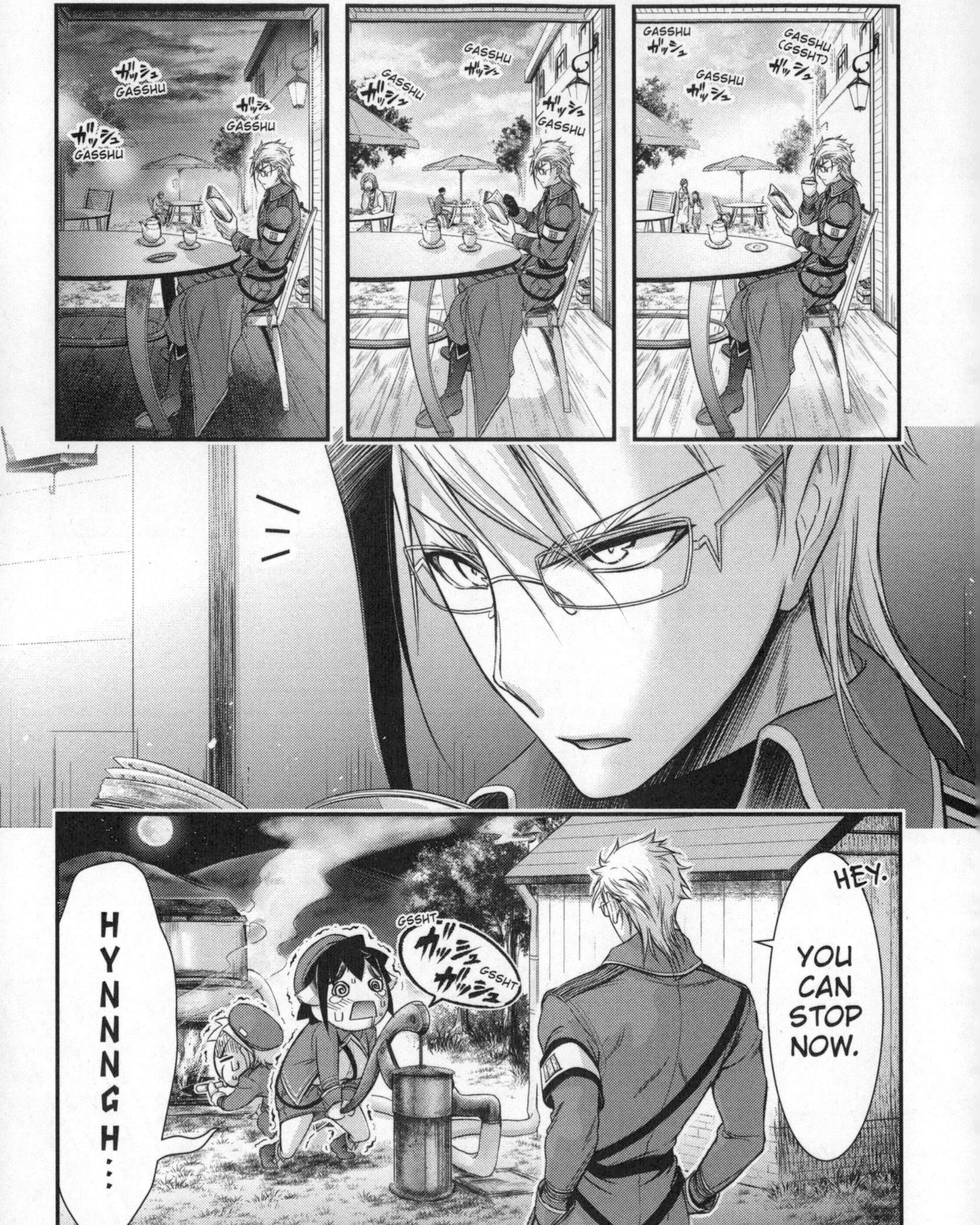
GASSHU (GSSHT)
ガッシュ
GASSHU
ガッシュ
GASSHU
ガッシュ
GASSHU
ガッシュ
ガッシュ
GASSHU
GASSHU
ガッシュ
ガッシュ
GASSHU
ガッシュ
GASSHU
ガッシュ
GASSHU
HEY.
YOU CAN STOP NOW.
ガッシュ
GSSHT
ガッシュ
GSSHT
HYNNNGH...

END

Plunderer

« E X T R A »

Extra

plunderer

3

ORIGINAL BOOKLET #3 INCLUDED IN BLU-RAY
BOX #3 OF THE PLUNDERER TV ANIME

Special Episode

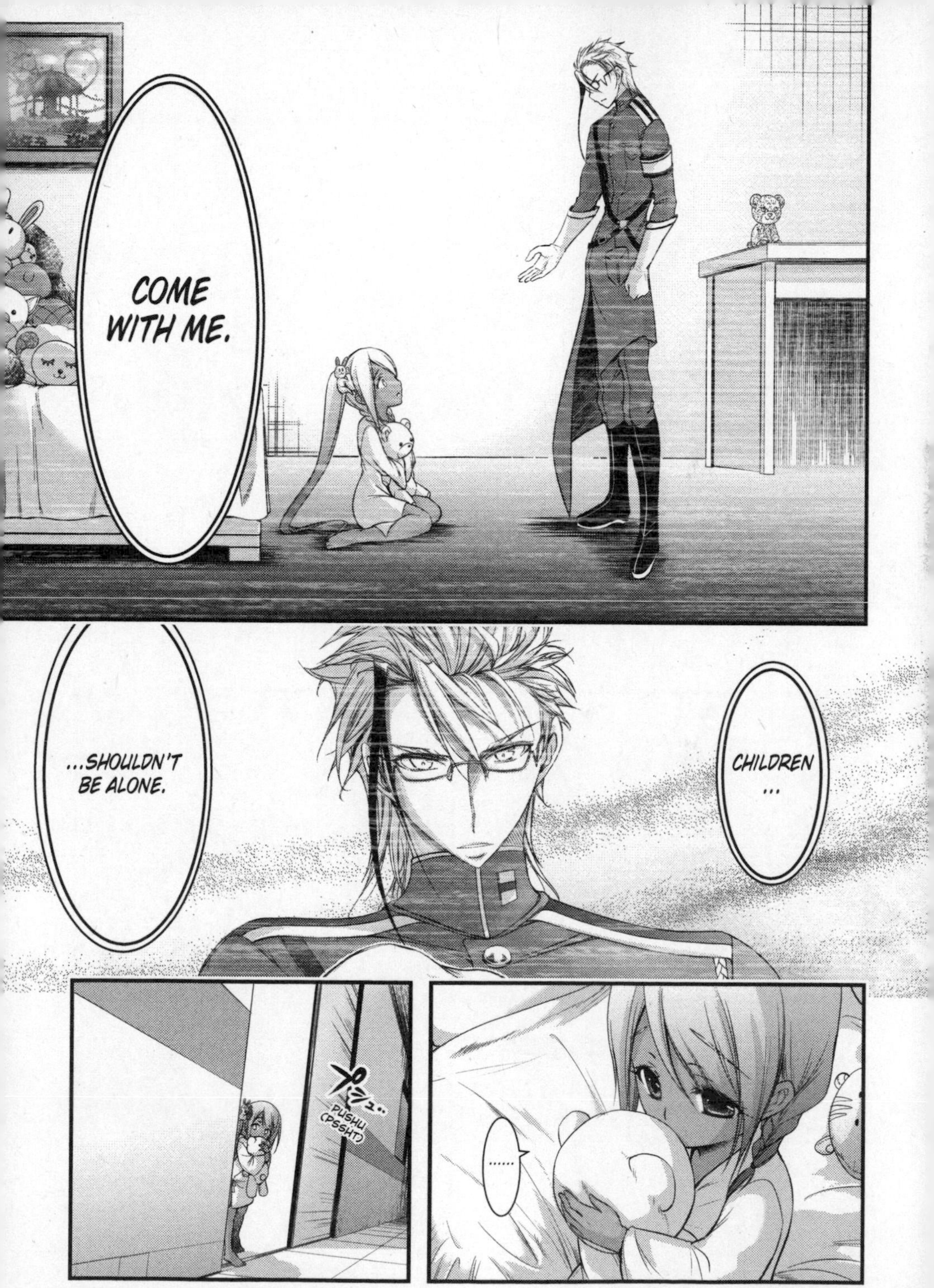
COME WITH ME.
CHILDREN ...
...SHOULDN'T BE ALONE.
......
プシュ..
PUSHU (PSSHT)

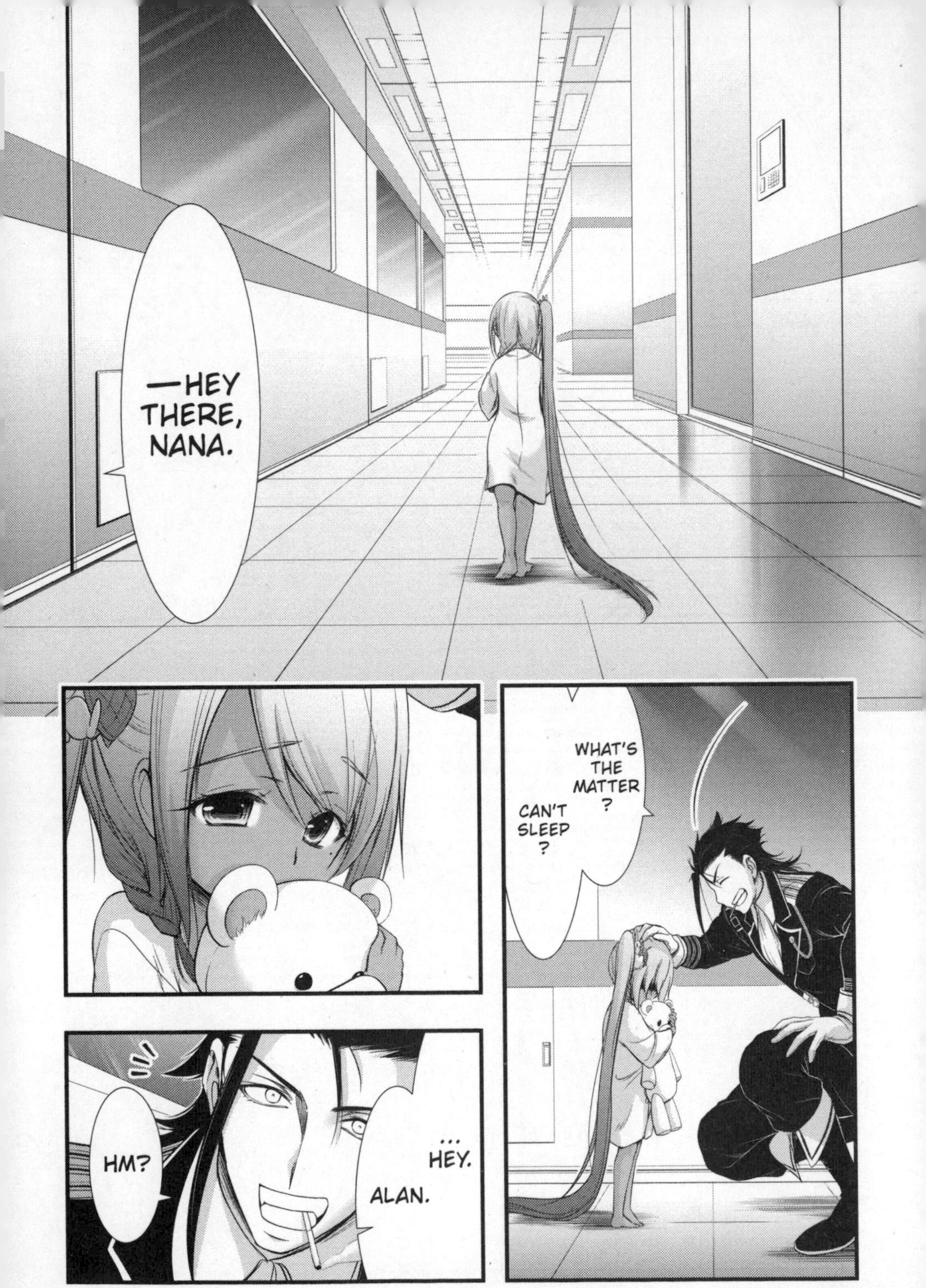
—HEY THERE, NANA.
WHAT'S THE MATTER?
CAN'T SLEEP?
...HEY.
ALAN.
HM?

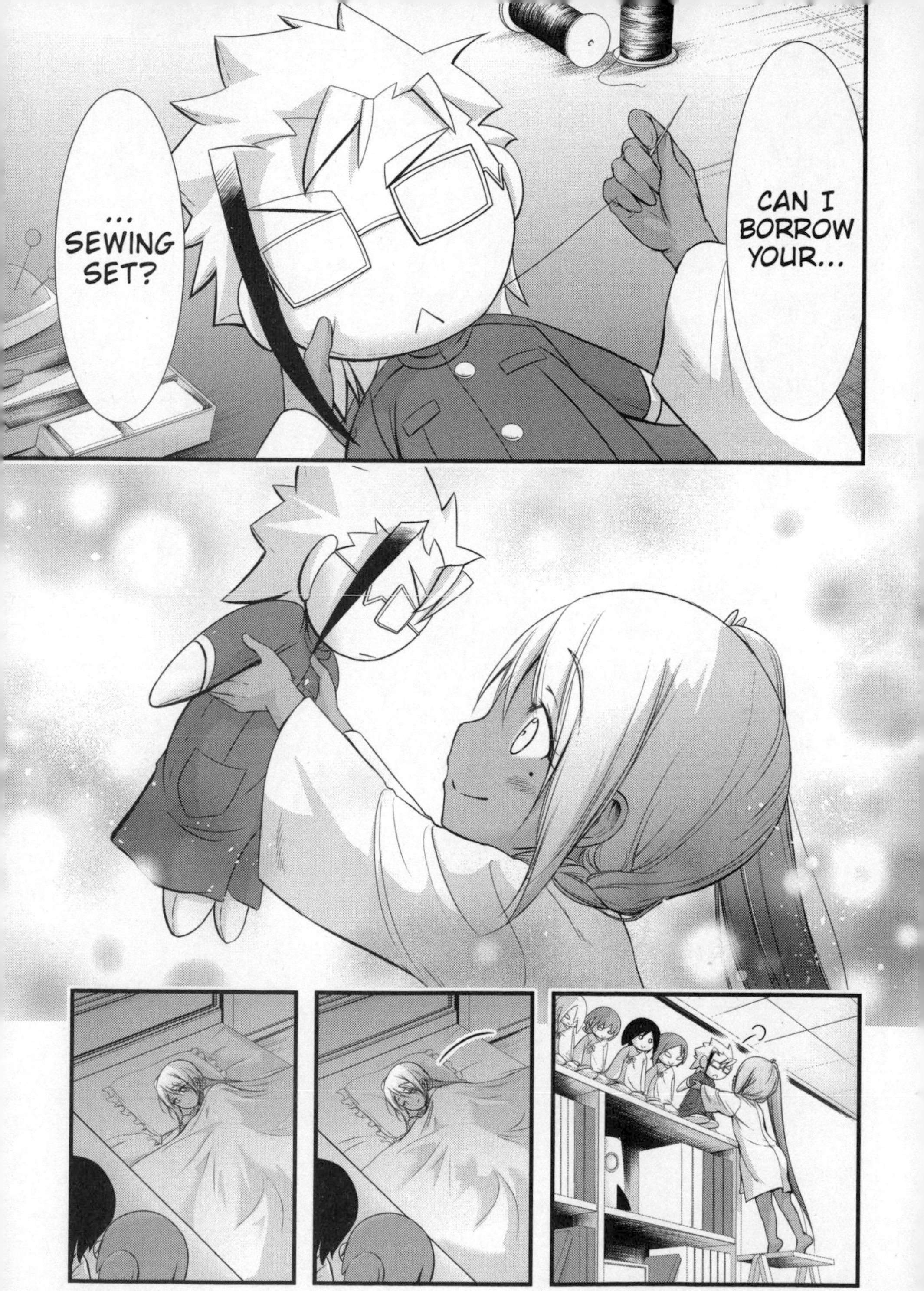
CAN I BORROW YOUR...
... SEWING SET?

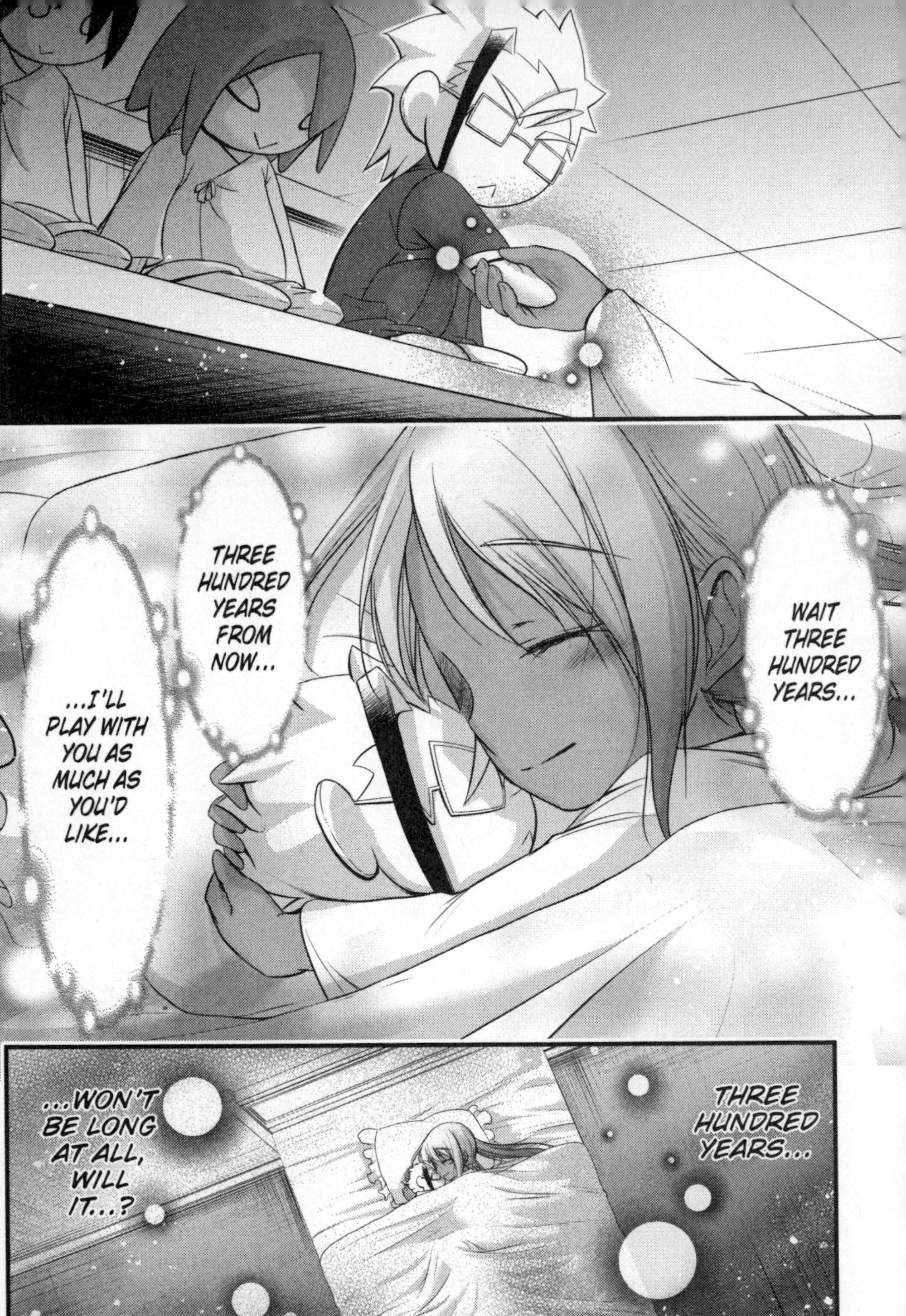
WAIT THREE HUNDRED YEARS...
THREE HUNDRED YEARS FROM NOW...
...I'LL PLAY WITH YOU AS MUCH AS YOU'D LIKE...
THREE HUNDRED YEARS...
...WON'T BE LONG AT ALL, WILL IT...?

END

Plunder

er

《 E X T R A 》

Extra

plunderer

ORIGINAL BOOKLET #4 INCLUDED IN BLU-RAY
BOX #4 OF THE PLUNDERER TV ANIME

Special Episode

SHUN
(SWOOSH)

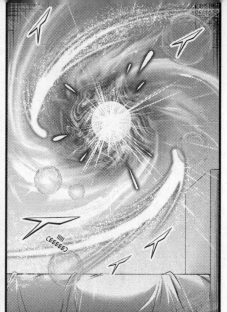

《EEEEE》

THEY EVEN HAVE AN ORIGINAL BALLOT...!

OOOOO 《WHOOSH》

☆32

I FOUND...

...AN ENEMY.

☆32

... LI-LI...
... RIGHT AWAY —

PUSHU (PSSHT)
プ/シ..

I NEED TO TELL...

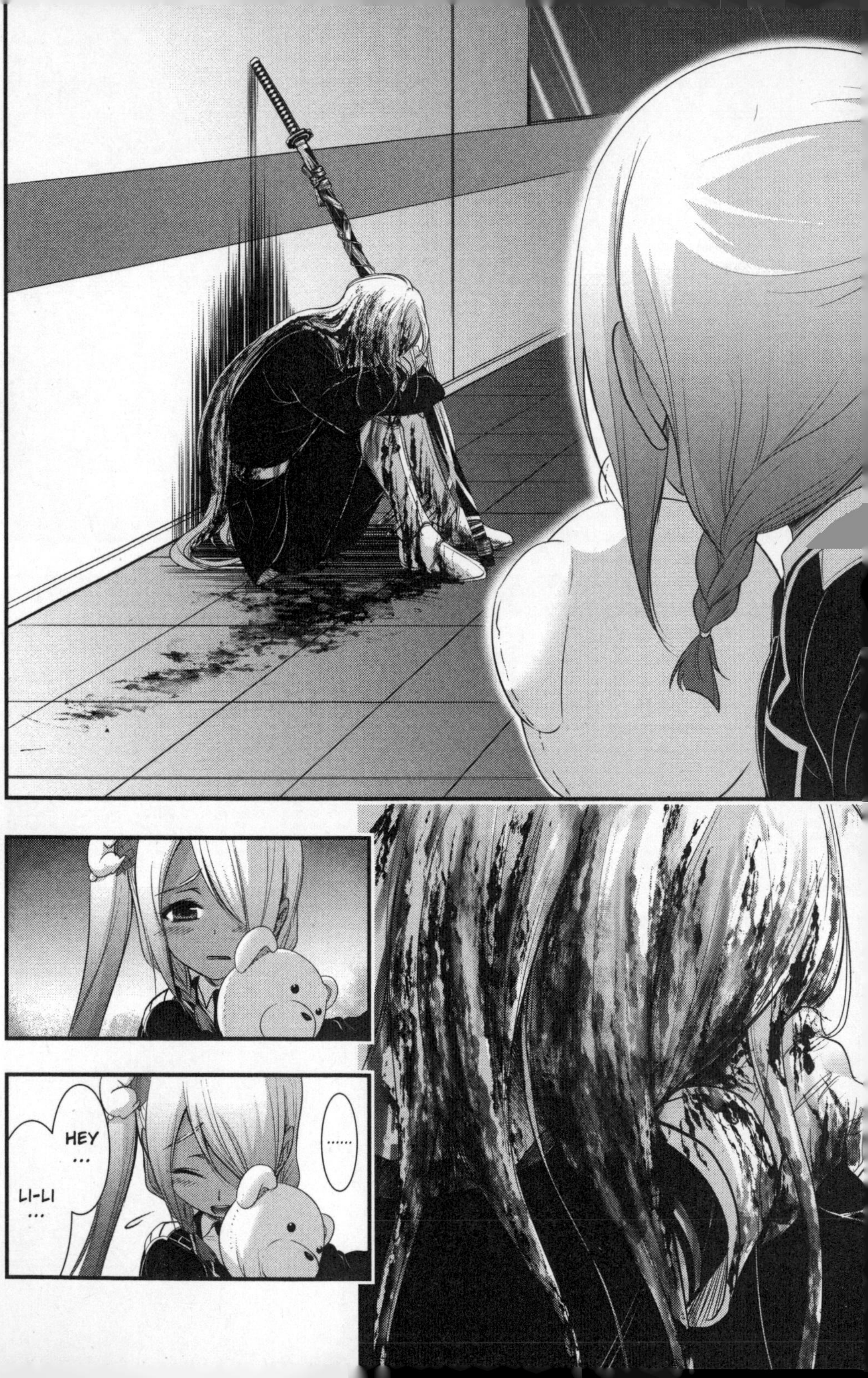
......
HEY ...
LI-LI ...

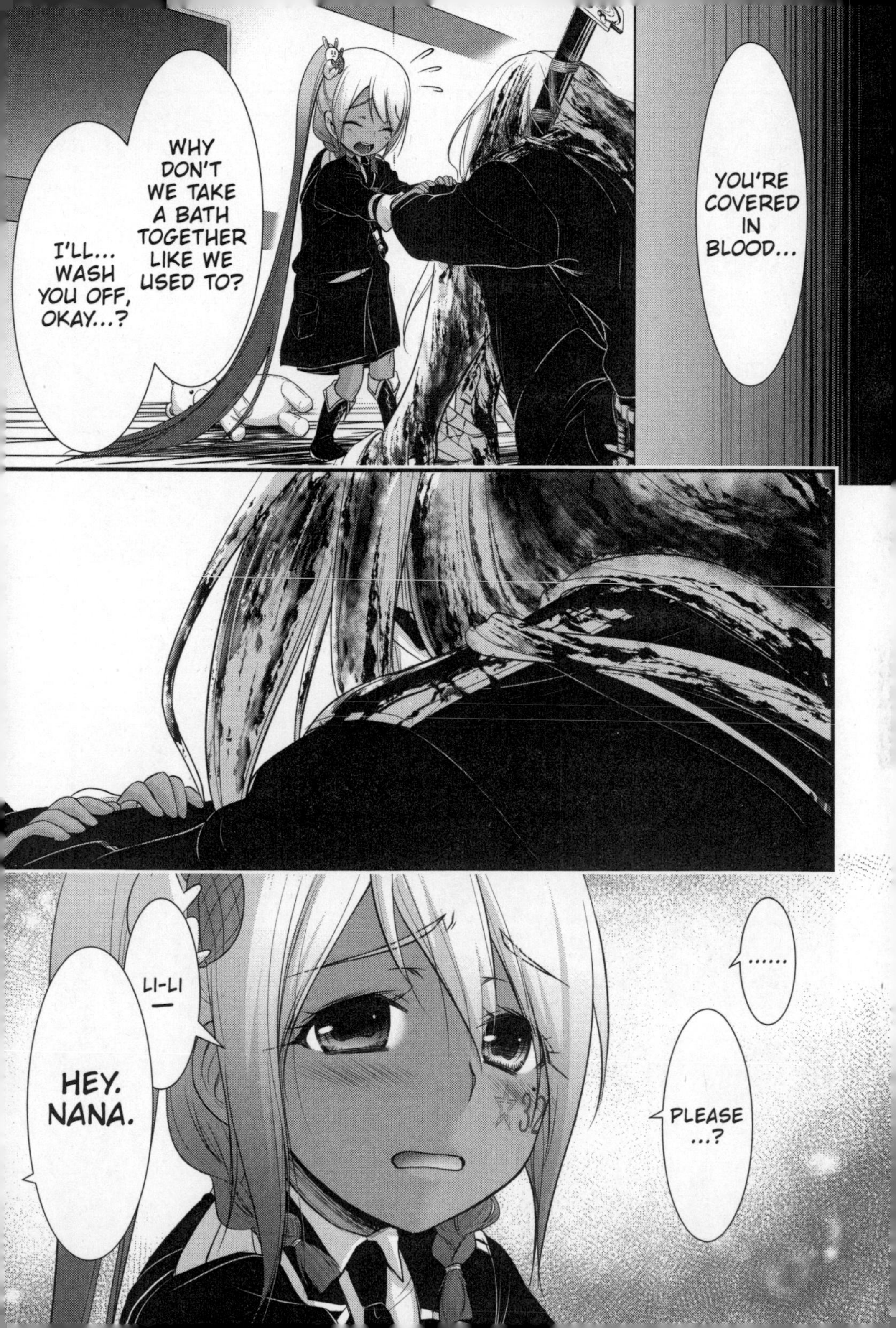
YOU'RE COVERED IN BLOOD...
WHY DON'T WE TAKE A BATH TOGETHER LIKE WE USED TO?
I'LL... WASH YOU OFF, OKAY...?
......
PLEASE ...?
LI-LI —
HEY. NANA.

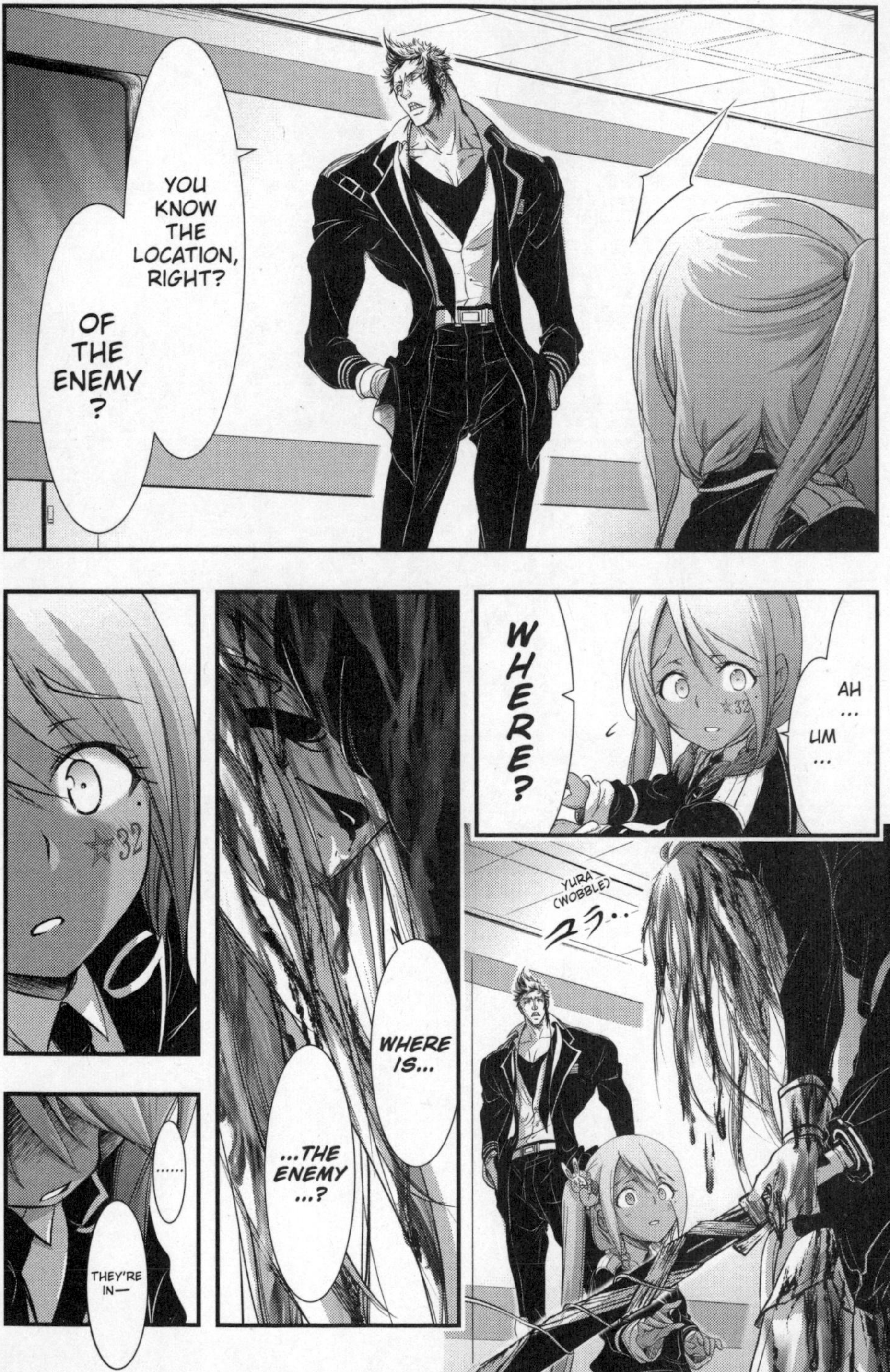
YOU KNOW THE LOCATION, RIGHT?
OF THE ENEMY ?
AH ... UM ...
WHERE?
YURA (WOBBLE)
ユラ…
WHERE IS...
...THE ENEMY ...?
......
THEY'RE IN—

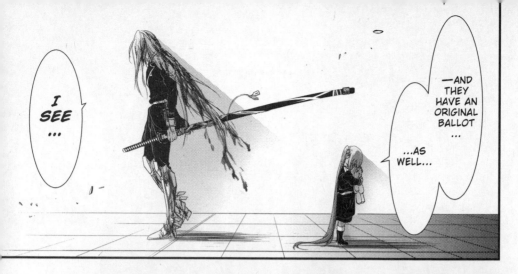

—AND THEY HAVE AN ORIGINAL BALLOT ...

...AS WELL...

I SEE ...

NANA ...

DON'T WORRY ...

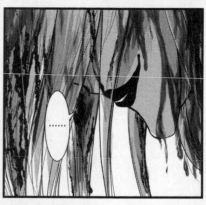

......

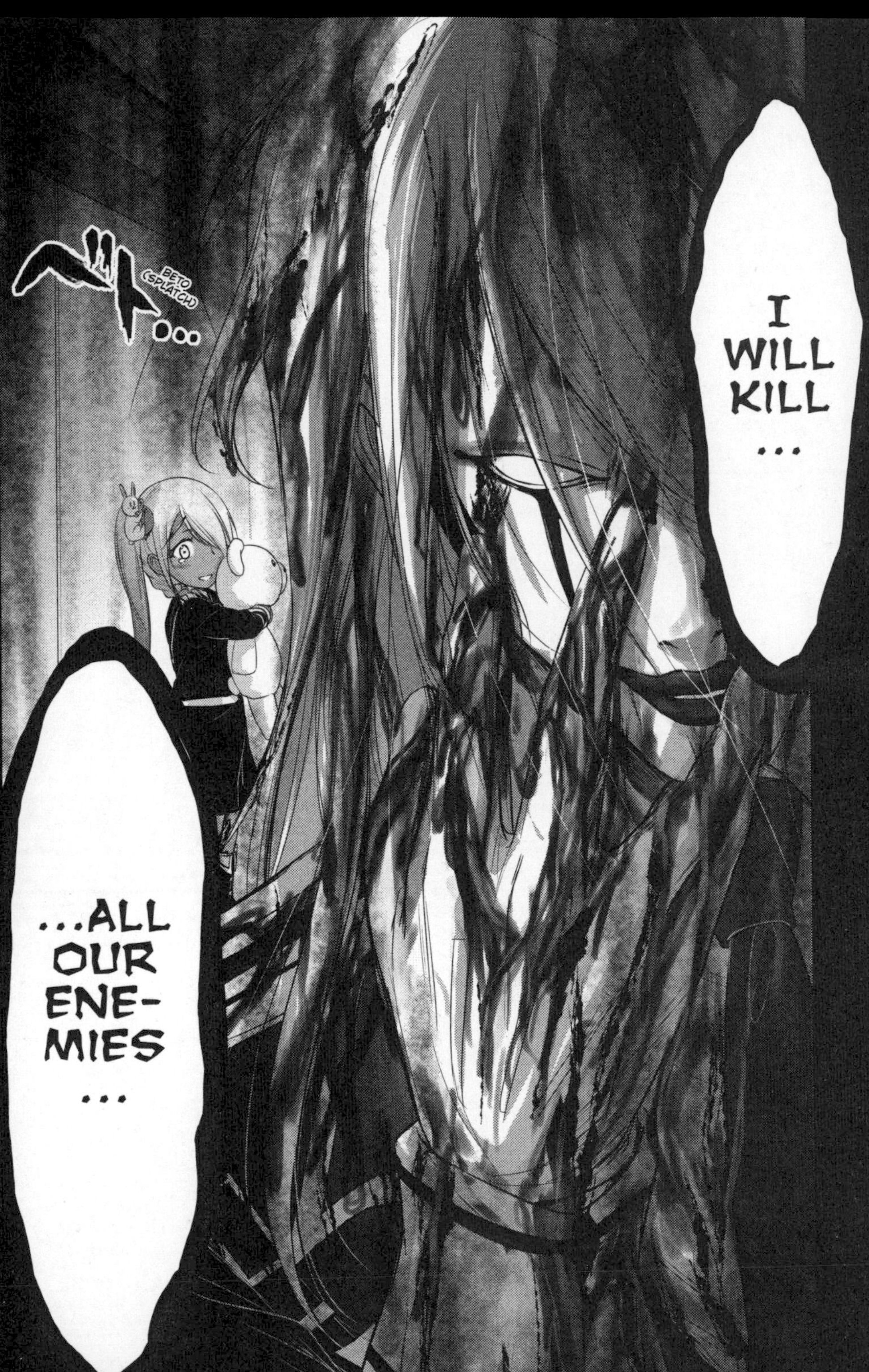
I WILL KILL ...
BETO (SPLATCH)
...ALL OUR ENE-MIES ...

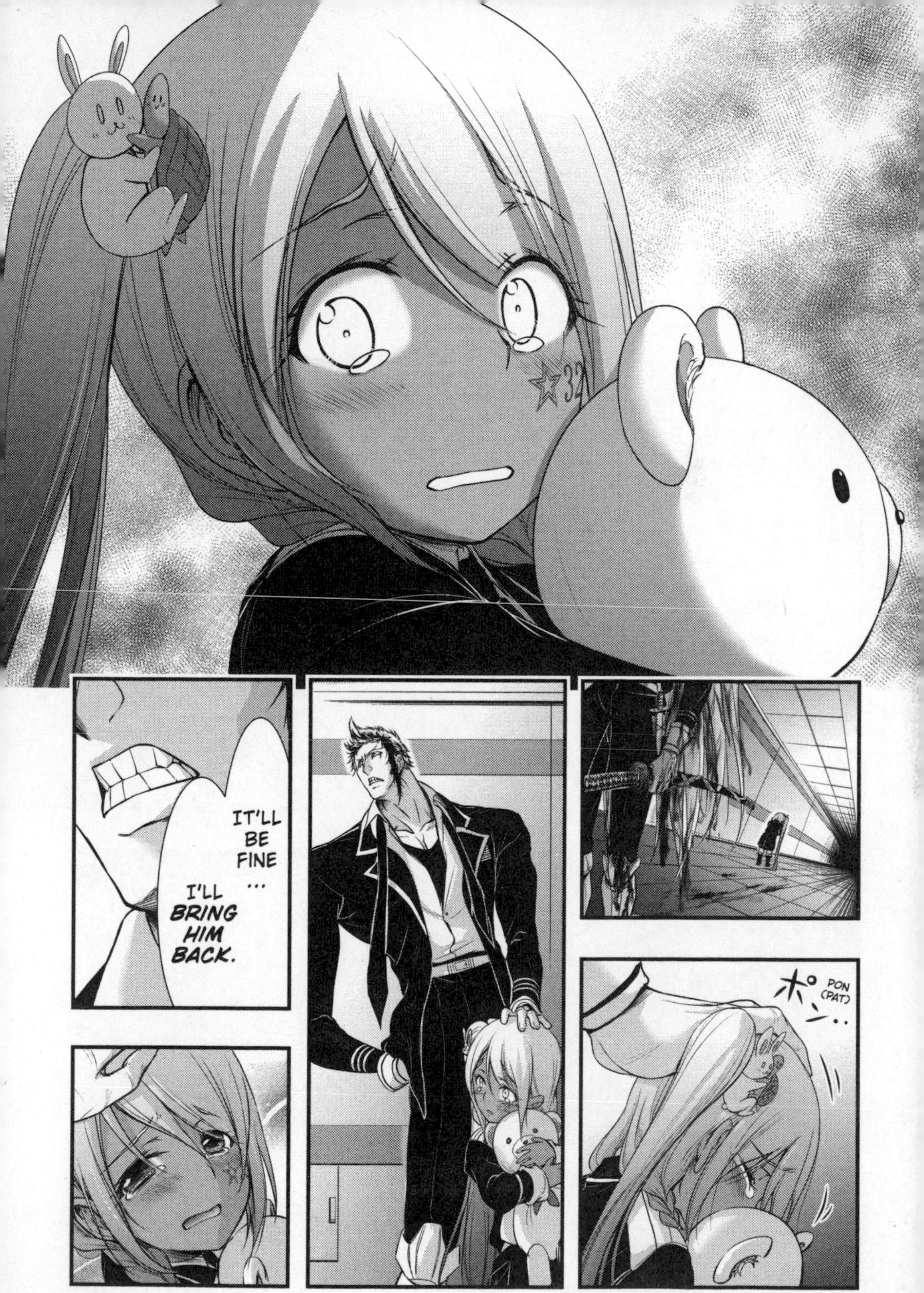
ポン
PON (PAT)
IT'LL BE FINE ... I'LL BRING HIM BACK.

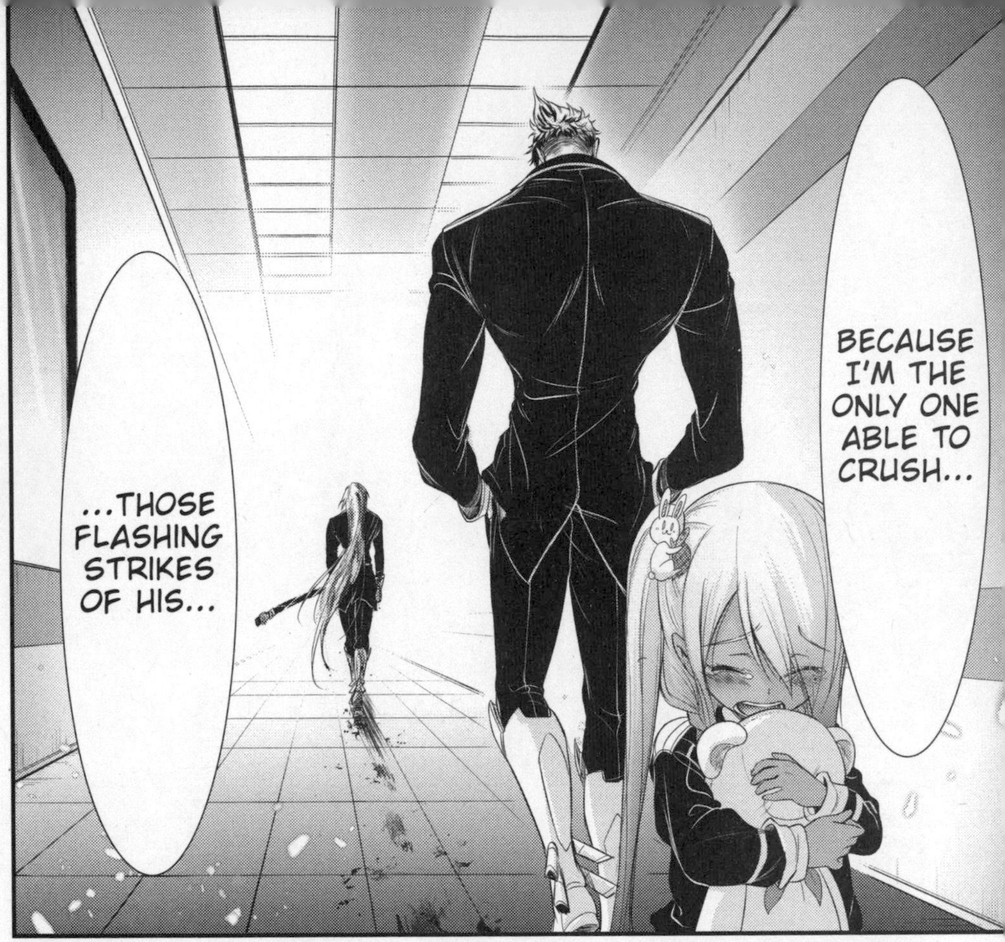
BECAUSE I'M THE ONLY ONE ABLE TO CRUSH...
...THOSE FLASHING STRIKES OF HIS...

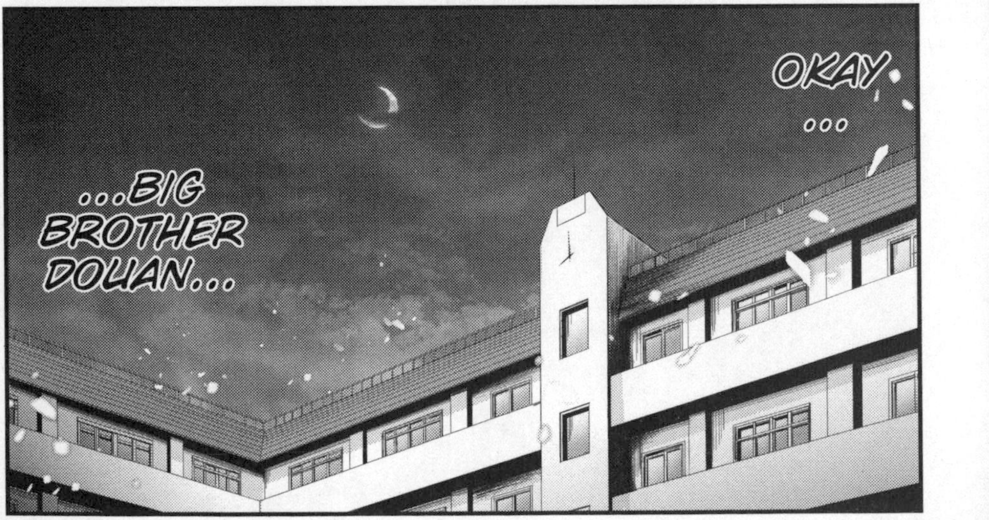
OKAY...
...BIG BROTHER DOUAN...

END

PLUNDERER

SUU MINAZUKI

Vol.
11

Translation: Ko Ransom   Lettering: DK

PLUNDERER Volume 21
©Suu Minazuki 2022
First published in Japan in 2022 by KADOKAWA CORPORATION, Tokyo.
English translation rights arranged with KADOKAWA CORPORATION, Tokyo through TUTTLE-MORI AGENCY, INC., Tokyo.

Yen Press
150 West 30th Street, 19th Floor
New York, NY 10001

Visit us at yenpress.com
facebook.com/yenpress
twitter.com/yenpress
yenpress.tumblr.com
instagram.com/yenpress

First Yen Press Edition: October 2023
Edited by Yen Press Editorial: Thomas McAlister, Mark Gallucci
Designed by Yen Press Design: Jane Sohn, Andy Swist

Yen Press is an imprint of Yen Press, LLC.
The Yen Press name and logo are trademarks of Yen Press, LLC.

The publisher is not responsible for websites (or their content) that are not owned by the publisher.

Library of Congress Control Number: 2018964275

ISBNs: 978-1-9753-6475-5 (paperback)
       978-1-9753-6476-2 (ebook)

10 9 8 7 6 5 4 3 2 1

WOR

Printed in the United States of America